Also by Godfrey Winn

Novels

DREAMS FADE
SQUIRREL'S CAGE
THE UNEQUAL CONFLICT
FLY AWAY, YOUTH
COMMUNION ON EARTH

Essays

I MAY BE WRONG
PERSONALITY PARADE
A MONTH OF SUNDAYS
FOR MY FRIENDS

War Books

ON GOING TO THE WARS
THE HOUR BEFORE THE DAWN
THE KIND OF PEOPLE WE ARE
SCRAPBOOK OF THE WAR
HOME FROM SEA
SCRAPBOOK OF VICTORY
P.Q.17

Travel Books

GOING MY WAY
THE BEND OF THE RIVER
THIS FAIR COUNTRY

Biography

THE YOUNGER SISTER
THE YOUNG QUEEN
THE QUEEN'S COUNTRYWOMEN
ONE MAN'S DOG
THE QUEST FOR HEALING
PERSONAL PAGES

Autobiography

Volume I THE INFIRM GLORY
In preparation Volume III HERE IS MY SPACE

In Russian Waters

The Positive Hour

GODFREY WINN

Volume II of his autobiography

'Because I do not hope to know again
The infirm glory of the positive hour.'

T. S. ELIOT
Ash Wednesday

London
MICHAEL JOSEPH

First published in Great Britain by
MICHAEL JOSEPH LTD
52 Bedford Square
London, W.C.1

OCTOBER 1970
SECOND IMPRESSION FEBRUARY 1971

7181 0669 5

Reproduced and Printed in Great Britain by
Redwood Press Limited, Trowbridge & London
and bound by James Burn & Co. Ltd. at Esher

FOR MY LIFELONG FRIENDS

ROBIN AND ANGELA FOX

AND THEIR THREE SONS

EDWARD, WILLIAM AND ROBERT

Contents

Illustrations

Acknowledgements

My thanks are due to the following for permission to use extracts from works in which they control the copyright: Faber and Faber Ltd., *Ash Wednesday* by T. S. Eliot; Methuen & Co. Ltd., *The White Cliffs* by Alice Duer Miller; Society of Authors and Jonathan Cape Ltd., *A Shropshire Lad* by A. E. Housman; Allen Lane, The Penguin Press, *Scapa Flow* by Malcolm Brown and Patricia Meehan; Constable & Co. Ltd., *Katherine Mansfield's Journal*; and Hamish Hamilton Ltd., *Vivien Leigh: A Bouquet* by Alan Dent.

The following have also been kind enough to grant me permission to use photographs in which they control the copyright: Keystone Press Agency Ltd., frontispiece, 35, 54, 55 and 56; Beaverbrook Newspapers Ltd., 13, 15, 17, 18, 19, 21, 23, 24, 25, 29, 31, 32, 41, 42 and 43; I.P.C. Magazines Ltd., 22, 45, 48, 49 and 51; Fox Photos Ltd., 20, 37, 38 and 39; Taylor's Press Service, 30; London News Agency Photos Ltd., 36; Angus McBean, 50; Anthony Buckley, 52; *Daily Mirror*, 60; and Lady McIndoe, 65, 66 and 67.

Part One
War Correspondent

The sound of the London traffic was suddenly so insistent and, indeed, so much stronger in my ears than when I had entered the building opposite an hour before, that the jumble of discordant noises now appeared to have acquired a special meaning.

In consequence, I found myself eagerly welcoming the barrage as a portent that my session with the ear specialist had had some positive success. After the preliminary mumbo-jumbo, when I had been instructed to hold up a finger the instant that I heard the least 'ping' in my right ear, the magician had performed his own series of mystic rites, soothing me before the slightly unpleasant ones and comforting me at the end of the performance with the assurance that it was unlikely my hearing would deteriorate much further. After all, it was only one ear that was really damaged. Yours is a very common condition, the expert pronounced. It is the war catching up with you at last. Too much gun blast.

Yes, there had certainly been that, I thought, closing my eyes in the street for a moment against the July sun. The midnight sun. Such an attraction on summer cruises through the Norwegian fjords. But for the scattered ships that were left of the convoy, whose code name had been 'P.Q.17', struggling through the Barents Sea during that very different July of 1942, that sun had been scarcely a holiday attraction. Instead, it had been an accursed sun, which had never totally disappeared beneath the rim of the horizon at any hour of the night to give us even a momentary cloak of darkness, and so a respite, however brief, from the enemy reconnaissance plane we had nicknamed Snoopy Joe, pinpointing the position of the ever-diminishing numbers, until the squadrons of Junkers 88s based on the Norwegian coast could make their final, obliterating attack. Admittedly to us, arching our backs on the bridge of the ack-ack cruiser, H.M.S. *Pozarica*, in which I was having a ring-side seat as the captain's guest, the German planes would have seemed minute – silver wings outstretched against the scarlet, batik sky, as harmless as flies upon the ceiling of the world – had we not all possessed too much knowledge already of what those small eggs leaving the under-bellies of the bombers had in store for us.

'Cor, what a day to spend a quid ashore,' P.O. Hynes from his searchlight platform had rejoindered earlier in the voyage when I had remarked that I would like to return to enjoy the panorama in more peaceful times. For there was no denying either the dramatic impact of the icebergs floating incongruously by, in the midst of the attacking sorties that were like a succession of Brocks' Benefit Performances, themselves having somehow absorbed all the colours of the kaleidoscope, or the Olympian grandeur of the ice-wall itself, stretching away endlessly on the port side, at once an implacable barrier and an unexpected protection against the submarines, eager for the kill but at the same time nervous of becoming enmeshed.

But all that was behind us; far behind us. There had been a last few precious hours ashore, when a little gang of us, including 'Florrie' Ford, the sixteen-stone chief gunner's mate, and his opposite number, Sandy, who had joined the Navy to collect stamps all over the world, and Bunker Hynes, with his undefeatable grin, had spent a beguiling afternoon bathing at Bangor before making a round of their favourite pubs in Belfast, with The Prince of Wales kept for the end. They had looked after their captain's guest in a way that they could not do once we were at sea. Then we had been anchored for the week-end at Seidisfjord, enjoying a brief glimpse of Iceland, before our rendezvous with the American freighters and their escorts.

That Saturday night I had received an invitation to dine in the wardroom of one of the destroyers, H.M.S. *Fury.* Much to everyone's surprise, a whaler had been despatched to fetch me with a crew of officers; a signal honour, so my own host for the voyage assured me – with, however, a slightly apprehensive glint in his eye. Not surprisingly, Captain David Lawford, who was to be awarded the D.S.O. for what he did later to salvage the losses of 'P.Q.17', knew more than I did about naval customs, since his own service days, starting at Dartmouth, stretched back to the Battle of Jutland. So this typical naval officer, whose ingrained reserve concealed a passionate concern for the welfare of his crew, was not in the least surprised when at breakfast in his day cabin the next morning I had to admit that I had returned without my shirt, lost and torn beyond repair in the climax of ritualistic rugger scrums which had followed the port.

High jinks in the wardroom? Just letting off steam before what lay ahead. After my week-end of unexpected gaieties which had included visiting, the next night, the cruiser *London*, Admiral Hamilton's flagship, I think I was first made conscious that this voyage wasn't going to be one long party when I came upon Mulley, the captain's devoted steward, stowing away all the family photographs. These were of Mrs Lawford, whom I had met in Belfast and who played her own part by doing her best to keep up the spirits of the other wives on shore, and of their two daughters, Joyce and Doris, both in the Wrens. They were the sort of rather shy, Anglo-Saxon pictures in silver frames that were duplicated in dozens of other ships. Only one was left out on the desk. This was an enlarged snapshot of a boy in khaki, serenely smiling, his face unlined by any adult experiences in the life that he had been destined to surrender before he had even had time to paddle in the water of experience. Peter Lawford had been killed on active service a month before we sailed. The loss of his only son was an extra burden the *Pozarica*'s captain had to carry with him throughout the bitter voyage. It was one more waking nightmare to add to all the others. The gun blast would throw the frame on to the floor, and whoever entered the cabin first would pick it up and replace it on the desk. But nothing was said between us till the night of the last great attack.

'This is it,' said P.O. Hynes tersely, when it came. There was no more time for larking around, for smart retorts in Service slang. We were all too tired, we all had grown so much, if not in stature – though in the eyes of all the crew the captain had certainly done that – then rather in the most unpalatable sort of knowledge, the acceptance that we ourselves were but pawns in a strategic game ineptly handled in high places.

Guns, who in peacetime had been a sporting journalist, had just reported into the captain's ear that, according to the R.D.F.*, fresh groups of enemy aircraft were approaching on the starboard beam. The R.D.F., in the bowels of the ship, a mysterious

* Radar.

panel of light to a layman like myself, which registered the imminent arrival of usually unwanted objects on its screen, was the province of a pink-faced, very young lieutenant named Pace, whom I encountered unexpectedly in that summer of 1968, strolling across the lawns of Glyndebourne in the interval. He looked surprisingly little changed, and had in tow exactly the kind of attractive young female that I would have envisaged from his cheerful and ever-hopeful conversation. Although we had not met for twenty years we took one look at each other, and simultaneously launched into the same chorus.

'I've got sixpence, jolly, jolly sixpence,
I've got sixpence to last me all my life.
Tuppence to spend, and tuppence to lend,
And tuppence to send home to my wife.'

Our voices were hardly of the timbre of those to which we had been listening inside the opera house. Still, we were unabashed; the song had been the vocal mascot of the ship and was invariably played over the loudspeaker whenever H.M.S. *Pozarica* was coming into harbour. But was that ever likely to happen again, I wondered, as the R.D.F. telephone rang again on the bridge announcing, 'Fifty miles . . . forty . . . thirty . . .'

I suppose the interval before the avalanche descended on our heads was about a quarter of an hour. It seemed interminable, long enough to re-live my whole life, but all I had in my mind was a confused picture of everything that had happened to us since we had left the deceptively calm anchorage of Seidisfjord, with its white woodwork church close to the welcoming quayside and the custodian mountains behind.

Once again in my mind's eye I saw the figure of the captain standing above us, as we gathered below on the quarter-deck that Monday morning; once again I heard him encouraging us. He was not given to pep talks, but now he was urging every member of the crew in words that all could understand, while 'Florric' Ford held up the map of the Arctic route ahead of us. I can still sense the feeling I had then of how the two men, side by side, the one with his carved, eagle's head, the other rubicund, barrel-shaped, made at once an unforgettable contrast and at the same time embraced between them the ubiquitous strength of the Service's tradition.

'I have been studying the reports of the last two convoys to go through, that is "P.Q.15" and "P.Q.16", and they are reports of increasing attacks. In a way, it is likely to be even more difficult going for us, because we shall have twenty-four hours daylight all the way . . . and though there will be cover by battleships and cruisers, an aircraft carrier can't be spared at this moment.

'And there's something else you must know. This convoy will be much the largest to sail for North Russia. Thirty-six ships altogether, and consisting mainly of American liberty ships. So for their sake as well as for the sake of our hard-pressed allies, the Russians, it has *got* to get through . . .'

Ironic words, in the light of subsequent events. But then it is only historians, some of whom, equally ironically, were scarcely born when these events on which they are passing judgment were taking place, and novelists with, reasonably, a purposeful eye on the possible film rights, who are fortunate enough to possess the hindsight then denied to us.

Alistair MacLean, in the first of his novels to hit the jackpot, H.M.S. *Ulysses*, used a very similar scene of a captain on the eve of a sailing exhorting his crew, and when his publishers brought their latest protégé to see me, at the time of the book's publication, the author admitted to me that he had never been on the Russian Run himself, though he had read my own documentary account of a particular disaster-ridden voyage.* Often a fiction-sized account will make a story twice as exciting to the reader, and Mr MacLean, who was an unknown Glaswegian schoolmaster when I met him, has deservedly discovered a rich vein in adventure yarns. However, I myself am only able in my writings to deal with what the French call *les actualités*. I am only at ease with reality.

In any case, there is no need to deck out, to add highlights to the speech I have reported, because the simplicity and straightforwardness of the captain's approach visibly stirred his men, staying with them and rubbing off on myself, so that I was still in the mood of Saint Crispin's Day when we had our first blooding. As I came up at dawn to the bridge from the cabin of Smithie, the navigating officer, which I was sharing for the duration of the trip, an extraordinary sight met my eyes. All the

* See Godfrey Winn's *P.Q.17*, first published 1948.

American freighters to starboard of us were hauling down their flags.

Now that usually has only one connotation at sea. Surrender. But how could they be surrendering? After all, we had only lost one ship so far; the real battle had not yet begun. Then why, why? The yellow muckers, muttered the Yeoman, and no one answered him because we were all too dismayed. Until a few moments later, someone shouted, 'Look'. And looking, we were faced with a sight which held us in thrall.

Now, instead of the scruffy flags, oil-stained and tattered from the Atlantic gales, fresh Stars and Stripes, seeming much larger in size because of their cleanness, were being hoisted at the masthead with one concerted movement right across the convoy. It was like a peace-time ceremony on a parade ground. But what did this defiant proclamation of national pride denote on this particular morning? Puzzled, we were unable to provide an answer, until one of the lookouts, mysterious behind their balaclavas and huge binoculars, called out excitedly, 'I've got it, sir . . . I've got it . . . It's July the fourth.'

July the fourth? Then suddenly to all of us the significance came in a rush. July the fourth was *their* Independence Day. And what a day it turned out to be for the crews of those liberty ships,* so far from their own homes and their customary celebrations. For, long before it was over, and while they were still licking their wounds from the waves of Heinkels coming in at mast height, our protective screen of destroyers were disappearing over the western horizon, to join the cruisers and the battleships. We only knew the reason later, much later; how they had been alerted to face a fresh menace, the *Von Tirpitz*, observed by our own reconnaissance planes to be stirring from its moorings in a Norwegian fjord. This was a strategic feint that was to produce a success surely far beyond the most optimistic hopes of the enemy. Whereas for us, left behind in the vacuum, steaming ahead of the two rescue ships, *Zamalek* and *Zaffarin*, who with total disregard to danger from the shadowing packs of submarines, had hove to, to put down their nets to haul up survivors from the four ships lost that day, there was the climax of the Admiralty signal that was to become a source of controversy in Naval circles for ever afterwards.

* American freighters.

I had just been exchanging greetings with a lad from Plaistow, whose utter spontaneity represented the spirit of all the cockneys I met at various battle stations during my time first as a war correspondent and later as an ordinary seaman myself. Ernie Davison was his name, and he had been blazing away all afternoon from his pom-pom platform, so that his face was as black as any coalman's, and his voice harsh from the cordite fumes he had absorbed. Still, nothing could quench his spirits.

'If I was at home now, d'yer know what I'd be a-doing of? I'd have both me feet up on the mantelpiece, the wireless on full blast, and my old lady she'd be cooking me something tasty for me supper.'

But he wasn't at home, any more than his American cousins, who had made such a challenging gesture in that dawn which already seemed a lifetime away. Or chiefie, who blinking at the brilliance of the eternal sunset, had come up on deck for five minutes of fresh air with a cup of tea in his hand.

I was startled at the change in our chief engineer since the last time I had seen him in Iceland. He looked like a prisoner kept in solitary confinement in a cell without even a slit of daylight.

'What's it like?' I asked him, 'in the engine room when there's a flap on?'

He told me in words which have stayed in my mind ever since. 'It's like being shut up in a hollow biscuit tin, with a lot of crazy kids beating at the side. And when they can't stand the din any longer, my own lads start beating time on the engine rails and singing choruses, like a bloody jazz orchestra. I'm sure I don't know which is worse.'

'It sounds like hell, chiefie.'

'It is hell,' agreed Lieutenant Ford in his dry, Scottish voice, before disappearing below decks again. And I went on my way to the captain's cabin, where I found Mulley clucking away with a brush, like a housewife – 'I don't know where all this dust comes from, it's quite disgraceful' – and Crisford, the assistant paymaster, who had already been sunk once in the war, entering just ahead of me with a signal which had that instant been decoded. It was on pink paper, and somehow you came to dread the pink ones, aware from their colour that they had come straight from the Admiralty and that they so seldom seemed to bring good tidings.

This one certainly didn't. It consisted of four words: *CONVOY IS TO SCATTER.*

I can see the captain now dropping the pink slip on to his desk, as though it were something loathsome. Something to be burnt because of the contagion attached to it.

There was silence in the cabin. Mulley had departed with his dustpan, and Crisford was back to help with the next decoding, for now the signals were to descend on us as thick as autumn leaves in Vallombrosa. But none of the others was quite as devastating in its intent as that first one despatched from the secret operations room, housed in the depths of that hideous concrete tower which still stands as a kind of wartime memorial at the corner of the Mall, close to Admiralty Arch.

I glanced at my host's face with its high cheek bones and bushy eyebrows, searching for hope and finding none. Although virtually still a landlubber, despite some small adventures in other ships, I had a glimmering that this must be about the most despairing signal that could be despatched to those at sea.

'What does it mean?' I asked feebly, still trying to pretend to myself that there must be some mistake, despite the earlier message received from the destroyer flotilla's leader, Commander Broome, on board H.M.S. *Keppel*, that *owing to threat from surface ships, convoy is to disperse and proceed to Russian ports.*

That did not sound quite so catastrophic. It was the ominous and deliberate use of the word SCATTER that stuck in one's gullet, like a fishbone that makes one choke.

'It means,' said the captain, reaching for his cap to go back on to the bridge, which he had left only a quarter of an hour before, and scarcely left again throughout the days that followed; 'It means', he repeated, choosing his words with a certain care, 'that you and I, Godfrey, would be better off picking groundsel in our back garden.'

The echoes and repercussions of that evening, that moment of history, still go on and on. A few months ago I was invited to speak at a dinner at Bakewell, in Derbyshire, in order to raise funds for the Royal National Lifeboat Association. As I have never been out in a lifeboat, it was suggested that I should talk about my time on the Russian Run. This choice of subject is one of which I am somewhat wary in an age when it is student battles and campus manoeuvres that tend to hold the attention of the world and attract the headlines. Not surprisingly, I was even more shy of, in any sense, holding forth as soon as I discovered that my chairman for the evening was to be Rear-Admiral Sherbrooke, who handled his destroyer *Onslow*, in the next-but-one convoy to run the gauntlet through the Barents Sea in December 1942, with such undefeatable skill and gallantry that he was awarded the Victoria Cross to add to the Distinguished Service Order he had won earlier at Narvik, in the Norwegian campaign.

However, like most genuine heroes, he wasn't in the least alarming. On the contrary, he had a most modest and disarming air, putting me at my ease at once over our drinks while the guests assembled. Quietly he stressed how important he felt it was that a new generation should appreciate exactly what sacrifices were made, and often what almost hopeless odds were accepted in order to keep faith with the Russians at the worst moment of the war.

'I tend to emphasize that point,' I assured him, 'and also how little the Russians did in return for us, either then or since, in the second volume of my autobiography. In a way, too,' I continued, 'there is a kind of link with the lifeboatmen. Because didn't you find on that run, in those Arctic waters, the sea itself remained the cruellest enemy of all?'

They were waiting for us to go in to dinner and I broke off, chiding myself because my companion would know so much more about such comparisons than I did; though, of course, he wouldn't have met Jimmy Campbell, who had received no official medals, and who has nevertheless always remained in my reckoning of those times as an example of supreme courage.

Jimmy Campbell had no inkling that his story would reach the world, that day I leant over his palliasse in the corridor of the hospital in Archangel, crowded with frostbite victims from the two previous convoys as well as our own. Jimmy, a Glaswegian lad of sixteen, whose first voyage in a merchantman it had been, had been in the water only half an hour. Nevertheless, they were forced to amputate one of his legs and one of his arms, to save his life.

Moreover, because the hospital had run short of anaesthetics, the surgeon had had to perform his salvage work like a butcher. It was nobody's fault, it was war, and the boy with the dark, curly hair and the wide grin had no complaints. On the contrary. When we asked if there was anything we could bring him from the ship, he shook his head and in a broad Glaswegian accent exclaimed, 'Och no, mon, the Ruskies are very good to us. There's nothing that we lack except, maybe, a football to kick around the ward.'

However, there's a postscript I can add to that, I told my audience that night. 'Only the other day I had a letter from one of my readers who has recently been on a visit to New Zealand. And in Rotorua she encountered Jimmy Campbell and his family. Yes, he is most happily married, he has teenage children of the same age as when I first saw him, and he manages his new limbs so well that he is teaching the "natives" soccer . . .'

As soon as I sat down, the wife of *Onslow*'s captain who was seated on the other side of me, had her own postscript to add.

'I was working in the Admiralty at the time of "P.Q.17",' Mrs Sherbrooke told me. 'As a matter of fact, it fell to my lot to type out the signal for the convoy to scatter. It made everything you said tonight seem even more vivid. Did you ever meet Sir Dudley Pound?' When I shook my head, smiling wryly at the immensity of the gulf between Ordinary Seaman Winn, as I later became, and such remote creatures as the First Sea Lord, my companion added, 'Generally he used to look into our room to say good night to those still on duty. But that evening I heard his step, which I could always recognize since he had a limp, coming down the passage. But it didn't stop. It went on.'

Because the decision he had just taken at the end of the conference – his responsibility and his alone – was such a terrible one, the devil's own choice between the havoc that the *Von Tirpitz* could create if allowed to slip through on a marauding raid into the Atlantic, and the probable destruction of all the freighters left to their fate, a straggling, sitting target, one presumes he could not face the bright, reassuring faces of the women staff at their typewriters. Too much on his mind, too much on his plate. No wonder his footsteps had retreated into silence. It was strange how the circumstances surrounding old battles could seem in retrospect sometimes more frightening than the actual participation. Now you were only conscious of the losses, the waste, like the twinges of a former illness recurring unexpectedly to remind you of the insistence of mortality.

'It must have been a tremendous strain for you, knowing so many secrets,' I suggested, remembering suddenly the evening, in the middle of the war, when I had dined with an old friend, who was a member of the Cabinet, at Boulestin's off the Strand. Jay Llewellin was always invigorating, because he had the kind of healthy colouring that never varied. In manner, too, he always appeared so confident and optimistic. Yet that evening he hardly spoke at all, and in consequence, the food seemed doubly war-time rations. When we emerged into the street to the sound of gunfire, with the searchlights bright overhead, and I asked if he had kept his ministerial car, not relishing the trek home to Victoria, his tone was unexpectedly peppery.

'Of course I haven't. How could I keep my driver hanging about in conditions like these? Ours wasn't an official dinner engagement. I sent him home to his wife at Harrow hours ago. Otherwise, she would have been worrying about him and he about her.'

We walked in silence along the almost deserted Strand until we reached the dark island of solitude surrounding Admiralty Arch. Here, as we parted, this man, with his open, English-squire face, relented. Such were his exemplary manners that he wanted to reassure me, I realize now, that the disappointing mood of the evening was not in any way my fault.

'I am afraid I have been poor company tonight. You see, I heard at the Cabinet meeting this afternoon that Singapore has fallen. I know you will keep it under your hat, Godfrey, till the P.M. announces it.'

Then he strode off towards Westminster and I continued my trudge through the Mall. Still, it was a peaceable stroll compared to the night when the whole face of Carlton House Terrace was coloured scarlet, with the flames leaping so high it seemed impossible to believe that anything could be saved from the wreckage. Today at my bridge club, which now embraces gambling, I gaze at the eighteenth-century splendours miraculously preserved, and then at the piles of chips in front of the players, and cannot help having a sour taste in my mouth as I compare the almost careless hazarding of hundreds of pounds with that utterly different kind of coin which had most value in the war years. I find myself remembering all those who gave up so much for the final victory, believing that this time the aftermath would be different. Just as I remember how I hugged with dismay that piece of good-night news to myself, not telling my editor, not daring to have a drink with a friend, lest my tongue were loosened, before on the Sunday evening the Prime Minister spoke to the whole nation over the air.

'I suppose being a Service wife, I was already conditioned to keeping secrets,' my fellow-guest at dinner was saying. 'It was such a relief to be doing something. Otherwise, all the time my husband was away at sea would have been so intolerable, so interminable. As it was, with a job in the Admiralty, somehow I felt so much nearer to him. Now that I look back the most difficult thing was not so much keeping to myself any inside knowledge that came my way in the course of duty, as never, never being able to pass it on to the people involved, to whom it meant so much.

'For instance, I remember meeting another Naval wife in Jermyn Street one day, just outside Floris, of all shops. Such a reminder of other times. Of course, she didn't ask me but she must have thought that I might have some idea of the whereabouts at that moment of her husband's ship. The awful thing was that I not only knew, but I knew that it had been sunk. I'd heard the news just before I came off watch but, of course, I could not say anything, no announcement would be made till the official telegrams had gone off to the next-of-kin. That was the kind of moment one never forgets. We talked bright nothings for five minutes, and then went our separate ways.'

'I would say myself that on the whole, women are better than men at keeping secrets,' I suggested.

'Despite what some men choose to say to the contrary?'

'Oh, but that is a myth my sex seeks to perpetuate in order to boost its ego. Whereas most members of your sex take a special pride in proving that they are to be trusted.'

To establish my point, to back up her own testimony, I also had an example to offer.

'One of the daughters of the *Pozarica*'s captain was stationed, as a Wren, in the secret underground Headquarters at Liverpool. By chance, it was part of her duties, during the actual progress of "P.Q.17" from Iceland to Archangel, to plot the convoy across the wall of the ops. room, moving on the plaques, which represented each ship, and taking them down as they were sunk. Day by day the numbers grew less, and each morning as she came on watch her eyes would go to the wall and she would climb the ladder to see if the disc with the name of her father's ship was still there. Her agony of heart must have been almost insupportable, but she continued to write chatty little letters, betraying nothing of her frantic anxiety, to her mother, left behind in Belfast, who in her turn was trying to rally the other wives of the ship's company at sewing parties. I often feel it was much worse for Joyce Lawford having to hide her feelings and maintain an unemotional front towards all the people in uniform round her, than it was for us battling it out as best we could.'

After the convoy's main escort force had disappeared to the west on that evening of July the fourth, all that was left besides ourselves and our sister ship, *Palomares*, another converted banana boat with four-inch armament, was a handful of corvettes and armed trawlers. The liberty ships, no longer in any sort of co-ordinated order, were disappearing haphazardly towards different points of the compass, while the midnight sun shone down on a scene so empty and desolate that it had assumed the strangeness of another planet.

I have described that night, and indeed the whole voyage, in detail elsewhere. However, you will not find any mention in my other book of one signal which my captain was to receive in the course of the next two days, and of which I have a copy beside me on my desk as I write, since it was marked MOST SECRET. In consequence, discretion warned me against publishing an extract from it twenty years ago. It surely does not matter now, especially as there have recently appeared in print contradictory accounts of this running sea battle – in which the enemy high command undoubtedly outwitted our own – written by others who, unlike myself, were not on the spot with a reporter's pen in their hands.

The last paragraph in this particular signal reads:

Pozarica and Palomares are not to take risks in rescue operations and are to proceed without delay to Archangel.

There was a certain anomaly in the use of the word 'risks', since, from the very moment that the heavy armour had turned back we had existed in the shadow of the imminent threat of an attack from enemy surface craft, as well as from the air and under the water. For had not another signal read:

Most likely time of enemy attack now tonight, fifth, or early tomorrow morning, July sixth.

Whereupon once again the captain had cleared lower deck, as in Iceland, and spoken with equal frankness to his crew of the situation in which we now found ourselves – was it a week or a century later?

'If we are sighted by a screen of destroyers, they may imagine from our silhouettes, spaced out . . . that we are a more impressive force than is actually the case . . . I cannot tell you for certain the exact composition of the enemy surface forces, but we must expect it to consist of the *Von Tirpitz*, certainly the *Hipper* and the *Von Scheer* . . . If we are turned to bay by the destroyers we shall engage, of course, and we stand a chance . . . while if we come within range of their capital ships I know you will agree that we should at once turn towards them and go on fighting as long as we can . . .'

At that there was a great shout, which I recorded, together with his words, in my diary that night; a kind of spontaneous belly laugh from the smudged faces below him, the release of their pent-up nerves which were forcing an outlet, before he quietened them once again into stillness with a sober peroration.

'I hope that those off-watch will get what sleep they can. I hope, too, that every one of you will make his peace with his Maker, as I intend to do myself. But I intend to bring you all back to port, with God's help.'

And with God's help he did, although there were both delays and diversions en route. Certainly not many travellers can have personal knowledge of a remote island situated at seventy-five degrees north, called Nova Zemblya. Certainly no one in the ship had, for it was scarcely on the direct convoy route to North Russia.

Sometimes today, when I become involved in a discussion over the difficulties of finding somewhere new and unspoilt for a holiday, and even start complaining at how all the popular places like Majorca and Malta, Corsica and Jersey and Elba, are becoming increasingly crowded, I come out with the name of the island where I spent a night at anchorage in the Matochkin Straits.

It is a certain conversation-stopper. 'Nova where?' I am asked, with a glint of hope in everyone's eyes. 'Can you reach it by air? What is the climate like? What travel agencies run package deals?' Alas, disappointment sets in when I explain the circumstances of my own brief visit, reciting what I found in the *Everyman's Encyclopaedia* in the wardroom that night, after the captain had passed on the information to one of the merchantmen, the *Samuel Chase*, that that was where we were temporarily heading and she was very welcome to fall in behind us.

'There is practically no animal life on the island, except for a few lemmings and brown and white bears. But on the coast abound birds, whales, walruses and dolphins. There is a small Russian colony on the south island.'

We had no chart for the Straits. But that was a minor hazard compared with all the others, and when gingerly and slowly we nosed our way in, it was to find that our sister ship had had the same idea, and immediately across the water flashed the Aldis lamp on their bridge.

'Welcome to our base.'

'May we anchor in your back garden?'

This kind of joking exchange at such a moment, deliberately intended to conceal the consuming tensions, will be understood at once by those who have ever found themselves in a situation of some danger. For 'back garden' one could more truthfully substitute 'back of beyond' and admit there was no semblance of real safety here. A brief breathing-space, no more. The tiny settlement on shore turned out to stare, but not to wave a welcome, pointing instead their only guns in our direction, preparing us in advance for the marked indifference we were to encounter later on the Russian mainland. The only friendly sign was of the washing fluttering in the breeze, to remind us that it was a Monday, when similar cleansing rites were being performed all over the world.

Far more insistent was the realization that what at first had seemed a haven was only too likely to turn into a trap the moment that Snoopy Joe discovered our whereabouts once more, and found, too, that the corvettes with the survivors they had picked up had also on their own initiative made for Nova Zemblya. Our pursuers had only to mine the entrance to the straits, and then bomb us at their leisure; for we could have no manoeuvrability at all. Better the open seas once more, where we would have a sporting chance.

So every ship's company, which now included three merchantmen, had one night in their bunks of blessed, undisturbed sleep, and then next morning, while a conference was being held among the senior captains as to how and when our little group should make a dash for it, I came into the *Pozarica*'s wardroom to find it full of strangers. Except that there was an instant bond between us, and always will be now; a bond of which I became aware all over again when a few weeks ago the voice of someone who had been rescued by the corvette *Lotus*, after five hours in an open boat, spoke to me over the telephone in London.

'This is Captain Charlton of the *River Afton*, do you remember me?' the voice began, in greeting.

The *River Afton* was one of the few British merchantmen in the convoy; her skipper came from Heaton, outside Newcastle. Yes, I remembered him, almost every time I was handed a bundle of crisp notes across the counter of my bank. I remembered, too, the story the *River Afton*'s skipper had had to tell me that morning in Nova Zemblya. How, after two torpedoes had hit the ship, the first boat they had tried to lower had overturned and all the sixteen men in it had been drowned. The smaller whaler, which seemed like a cockleshell, and in which the captain found himself with two other members of his crew, also capsized twice. Somehow they got it righted again, and it was as they were desperately seeking something, anything with which to bale out, that the captain became conscious of the brief-case tied with a cord round his neck. It contained all the money for the crew's wages. At once he emptied it and made a bucket of sorts, while behind him like a bizarre version of the Milky Way the very clean notes drifted until their passage was arrested by the body of a fireman, with his head burst open. Now that the level of the water in the boat was decreasing, they could risk stretching out and lifting him on board. But he died almost at once. Then Captain Charlton took off his oilskins and, wrapping them round the body dropped it back over the side. It was the best that he could do.

'I had nothing to weight the body down with,' he explained to me that morning in the *Pozarica*'s wardroom, 'and I couldn't remember how the burial service went, except the bit about dust to dust and ashes to ashes. So I said that twice over, though it sounded strange surrounded by all that water. When I looked back over my shoulder to see if the body was decently sinking, it was still floating in the middle of all that money . . .'

We had been thrown together by such a macabre twist of Fortune, and had never met again in peace time, and now as I heard his strong northern accent over the telephone I saw him as he was then, with a fiery ginger moustache and dressed in the incongruous but dry clothes that had been provided for him out of a bundle sent by the Merchant Navy Comforts Service. For he was wearing, of all surprising things, a pair of pepper-and-salt trousers, such as an elderly member of The Carlton Club might sport. As though in explanation, the recipient produced the label from the rescue kit, giving the donor's name, and it read, *Lord Yarborough, Harston, Lincolnshire. Good luck and God speed.*

Captain Charlton needed the luck, for I discovered that this was his third trip to Russia, and his third ducking. And his luck had stayed with him, for it was good to hear that he was still at sea, still in command, and still in the same unquenchable spirits as when he had raised my own morale by exclaiming, 'I hope you've got a survivor's gun on board.'

I did not remind him of that but, instead, he reminded me of something of which I have no recollection. This puzzled me, except that I have never visualized myself in an heroic role. Simply as an observer, and a kind of messenger, absorbingly interested in how the rest of the world lives and has its being.

'Do you remember when you and I took turn and turn about with a Lewis gun on the searchlight platform? Most of the time you blazed away, as I did the loading.'

Did we? Did I? If you did, that must have been during the night of the final showdown, I thought as I put down the telephone, when two out of the three merchantmen went and only the *Ocean Freedom* was left and I kept on saying desperately to myself over and over again, they can't sink a ship with a name like that.

At first, after we crept out of Nova Zemblya we were protected by a thick screen of fog, and it was only when that cleared and what was in a sense our ultimate enemy, the midnight sun, took possession once more out of a clear sky that we were picked up by the waves of Junkers 88s – the crack squadrons, we heard afterwards, which had been specially transferred from Sicily.

'At ten thousand feet, bombs drop three hundred feet a second, and to hit their objective should be released a mile-and-a-half in advance.'

This piece of information, unusual for me to possess, I had heard being impressed on a class at Millom R.A.F. Training Station on the Lancashire coast, which I had visited earlier in the war, and now it kept repeating itself in my mind as I pressed my palms to my ears, because one of my drums had been pierced by the blast. The pain was so intense that I was terrified not so much of the bombs that were scoring near-misses all round us as that I might faint and make a fool of myself in front of everyone on the bridge.

It was the captain who saved me, as I kept my eyes on him, savouring his quiet authority, his absolute calm. I suppose it was a lifetime's training behind him, but all the same I still don't know how he had the nerve to hang on till the last split second when he sensed the eggs were actually leaving the planes directly overhead, and then he gave the signal to Mac, the quartermaster in the wheelhouse below, who came from the Outer Hebrides and was my favourite partner at solo in the P.O.'s mess. 'Hard to port' or 'Hard to starboard.' But despite the shrill whining of the bombs themselves, distinct above the cacophonous din of the guns, the captain never spoke more loudly than if he were asking me to pass the salt at a meal in his cabin.

How slowly the ship seemed to turn; so slowly that I would rise on my toes, willing it to swing round faster, faster, or surely this time they must score a direct hit, especially now that they were making us their special target because of the cover we were seeking to give to the rescue ship, *Zamalek*, packed with survivors, on our starboard beam.

It was four o'clock in the morning when the R.D.F. was finally silent and the radar screen was clear. I was too spent to go in search of the Doc to ask what he could do for my ear. Besides, what did it matter compared with the losses? I was still standing disconsolate on the bridge when something happened which poured a fresh supply of adrenalin into my veins; something which must have meant as much to the master of the mercy ship, *Zamalek*, as the D.S.O. that Captain Morris was to wear subsequently on his tunic. To be spontaneously cheered by your comrades at sea, after passing through a tremendous test together; is not that a tribute beyond price?

It was our captain who, casting aside his customary reticence, started the acclamation. Taking off his cap and holding it aloft, through the loudspeaker he rallied everyone's spirits; 'Let's give them a cheer'. And instantly across the fifty yards of intervening water and beyond, echoing into the wastes of the Arctic, went volley after volley of a different thunder from that of the guns. I don't know how they managed to produce such a volume from their scorched throats, with the temporary passengers, including the Yanks in their yellow Mae Wests, that made them seem like creatures from a Wellsian world, joining in most vociferously of all.

Then, in turn, the eyes of the *Pozy*'s crew beheld something which must have made them all feel, at last, at peace with themselves, all the weight of the abortive alarums and excursions of the last few days lifted from their shoulders. Every man of them, just as much as their captain, had been haunted by the sight of the convoy miserably disintegrating like a flock of lost sheep, and hated the inference that, through no fault of their own, but because they had to obey the direct orders from the Admiralty, they were leaving the virtually unarmed merchantmen in the lurch. But now, through the purging of tonight's pitched battle, they had regained their manhood. So no wonder they cheered, and then were as swiftly moved to silence as they watched the small ship make a gesture in return which is very rare. The *Zamalek* dipped its ensign in recognition and gratitude for the protection it had received during the long hours of concentrated attack. Not in vain, after all, had they risked so much in putting down their nets. Their human flotsam of the sea was safe. Or rather, the prospects had considerably improved. For we were only a short steaming time from Iokanka; and was not Iokanka on Russian soil, at the very tip of the White Sea leading down to the secure anchorage of Archangel?

I am often asked what memory from the extremely mixed bag of adventures which came my way during the war years has become most insistently part of my consciousness. It was the cheering in that dawn of a new day and the answer which it evoked – in a code unrecognized by those students of Sussex University, just down the road from my country home, who chose not long ago publicly to burn the Union Jack on their campus. This was, presumably, in protest against the standards of behaviour and the beliefs of men like the captain of the *Pozarica* who himself, though already in his fifties, refused to surrender the command of his ship for a shore-based appointment when he learnt that they were to exchange what they had nicknamed The Milk Run, between Belfast and Milford Haven, the last lap of the Atlantic convoys, for the infinitely greater challenges of the Russian Run.

'Well Godfrey,' he said when at last the cheering had died away, 'what about supper? It's been rather noisy tonight, so I suggest somewhere without a band. What about the Ritz Grill?'

'No, let's try the Savoy Grill. It keeps open longer,' I replied, doing my best to maintain the exchange of banter which had become a private joke between us during the voyage. For our supper always consisted of the same menu, a cup of kye.

As I followed him down the companion way, a figure in singlet and dungarees, soaked through, came stumbling out of the wheelhouse. Mac . . . I took his arm and he swung round, rocking on his heels. I scarcely recognized him as the consistent winner in the solo school. I used to marvel at the depth of his concentration over the greasy cards, undisturbed by all the gregarious chaffing round him in the mess, but what must it have been like for him trying to separate the captain's orders coming down the voice pipe, from the confused clamour of the battle itself? The heat in his extremely confined space must have been almost insupportable, but equally so the strain on his two arms, huge though they were, incessantly hauling the wheel now this way, now that. Still, Mac had come through, and the two men who between them had saved the ship that night looked deeply into each other's faces. But they did not speak. They simply shook hands and went on their way to their own domains.

In the captain's cabin, Mulley had once again just picked up the solitary photograph frame off the floor, and was setting it on the desk as we came through the door. 'Where are the flowers?' my companion unexpectedly asked. They were the geraniums that Mrs Lawford had brought on board at Belfast on the morning that we sailed; bright, scarlet geraniums, such as you see in public parks or in front of Buckingham Palace in the tourist season.

She must have sensed my lack of enthusiasm for them, for she had explained, 'I thought they would last longer'.

'Oh, they've had it, sir. I threw them away in blooming Nova Zemblya.'

'Did you? I didn't notice.'

He slumped down heavily in a chair, still in his padded coat, and Mulley poured the cocoa for us, the Naval cocoa made from the kind of concentrated chocolate essence you never appear to get on shore. It was one of those pleasant perks, like the rum ration which equally seemed so much more fiery, as I found when in due course I myself had the right to draw my own daily ration.

At first we sat in silence, and then with a sudden movement my host reached for the picture of his son and held it in his hands. 'I never told you about Peter, did I?' he said at last.

'No, only that I know he was . . .'

Again the silence between us before he began again.

'Of course, you know he was our only boy, but he had a friend called Richard, who was as close to him as an elder brother. They always used to spend their summer holidays together, until the balloon went up. Then Peter decided he didn't want to go into his father's Service – and I can understand his point of view – but to be a soldier instead, while Richard opted to be a pilot. You see he had already done some peace-time flying and a first-class pilot he made, too, till they shot him down in his Spitfire, in the Battle of Britain. He was twenty-three, two years older than Peter.'

My companion reached for the silver box filled with cigarettes that were to run out during our enforced sojourn against the woodpiles outside Archangel, and offered his guest one, forgetting that I did not smoke. He himself was far away.

'Before I took command of the *Pozy*, I was working at the Admiralty, and it was there that Richard's mother phoned me. It was a glorious July day, I remember, and I asked for short leave so that I could go and visit her. She lives in the Weald of Kent, I expect you have seen what the blossom is like there in the spring, and they were still fighting the battle over her head. But that hadn't stopped her being out in the garden, and she came across the lawn to greet me, her gardening basket over her arm and her hands full of the flowers she had just picked. And she was actually smiling. That is something I have never got over. She was able to smile at me, and before I could try to tell her what I felt about Richard, who would have made such a grand leader, she said, 'I know what you've come to say, David, but don't say it. Don't pity me, please. Richard is my contribution to the war effort.' So I could only go away marvelling . . . but when it was our turn, Richard's mother sent us a telegram. . . .'

Instinctively he reached towards the pocket of his zipper suit, searching in the same pocket where all the crew kept their last letter from home, but he really did not have to look down at the piece of crumpled paper. The contents of the telegram were already engraved on his heart.

'Peter is now with Richard. Invincible and invulnerable they will return to succour us.'

Then he put down his son's picture and left the cabin to go on to the bridge, and I fell asleep instantly in the chair where I was seated, and started to dream.

I was back in the *Freebooter*, in which I had been doing a trip exactly a year before. The *Freebooter* was a much smaller boat even than the *Zamalek*, an ocean-going tug which in company with two others had been given the unusual assignment of towing a floating dock, with a twenty-thousand ton displacement, from Plymouth, round Land's End to Greenock. Progress could only be made at three knots, and before we started I had been warned by the Admiralty department which gave me my marching orders to expect fireworks. In actual fact, it turned out a picnic, the Irish Sea was like a mill-pond, we never sighted an enemy plane and the boys on board spent their time gleefully getting brown for leave, while the tug's master, Captain Bond, who came from Hull and sensibly never shed a single garment the whole week we were on board together, indulged in a series of cat-naps.

But now, in my nightmare, the floating dock instead of resembling Tower Bridge proceeding majestically behind us, had turned into a wicked-looking battleship, bristling with guns, and I heard myself crying out, Wake up, Captain Bond, the *Von Tirpitz* is behind us and we must go faster, faster, faster. Then the scene changed and I was in the water, choking, drowning, in the depths of my sleep of utter exhaustion until I was rescued by a net let down, not by the *Zamalek* but by the *Pozarica*, and the reason I know it was my own ship was because I was being welcomed at the top of the gangway by her captain, to whom I was apologetically explaining how sorry I was that I hadn't a clean white shirt, but I hadn't needed one on board the *Freebooter*. Never mind, he said soothingly, I expect you lost it at the Astor. Whereupon the whole ship's company took up the chant, singing the words of the refrain which was always played, as a variant to *I've got Sixpence*, over the loudspeaker, sailing in and out of harbour.

But surely that came later? This was our first meeting, when they were our escort, guarding the floating dock, an exchange of greetings half-way from Plymouth to Greenock, ending with an invitation at tiffin time to be their guest for a longer visit on another occasion. This I accepted in due course, and greatly enjoyed.

There are some ships, like houses, in which you feel at home at once. I found myself longing to be a member of the crew. Especially after Sandy, who looked too mild a man to be a gunner's mate, had announced that they'd like to have me on board as their mascot, as I seemed to them to have a charmed life. I wasn't so sure about that myself, but when I finally decided to give up trying to fight the war with my pen, and to disappear anonymously instead into a seaman's uniform, I accepted with alacrity the further invitation of my favourite ship to spend a few more days on board, not officially this time but as a private guest, before reporting at the depot where so many thousands had done their training before me, H.M.S. *Ganges*.

As soon as the *Pozarica*'s captain had greeted me in his cabin, this time in Milford Haven, it was he who asked the first question; rather a far-reaching one. 'Are you going to come with us to Russia?' Apparently the orders for a change of course had come through, even as I was proceeding overnight by train from London, expecting to be put ashore again at Belfast. And so, instead, this bonus, if that was the right word, which seemed too pointedly part of my personal destiny to refuse if permission from 'on high' was granted. In Belfast I waited for my masters to make up their mind and those extra, unforeseen days while the ship was packed with provisions, and extra fuel tanks added, were one of my precious, most care-free interludes during those six surprising years.

'But you'll be late now arriving at the *Ganges*, you'll be late now arriving at the *Ganges*, and it would never have happened,' Captain Bond was admonishing me, in my uneasy dream, 'if only you'd taken my advice about indulging in cat-naps, cat-naps . . .'

I was being gently shaken awake by Mulley with a cup of tea in his hand. At once I sensed that the ship was no longer moving, and feeling like a sleep-walker I staggered up on deck and started to wade through the carcasses of shells, of which in the five hours of continuous attack we had used twelve hundred rounds of four-inch, to discover that we were riding at anchor. We had put into Iokanka, in the hope that our allies might have some ships there that could go out at once to look for survivors. But we were met with the first of many refusals. Both the sloops that we could see tied up against the miniature quayside were there for 'boiler cleaning' and there was no other suitable craft available.

We had to accept these excuses at their face value. We hadn't sufficient fuel to turn back ourselves, and no ammunition left at all. This was the morning-after, with a vengeance. As we began to sail on towards Archangel, I was depressed and dismayed by the lack of colour on the shore. No flowers or vegetation, nothing but piles of wood awaiting transportation and the whole landscape so barren of habitation. Yet at the same time it had a kind of oriental watchfulness, as though a thousand unseen eyes were scrutinizing the silhouettes of our ships, mocking our sorely diminished numbers.

At the junction of the White Sea with the Doina River, we were met by the leader of the minesweeping flotilla, based on Archangel. Her captain, hailing us through his megaphone, announced in the most pussar of voices that we might expect a pilot to take us on down the river, in five hours, five days, five weeks, five years.

Here was our second warning already that Russia might not turn out to be the welcoming paradise that most of us, especially the members of the lower deck, had expected. After all, at home, at this zero point in our struggle for survival, we had been subjected to the most intense propaganda concerning not only the bravery of our allies in defending their own soil but their superb efficiency and their total selflessness in toiling for the common cause. Yet when the pilot did appear, he scarcely proved a spectacular advertisement for the Soviet régime, since he proceeded almost immediately to take us aground, where we had impotently to remain for several hours till the tide itself refloated us once more.

Two men had come on board, both dressed alike in coolie jackets that made them resemble Chinamen. One was the pilot, the other a member of the commissar's staff, who could speak a few words of English. However, he was not so much there as an interpreter as to watch his comrade to see that he wasn't corrupted by Western bribes, or by such a very different way of life. With typical naval hospitality, our first Russian contacts had both been escorted below to the wardroom and offered their choice of whisky, gin or beer. There is an iron rule that no officer drinks at sea. So everyone stood round, watching the eyes of our guests boggle. Alas, the festive mood did not last long, for when the absurd anti-climax happened, through sheer incompetence, and we were stuck, the man who had brought us all this way without mishap lost his temper for the first and only time on the voyage. And how formidable he became. I began to feel almost sorry for the cringing figure in front of him, now looking more like a half-starved coolie than ever, especially when his chum took up the harangue and pursued his opposite number to the back of the bridge, with the hissing noises of a gaggle of geese. In the end it was too much for the one in disgrace, who burst into a storm of hysterical weeping.

'What will happen to him?' I asked Charlton, not a newcomer as we were to these parts, who had been a witness of this unedifying tableau.

'Well, one thing is certain. However many times you come up and down this river again, you will never set eyes on this particular pilot. Because he has committed the one unforgivable crime in their eyes. He has let down the side in front of foreigners. National face, and all that. So our friend will be despatched for a long week-end in the Urals.'

'A long week-end in the Urals?' I echoed, puzzled.

'Haven't you heard that expression before?' the veteran at my side persisted. When I shook my head, he stroked his ginger moustache and assured me cheerfully, 'You will, laddie, and many times if you stay here long enough.'

The next time I heard mention of the Urals, and on this occasion with more sinister overtones, was from my stable companion, Smithie. As navigating officer of the ship, it fell to him to report every few days our exact moorings at the Port Controller's office, situated at the side of the wood wharves at Ekonomia, outside Archangel, where we found ourselves berthed close to the corvettes and the minesweepers.

To walk across the wood wharves and back was not exactly an exciting expedition. All the same, his fellow officers envied Smithie his prerogative, since the interpreter on these occasions turned out to be an attractive young student from Archangel University. Anya was naturally delighted to have this opportunity to practise her English in such a legitimate manner, while Smithie, in his turn, just as any other man in the ship would have done, welcomed these brief feminine encounters as a change from the growing monotony of nothing but masculine company and wardroom conversation that was fast becoming like a gramophone record, repeating itself *ad nauseam*.

Not surprisingly, therefore, Smithie suggested that Anya and he should continue their English lesson, out of office hours. Gladly she accepted his invitation one evening to go for a walk along the quayside and back. For what could be more harmless than that? They were in full view of all the ships' portholes. Yes, but equally of the ever vigilant eyes of the Ogpu. The next time that Smithie arrived to make his routine report in the Controller's office, he found a very different Anya. Now, instead of a welcoming smile, she gazed at him with terrified eyes and poured out in a hurried rush, glancing nervously at the door, 'You must never try to see me again, except here in the office. I have been warned that if I go with you on the quayside, I shall lose my job and my parents their apartment, and they have two rooms to themselves, and I shall not be permitted to finish my studies at the University. So please, please be careful.'

'But in actual fact, there was absolutely nothing to be careful about,' he summed up that evening, lying in his bunk, before we turned out the light, with his wife's smiling picture on the chest of drawers between his bed and mine. 'Of course, I told her that I was married. That was the point, really. I mean, just to walk beside an attractive girl like her somehow brought my wife closer. And I promised Anya that when we get back to England – if we ever get away from this dump – I would ask my wife to send her a lipstick and some powder. She said that's what she'd like more than anything. You should have seen the way her face lit up, as though they were luxuries beyond compare.

'Anya asked me all sorts of questions about England,' he went on, 'and I felt I was doing a good bit of propaganda. You know, they have been fed with an awful basinful of lies. They imagine we all live like belted earls – can you believe it? – and they are deliberately told nothing about the war effort on our side. Take this convoy, for instance. Although Anya works in the Controller's office, and must hear a lot of private information, she swore that she didn't know anything about the tremendous losses of "P.Q.17" and the previous convoys, too. She imagined that the ships which arrived were the only ones which had been sent, that we simply weren't trying to get through all the machinery, etc., that they need. Can you beat it?'

When I last saw him, Smithie was a river pilot, happily based on Gravesend, and here I visited him one post-war July to open a summer fête in aid of his wife's church. After I had made the round of the stalls and the side-shows, we talked again of that extraordinary summer when we were marooned at Ekonomia, and we wondered what had happened to Anya in the years between, and whether she had successfully escaped being banished to the Urals.

Smithie's charming lady looked a little incredulous that such a threat could ever have really been a positive one. And I can readily understand her reaction. Because what her husband and I and all the others experienced is a long way off now, both in time and latitude. Yet in their ruthless attitude in regard to human expendability, their inbred distrust and dislike of everyone on our side of the Curtain, are their leaders any different today? I wonder.

People often expound their views on Russia to me at length, and as the proof that a genuine thaw has set in they cite the pleasure they have had themselves in watching a performance of the Bolshoi Ballet. However, when at the end of their harangue I always ask politely if they themselves have ever set foot on

Russian soil, the answer is almost invariably a negative one. Whereupon I shrug my shoulders and change the subject. For it is almost impossible to seek to recapture in a few sentences the overriding impression we all had of being regarded not as allies, brave or otherwise, but rather as a species of political prisoners, let out on parole. One false step and we would be incarcerated, despatched to the salt mines ourselves.

Once, but only once, did I chance my luck in Archangel itself. The Russian authorities did not encourage such trips. In any case, there was scarcely anything to buy in the shops except gramophone records of Stalin's speeches, while we in our turn had precious little currency to spend. All the same, we were possessed of a great longing to venture forth, however short a distance, so that we could escape, even for a few hours, the uninspiring backcloth of wood piles to what was virtually a prison camp, with robot-like guards at the entrances facing inland.

In consequence, it was rather pleasant to come within view of a Mosque, uncared-for though it only too clearly was. I was standing there quietly in the roadway when I felt a tap on my shoulder. Turning, I found myself staring into the frozen features of a policewoman, with a belt round her massive waist that might have been borrowed from a blacksmith. She did not try to communicate with me, except in sign language. It was enough. Her thumb denoted that I was to move on, and move on I did most hurriedly with my heart beating uncomfortably fast against my ribs.

To this day, I cannot imagine what dangerous impact she read into the sight of a young man in a dark blue blazer, peacefully occupied in trying to put a date to the onion-shaped, copper-coloured dome.

It may seem absurd, but I felt more frightened at that moment than all the time I was rooted to the bridge of the *Pozarica* and the near-misses were being recorded in gargantuan spouts of water all round us. How could you have been, I am sometimes questioned on a note of incredulity. I can only write and speak as I recall it all, deep in my bones. As the weeks went by and our sense of isolation inevitably increased, there is no doubt that the crew of the assorted collection of ships marooned at Ekonomia began to share the same sensation of there being something as grim and as inhuman about the inhabitants of this corner of an alien empire, as about the landscape itself.

I had a rather disturbing confirmation of my original allergy, my instinctive wariness, a quarter of a century later when I was flying to Australia just before the Christmas of 1967. On its first lap, our Air India plane reached Moscow at midnight, and against my better judgment having sworn to myself never to risk finding myself on Russian territory again, I weakly followed the other half-dozen passengers in the first-class compartment down the gangway. To my astonishment, we had to surrender our passports, and at once the old familiar sense of unease gripped me. Surely one did not usually have to hand over one's passport in exchange for a worthless piece of cardboard, which was all the transit passenger ticket really was? By the time our bus had ploughed its way through a mantle of thickly-falling snow, to the main buildings, the hairs on the back of my hands were standing up on end, like those of a dog scenting danger. Nor was I appeased by the vast, grandiose lounge in which we now found ourselves, with colossal propaganda posters screaming at us from the walls.

In our plane there was a large group of school children returning for their Christmas holidays to their parents stationed along the line, mostly in Singapore. As though the strangely empty spaces, with little furniture, had been provided specially for them as a playground, they ran around, laughing and unafraid, in infectious high spirits. In contrast, our little lot seemed somehow to find it difficult to relax, as we stood in a small, mutually-reassuring group in the centre of nothingness. Why had we troubled to leave our warm seats? Of course, the name 'Moscow' had always had an exotic connotation, but there was nothing here to remind us of Stalin's tomb or the Red Square. As an anonymous figure passed us, who might so easily, I decided, have been a member of the secret police, I remarked in what was intended to be a bantering tone, to keep up my own spirits as much as theirs: 'What a splendid setting this would make for a thriller by Eric Ambler. Someone would come up to us, offering us free refreshments, and while we were choosing what we would have another attendant, taking advantage of the diversion, would get busy with a concealed syringe. Whoever was the quarry would scarcely notice the faint pricking on the wrist, being so enchanted with the liberal offering of caviar. Then five minutes later, with the sound of many waters in his ears, and all the lights crashing in his head, he – because it is more likely to be a he – would pass out into darkness, on the floor. At once, yet another ubiquitous attendant, this time dressed in the uniform of the International Red Cross, would glide on the scene to supervise the removal of the one who had unexpectedly fainted, to the First Aid room . . .

'The marked-down victim would never reappear, and our plane, with one seat empty, would sail on into the night. Later, again, when the one who was, shall we say, acting as a private courier for important diplomatic dispatches, or had some specialized knowledge of the latest Atomic secrets, came-to, what chance or hope had he of ever proving his real identity? Remember, they have taken away our passports. At this moment, every one of us is Stateless, without any rights as a citizen of their country, without even an identity card in our wallet, such as we used to have to carry in the war. But the cold war itself has never had an armistice. . . .

'Of course,' I added, the jocular tone now eroded from my voice as my traveller's tale, made up on the spur of the moment to serve as a diversion during our tedious wait, began to assume credence in my own mind, 'Of course,' I repeated with some emphasis, 'I have no idea if any of us merits such attention from their own Secret Service.'

It was inevitable then that we should introduce ourselves, and I thought: this is rather a good way of breaking the social ice. One couple had come from Skye, and another couple were on their way to Fiji, where the husband, I gathered, was in the Civil Service. But at that point, I am afraid I wasn't very interested, because a tall, rangey young Australian was telling us excitedly how much it meant to him to get home for Christmas, as his wife was expecting their first child. I took it for granted that his destination in Western Australia was a sheep station, since, in his tweed suit and with his loose tie and long thin legs, he had the look of someone used to riding and being out of doors all day. So it was something of a surprise, I think to us all, when he went on to explain that after working for several years at the atom plant at Woomera, in his own country, he was now on loan to the Americans. Was it my imagination that we all drew closer to him protectively? Certainly we regarded him with a new interest and respect.

At last the call came for the passengers from our plane to re-embark, and the children became muddled up at the exit gate with a group of natives, themselves departing, one felt, for the furthest steppes. For the men all wore fur hats and, in contrast to those of their compatriots that I had encountered in Archangel, were tall with swarthy, Tartar features, and a striking, almost theatrical, panache which reminded me of the dancers in *Prince Igor*. What was this exclusively male party? A returning Trade Mission from Outer Mongolia, or the Urals? A group of first-class workers from The Caucasus, who had been rewarded by a sight-seeing tour of the Capital? I shall never know, nor the English boys and girls who stared at them with wonder in their eyes, giants and goblins from another world, as we waited for the usual sullen-looking pair of de-sexed women officials to let us grudgingly through, two by two, like couples entering the Ark.

Into the bus again, and across the airfield, until only fifty yards from the plane we stopped, and there was a hiatus, a sudden tightening of the atmosphere. Now we were all conscious that we were crammed together in complete darkness. Why did not someone open the door and let us out of this airless oven, and on board? I had had the same experience of being treated like cattle, in a B.E.A. bus, but that at least was in daylight, and in my own country. It was at this moment that I discovered to my horror that I must have dropped my transit pass on the floor, and my little group all bent down in the blackness, and searched round everyone's feet. But in vain. Meanwhile, the children had gone very quiet, ominously so, until suddenly there was a scream, followed by another, and then a crash of breaking glass, which inevitably became the sound of doom in my own ears. Why hadn't I kept my pass safely in my pocket till the actual moment of boarding? On this night of all nights, with so much knowledge from the past, how could I be such a fool? My mouth was so dry I could not even thank my new friends for their unselfish efforts on my behalf. I have a confused recollection of the door of the bus being opened at last, in answer to the continuous tattoo beaten on the blind, frosted windows, and of our streaming out, with our heads down against the blizzard like a curtain separating us from the lighted gangways, our havens of security.

We were not safely inside yet. I imagine I knew what was going to happen, before it did. It was not simply my instinct as a teller of stories that insisted on a climax. In effect, the hold-up was exactly as I had imagined it would be. At the top of the stairs leading to our end of the plane, there was yet another female official, with a shapeless fur skin draped round her shoulders, all set to play her part. Directly in front of me was the unobtrusive, middle-aged civil servant, and in front of him again the Australian passenger for Perth. The others had been given back their passports in exchange for their transit passes, and disappeared inside. We were the last three, bringing up the rear. As soon as the Australian drew opposite, and held out his hand for his passport, announcing his name, I leant forward so as to have a visual picture of the dumb play which followed. The lifting of her shoulders under the shaggy, smelly rug, the elaborate gesticulation to imply that she could not find the Australian's passport to return to him, the increasing insolence of her manner. The civil servant allowed her to complete her ploy, and then before the situation could worsen further he gave his fellow passenger a sharp shove, urging him into the plane. 'I'll cope with this lady,' he said. And did.

The amazon made an angry movement to restrain him, but she was too late. To my amazement my fellow-countryman seemed now, instead, to tower above her. In an instant he had become more than six-foot high, with all the majesty of the Raj, in its palmiest days, surrounding him. 'Give me my own passport,' he demanded curtly, 'and give Mr Winn his. And find the other one. *Quickly*.'

Our adversary was too surprised by the weight of cool authority displayed to demur. It was only afterwards that I realized my lack of a boarding card had passed completely unnoticed. Pocketing the two passports, and repeating his terse command about the other one, our self-elected leader took me by the lapel of my overcoat and pushed me ahead of him into the plane's interior where a hostess in a sari, made to seem twice as elegant and exquisite by the contrast with the creature with whom we had just had a confrontation, offered us champagne and caviar.

At first we were too shaken by our encounter to enjoy our midnight feast. The gangway door was still open, and a piercing draught of cold air blew menacingly in upon us. Once more, the unexpected hero of the evening assured the Australian that he was safe now, on neutral ground, and could not be taken off the plane. 'Never fear, they will produce your passport in the end,' he said quietly, his tone implying that they had lost this round and would be compelled, grudgingly, to admit it. And indeed, just as he prophesied, though after what seemed an interminable pause, the sari lady, her smile unchanged, made a reappearance with it in her hand.

'Now will you have some champagne?' she suggested.

'I certainly will,' I called out, lifting my glass to toast my fellow-passenger, his long legs stretched out beside me. 'At least now, you won't be spending your Christmas, or at any rate a long week-end, in the Urals,' I assured him.

'A long week-end in the Urals?' he echoed, in his deceptively guileless voice. 'Why the heck the Urals?'

I thought it best not to enlighten him or pursue the theme further. Everyone was settling down to sleep and, after all, I had produced one yarn for the company that night. Although I suspect that the civil servant, reverting to type, and rather shyly confessing how he found that the best antidote to a diet of familiarity in his peace-time station was to listen to classical gramophone records sent out from home, would have appreciated hearing about the episode of the cabbage.

Did you imagine that the cabbage had a lowly place in the list of vegetables for the table? Not to us it hadn't, as the summer of 1942 had dragged on from July into August, and still not the least prospect of sailing for home until more ammunition and provisions could be sent out to us under the cover of the early autumn darkness of the longer nights. Meanwhile, only too plainly, Britannia did not rule these waves.

Already the midnight sun had vanished, but that was almost a relief for us because of its unhappy associations, even though in its place a molten sky pressed down upon us. How steamy and enervating the atmosphere was, and now instead of the Heinkels and the Junker 88s there were the attacks of mosquitoes, based on the river, to plague us. It was astonishing that morale did not crack, but in actual fact it remained surprisingly high. When a situation has become completely static, and things are at their lowest ebb, the British Navy has long since worked out its own remedies for killing time and too much useless speculation. Paint ship, in working hours, exercise and more exercise during all free periods.

The wharfside became our Wembley Stadium. Improvised football and cricket pitches were marked out, and a series of inter-ship hockey matches were arranged, with my own team appearing on the fixture list. We were short of equipment, and had to play with an improvised ball made of twine from the ship's stores, but somehow we made a game of it and got up a lather, and that was what mattered. Meanwhile, from a safe distance stray members of the local population, attired in dun-coloured garments to match the landscape, would watch all our efforts with complete impassivity. They must have wondered where we got our energy from, since we were down to hard tack. Bully-beef was the order of the day. The crew nicknamed it Churchill's chicken. Mulley served up what he lugubriously announced as Bully Beef Surprise. But it still remained Bully, hot or cold, and tasted like Bully, until sometimes I wondered, as I sat seated opposite the captain in his cabin at every meal, whether I was going to choke on it.

What saved me was the patina of his own good manners, so much a part of the Navy's heritage. The same good manners were instilled into junior snotties in the Gun Room until they had learned that though their days in the Service would take them into many outlandish places and confront them with all kinds of extraordinary challenges they must never flag in making polite conversation with the other fellows in their mess, because that was both civilized and life-saving.

'Where did I sit at lunch?' my host would say, coming into the cabin after his evening stroll along the wharf. 'Then I will sit *here* tonight.'

After that one glimpse he had given me of what lay in the secret places of his own heart, he elaborately avoided any further reference. Instead, he would try to interest me in some safe, impersonal subject, like the pleasures of salmon fishing, of which unfortunately I knew less than nothing. Drawing a blank, undaunted, he would persevere. Somehow, we got through the meals, the days passed, he tore off yet another page from his calendar on the wall, and remarked cheerfully:

'Ah, grouse shooting starts tomorrow.'

With Captain David Lawford, D.S.O., on the bridge of H.M.S. *Pozarica*

The start of an historic voyage

Mulley, the captain's steward. 'I can't think where all the dust comes from'

Sandy, gunner's mate. 'I've got sixpence, jolly jolly sixpence. Sixpence to last me all my life'

The dawn after the final attack on the remnants of 'P.Q.17'

Funeral pyre for an oil tanker, July 4th, 1942

'Oh does it, sir?'

'Yes, it would be pleasant to be in Scotland at this moment, Godfrey. Do you know Scotland well?'

'I am afraid I don't. You see, I don't shoot. But I did go to Braemar once though I missed the Games. And I love Edinburgh. I've always promised myself that one day I'll take a house there for a year, in one of those squares off Prince's Street, and write a book.' I could feel the sweat on the palms of my hands under the table. How boring my voice sounded, even to myself, and how studiously courteous he himself remained. 'And the Clyde,' I went on desperately, 'I can never decide whether coming up Southampton Water, or reaching the Clyde, gives one a bigger impression of coming home. It must have been about a year today we arrived at Greenock ourselves with the floating dock. I wonder where the *Freebooter* is now? We never thought then that. . . .'

'No.' There was a pause, and then he added, but still without any emotion in his voice, 'I hope we get back in time to have one more bathe in an English sea.'

I nodded my agreement, though how cold and unwelcoming the North Sea had been in the days of my family childhood when we had rented a bungalow at Hunstanton every summer. Even in June the temperature of the Wash had seemed to be far below freezing point, and I had vowed to myself that I would never bathe again in an English sea, once I was grown up and could make my choice. It was warmer, of course, in the rivulets left behind by the tide, where we used to shrimp for our tea, and nostalgically I was filled with a longing to be back there with my brother and my Ludlow cousins, looking for peewits' eggs in the dunes beyond the golf course, that were such a prize – and such a delicacy in the eyes of the grown-ups.

It was a relief when Mulley came in to clear away the unappetising plates, for this was always the signal for me to escape to the P.O.'s mess for my evening session of solo with Mac and Bunker Hynes, and Percy Price, who by a self-concocted recipe had succeeded in dyeing his overalls the most brilliant Mediterranean blue, and was for ever washing them as a kind of therapy. To each their own booster. Using the talent for improvisation that all matelots, whatever their rank or length of service seem to possess, Captain Crombie,* the officer commanding the mine-

* Later Rear-Admiral Crombie.

sweeper flotilla, and the captain of the *Bramble*, increasingly reconciled to spending another winter in these parts, had decided upon his own source of recreation, in re-reading old copies of *The Times* propped against the teapot at breakfast. A different copy for each day of the week, Sunday included. The fact that they had first reached him several months ago, and that their topicality was nil, did not worry him in the least. By this ingenious charade, he bolstered himself against whatever local rumours or vexations another day might bring.

Of course, there was no mail or authentic dispatches from home, and the wireless maddened us by invariably picking up nothing but gibberish. In the dog watches, the crew wrote endless screeds to their families, which they could not post, encouraging themselves by opening their pocket books or their ditty boxes and taking out once again the thumbed and fading snapshots that to them were their testament of faith, their tiny stake in immortality.

'That's the missus, Goff, but it's not really a good likeness, she's got her eyes all screwed up, 'cos of the sun, and that's our garden, it's nothing like yours, just a strip between us and the railway line, but all the same we grow smashing chrysanths – do you think we'll be back in time to see them this year, what's the latest buzz from t'other end of ship? – and that's Willie, he's a bit of a mongrel but the kids love him. . . .'

I would pass along the messdeck, hailed and made welcome, till I came to Tom Brooks' cabouche, the equivalent on board of a village store. Every day Tom would elaborately go through the motions of opening up shop, even though his shelves had been stripped of everything appetising and now only a few tired bottles of HP Sauce remained. Cigarettes had long since run out, and so had nutty; Mars bars and Rowntrees' clear gums were simply a delicious dream from the past. But still would-be customers gathered, nattering away, like housewives exchanging greetings in a grocer's shop in Tom's native Darwen. I suppose they found a kind of reassurance in the aroma of the cubby hole. Besides, there was always the latest buzz to mull over, discounted though it usually was a day or two later. In consequence, when a wild rumour ran around the ship that the Second Front had started at last and allied troops had landed in France, no one took it seriously, least of all the parochial storekeeper himself, until the first load of fresh green cabbage appeared, and even then we didn't at first connect the two events as being one more example of cause and effect. Why should we?

Soon after our arrival at Ekonomia we had received an official visit from the local Commissar, who drew up beside our gangway in a very swanky American car. This we all agreed must inevitably devour petrol, and all expenditure of petrol was a touchy point with those who did their wartime service at sea. After a few preliminary politenesses, exchanged through the interpreter, he came to the point of his visit. He had fur-skins to offer, remarkable both in quality and quantity, what had we to barter in exchange? As soon as the *Pozarica*'s captain explained blandly that he was completely without resources in kind, unless a cheque on Coutts, cashable presumably after the war, would be acceptable, the interview swiftly came to an end. In turn, my captain's own request for any kind of diet variation, especially in the form of vegetables, fell on deaf ears. Very soon our doctor was dishing out doses of lime juice, a shipboard precaution against scurvy from the days of sailing ships. With affection the wardroom mocked him, saying they couldn't bear the taste of the stuff without gin, and the gin was disappearing as fast as everything else. All the same they drank up obediently when he warned them that several members of the crew had already come out in ugly sores. I myself was nagged by a skin rash which had appeared over the back of my hands. After my encounter with Jimmy Campbell, however, it seemed of no account.

And then, unheralded, one morning a lorry drew up alongside to deposit a consignment of cabbage rich in the minerals and vitamins our bodies craved. Every man on board wolfed down large helpings, as though enjoying the kind of 'Big Eats' they'd have 'up the smoke'.* It was indeed fortunate that none was kept back in cold storage for a second menu. For believe it or not, and we ourselves were pretty incredulous at the time, two days later someone from the Commissar's office arrived in person to demand back the gracious present of greens.

'You want it back?' repeated the *Pozarica*'s captain, half-imagining at first that the interpreter must be at fault. 'You say it was delivered to the wrong ship? That it was really intended for one of your own boats tied up at Ekonomia? Well,

* Naval slang for London.

my dear fellow, I am afraid that you must report back to your Lords and Masters that they will have to provide stomach pumps. . . .'

Once again the interview ended on an inconclusive note and it was some time before, as Mulley put it, the penny dropped. The Dieppe Raid, of course, that was it. The buzz about The Second Front had had a greater measure of substantiability than was usually the case. The coastline of France had been invaded, chiefly by Canadian Forces who suffered bitter losses as guinea-pigs. The planners had only intended the raid as an experiment, to test the enemy's defences. Forty-eight hours later the assault was over, and equally, all positive signs of a real Second Front in Europe had receded. We were back to square one. In consequence, in Russian eyes, no allied ship's company deserved a single helping of a fresh vegetable, even as humble and proletarian a one as the cabbage.

How childish, how utterly absurd? I agree, and yet it didn't seem so funny at the time. Or, for that matter, even now, if one seeks seriously to analyse the underlying motivations of that incident. For my own part, I would suggest that seen in the light of subsequent events, taken together with our present-day relationship with the Soviet régime, the episode of the cabbage was one of the most illuminating clues which came the way of those of us who, for a time, were the uninvited observers of the curiously devious manner in which the Russian mind works at an official level.

There was also a sequel, equally fascinating, equally having as its background the basic ingredients of the art of hospitality.

In the harbour basin of Archangel itself there rested at perpetual anchor a glorious white yacht, which seemed to have strayed from the Monte Carlo skyline in peace time. It maintained its pristine appearance, so it was said, because it had prudently refrained from venturing even a few miles down the river towards the open sea since the day hostilities had begun. In it was berthed the Admiral in charge of the White Sea fleet. One might have expected Admiral Stefano at least to have put in an appearance at Ekonomia to inspect the most recent batch of ships to survive the Suicide Run. Instead, he made a different gesture. While the flavour of the boiled cabbage was still in our nostrils he summoned to his presence our Captain, who found the

Admiral seated on a kind of throne, his pate shaven, and looking every inch an Oriental potentate. Having extended an ice-cold hand he proceeded to give an audience, after first offering his guest all sorts of delicacies: champagne from the Ukraine, caviar from Moscow, and Caucasian brandy which looked like cabbage water, I gathered later, but had the authentic fire. The visitor was as amazed as Aladdin at the riches set out in front of him. Having heard such endless talk of privation and shortages, having seen with his own eyes the empty shops in Archangel, it seemed incredible that such an example should be set by someone raised on high. He himself – though it was Mulley who told me – had even surrendered his daily allotment of twenty cigarettes in order to eke out the dwindling rations of his crew.

Captain Lawford was by nature the most abstemious of men. On this occasion, however, depressed by the absence of human warmth in the cabin, he gulped down one glass of brandy and then another, so that his tongue was loosened and he proceeded to give a day-to-day account of everything that had happened to the ill-fated 'P.Q.17' since we ourselves had left Seidisfjord. He explained the giant strategy, so far as he had been briefed, he admitted where it had gone wrong and where we had – as was becoming increasingly obvious – been outwitted by the Germans; deliberately he made no attempt to excuse or minimise the shambles that followed. Yet as the pieces of the jig-saw puzzle fell into place, and he paid his own tribute to the courage of the two rescue ships and of the corvettes that on their own initiative were eager to turn back whenever they received an S.O.S. from a sinking freighter, ending up with a graphic account of the stepped-up assault on the convoy remnants that were left, and giving throughout the kind of technical description which he imagined that a fellow-professional seaman would understand and gauge, he was at first surprised and then dismayed by the complete impassivity with which the man with the ochre-coloured skin and the small oriental eyes, seated above him, received his dispatch. For all the effect it appeared to have, he might have been giving a long range meteorological report. At the end of the recital the Russian Admiral, his expression still inscrutable, lifted his own glass, gargled the rest of its contents round his throat and gabbled at the interpreter. The Englishman, waiting for the translation, expected some show of regret for the loss of life as well as of material, a grateful reference, too, to the almost crazy loyalty to the common cause displayed in these desperate efforts to keep the northern route open for supplies at this time of the year, without any cover of darkness, but instead, this was the exact answer that he received and which I take from my diary:

'You should send bigger convoys and provide better means of protection. There should be fighter cover the whole way.'

'Of course, there should be Godfrey, we all know that,' my host added his own postscript at breakfast the next morning. 'We were all only too much aware of that from the start. But Winston, because he is being pressed all the time for the opening of a Second Front, has promised as a sop to our Eastern allies that he will speed up the northern convoys and keep this supply route open, even during the reign of the midnight sun, and this is the result.

'I suspect our friend in his Hollywood yacht is precisely aware of the odds against us,' he continued. 'Personally, I don't mind his taking such elaborate care of his own skin, because the Russians never were sea animals and never will be. No, what really worries me is that when this show is over at last and we are left in peace to grow our own cabbages in our own garden, and our children's children read in their history books about the far-off Murmansk Run, the Russians will get all the glory for their scorched-earth policy, and we shall get the big stick for failing them with supplies. For example, thirty-six freighters were there at the mustering, packed to the decks with tanks and every other sort of fighting material, but less than a dozen reached harbour for the unloading, at this end of the voyage. It will be the pathetic fewness, the meagre trickle of what got through, that will be emphasized. You see.'

Then he shrugged his shoulders and was smiling, as I remembered him the first time that we had met halfway across the Irish Sea, so far away from these inimical waters.

'I wish I could have pinched a jar of caviar for you, Godfrey, but you know how suspiciously they watch us the whole time, waiting to catch us out. What a pity you couldn't have been at the party. Such a waste. I don't like the beastly stuff myself, but I know it's your weakness.'

Yes, but how did Colonel Ivanov of the Profumo affair know that, too? I have often wondered since, hovering between the flattering explanation that he had deliberately taken the trouble to acquire that seemingly trivial piece of information, which nevertheless in his eyes opened up possibilities, and the more obvious explanation that he had been merely pursuing the customary technique that his Kremlin tutors have found to produce the most rewarding results; the technique of seduction through the human appetite for sex and the expensive luxuries of living – the exploitation of greed being the keynote of such wooing.

I must explain that I never actually encountered Colonel Ivanov in the flesh. I am unaware to this day whether he was a short man or tall; with the conventional grooming of the career diplomat or the facelessly anonymous look of the contemporary spy. He was simply a name to me, mentioned first in a conversation that wasn't as casual as it appeared to me at the time, later confirmed as belonging very much to a real person when this member of the Soviet Embassy staff in London took his place as one of the central characters in the most heart-searching – and I use the adjective with some deliberation – political scandal of the post-war era in Britain.

The blandishments of the colonel, presented by a go-between, were resisted by me as a result of a modicum of common sense plus the instinct for self-preservation which has been very strong in my nature throughout my life. Had I succumbed to the initial bait, so apparently innocuous, would I have been drawn further and further into the net?

Such speculations were not even remotely in my mind, since the name had not yet entered my consciousness the week-end in the late summer of 1962 that I drove out of London to stay with friends who lived at that time in a pink-brick house that was a particularly satisfying example of Caroline architecture, near to Great Missenden. Great Hundridge Manor had two matching wings stretching out from behind its delicate formal front towards a spectacular herbaceous border, the tennis courts and swimming pool, while in the near distance at the end of a long grass-walk was, I recall with pleasure, a gazebo. This gracefully rounded off the scene to give one the sensation, strolling towards it, of living in another century. One could not have wished for a more pleasant setting in which to recover from the week's labours.

My hostess that week-end is considered by many to be one of the outstanding beauties of our era. As Maureen Swanson, she had at an early age appeared in many films and on the stage before her marriage to Lord Dudley's heir. Maureen and Billy Ednam* are both enthusiastic and skilful card players and the week-end had been planned round the bridge table, one of my own favourite forms of relaxation. I had also promised to knock-up on the tennis court with my hostess who was anxious to add yet another arrow to her growing quiverful of accomplishments. And having found her already a most conscientious pupil I was pleased to be again of some small use in guiding her forehand over the net.

It looked like being another agreeable but completely uneventful week-end. Originally the party was to have included the Dartmouths, but Raine at the last moment was indisposed and didn't arrive. However, if her husband, Gerald, had cried off too, we would still not have been deprived of our bridge four because there was another house guest, the only member of the party who was a stranger to me, though I had heard of his talents in two totally different spheres. This tallish man, with a face free of fat to match his thin body, I suspected was already in the forties though his manner was consistently more youthful, at times almost coquettish – though in an entirely masculine way. His facile smile turned on and off like a light in a dark room – in momentary repose the skin of his face had a peculiar emanation of deadness; above all, his elaborate attentiveness gave the impression of someone who though eager to please, through not being absolutely sure of himself, yet at the same time had an equal desire to manipulate the company, and even to command.

Stephen Ward had at that time a fashionable practice as an osteopath, but was equally well-known for the stream of flattering crayon drawings he produced of his many Society friends. On several occasions I had seen his sketches auctioned at charity affairs, and his face, with the questing eyes, was a familiar one to me, at a distance, at other people's parties, though I had never had cause to put an identity to it until that August Saturday. During the rest of the week-end, each time he was cut out of the

* Now the Earl of Dudley

four he occupied his wait with a pencil and pad, looking from one to another of our intent heads over the bridge table. Later, when the entrails of his secret life were spattered across the headlines, day after day, during his trial, I was naturally curious – and still am – as to what happened to that particular sketch book.

After lunch on Sunday, announcing that he intended to drive over to give an airing to the rooms of his own week-end retreat, beside the river in the grounds of Cliveden, Ward enquired if any of us would care to accompany him. Gladly I accepted to be his companion on the drive. I had found him already a stimulating and amusing conversationalist, and now he continued to talk with an airy familiarity about all kinds of people in the public eye. I was both puzzled and fascinated by the breadth of his acquaintanceship, but put it down to his working connections. The contacts would start in his consulting room, and end? The answer to that question mark was provided for me, long afterwards, by someone rich, powerful and of a reputation so imperatively impeccable that he could afford nothing even remotely approaching an indiscretion. To his London house was summoned one evening the osteopath with the magic touch, to ease a back-strain caused on the tennis court.

When Ward arrived he had with him not only his professional bag but also a most attractive young lady. He explained to the butler that he was going straight on out to dinner afterwards. Might his guest for the evening wait downstairs while he was attending to his patient? It seemed a most natural request. After all he had come out of what were strictly his working hours. The session over, his client politely accompanied Ward downstairs to offer him a drink. Opening the door of his library he found himself, clad only in his dressing-gown, confronted by a fetching blonde, discreetly dressed but with a beguiling smile. Again Ward offered his explanation as to why she was there. But this time he added, on a slightly interrogatory note, 'I wonder if you would care to join us this evening?'

'I explained,' my friend continued 'that I was already dining out myself. But Ward was not easily put off. "Another night perhaps," he persisted, looking from me towards the girl he had brought as his bait. Of course until that moment I hadn't suspected anything. Why should I? But the message of his look was so blatant that I heard myself exclaiming loudly, "Not to-night or any other night." And having rung for my butler to see them out, I beat a hasty retreat upstairs to have a bath. . . . He was a most excellent osteopath . . . but I didn't employ his services again. It could have been too – expensive.'

After the *débâcle*, there were a number of such stories going the rounds. However, the authenticity of this one, having heard it at source, I can certainly vouch for. Just as what I am going to recount now I know to be equally so, since I was the spectator myself.

We had reached the bend of the river, where on the edge of the grass stood the white Edwardian boathouse that the owner of the property, Lord Astor, had rented for a peppercorn to his old friend, who had done little to convert it into conventional living quarters. Instead, it seemed more like a suitable place for a picnic than for spending a whole week-end. But the very fact that there still clung to it the aura of its original use only added to its charm. There was a feeling of tranquil isolation. I was enchanted, too, by the view itself, the mating of the river with the woods, so lush, so green, creating the kind of dream picture of England that exiles in far-off countries conjure up when the thermometer soars above the hundred mark, and a fresh shirt is drenched within an hour.

A writer looks at any dwelling place through the eyes of his craft. At once I started planning in my mind's eye where I would put my desk to get the best view, where I would sunbathe, in complete seclusion, between working sessions. However, as soon as I exclaimed aloud to its occupier how much I envied him his sequestered week-ends here, his reaction was one of surprise. A moment later he was assuring me, with some vehemence, that he disliked his own company and took care never to be alone here.

'Whenever I come down, I always ask a whole crowd on Sundays. If it's wet, we dance to a transistor set. As you can see, there's plenty of room. And more people keep arriving all day, bringing fresh supplies of food and drink with them. It's a kind of non-stop serial. And if it's fine and warm on Sunday afternoons, I usually take my guests up to the house to bathe and have drinks. Often we stay on to supper with Bill. He hates being alone as much as I do.'

In due course we walked up the hillside to the pool. As we stood beside it, with Cliveden itself so close at hand, a different kind of picture began to take shape in my mind. Although it was very quiet, because the house was unoccupied at that moment, with the family away in Scotland, it was not difficult to envisage a laughing company of bathers jumping in and out of the water, and the eternal spectators like myself standing on the edge, drinks in their hands.

'I suppose it is mostly a young crowd,' I said tentatively.

'Oh, lots of attractive girls, models and would-be models, but no scrubbers unless they look particularly good in a bikini. Then of course Bill will often have a house party of his own, with people like Valerie and Jack Profumo staying. In my turn, I have a great chum in the Russian Embassy who comes down a lot, called Colonel Ivanov.'

Up till that moment I had had no suspicions of any kind. I was simply enjoying the afternoon and this beautiful pleasance. I was a reporter off-duty. It was something in my companion's face as he spoke of his Russian week-end guest which alerted me. The greyness of his skin was suddenly flushed. Now he had the self-satisfied air of an entrepreneur who has just brought off a most advantageous deal. Yes, that was it, (the pieces of the puzzle were beginning to fall into place) that was his real motivation in life. He really saw himself as a kind of entrepreneur, introducing people from different worlds to each other. Then he would sit back and see what happened, and what happened would give him the sense of power that he sought but could not obtain through the use of his artist's hands. Even so, many hosts mix up their party guests with completely harmless results. I don't imagine I should have felt so perturbed at that moment had he not boastfully emphasized the recurring presence of someone from the Soviet Embassy among his week-end guests.

'Is it wise?' I began, and then stopped. For it was really none of my business.

'Wise?' he echoed, and the note of arrogance was still strong in his voice. 'What do you mean?'

'I mean, supposing one of the girls who comes down to your parties from the King's Road, Chelsea, – or wherever her background may be, – was a bit pushed for money. Or just out of vanity, a liking for publicity, hoping it might land her some modelling or photographic jobs, decided to give an interview to a scandal sheet. You know the sort of thing. *Week-end Bathing Parties at Cliveden. The new Cliveden Set. 'One of the charming men I meet there a lot, and who is most interested in everything and everybody is Colonel Ivanov, the military attaché (or whatever he calls himself) from the Soviet Embassy.'* Oh, you know the sort of thing. Decked out with a few of the snapshots someone must have taken down on the river bank of you all. Of course, I am sure there's no real harm in any of it;' I added hastily, 'but all the same, I would have thought it could be tricky. . . .'

'But why on earth tricky? It may interest you to know I have been vetted by MI5 regarding my friendship with the colonel and been given the go-ahead.' All the same, I thought I detected behind his insistent rebuttal a contrasting wariness. Then the next moment he had flung his arm round my shoulder in a gesture of friendship, and was suggesting that I must meet the Russian myself and form my own judgment. 'It is you who can do the interviewing. You will find that he is mad about England and everything and everyone that is English. That's why he loves coming down to Cliveden so much. And he is a first-class bridge player. We'll have a four at my flat one evening.'

In the end, that particular bridge four never materialized. Instead, I invited Stephen Ward to my birthday party that October, as the Ednams were coming, though the only time I remember catching sight of him across the crowded room he was deep in conversation with the mother of Lord Astor's second wife, Philippa Hunloke. On the next occasion I was staying with Philippa's mother, Anne Holland-Martin, as she then was, my hostess volunteered how pleased she had been to see Stephen Ward. It gave her the chance to thank him for something. 'When Philippa was unhappy, as the marriage was breaking up, Stephen Ward was always so kind to her, at week-ends. She has often spoken of it.'

Soon after my birthday party the entrepreneur rang up to suggest a date for bridge, but I was already engaged that evening and he promised to ring again – which he did a week later. Now he put the onus on to me to suggest a free night. While I searched in my book, as I was in the middle of a lecture tour, he became more pressing, more insistent. 'Colonel Ivanov says he will produce a big jar of the best caviar for you, if you will come.'

'Why?' I demanded involuntarily, and had the sense to ring off. It was the last time we spoke to each other. The mention of the caviar, instead of making my mouth water had had exactly the opposite effect. For why should this Russian wish to present me, a complete stranger to himself, with a lavishly expensive present from his native land? He had, I decided in due course, worked it out in collaboration with his pawn that the 'bring-on-the-dancing-girls' approach would leave me cold. Then try the alternative. Having accepted his present, I would have felt it only polite to answer his questions, so subtly phrased and spaced out that I would not have been conscious of being led to the brink of verbal indiscretion, encouraged and flattered to boast of any inside knowledge I might possess through the environment in which I worked.

Of course, it wasn't as absolutely clear as that on the day I put down the telephone and gave instructions that in future I was not at home to that particular caller. I was simply on guard, my suspicions strongly aroused. But even so I had no inkling – how could I have? – of the final outcome, the suicide that was not so much a private escape as a public crucifixion, on that day the next spring when I went to lunch with the B.B.C. Television Director, John Irwin, who was putting on the annual show to choose the Post Office Girl of the Year. For 1963 he had invited Valerie Hobson, married to the Secretary of State for War, and myself to be the two judges. The object of the lunch that May day was to discuss our respective roles. By this time Fleet Street was seething with rumours, coupling the names of Christine Keeler, Ward and John Profumo, though it was another month before the cauldron finally boiled over.

John's other guest at lunch in the expensive West End restaurant had never looked more beautiful or poised. There was not the slightest hint of any underlying tensions. If it was a bluffing performance she was giving, it was certainly a first-class one. I was filled with a fresh admiration for her as we laughed and joked and all chose strawberries and cream to end our meal and herald another summer just over the horizon. 'If they're your first strawberries of the season, you must wish and wish hard,' I told them both, and as I did so myself I recalled the evening that I had taken Valerie to one of the Rodgers and Hammerstein first nights at Drury Lane. She had created something of a furore by wearing a sari, in which she had posed dutifully for the photographers. She was then at the height of her career as a film star and this was part of her life. The next occasion I went to a Drury Lane première it was to applaud her singing debut as leading lady in *The King and I*. Although she made an outstanding success in the role, she decided it would be her signing-off performance. From then on she would devote herself solely to being the wife and supporter of her husband. Instead of the theatrical world it would be the political stage that she would seek to understand and conquer.

As I drove her away from the restaurant in my car I asked her if she would come to a lunch party I was giving in my home on the thirtieth, but when she looked at the diary in her bag she found she was already engaged. 'Jack and I are lunching with the Queen Mother that day. The Whitneys are going to be there. I am so sorry. Do ask me again.'

As it happened, in her turn she had already made another rendezvous with myself of an utterly different kind. Actually, it was some months before that Valerie had first asked me if I would be willing to accompany her on a visit to a Home in Worcestershire dedicated to the care of mongol children.

'Sunfield does such wonderful work, but they need to raise more voluntary funds in order to be able to go on expanding and to maintain their unique standard. I know about all this from personal experience,' she had explained to me. It transpired that a son by her first marriage had been looked after there for years. 'If you could write something about the understanding that is shown and the constructive help that is given, above all the feeling of optimism and love, I am sure that would be a tremendous help. And I am perfectly willing for you to refer to my own involvement, why I particularly wanted to be your guide, why I myself will, for the rest of my own life, always have such deep feelings about Sunfield.'

Now I saw another face; the one of the three faces I had never seen before. I was only too familiar with the face of the glamorous film star, and again the face of the socially successful helpmate to the ambitious and able politician. But this was something utterly different. This was the real person beneath the trappings of the façade that we all wear in self-protection, or from shyness. Moved and stirred, I gladly concurred. So Friday, June the fourteenth, was fixed. Both of us already had commitments that week-end in the Midlands. Valerie was to speak to the Conservative ladies of Edgbaston, the suburb of Birmingham where I was born, I had promised on the Saturday to open a fête at Butlers Marston, in Warwickshire.

We were to join forces on Friday morning, at a hotel in Stratford-on-Avon, her husband's constituency at that time. But the rendezvous was never kept; and as for our television partnership, although it was too late to take her name out of the *Radio Times*, a deputy had to be found at the last moment. In the circumstances, it was extremely sporting of Mrs Bernard Braden, who as Barbara Kelly is very much a star in her own right, to step into Valerie's shoes. Tactfully, at the lightning rehearsal no reference was made to the reason for the substitution, though I could only think of the agony of heart which the original choice for my fellow-judge must be enduring at that moment. The relaxed atmosphere of our strawberries-and-cream luncheon and what had been planned as an equally enjoyable occasion, had unexpectedly deteriorated into a cruel and mocking charade, the contrast bitterly emphasized as far as I was concerned when, just as the red light was about to flicker, reminding us that for the next half hour we were on show in front of a vast audience, the experienced performer at my side murmured with a dead-pan expression, 'Be careful. Don't call me Valerie'.

I am never completely at ease in front of the television cameras. In fact, my nervousness only seems to increase with familiarity, since I am only too conscious of how many thing can go wrong. But on this occasion I had hoped to get by unscathed with the help of an old friend at my side. Now as the area winners in the contest paraded in front of us and we did our best to encourage them to show themselves off to their best advantage by asking the kind of questions which are not too clever on the one hand and not too banal on the other, everything seemed to swim in front of my eyes. Even as my mouth uttered polite invitations to self-projection, a confused kaleidoscope revolved in my mind of other girls in bathing dresses beside the pool at Cliveden, all mixed up with my impressions of the day that I had spent as a guest at Sunfield. Inevitably, that had been something of an ordeal. Although every member of the staff made me feel as welcome as they could, their charges gazed back at the stranger in their midst with eyes that only recognized familiar shapes and voices; they were not accusing eyes, just blank, ageless eyes. Nevertheless, I had felt accused, and increasingly inadequate, as the day wore on and the silences began to stretch out and the question marks – why does it have to happen to this family, and not to that family? – which can never be authoritatively answered or explained, were frozen within me.

Earlier that week the parent who had intended to be my companion and my interpreter had written to me:

'I know you will forgive me for not having phoned myself. I am dreadfully sad at not being able to come with you to Sunfield and the Home. But perhaps we'll go one day. My love, Valerie.'

We have not met since. I was shy of suggesting a meeting lest it might seem as though I were in search of a postscript to that moment six years ago when by chance I became close to but not scorched by the flames of a *danse du feu* whose steps, reverberating with such self-destructive sexual overtones, have left footmarks upon a page of contemporary political history.

The Profumos have withdrawn entirely from the kind of life they once led; they refuse all invitations except from a very intimate circle of close friends. There are some wounds that never completely heal, but it should be recorded that there has been no whining, no alibis, no seeking for sympathy. On the contrary. He has sought a refuge for himself and found the means of rehabilitation by working full time in an East End Settlement, where his fellow volunteers speak with universal respect of his enthusiasm, his experience and his dignity of bearing. But for her, the utterly guiltless one, it has surely been the harder way back. A woman at the height of her looks, frankly enjoying the fruits of her social position as a political hostess of the party then in power, is suddenly completely cut off from all the symbols of being a member of the Establishment. That hers has been a self-imposed withdrawal cannot make the days as they pass any easier to fill.

Many times it must have been suggested to her by well-wishers that she would find her own form of escape from a situation that was so utterly not of her making by returning to her previous acting career. Her fellow players would have

'Nearer and nearer we reached to the ice wall stretching to the North Pole'

The *Pozzy* is caught in the ice

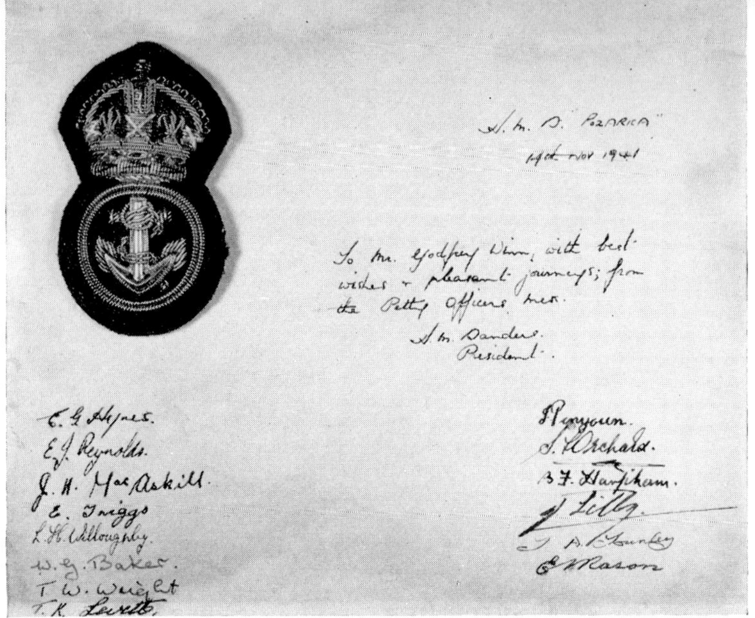
H.M.S. "Pozarica"
19th Nov 1941

To Mr. Godfrey Winn, with best wishes & pleasant journeys; from the Petty Officers' mess.

S.M. Sanders.
President.

E. G. Hynes.
E. J. Reynolds.
J. H. MacAskill.
E. Triggs
L. H. Willoughby.
W. G. Baker.
T. W. Wright

S. H. Orchard.
J. Lilly.
E. Mason

The kind of memento one does not discard

The keenest battle of all. The solo school in the P.O.'s mess

welcomed her, for in the World of the Theatre the most widely shared code of ethics is solely concerned with the difference between a professional and an amateur attitude to one's work. And there are many stage and screen roles that she could have played with a fresh depth of feeling through all that she has had to endure; not least in the protecting of her younger son by her present marriage.

But Valerie Hobson could not face performing in front of an audience again. Perhaps she felt her acting ability would be ignored, other things unfairly remembered. So instead, the Profumos have exchanged their London house for a home in the Berkshire countryside. Had they decided to go and live abroad for a time, it would have been readily understood. Instead, they showed a courage which must have silenced by now even their most virulent critics. For to choose to go into self-imposed exile within your own country, surely that is the most exacting test of all?

Honours and awards. For those in office, for those who have performed outstanding services to their country or their community; but just sometimes, though not often, for those in exile, too. I have no hieroglyphics, to be translated in terms of public recognition, to place after my name on an envelope; no collection of official scrolls, either, to prop up my self-esteem, no positive proof of official acclaim. But I am not unduly cast down. For instead, I have a drawerful of souvenirs that are infinitely precious to me and among them is a page torn from a ship's log book with a very imposing seal attached at the bottom of it. Holding this again in my hand after the passing of so many years, I am conscious that the combination of that once very familiar piece of bumph and the seal that is exclusive to all Her Majesty's ships, the mock-up, but the meaning behind the mock-up, exactly mirrored the mood of the evening when the only guest from another ship I made my way, prudently wearing the oldest of my shirts, over the gangway of H.M.S. *Leda*, one of the flotilla of minesweepers that were our companions at Ekonomia. For us a temporary resting place, we hoped, for them a permanent base. And as the weeks passed, I came to marvel at their resilience, their uncomplaining cheerfulness and, off watch, their ability still to create the party spirit from such slender material resources and, on this occasion, for such a fugitive reason, the news filtering through of the Dieppe Raid which they determined, unlike our Russian allies, to welcome and salute as the passage of more aggressive action to come.

At once I was enveloped in the same cocoon of unconquerable gaiety as I had encountered in the wardroom of H.M.S. *Fury* at Seidisfjord. But this time there was little if any alcohol to enhance it. Instead of being greeted by a glass of pink gin being pressed into my hand, there was simply a sheet of paper headed HONOURS AND AWARDS.

Underneath I read, first with bewilderment, then with delight: '*H.M.S.* Leda *gazette. Wardroom officers of H.M.S.* Leda *have been graciously pleased to approve the following appointment. To be an additional Member of the Most Excellent Order of the "Old Sock". Signed: By order of the Old Sockites.*'

By the end of the evening I had a dozen naval blue issue socks festooned round my neck, like an Hawaiian lei. A small, silly, private joke of long ago, with no meaning in a world that is today dominated by the insignia of student unrest? I suppose it could be argued thus, but the reason that I recall the occasion now is not because of the affection shown me by my fellow exiles; or again, because of the pride I felt in the scroll of membership bestowed upon me by Lt. Pengelly, the *Leda*'s opposite number to Smithie, our own gunnery officer. This Cornishman used to take me sailing sometimes in the dog watches in a dinghy, seeking his own form of escape from the inimical aridity of our present surroundings by enthusing to me about Looe with its absurd toy pier shaped like a banjo. With a captive audience he was able to savour to his heart's content the picture he lovingly described of the fishing boats with their brown sails filled out with a friendly breeze, entering harbour on the smooth milky tide of a summer's evening.

On this contrasting evening of brooding heat, so utterly at variance in temperature from those at home, there was in the company an odd man out. His name was Aarl – Lt. Aarl of the Norwegian Free Forces, seconded to our own Navy – and of all the people with whom I was thrown together in the war, and for this reason or that have never met up with again in the years of peace, none has left a more lasting impression on my mind than this modern version of a Viking of old, who had escaped in a fishing smack under the cover of darkness when the Germans had overrun his country.

Until that evening I had known little about him except his nationality. He spoke haltingly in the mess, for his English was still imperfect, and in any case it was clear from his manner that the coin of small-talk was not the kind of exchange he favoured. He never joined any of the sorties ashore to the misnamed 'Welcome Inn'; instead I would see him walking up and down, up and down the quarter-deck like a caged lion. All that his messmates had told me about him was that he made a vow never to drink even a glass of beer, in harbour, until he was reunited with the wife – she had won a competition as 'Miss Norway', but what was the use of that now? – that he had had to leave behind him in Oslo. It was he who unexpectedly volunteered the rest.

It happened after I had tried to make conversation in a corner of the *Leda*'s wardroom, though it was difficult to be heard above the gregarious din, explaining how I had never visited his country in peace time, while the nearest I had got in the war was a rather abrupt aerial view of Stavanger and the Norwegian coastline in a Hudson on a reconnaissance trip.

'But we'll have a reunion party one day in Oslo, Pilot,' I assured him, 'and you'll be free then to drink all the schnaps you like, and we'll go on saying *Schol* to each other till we fall over.'

I am not sure if he appreciated my rather self-conscious effort at *camaraderie*, because his face did not change. But then I never once saw him smile. There was an iron band round his heart. Nevertheless, something must have reached him – perhaps it was the mention of the names so dear to him – because he abruptly announced that he had something he wanted to show to me, in his cabin. I have a feeling now as I relive it all that he had reached the point when he must unburden himself to someone and it was easier with me because I was not a member of his own wardroom. He did not have to live with me day after day in cooped up proximity. Or again, it may have been that he recognized in myself, dressed in civilian clothes, another outsider as vulnerable as himself.

It was very still and quiet in the small cabin at the other end of the companion-way. I stood uncertainly in the open doorway while the young man with the mane of blond hair fished under his bunk for his suitcase.

'Pilot, when you get back to England I hope you'll look me up. I'll give you my address, and even if I am not there you can borrow my flat if you like. That is if it's still standing when we get back. But my housekeeper is a splendid woman. She will look after you like a mother.'

Mrs Hubbard's successor had an equally suitable name to fit her domestic tasks. She was called Mrs Bone, though as the bombing raids on the capital increased, and the sirens followed by the barrage from our own guns became an almost nightly ritual, I had secretly rechristened her Britannia of Ebury Street. Whenever I returned from one of my trips as an observer, especially if it was after a night journey, I always seemed to find her cleaning from the front steps the aftermath of last night's blitz. A big, strong woman, with the complexion of a girl, though she had a grown-up daughter, Vera, nothing seemed to deter or surprise her. Even when a direct hit from a bomb completely gutted the house opposite and blew out all the windows at number 115, her only reaction was to exclaim that a miss was as good as a mile and obviously the bomb hadn't got our name on it. If she ever suspected that there might be another bomb which had, she kept her thoughts to herself. Little by little she so infected me, too, with her own philosophic calm that I refused to move any of the pictures in the collection I had already begun to build, and so greatly prized, to a safer resting place. If they went, they went. Mrs Bone would still be scrubbing her steps clean and providing me with a hot meal from somewhere. As far as I know, she never left London once during the siege from the air, and as long as I was under the same roof as herself I felt safe.

However, my portrait of a London housewife under duress, that could be duplicated a thousand times over, did not appeal to my companion. For one reason, and one reason only: 'I do not want a mother, I want my wife,' he answered simply.

In my hands now were the faded, crumpled newspaper cuttings he had produced from his suitcase, proclaiming his bride's triumphant victory in the Beauty Stakes. The inevitable picture of her in a bathing dress parading before the judges reminded me of the times I had been an adjudicator myself at a Butlin holiday camp. As far away as Oslo and Stavanger were to him, Skegness and Clacton were to me as I looked now at the picture of Miss Norway with a welcoming bouquet in her arms, after a civic reception in her home town. But the photograph that had the most reality was the one of her leaning on her groom's arm after their wedding, in the days when he had been the navigating officer of a luxury liner on the Atlantic, not the Russian, run.

'Did you never hear anything, Pilot? No news, no message of any kind?'

He shrugged his shoulders and the gesture was more expressive than any words. 'How could there be? She does not know where I am, or even if I am alive. I escaped. . . .'

And then there was silence. I again looked down wonderingly at the cuttings in my hands; in such newsprint tomorrow's fish and chips are wrapped. Yet, travelling light, he had found room for them in his knapsack.

'I wish I could do something,' I exclaimed. 'Supposing I put a message on my page when I get back?'

'Your page? What do you mean by that?'

'I mean the page I have every Sunday in the newspaper in which I write. Or did, up till now.'

'No, no. You must not do that.' His customary phlegmatic demeanour cracked into a thousand pieces and immediately his excess of fear, not for himself but for the one person in the world whom he loved with all his being, enveloped me, too, so that I braced myself even before he took me roughly by the shoulders. 'Don't you see what would happen then? They would search her out, they have spies everywhere, they would torture her. I would never see her again. You must promise me . . . never to write my name.'

'Of course I promise,' I assured him, furious with myself for my stupidity. And I kept my promise, until it did not matter any more.

Satisfied, he took the newspaper cuttings in the language I could not understand, and carefully put them back into his suitcase again. I sensed it was a nightly vigil that for once he had chosen to share. Even so I was doubtful if it had lessened his burden of isolation, intensified unwittingly at that moment by the rollicking sounds from the wardroom down the passage. Must we go back and play an over-hearty part in the scrimmage? The odd-man-out stood with his back to me, straightening himself. When he turned again towards me, his face was the stone-face of a naval war memorial.

'It is not so bad at sea,' he said softly. 'They always want to come back into harbour, because of the mail, but I know there can never be a letter for me. So I do not want to be in harbour. And now like you and your ship, we wait and wait. It is bloody bad. But next time there should be battle and that is good. They say that our ship and your ship will go back together, in the next convoy. It is our turn, with the *Seagull* and the *Bramble* from the flotilla to help out as escorts.'

The *Seagull* had as its Number One James Phillipson, a coal-mine owner in peacetime, who had generously conferred on me the freedom of the bath, since they had hot water and I still possessed a bar of soap.

'But when?' I demanded, my sympathy for him and his wife swallowed up in a returning wave of acute frustration.

'You ask me. I ask you. When?'

Then, as there was no answer that either of us could provide with any certainty, we made our way back to the wardroom where by now the *Leda*'s captain, Lt. Commander Wynne-Edwards, was acting as a rugger ball and the scrum was closing in mercilessly overhead, chanting 'Tallyho'. Despite all their welcoming, unquestioning kindness towards me, I had no stomach to join again in the fray, and slipped across the gangway with my shirt intact this time, and carrying the Old Sockites' award in my hand.

Walking back towards the *Pozy* along the deserted quayside, I heard my footsteps echoing mockingly behind me, urging me to hurry, hurry, or you'll miss the boat, just as they used to do once upon a time when I had been a seventeen-year-old student at The Playhouse, Liverpool, returning to my digs off Rodney Street for supper, after taking off my greasepaint. All my ambitions in those days had been centred upon becoming a successful actor and now here I was in the centre of a Greek drama in real life; yet doubtless everything that I passionately desired to write about that drama – if and when I got back and made my own report to the Admiralty – would be censored for publication, as so many of my other dispatches already had been.

That pre-knowledge hardly made me quicken my pace. It was cooler now, and in a way it was a relief to be alone, even though as well as my own footsteps the Pilot's voice also pursued me. '*It is not so bad at sea,*' ending with his imperative echo '*When, when, when. . . .*'

I stopped and gazed out towards the river, as wide as the ocean and yet so unimpressive compared, for instance, with the lower reaches of the Thames. There was no mystery about it, even in this half-light that was neither day nor night. Whatever the time, it remained as flat and sluggish as my own mood was becoming unless I was shaken out of myself, as I had just been by someone whose own unyielding, one-track attitude had without intention made me feel almost like a deserter, guilty that I was not already half way through my training at H.M.S. *Ganges.*

We had expected to be back in home waters within a month. It was neither my Captain's fault nor my own that I was trapped and idle, I reminded myself yet once again. And once again, searching endlessly for reassurance, I compared the situation in which I was now embedded with that even more lost, hopeless feeling of despair, engulfing me on the Sunday morning when the Prime Minister's voice had informed the nation over the radio that we were from that moment at a state of war with Germany. Surely that had been much, much worse.

For however hard I tried during those unreal, haunted summer months of 1939, I could not envisage myself as an active combatant, khaki-clad. As a schoolboy of fourteen, I had been compulsorily enrolled in the O.T.C. and swiftly became the butt of the corps, a notorious duffer. My puttees, however tightly I strapped them round my calves, persisted in coming down on parade. I turned left when I should have turned right, I could never present arms in a really soldier-like manner, let alone fix my bayonet in the seconds allotted to the command.

The pen mightier than the sword? In those first few weeks of what is now designated the phoney war, the deceptive lull before the bombing really started, and before Dunkirk and the Fall of France, when Churchill rallied his countrymen and women in the most historic of all his exhortations, reminding us how we might find ourselves at any moment fighting on the beaches of our own island, I found no solace any longer in that hackneyed phrase about the might of my fountain pen. Yet, ironically, I had produced a multitude of variations on the theme of war's futility in the days when like the majority of my generation, shocked by the indiscriminate carnage of the First World War to end all wars, I had been a pacifist, genuinely believing it was better to live for one's country than to die for it.

No one wants to die if he is young and ardent. I certainly didn't. All the same, surprised at my own eagerness, I longed to be blooded and as swiftly as possible. And you have been blooded. You have been blooded. The mocking refrain repeated itself over and over again in my mind, as staring down at the sheet of paper in my hand I compared it with all the other souvenirs I had acquired in these three surprising years; such as the pair of Royal Air Force wings that another kind of pilot from the *Leda*'s navigating officer had cut off his tunic and given me as a mascot for the rest of the war, inviting me at the same time to accompany him and his wife on the day that he went to the Palace to receive the D.F.M. for bringing his plane safely back from the trip we had shared, a rather dicey day-excursion over Stavanger. Again, there had been the enamel regimental badge that was presented to me by the officers of the fort that I visited in the Maginot Line.

You could hardly call that a battle honour, I had to admit, communing with myself beside the uncommunicative waters of North Russia. All the same, this positive proof of my sojourn, however brief, in that mysterious robot world below the ground, had meant a great deal to me at the time, if only for the proof that I had been the first observer attached to an English newspaper permitted to explore what was too readily accepted, both by the French and ourselves, as an impenetrable line of defence.

Almost as impenetrable, though much closer at hand, were the inner sanctums of the Whitehall Wallahs. However, in dealing with them I had an initial stroke of luck. The head of the Public Relations Department at the War Office, to whom all applications for press facilities had finally to be submitted, was himself a fellow writer of considerable fame. Now, for the duration, Ian Hay – author of that classic work about the 1914 campaign in Flanders, *The First Hundred Thousand* – had become Major General Ian Beith once again, with a wife who was as enthusiastic a bridge player as myself. It was a link, if a tenuous one, strengthened, most fortunately, by the General's P.A., a frail-looking young man with fair hair and a shy manner, who talked in a gentle voice and looked as surprised by the pips on his shoulders as I would have been had I suddenly been made a captain even in the Press Corps.

David Heneker was, I imagine, a regular soldier at that time. However, it was not difficult to discover that his real aspirations lay in quite a different field. He was a musician *manqué*, I was a war reporter equally so. We got on splendidly. I poured out my hopes and longings to get across the Channel, so that I could make contact with the advance units of another expeditionary force once again settling into their billets amid the familiar landmarks of yesteryear; David, in his turn, confided in me how he was hoping, in his spare time, to write the music for a song that would be as famous as *Keep the Home Fires Burning*. That was my cue. 'But it will help to keep the home fires burning if I can send back messages to their families from our chaps digging themselves in for the winter. Won't you explain that to your boss?' I pleaded. Clearly he did, and with such sympathetic persistence that early in October the first of my War Zone passes came through, to the surprise of everyone in my Fleet Street office, since the official list of war correspondents had not yet been posted. I was to be despatched, on my own, and I could scarcely believe my good fortune and longed to share it with my benefactor. Even so, when I was summoned to David's outer office at the War Office to pick up my permits, it scarcely occurred to me that almost the next time we would meet would be at the première of the Musical, *Half a Sixpence*, in which Tommy Steele put over all his numbers with such charm and brio that the composer of the score was acclaimed and the fortune and fame of David Heneker finally assured.

Today David and his wife, who possesses green fingers, have come to live a few miles from my Sussex home, in one of the most attractive terraces in Brighton, standing high above the sea. Here their garden is the envy of all the other occupants of Clifton Terrace, including the talented playwright and librettist, Alan Melville whose war-time revues at the Ambassadors, starting with *Sweet and Low*, exactly captured the mood of those on leave, as well as all the civilian population seeking temporary amnesia between raids. In these ventures, his irrepressible ally was, of course, Hermione Gingold. Now, through their unexpected proximity, perhaps these gardening neighbours will get together and produce a peace-time show that is melodious and witty, rather than one depending, as so many seem to do today, on nudity and noise. It is as though we were all adolescents, demanding that our capital should emulate the mythical licence of the French one, and envisaging Paris solely in terms of naked breasts displayed in Montmartre night clubs.

If there was an abundance of nudity to suit all tastes still on display behind the embracing black-out in Paris, that autumn,

I had neither the time nor the inclination to search it out. For it would have seemed like dalliance, the betrayal of my mission; while as for noise, though the repetitive screeching of the taxi-drivers' brakes presaged a certain kind of disaster, I was not, ironically, destined to hear a single shot fired in anger when, ahead of the other correspondents, I reached the so-called Front Line.

Nevertheless, I became increasingly keyed up and expectant as I found myself being driven down one of those endless straight roads, bordered by sentinel poplars that are such a monotonous feature of the Northern French landscape. Suddenly we came in sight of a ruined fort, a landmark left over from the tide of the previous holocaust. On an impulse, I asked my conducting officer if we might stop, and we got out and explored its multitudinous stone passages, its turrets pitted and scarred, its grass banks, where in the hollows made by ancient gun-fire shrubs and undergrowth had mutiplied exceedingly once more, in the waiting years between. At the time I regarded this brief interlude as a prologue; the curtain to the real drama was about to go up, I told myself with a stabbing of excitement, as I traced with my finger the names of all the couples, Jacqueline and Robert, Marie and Jean, José and Charles, pierced with Cupid's arrows or entwined with lovers' knots, that were scratched everywhere on the walls so cold to the touch. Were all the men already recalled to their regiments? Would I meet some of them in the Maginot Fort I was about to visit? Evisaging it as a replica of this one, but on a giant scale, I retraced my steps, and across the road, before we got back into the car, discovered, like a portent for all that was to come, a tiny cemetery. On one of the plaques that had been erected, presumably during the uneasy armistice, was an inscription that I had never been able to erase from my mind.

ANNIVERSAIRE. TOUT PASSE: TOUT S'EFFACE, HORS LE SOUVENIR.

Everything passes, everything vanishes with time, except remembrance. At my birth I was granted the gift of total recall. Sometimes I have blessed it, sometimes I have cursed it. Sometimes there has been so little to recall, anyway; to write down, then or now. For instance, today it is universally accepted, in the light of subsequent events, that the Maginot defences were the greatest sham of all time. Even I, amateur strategian though I was, could recognize the glaring defects in such immobility, and when I returned to London and lunched with the then War Minister, Mr Hore-Belisha, I asked ingenuously: but what happens if the enemy by-pass the forts completely, their tanks worming their way round behind? What then? What indeed. In due course, the Minister, paying an official visit to the Maginot Line, was to ask the same question, though with more emphasis, of the French generals, and several equally pertinent ones, of our own. Whereupon he was quickly removed from office, for dabbling in affairs outside his political brief. It was still that kind of war: static, ritualistic and bogged down by the 1914 mentality.

On the other hand, as a toy for grown-ups, the Maginot forts had a certain mechanical fascination. I remember when the staff car eventually reached its destination, I could not understand why we had stopped at that particular spot. All my eyes could register ahead was a grassy hillside. Where *is* the fort? I asked, perplexed that we were not confronted by massive turrets silhouetted against the skyline. Smiling cryptically, my guiding officer started to walk ahead of me. Lo and behold, after about a hundred yards, and at the point where we should have had to start climbing, a huge camouflaged door slid silently sideways, reminiscent of the cave entrance in the pantomime *Ali Baba and the Forty Thieves*. We crossed the drawbridge and there before us was a long tunnel that reminded me now of our own Underground railway in the metropolis, except that there were no bays with platforms; instead you walked forward along the single track, hoping not to meet too many trucks en route. The first one we encountered was stationary and I peered eagerly over the side, expecting to find it full of ammunition. Instead, it was loaded with apples, the first sign in the bowels of the earth that human needs had to be catered for, health maintained. My guide explained to me that the fort stretched for fourteen kilometres in circumference, and was planned on a system of criss-cross passages. This meant that the men lived their whole life in a corridor. They had their cinema shows in one, their Mass with a miniature altar on wheels was celebrated in another, while in yet others they ate, seated back to back at tables, which when not in use folded up against the impersonal walls. No scribbled messages yet of love or hate.

The sensation of being dehydrated increased as we advanced down the tunnel until we came to more gates, which in turn slid back at the flashing of a green light, such as one finds outside each B.B.C. studio. I longed to sit down, for it seemed that the walk would never end; indeed, I was not surprised to learn that the officers used bicycles in their trek from one gun emplacement to another. Inevitably it was presumed that for the visitor the highlight would be the permission to press the button that set in motion the machinery for the guns to proceed majestically upwards in their hydraulic lifts to the surface of the surrounding landscape. I could hardly explain, in my schoolboy French, that I have never been sufficiently interested to discover even what the carburettor of my car looked like. In consequence, what should have been a moment of supreme power tingling through my veins, left me completely unmoved. It is the changing beat of the human heart which never fails to arouse my imagination; and, in consequence, what still impresses me most about that extraordinary Jules Verne world beneath the earth has no connection with the weapons of war but a great deal with the fundamental props of life itself.

In the officers' mess, where I was fed and welcomed as a new face, they had done their best to disguise the fact that the surroundings were still virtually a corridor by building against one wall a dummy fireplace, its mantel decorated by Victorian busts of two ladies representing Alsace and Lorraine. Of course, there could be no fire, no chimney, because not only the guns but everything else, including the air we breathed, was electrically controlled. All the same, as the members of the mess gradually assembled from their respective duties, and poured themselves out an aperitif, I noticed that automatically they joined the circle round that deceptive façade, in front of which two or three already had their hands outstretched behind them, as though they were warming themselves in their own homes.

It is true that I am writing this in a room that has no fireplace in it, but I would never willingly sit in one, at leisure, that lacked such a central focal point, symbolizing at once the peaceful security of the hearth and its traditional welcome. Again and again during my trips as a war commentator, I came across similar efforts at conjuring up the mere semblance of a home atmosphere, often under equally bleak and forbidding conditions. It is only natural, therefore, that the first example I encountered should remain most vividly in my mind, and seem so real and, in its own way, as important as it did at that moment when, after our meal together, my companions crowded round their make-believe fireplace once again, to sing for the stranger in their midst the song of the fort. Though their voices and their faces have long since faded from my consciousness, the words remain, an ironic footnote.

Au fond de l'Ouvrage,
Nous chantons et combattons.
Ils sont du courage
Les gars du Beton.

Pour défendre la France
On nous fait venir.
La peine et la souffrance
Sauront nous aguerrir.

(*In the depth of the work*
We sing and we fight;
They are filled with courage,
The lads of the cement.

(*For the defence of France*
They have brought us here.
Trouble and suffering
Will serve to sharpen our warrior spirit.)

I might have tried, out of politeness, to match the optimistic tone of their chanting with the equally cocky refrain of the first of our wartime songs – one that, not surprisingly, had a short life; *We'll hang out our washing on the Siegfried Line.* Fortunately, as I have no pretensions to a singing voice, I refrained. Not, I hasten to add, that we weren't all at that time equally enveloped in a blanket of euphoria. The inhabitants of both capitals had braced themselves for massive air attacks. When nothing happened, the relief of the anti-climax was overwhelming.

Returning to Paris for week-end leave between visiting the French and joining the advance striking force of the Royal Air Force stationed at Rheims, I heard the expression '*il faut en finir*,' repeated over and over again; fiery, aggressive talk which was only to be expected from a nation that had been called upon to fight three major wars against the same aggressor within a hundred years. At the same time I could not help feeling uneasy at the amount of chatter there was about such unimportant appendages as the special air-raid-shelter clothes Schiaparelli had created in shiny black oilskin for her clients, as though for a wet but still *chic* day at the Races. Again, that unfailing barometer, the bar at the Rue de Rivoli entrance to the Ritz, was just as full as in peacetime, and the few men in uniform were peacocks taking part in a fashion parade.

On the Sunday I went to visit an old friend, Elsie Mendl, who in the 1914 war had run an American hospital under fire. Elsie now lived in a house at Versailles, full of exquisite *objets* which she had acquired in the course of her successful career as an interior decorator. Although considerably older than my mother, she had the figure and the supple limbs of a girl and enjoyed standing on her head at the least provocation. Her inner fires were inexhaustible, perhaps because she was extremely careful over her diet. Pushing aside a soup plate in someone else's house, I once heard her comment sharply, 'Who wants to start a meal with the foundation of a lake?' At first sight, with her blue-rinsed hair and a French accent possessing strong New York overtones, you might have mistaken Lady Mendl for any modish American matron in search of culture in Europe. However, such a judgment would have been mistaken. There was a great deal more to her than that, or the English diplomat, Charles Mendl, whom she married late in life, would not have been so adoring. Elsie welcomed the young and their ideas, however startling. She was a lioness in defence of her friends, and as for her personal philosophy, in her drawing-room there were embroidered cushions on the sofa which stated it in concrete terms. '*Never complain, never explain.*' '*He who rides on a tiger cannot descend.*' '*Failure only begins when you give up trying to succeed.*'

I had long since forgotten about the cushions and their rallying mottoes until I discovered them again, this time in the drawing-room of the Moulin de la Tuilerie, the home of the Duke and Duchess of Windsor, outside Paris. Elsie had left them to her in her will, my hostess explained, as a souvenir of a friendship that had never wavered. As the Duchess went on to answer my other more searching questions, in the first interview in depth that she had given in the thirty years since the Abdication, with a candour that was disarming – 'Every morning of my life when I wake up, I am conscious over again of all that the Duke gave up for me' – I was forcibly struck by how little she had changed in appearance from that Sunday night at Versailles early in the war, when she and her husband had come to dinner and afterwards we had amused ourselves with a childish game of Chinese Chequers.

On that occasion the Duke had been dressed in the dark-blue mess uniform of the Welch Fusiliers, and the aura of gold round his head was exactly the same as when I had followed in his wake during his tour of the Welsh villages at the height of the depression of the 'thirties, and at the end of a day of brutal knowledge gained at first hand, he had been so aghast that he had announced to the world at large, 'Something *will* be done'.

What was done was to pack him off into exile as quickly as possible, and provide no official post for him abroad. Now through a fortuitous change of circumstances, caused by the outbreak of hostilities, he was back in harness, exulting in having something to do, even if it was the modest job of being some sort of liaison officer between the French and the English. That did not matter. What was important to his *amour propre* was that he was in uniform again, back up the line. At half-past ten when someone suggested a final game, he shook his head. He must be off again in the dawn. As he stood waiting for his car to come round, he touched the waistline of his tunic and remarked with a reasonable sense of pride, 'This was made for me twenty-six years ago, and thank goodness it still fits me'.

I went to war myself in a thick blue suit of barathea cloth, and I still wear it sometimes, thirty years later, on a cold winter's day. I am glad to say that the trousers continue to meet round my waist, even though my chest has broadened somewhat.

Although I wasn't attired in any uniform for the first three years of the war, no one presented me with a white feather. I sometimes wished it might happen, since as the months went by I had acquired a reasonably good alibi, sufficient to confound any accuser. But it didn't turn out to be that kind of war.

Something in me revolted against the idea of being dressed up in uniform, like the other correspondents. I felt I had no right to the captain's rank, or whatever it was that they were given, and although I appreciated the complications if I was captured, after being sunk at sea or baling out over enemy territory, I still preferred that risk to a sense of resentment the ranks might feel towards my fancy-dress clothes. Besides, as I was anxious to report from every front in turn, was I to be decked out in a whole series of uniforms – one to wear in France, another when I was at sea in a mine-sweeper, yet a third during my visit to the airfields or on my occasional operational flights with bomber crews? It was palpably absurd. So I stuck to my blue suit, exchanging it sometimes for flannels or slacks, according to the given assignment. And because it was to turn into a total war, in which the Civil Defence Services and the civilians on the home front had to withstand, in the end, the most searching challenges of all, the unorthodoxy of my attire went, if not unnoticed, at any rate unfrowned upon either by my succession of hosts or by my official sponsors.

As winter deepened, it was all quiet on the western front once again, and I returned to my home base feeling like a schoolboy after his first term at his public school. Displaying my Maginot Line badge on the lapel of my jacket, I found that it became a pleasing source of conversation wherever I went. *Il faut en finir*, I repeated like a password, glossing over the fact that I hadn't heard a single shell yet whizz over my head. My civilian boss, Lord Beaverbrook, telephoned me to congratulate me on my dispatches – 'Capital, Godfrey, capital' – but I sensed that there was another reason for his call. I was right. After a moment's pause he barked down the instrument, 'Did you see Noël Coward in Paris?' 'Yes,' I replied. 'Was he in uniform?' 'No,' I replied, equally warily, with a picture in my mind of The Master, as his entourage chose to designate him, popping in and out of the Ritz bar in a bow tie, and with sealed lips. 'Ah,' continued the inquisitor, 'what do you think he is doing?' 'I have no idea,' I was able to report truthfully. 'Probably some hush-hush intelligence job.' My boss gave a final snort and rang off.

I still have no idea what brought one of our leading performers to Paris at that suspended moment of the war. Perhaps it was too secret a mission even to be mentioned now. Whatever it was, he himself was still giving a splendid performance, a character out of Ruritania come into his own.

The truth was, the real breath of war had not touched any of us yet. On my first day back in the Glass House I travelled up in the lift with the air correspondent for the *Sunday Express*. Victor Burnett and I had been fellow spectators at air rallies in peacetime, and during the course of one of them at Lympne he had persuaded me to go for a flip in a biplane with a German acrobatic ace, who proceeded to throw me about the sky until I almost prayed for death. When we eventually came in to land, and the prisoner was unstrapped, I stumbled away from the crowd, across the airfield, and was violently, humiliatingly sick. German revenge for the last war, Victor had pointed out. It was some time before I saw the joke against myself, and joined in the laughter, my convalescence quickened by the sympathy of another member of Jeanne de Casalis's house party. I was hypnotized by my fellow guest the whole week-end, for with her heart-shaped face, swan-like neck, and the smoky-blue eyes of a Siamese cat, she was without doubt the most beautiful young woman who has ever come my way. To my astonishment, she seemed completely oblivious of the devastating effect she had on every male in sight, and I in my turn could only stare and stammer, equally unaware of what close friends we were later to become, and that one day a nostalgic picture by Sickert, called *The Belle of the Ball*, would hang on the wall of my home, bequeathed to me in her will. That week-end it seemed utterly impossible that mortality should ever strike her down, for she was not merely flawlessly lovely but also so young. I sat at her side, enraptured, while she described the film she was at that moment making, *Fire Over England* – though she made no reference to the young man playing opposite her, or to the overwhelming attraction they felt for each other and which was to have so many consequences both for herself, Vivien Leigh, and for Laurence Olivier.

It was almost inevitable that Victor and I should speak of Vivien and of the stories that were seeping through from Hollywood of her meteoric success as Scarlet O'Hara in *Gone with the Wind*. Then after the lift had reached our floor, and we were walking along the corridor to our respective rooms, he said with a smile which lit up his whole face, 'I've just had a raise. I heard about it this morning. And do you know what I am going to do, Godfrey? As soon as I get home tonight I'm going to tell my wife to buy all the bulbs in the world . . . to come up next spring.'

Whereupon he held out his arms as though to embrace the whole world, but when the spring came it was his body that was under the ground, a casualty of the war in the air, and the first to have a special meaning for me. Again, before the spring and the evacuation from Dunkirk, the final stage of which I had to watch impotently from the cliffs of St Margaret's Bay, one of the ships, the *Royal Archer*, in which I sailed that winter in a North Sea convoy, sank, hit by a mine, on its very next voyage. When the news was telephoned to me in Glasgow, where I had just returned after a trip in an Aberdeen fishing smack, the matter-of-fact tone of the news editor from London was overlaid by Captain Piper's voice on the bridge, as gingerly, hour after hour, we had edged our way through the minefields, in the darkness, and softly, in his Hull accent, he had muttered, 'You know, the time I like is the spring, when the birds begin to sing again and you can imagine there are other things in the world beside Hitler. . . .'

That first Christmas most of us made an effort at imagining that, too. I took my mother to Brighton, and over the holiday we stayed at The Old Ship on the front, where once upon a time Thackeray had had rooms and written part of *Vanity Fair*, setting a honeymoon scene in the hotel; while on another occasion Paganini had played his violin in a rather more fastidious style than that displayed by the scratch orchestra who at that period encouraged the patrons to dance, dance their troubles away.

There was a hearty effort at business as usual; crackers and caps and plum pud. Over by Christmas? Hardly, but all the same, surely Hitler would come to his senses in the spring, and there would be a get-together round the conference table with, perhaps, America in the chair. It was all right for the French to talk so belligerently about finishing it for ever this time, but too many members of an older generation than myself had ghostly memories of the previous decimation, that unholy holocaust, to have any stomach for even the semblance of such a repetition stretching endlessly ahead. So pushing that nightmare possibility away from them, like a confrontation with Banquo's spectre at the feast, they gave way to a spirit of untiring frivolity. Even my mother, who usually disliked staying up late, now, to her younger son's surprise, was loath to leave the dance floor at midnight.

Drink up, drinks galore. But whenever it was my turn to order another round, I had a stabbing picture in my mind of the Cameron Highlanders, marching back to their billets with, incongruously, their billycans in their hands, to pick up their evening meal, chocker – the new slang of a new war, which I had begun to acquire – because they were about to be stripped of their distinctive, traditional kilts and put instead into anonymous batttle dress like all the other British units attached to the Maginot Line. We shall feel like eunuchs, the jocks had vehemently protested.

Their rumbling revolt had seemed so imperative 'over there'. Now who except a former member of the regiment would be interested in their dilemma, back home on the so-far phoney civilian front? I visualized myself as a messenger between the two fronts, but some of my tidings I suspected would fall flat, and others I kept cautiously to myself, surprised by the depth of my own longing to be back in the bar of the Lion d'Or at Rheims. Here everyone had foregathered who was billeted anywhere in the vicinity, and all ranks had been made welcome in that waiting room, with a variety of anaesthetics at hand for whatever tomorrow might bring.

The casual, transitory encounters of war; the friendships burgeoning so swiftly and so swiftly shrivelled by death or departure. If I could walk in again at this moment, discarding my dinner jacket, would I already look in vain for the baby-faced pilot with whom I had established an instant link when we discovered that we had spent our childhood in the same county of Worcestershire? We had both been brought up in the shadow of the Malvern Hills, and over and over again, above the friendly, embracing din, we repeated to each other, like a charm, what it is always like in the spring when the banks of the Avon overflow with a fresh pink tide of blossom. Although he himself was in Air Force uniform, with as yet the one thin line on the sleeve, we were able to dismiss the existence of war until, stupidly, the eager reporter in me had demanded, 'How are things with you in your squadron?' Whereupon instantly his face had changed, the boyishness vanished, the mask carefully slipped back in place. 'Oh, things are very quiet. Nothing has happened at all.' It wasn't that he was deliberately snubbing me; it was simply that I had reminded him of his other self; and it was left to 'Poppy' Pope, a senior officer in his own Service, whom I was to meet up with again later, at Leuchars, on the Scottish coast, to fill in the reticent gaps in his story.

A few days before we had met, that particular pilot had been surprised by an overwhelming number of Messerschmitts on the German side of the frontier. His cockpit had become full of flooding petrol, his instrument board was shot away, but still, flying blind, he had somehow, miraculously, succeeded in getting back to his base.

'He made a perfect landing,' the narrator continued in his clipped, unemotional voice. 'But because of the damaged undercarriage, the machine turned over. Fortunately he was thrown clear, and only momentarily stunned. Coming to, his first instinct was to go back and risk death all over again, in the furnace his machine had become, to rescue his gunner and drag him clear.'

And that was what my countryman, my fellow native of Worcestershire had described as being 'very quiet'. If I sat rather silent and glum myself, at the Christmas feast, it wasn't that I was sulking, as my mother suspected, at having to play the dutiful son. On the contrary. I had welcomed eagerly this opportunity for us both to be together again for a few days for the first time since I had left for France. And now to my dismay I found it difficult to make conversation about such small domestic items as changing the diet of my Sealyham, Mr Sponge, since it was likely to become increasingly difficult to procure a ration of meat for him. I had moved on a little along the road and was full of doubts I could not express aloud, with a paper crown on my head, as to how I would respond myself to any similar challenge, in the air or at sea. In the 'Lion d'Or' bar, another pilot had come up to me and introduced himself, with what I mistook as a mocking smile, as a member of the audience in the concert hall at Felixstowe, where I had spoken on the last Sunday night before we had been informed, over the radio, that we were at war with Germany.

'My girl friend dragged me along, because she is a fan of yours. I was recalled to my squadron the next morning and had a boshed leave. You said something about the three things you considered took you furthest in life. A sense of humour was one, and sincerity and having faith in something or other was another, but what was the third? I have been wracking my brains ever since I heard you were out here. I hoped I might run into you somewhere.'

'Self-discipline. Actually, it was the first on my list,' I answered, hoping that he didn't consider me a pompous ass. To my surprise he agreed with my assessment. 'It's the first, too, on my own list,' he told me, unconsciously proving his point by shaking his head at the offer of another drink from someone in our group. 'I must be getting back,' he explained, 'just in case I'm wanted half-past four tomorrow morning.'

Wanted in that foundling moment between night and day. In that same hour I had stood at my bedroom window at the 'Lion d'Or,' on my last evening in France. Tired and stiff from writing my final dispatch, I had drawn aside the curtains and stared out at wispy, insubstantial nothingness. Overwhelmingly aware I had been at that moment of all my fellow pilgrims who had stood at other windows at the same hour before the dawn, drained of all self-esteem, bereft of all props to their ego, barrenly conscious themselves that in the end neither possessions, nor a substantial balance in the bank, nor even the love of one's friends, is of any avail. First you must confess all your fears to yourself, and then you must conceal them again, so as to go forth, apparently unafraid, to take the wings of the morning.

Again and again, I had asked the operational pilots I had so far met the same question. What did they think of, as they walked across the tarmac to climb into the cockpit? All had given me, stubbornly, variations of the same answer. Either they had thought of nothing. Or else they had forgotten. Would it be the same for me, if and when my chance came to fly with them? Would I be equally able to keep my mind a blank?

At that same hour, on our last night at The Old Ship, I found myself standing in the same position at my hotel bedroom window, gazing out to sea. However, this time I was specifically searching for something in the half light: the silhouettes of any small ships, bobbing up and down on the horizon. I was still absurdly ignorant of the mystique of maritime tonnage; a trawler, a fishing smack, a freighter, all looked alike to my queasy eye. But since I had chosen to christen the New Year by spending it on board a minesweeper of the Dover Patrol, I had come to regard anything I could espy these last few days, far out at sea, with an increasingly sinking stomach.

In an effort to drown my anxiety for what might lie ahead, I had purposely taken a box at Brighton's affectionate playhouse, The Theatre Royal, as a climax to my half-term break, in the first term at a new school, and invited to join us the mother of the latest addition to my brood of godchildren. This one had been born the previous May and christened William Francis Winn Fox. Today he is known by none of those baptismal names, but simply as James Fox, a screen actor of considerable range, chosen to play opposite such diverse leading ladies as Julie Andrews and Vanessa Redgrave, and yet at the same time very much someone in his own right. All the same, I am certain that he would be the first to agree that he owes a considerable proportion of his spectacular success to the continuing influence of his parents.

That unreal summer before the die was cast, I would visit his mother almost every afternoon. Angela and Bob Fox at that time had a flat overlooking the river at Chelsea. I would sit on a window seat, looking out on to the Embankment, idly watching the tops of the barges softly drifting by, while the refracted sunshine lay on the water and filtered through the trees like the points of paint on a canvas by Pissarro. How reassuring it was, how peaceful. I suppose all mothers, once their baby is safely delivered, pass through a period of euphoria, of being spoilt and showered with congratulations, all the pain and discomfiture of the months of waiting obliterated in the satisfaction of having produced something at once so helplessly craving protection and love, and so unique.

Which qualities would this baby inherit from his parents? His father's already keen legal brain, his mother's romantic disposition? Angela, with her untinted hair, her strong Saxon colouring, was so utterly English-looking that she could have represented her country at a Trade Fair, and both her sons – Edward, the elder by two years, has also made his mark in the Theatre – were to inherit her natural fairness, but at the same time something far more important: the unwavering conviction that so long as a family remains sufficiently close-knit, it is undefeatable and invulnerable.

Nevertheless, I was astonished by the confident manner with which Angela brushed aside all references to the possibility of war. She knew that Bob, as a gunner in the H.A.C., would be called up at once, and indeed he was already preparing at that moment to spend August under canvas. She would be left with two small children to look after, on her own. And yet when I had asked her if she had not been apprehensive of all the hazards in bearing another son at such a moment as this, she had shaken her head with a decisiveness that silenced any further argument.

'Whether this war happens or doesn't happen, it is only an incident in the ultimate scheme of the universe. It has no lasting significance. It cannot hurt my baby. By the time he grows up, the skies will be clear again. The future belongs to him, as it belongs to every human being born into this world.'

It wasn't bravado; it was absolute belief. Recognizing this, I marvelled at her words at the time; and as we sat in our box in the packed theatre, joining in the applause for the revival of an Ivor Novello comedy, with its author heading the cast, supported by two leading ladies, Isabel Jeans and Dorothy Dickson, I marvelled again at her composure, her serene, smiling acceptance of her changed circumstances. In a moment, her husband's earnings as a solicitor had been slashed to nothing, and she and the children packed off to a cottage in Cuckfield, to exist from then on, like a multitude of other families of professional men, on a soldier's woefully inadequate pay.

This was the side of the upheaval that no one dwelt much upon; it was so dull, so ordinary beside the battles yet to come. However, stubbornly, I feel this chronicle would not be complete without some reference to it, even though that evening Angela deliberately made a joke of her lot, recounting what an eight-year-old East End child had written home, on being evacuated to a farm in Somerset. *'I have arrived safely. I like the man's face. I don't like the woman's face, but p'raps she'll look better in the morning. I like the dog's face best. Love from Johnny.'*

In many cases, the mass evacuation was to turn out a blessing, for I have noticed again and again that urban children who were despatched to the country for the duration have grown up with far greater staying power than they might otherwise have had. I am equally certain that the fact that my own earliest formative years were spent in a Worcestershire village have strongly fortified my constitution. When sometimes I have been asked how I was able to stand up to the cold of the Russian Run, I have answered, truthfully, that if you can withstand the rigours of a Midland winter, you can survive anything. In her own way, Angela was equally determined that she and her sons would survive the war, and under her innate skill at home-making, Ockenden Cottage became so inviting that it is still, today, in an utterly transformed state, serving as a week-end meeting place for all the family, with Edward's enchanting small daughter, Lucy, her own fair hair flowing over her shoulders, running about on the lawn, where once I watched my godson take his first wobbly steps. While in the church opposite, at whose lichen gate you will find the whole of Sussex towards the coast spread out before you in a melting view that catches at your heart, Bob and Angela's third son, a peace offering after the war, a reaffirmation of so many things, was christened with, this time, Robert Morley as his god-parent.

On both sides, the children had grease-paint in their veins. Lucy is the great-granddaughter of Fay Compton, Bob's mother was a celebrated Edwardian beauty and actress, Hilda Hanbury, while Angela's own father was a famous playwright. Thus it was not surprising that she, too, should have tried her hand at acting, before she married, at a very early age. Yet how undramatic, at first sight, was the role that she deliberately chose to perform during those six long, testing years. 'What did you do in the Great War?' is a classic quip from my own earliest childhood which has long since had a sour and mocking connotation attached to it. My godson's father was to win a Military Cross, later, in Italy; on the other hand, his mother did not seem to do anything. She did not dress up even in a home-front uniform of some sort. She simply stayed at home, dutifully put up the black-out curtains, queued for her rations, like everyone else, and again like other mothers with young children automatically sacrificed her butter ration. She stayed put and prayed quietly every night that a marauding bomber, bound for the capital, would not jettison its bombs over her unoffending village; and again, that tomorrow would not bring a telegram from the War Office. Up and down the country, other wives and mothers were behaving in the same disciplined, self-deprecatory way. All this is unsensational compared with the exploits of someone like Odette, who has become a legend in her own lifetime as a heroine of the Resistance, and who told me once that when she had been tortured and in solitary confinement in a German concentration camp, the one thing that had saved her reason was a leaf that was, miraculously, swept in through the tiny grille, high up on the wall of her cell. She held it cupped in her hand, and the sap of the burgeoning spring that it contained, its unfurling green, gave her fresh hope and strength to hang on a little longer.

Angela's own fortitude was of a more modest kind. She never wavered in her other belief, and firmly held as the one concerning her sons' future, that her husband would come back to her, and whole. This he did, though it was a narrow shave. Dangerously wounded, Bob was lying in a makeshift clearing station in Italy, unaware that a doctor, who was to become a life-long friend, was at that moment scanning the latest list of casualties, with their unit and home address set against their name. When he came to the words 'Ockenden Cottage, Cuckfield', he paused and his interest quickened. For this was his home ground, and he got up and there and then, on a sudden impulse, he went in search of the wounded man whose next-of-kin lived in the unspoilt corner of Sussex which he himself knew so well and loved. At once, from an instinct trained fine, he realized that this was no moment for a reminiscent, nostalgic exchange; this patient, with his very dark hair enhancing the pallor of his skin, was desperately in need of a blood transfusion to save his life. It was given, and just in time. How does one explain such quirks of Fate?

Today that same doctor, now the head physician of a London hospital, and his wife, herself a member of Archie McIndoe's celebrated team at East Grinstead, are week-end neighbours, and last Easter we were all together, children and grown-ups of the two families, and myself, picnicking side by side in the Foxs' garden. It was exceptionally warm and the air was full of the promise of summer. And yet, almost inevitably, the talk was still of war, since Philip and Barbara Evans had recently returned from spending a year setting up an English medical unit in Saigon. On Christmas Day there had been a bombing truce, and they had sat in the courtyard of their rented house sharing their capon with their Chinese servants, An Tu, Chi Chai and their five soft-footed little girls, who instead of using their fingers, or their usual chopsticks, struggled with a knife and fork so as not to put to shame their hosts, to whom the sudden silence under the canopy of stars had as much a mystical quality as a religious significance. Listening, I thought how infinitely further away that other Christmas at Brighton now seemed. A tableau from a different century. Yet Angela seated quietly on the sideline, in her chosen attitude, watching her husband and her sons partner me on the tennis court, appeared no older in my eyes, but still perenially young, because of her unquenchable optimism and trust in the bounty of life.

'I have given everything to my family,' she once confided to me. 'But I have sacrificed nothing. On the contrary, I regard myself as a very fortunate woman.'

Did my mother feel the same? With two marriages behind her, the one to my father a disaster, the one to my step-father ending in tragedy, I never heard her once ask for sympathy and perhaps, for that very reason, I never ceased to be aware of the uncountable sacrifices she had made, at an earlier stage, for her own two sons. Angela had a considerable admiration for my mother who, in her turn, approved wholeheartedly of the younger woman's matriarchal quality. Equally she was grateful for the spontaneous manner in which the Fox family had adopted me, absorbing me into the kind of utterly normal environment that she was delighted for me to share.

Yet somehow the evening was not the success I had hoped it would be. Although the two women talked brightly to each other in the intervals at the theatre, and at supper afterwards, at the hotel where I tactfully danced with each of them in turn, I began to sense a growing wave of maternal irritation, on my side of the fence, because my guest for the night would persist in treating me as a warrior on leave, so soon off again on another hush-hush assignment. I had simply stated that I would be seeing the New Year in, at sea, and left it at that. But Angela, by nature, was a 'builder-upper', whereas my mother believed firmly that you should always prepare your offspring, as well as yourself, for the worst. It became only too clear as the evening wore on that she could not envisage her younger son as anything but a chocolate soldier, so that I sat miserably deflated, while the contest sharpened over my head, only to be thankful when *The King* was patriotically played and the party broke up.

After taking Angela to her room, I knocked on my mother's door and found her, in her dressing gown, seated in front of the mirror, brushing the very soft fine hair that had begun to turn white when she was still a young woman. The familiar position made my heart turn over, and as I bent to kiss her good night I was full of love and gratitude and pride, hoping so eagerly, too, that she would take this opportunity to make some comment about how much she had enjoyed this week's respite, and her rest from household chores, in almost pre-war luxury.

Instead she continued relentlessly. 'I forgot to tell you that when I was changing for the theatre Joyce rang up to say that poor Rodger has been on duty the whole time over Christmas at The Admiralty. Sometimes he doesn't get home till four in the morning, and then the telephone will ring beside his bed, just when he's got to sleep. I don't know how his health is going to stand up to it. He is in the Submarine Room.'

Deliberately she made it sound as though he was out at sea in a submarine on patrol in mine-infested waters at this moment. I had an awe-inspired respect for my elder brother who, although crippled by polio, had surrendered his extremely successful career at the Bar on the day that hostilities broke out and was to rise to the rank of Captain, an almost unique honour in the 'Wavy' Navy. All the same, at this moment I was stung and hurt by the obvious implication that I had been enjoying myself over Christmas and blurted out the details I had intended to keep secret.

'This time tomorrow, I shall be out with the Dover Patrol, in a minesweeper.'

Her brush suspended, she turned towards me. Her reaction was instinctive. 'Oh dear, I do hope you won't be dreadfully sick. You know what a bad sailor you are, and it will be so embarrassing for you in front of the crew.'

It was not surprising if, after that, I could not sleep. I tried to comfort myself with the memory which had long since been regarded as a family joke of the time when I had come home to Worcestershire for the week-end, and announced that the typing bureau which had just completed the manuscript of *Dreams Fade* had assured me that they had never had a failure yet with a first novel. At which automatically my mother had pronounced: 'What a pity you will break their record'.

True, she had been wrong on that occasion; yet even so, increasingly my head seemed to be heaving up and down as though the ship's deck was already beneath me, until, defeated, I got up and stood beside the window with a passage repeating itself over and over again in my mind from the journal of Katherine Mansfield in a book which, instead of a field-marshal's baton, I carried in my gas-mask container.

'Honesty is the one thing one seems to prize beyond life, love, death, everything. It alone remaineth. You who come after me, will you believe it? At the end, truth is the one thing worth having. It's more thrilling than love, more joyful and passionate. It simply cannot fail. All else fails.'

It is terrible to think how this supremely gifted writer, who suffered so much from ill-health and privations of every kind, on one occasion was obliged to give up writing her Journal, not for shortage of inspiration but because she lacked the few pence with which to buy another bottle of ink. Yet her work has survived and should be prescribed reading for all sixth forms. Nevertheless, I suspect that this New Zealand artist would have been defeated by the British Censor in the Second World War. I certainly was on many occasions, having my dispatches returned either to myself or my newspaper office, with whole passages scored out in blue pencil. However, I learnt to be cunning.

Fully aware that I should not be allowed to name the minesweeper in which I spent the first New Year of the war, as being the *Polly Johnson*, I made some play of the fact that her captain who hailed from Grimsby, and like his father and grandfather before him regarded the sea as his birthright, was affectionately known to all the crew not as Skipper Miles, but as Captain Polly. Surely that should provide a strong clue, at least to Grimsby folk.

Not simply because Skipper Miles was the first captain with

whom I sailed in the war, and into whose hands I entrusted my landlubber's body, does his personality stay so vividly still in my memory. There was something invincible about him. Even when he jerked his thumb towards a buoy a hundred yards away, and explained to his guest that this was the spot where his last ship, the *Atagonite*, had blown up, I had no qualms except for my stomach. It couldn't happen to us again – at least, not on this voyage.

Short and square, with a broad grin that was seldom absent from his face, he made me feel instantly that all his life he had taken the watch and stayed on. And that was so. For he had been apprenticed to the sea when he was twelve, and for the next five years he had earned sixpence a week. In contrast, later on, he reckoned that it was a poor year if he did not make a four-figure profit between the wars, when a thousand pounds still had considerable purchasing power. And he described to me also how, on his return from service in a trawler, at the end of the 1914 war – he had been stationed at Alexandria for three years – he had been looking forward with all the passion of his youth to an accumulation of sixty days leave on shore. 'Get down to the docks, there's money to be made,' was the homecoming greeting he received from his father. It did not occur to him to argue, to demur. At once he signed on, and that first voyage of twelve days, as a civilian once more, brought back to dock a haul of fish that in the market raised two thousand five hundred pounds.

Although I was piecing together the story of my host's life, in the wheel-house of the *Polly Johnson*, which hadn't exactly the amenities even of a cross-channel packet, with the wind freshening as we reached the open sea, yet the astronomical figures he produced sounded like cushy money. Until, a few weeks later, I found myself doing a trip in one of the Scottish fishing boats that put out from Aberdeen and sail up the north-east coast to Wick and back. This one was named the *Barness* and had had her decks raked with machine gun bullets from a marauding plane on its previous voyage, so that the crew were not surprisingly a little jumpy.

For my own part, setting sail from a city that does not deserve its music-hall reputation for meanness, since its handsome granite buildings shine like diamonds in the spring light, and its citizens freely subscribed over a million pounds for the building of Aberdeen's Infirmary, my mind was principally occupied as to where I could bunk down, between lurching excursions to the rail side. I would say that the corvette in which I sailed from Londonderry into the Atlantic, H.M.S. *Arabis*, so deceptively named after a delightful small flower, had the most fiendish motion of all that I personally encountered; it somehow managed both to roll and to pitch at the same time. However, the *Barness*, as soon as it hove to and put down its nets, had the only passenger on board almost inviting another raid, anything to divert his attention. To my dismay I had discovered that there were no cabins on board, no proper bunks, just holes in the wall, like rabbit hutches without the wire, placed round the space below that was sitting-room, dining-room and everything else to the nine members of the crew. They gave me a blanket that was none too clean, and I dossed down, opening one eye and closing it again hastily, for the sight that lay revealed was of the off-watch fishermen, enjoying a hearty supper of soused herring, their hands and bare arms splashed with blood from the haul they had just shipped on board.

Harry, the ship's mate, grizzled and muffled up in two fair-isle sweaters that one suspected never left his back, kept on reassuring me that the landing at Gallipoli had been chicken-feed compared with the life on board a fishing trawler, in peace and war. I didn't need the constant reiteration of the comparison to believe him. As a welcome variation, the next time he summoned me to leave my hole in the wall and come up on deck, he was chanting in my ear, in a dialect as strange and difficult to decipher as that of a Geordie, 'We've had two record hauls. Fourteen boxes in all, four boxes of lemons. Aye, that's the stuff to give the troops.'

Aye, in either war, I agreed, rolling up the companionway through a mist of cooking cabbage and the backwash of oil from the engine room. Overwhelmed, I just reached the side in time. 'Never mind, lad,' called out the chief consolingly, 'we all reckon you've been jammy for us.'

'Jammy,' it was explained to me, meant 'lucky', and there were to be many other occasions, in the testing times ahead, when I was to hear again that flattering suggestion that I brought luck with me. It was a comforting idea to account for the charmed life I certainly seemed in due course to possess, but how was one to gauge if the theory had any real substance? Today I still enjoy the reputation of being lucky for my friends, and I am gratefully proud of that. On the other hand, during the war itself, I was to be precipitated again and again into situations at once so bizarre and so alien to my previous way of life, that my overruling reaction was one of astonishment rather than of fear. I suppose surprise made me speechless. In consequence, I gained a largely undeserved reputation of possessing nerves of steel. How I wish that were true. Especially in regard to my stomach muscles.

The skipper of the *Polly Johnson* must have sensed my weak spot, without any briefing from me. I was trying to comfort myself with the item I had come across somewhere about Nelson always having a bucket beside him on the bridge, but it didn't make me feel any less apprehensive.

That first morning, as we nosed our way out of the harbour to the open sea, Charlie-the-cook every half hour brought up steaming hot mugs of tea, so strong a brew that had there been a teaspoon provided, it would have stood upright in the centre of the glue-like concoction. After one sip, caution made me leave mine untouched. My companion appeared not to notice, but the next time the service was repeated he growled fiercely, 'Can't you make it a bit weaker, Charlie?' as though all his life he had been a connoisseur of the delicate aroma of *Lapsang Souchong*. What had come over the skipper? The expression on Charlie's face was so comical, it raised my spirits.

When we were alone again in the wheel-house, I looked towards my host gratefully, conscious not for the first time how it is the genuinely strong who can afford to be gentle, and so often possess much better natural good manners than those who pride themselves on their background and the accident of their birth. It was the same with all the *Polly Johnson*'s crew. Their instinctive effort at making me feel at home was to invite me to join in a dart's match, in the dog watch. In vain did I protest to my partner, the gun-layer, whose peacetime home was in Guernsey, that I was a complete duffer at the game. To cover up my awkwardness he confided to his captive audience that this wasn't his first ship in the war. No, at the outbreak he had been posted to another trawler called the *James Ludford*. After three

All Fords are called 'Florrie' on board naval vessels. 'Florrie' Ford, Sandy's opposite number, in war and in peace

Skipper Miles of the *Polly Johnson,* in which I received my baptism, January 1st, 1940

Where are they now? The crew of the *Polly Johnson*

months, he had been sent off to Whale Island at Portsmouth to take a course in gunnery, just completed. The very day after he had left his previous ship, the *James Ludford* had hit a mine and gone down with all hands.

Sharply I drew in my breath and picked up the dart. 'Double Four,' I repeated. 'Why, that's easy. Just show me where it is on the board.' They showed me. The board swayed with the motion of the ship and I felt my entrails stirring uneasily. Taking another, even deeper, breath, and holding it, as Marie Tempest* had taught me in the days of my apprenticeship in the Theatre, I closed my eyes, at the same time flicking my wrist in an endeavour to ape the professional skill of the little friendly group surrounding me on the stifling hot mess-deck. Now. And I can still hear ringing in my ears the joyous shout that went up as my dart, like a homing pigeon, buried itself bang in the middle of the double four. I did not chance my beginner's luck in a return match, and I don't think I have ever played since. But the memory and the sense of exhilaration remain, and at the same time, with a certain wonder, like looking through a telescope at a far-off scene, I see myself later that evening feeling my way in the darkness along the narrow bridge outside the wheel-house, and clambering up on the rail.

There is five minutes left of the old year and I have been chosen, as a temporary mascot, to ring the New Year in on the ship's bell above my head. It was the skipper's idea for a brief spell to ignore the war, and instead to give a double chime of sixteen bells, as is the custom in all ships at sea at midnight on New Year's eve. Above my head, on the look-out platform, the watch calls out 'Half a minute to go', as I take hold of the bell's clapper with one hand, and gingerly hang on to my perch with the other. In those last seconds of waiting, across the screen of my mind flash pictures of the two previous New Year celebrations. The year before I had ended up in the Sporting Club at Monte Carlo, where everyone was inevitably raising champagne glasses in the air, in a self-conscious tableau from a B Class movie. Whereas the year before, I had ironically been on board an extremely luxurious German cruise boat, the *Cap Arcona*, in the harbour of Madeira, where there is a tradition of many decades standing now that as the clock strikes twelve the whole

* See page 230, *The Infirm Glory*.

island goes up in a blaze of fireworks, making your heart leap towards the rockets, as a symbol that this year only the sky will be the limit, for your happiness and success.

How different it was this time, in the silence and the darkness. At first my efforts as a bellringer were rather muffled and tentative, but then gradually the knack came to me so that the second eight went forth strong and clear across the water. Afterwards, everyone hastened to assure me that that was a good omen for the future. Having done my best, I joined the little group aloft, on 'monkey's island'. There was my darts' partner, the gun-layer, who was taking the watch, and a fair, fresh-looking boy from Bristol, John Smith, who was changing the recognition lights. In that moment of shared communion with the ship suddenly very still beneath us, anchored till the dawn, Smithie announced that he had got married a month before, and that his reason for choosing the Navy, rather than one of the other Services, was that he had acted in an amateur production of *The Pirates of Penzance*. Just as I was thinking what a very odd reason that was, we were joined by Paddy, whose instinct had brought him up from his beloved boilers at exactly the right moment, since the flask that I had smuggled on board, strictly for medicinal purposes, of course, was now passing from throat to throat. As Paddy took a swig and smacked his lips, I asked the question that I imagine was hovering in all our minds. 'Where do you think we shall all be this time next year?'

'Oh, for sure, we'll be pushing up the daisies.'

Although Paddy's accent was cheerful enough, and stage Irish rather than bog Irish into the bargain, I felt a shiver touch my spine. Alas, I wasn't to prove such a lucky mascot for the ship, after all. Or perhaps I shouldn't have left her after only two nights on board. Anyway, the *Polly Johnson* was destined to go down during the evacuation from Dunkirk, and when someone from the Admiralty telephoned me the news, his voice was blotted out by a particular exchange I had had with her captain.

'When you first went to sea, like I am doing now, did your father give you any advice?'

'Yes, he did. Two words.'

'And what were the words, Captain Polly?'

'Don't worry.'

Now the harsh breath of war had come so much closer with the threat of invasion only twenty miles away, that you could not escape the look of worry in everyone's eyes. There are poetical phrases that are popular with a certain type of gardener about the slow awakening from the winter's long sleep. The exeunt from Dunkirk that spring was a very sharp awakening indeed. I still do not understand how it was hailed as a victory, even at the time, except for purely propaganda reasons. I can even now too vividly recall the mood of utter impotence I had to endure myself. The sole volunteers whose services were of any use, apart from the nursing and feeding services, were those who in peacetime had spent their week-ends messing about in small boats along the coast. Anything that conceivably could make the journey there and back was gratefully enrolled in the most extraordinary Armada that ever set sail. My whole being ached, as always, to be in the thick of things, right on the spot. But the friends in the War Office who had got me out to the Maginot Line could not help me now. I should be cheating if I offered my services as a member of a scratch crew; for I should not only be in the way but take up valuable human cargo space.

Nevertheless, almost inevitably, I found myself making for Dover, where at least I could watch the survivors being brought ashore, looking like sleep-walkers, their eyes red-rimmed, unshaved for days, noticeably taciturn too. No thumbs-up for victory signs. None of that lark. Only an overwhelming relief that it was over, that they were no longer being dive-bombed on the French beaches, but were at least in their own country and had survived to fight another day.

I kept on looking for the faces of the friends I had made out there, like my conducting officer, Bobby Hartman. One face in particular was stamped upon my memory. The face of someone in battledress, who had come across to my table one evening in the brasserie of the Hotel Universe at Arras, where I was having my supper. I suppose it made me feel a little less isolated to peer into the faces of the rabble host, being given hot drinks and food by the W.V.S., always among the first on the scene in any national emergency. How I envied them their right to be there. After many hours had passed, my own sense of futility became so unsupportable that I got back into my car and drove on a little way along the coastal road, having decided to take up a watching brief, instead, from the headland of St Margaret's Bay, which possesses an unparalleled view of the Channel. Indeed, I have always intended to pay a return visit, part of the promise that we all make to ourselves, in times of war, to go back; in my case also to Londonderry, where the banks of the river seemed so unbelievably green after the monotonous grey of the Atlantic; and to Campbeltown, nestling on the west coast of Scotland, used as a base for the rescue tugs, one of which took such a battering from the storm we had to ride through to reach the wreck which had sunk by the time we found ourselves in the right area, that all my other doses of *mal de mer* seemed, in comparison, like an afternoon's rowing on the Serpentine. Still, Campbeltown itself was a bonny little place, linked in my mind with the visit I made to the lighthouse-keeper and his family on the Mull of Kintyre.

Actually, it is the only lighthouse in which I have ever spent the night. However, it is not for that reason that I find no difficulty in recalling the cluster of white buildings, with the washing hung out and the giant cabbages in the garden, and in the sitting-room the only books in the case, leather-bound volumes of *Good Words, Welcome Guest* and *Leisure Hours*, dated 1860 and 1857. Rather, it was the lasting impression which Mr and Mrs Andrew McMillan themselves made upon me. There was such a sense of peace between them. They had already lived in half a dozen lighthouses during their thirty years of married life, yet when I asked Mrs McMillan which she liked best – had it been Buckaness or Sule Skery, Inch Keith or Ailsa Craig – she simply gave me a sweet smile and replied, 'I liked them all'. I could sense that she was gazing back across the years to the time when her first son was born, and they sent a pigeon with a message and it flew the ten miles to the mainland so swiftly that within half an hour the doctor was climbing into the boat. Now that son wore the coveted NL in his cap like his father, and his mother could say with honesty to their guest:

'If you are happy as we have been, I don't think you notice the place very much. It is our home. You and your man are together. And the days seem to pass so quickly.'

At that I remember how her husband broke in, pretending to be embarrassed, though I could see the pleasure at her declaration in his eyes, so used to staring out to sea. 'Sometimes in the summer visitors like to have a peep at what we ourselves call "the edge of the world". They come scrambling down the side of the hill, puffing and blowing, and then seem quite disappointed and surprised to find that we haven't heather in our hair...'

The heather in the late summer, carpeting the Mull, must be a bonny sight, too. I often wish that that corner of Scotland wasn't so far away from Sussex, since in another direction lies Milford Haven, particularly dear to me because it was there that I joined the *Pozy*. There are so many places one promised oneself the pleasure of revisiting once the blackout curtains were down and discarded and all restrictions on petrol lifted. But somehow, one has never seemed to have the time for that nostalgic leisurely progress through Britain, with a rather special and entirely personal map at one's side. In consequence, one is left with the sometimes blurred, sometimes still sharp, impact of one's original visit, as I am of that evening on the cliff's edge, with the sea, that week-end of early summer, like milk beneath me poured into a mill pound. The last of the boats with their amateur crews, so tiny from that height and distance, were still straggling across the intervening but now dangerously narrow waters, pursued by the recurring flashes of flame towards the horizon. Gazing back at this distance of time, I am surprised that I should at that moment have hardly been aware of the vital importance of the dog fights over the French coast, the preliminary tests of strength for the Battle of Britain just ahead. I suppose it was that all my thoughts were still concentrated on the expeditionary force that had been compelled to leave our French allies to their fate. To me at that moment the whole messy business was epitomized by that anonymous soldier who had tackled me so urgently, while I was still able to enjoy the pleasures of French cuisine. Was he safe? Was he still alive? Was he already in the half-and-half state of being a prisoner of war? I could not write to his family for news because, unlike the majority of the chance encounters I had had in my role of messenger, he had been reluctant to give me either his home address or even his own name.

'That doesn't matter. Just call me Private Blank,' he had said, as he made his unexpected request. 'I want you to do something for me. You have a platform every Sunday.' (He was referring to my page in a Sunday newspaper.) 'Will you lend me that platform one Sunday? Not yet, it is not the right moment. They still talk about this as 'The Bore War', but the days will come when all that is changed. We shall be in it here, hot and strong. It is then that I want you to tell them what we really feel out here.'

He sat down at my table and took off his forage cap, and lit a cigarette.

'This afternoon I went to see the memorial that was built on a hill outside Arras, after the last war, in memory of my father's regiment. The East Ridings, he was in. I cannot remember him. You see, I was only a baby when my mother heard. And today, somehow I could not connect that monument with my father. Instead, I could only see the back-to-back houses in the street at Leeds where I was born. They are some of the foulest slums in England. If they had pulled them down, every house of them, after the last war, that would have been the best memorial of all.

'But they didn't. Everywhere they fell back into the same old complacent ways, seeing only what was under their nose, glossing over the rest. This is not the first war I have fought in. All my life I have been fighting, like millions of others in Britain, to get a chance to spread my wings a bit. I didn't get very far, I ended up as a clerk in an insurance company and I joined the Territorials more for the fun of going to camp each summer, than anything else. I never believed the politicians could be so mad as to let it all happen again. Do you remember that bit in the film of *All Quiet on the Western Front* where the soldier says, "I did not want to kill you, brother."?'

He paused for a moment and opened the pocket of his khaki blouse. I thought he was fishing for his cigarette packet again, but he was not. He wanted to show me something as precious to him as to them all. Gratefully I was to grow accustomed to such repeated gestures of confidence, the producing of a passport that was valid across a universal frontier, and meant so much to me, too, particularly when I was marooned in the *Pozy* against the Russian woodpiles. But this was the first time I had held the passport in my hand, and the moment struck deep into my consciousness.

The snapshot was of a strip of garden, with just space in it for two deck chairs. With himself in one of them, wearing a self-conscious smile and grey flannel bags, and at his side a girl with fair hair and a baby on her knees. 'We got married the week after Munich,' he was explaining. 'We had a year's happiness, anyway. It was worth it, whatever happens. And if it should be destined that I do not get back to see my son grow up, I cannot believe that they will make a mess of the second peace. Surely those who do survive wouldn't let them?'

When I did not answer the question-mark in his voice, because I did not want to interrupt the flow of his testimony which, later, I would record in my notebook, not for posterity – that pompous phrase – but nevertheless having its place as a genuine footnote in the final record, he went on:

'I expect you read Rupert Brooke, like I read him at night school. You remember the bit which we used, in our class, to think so corny, about *"If I should die, think only this of me; That there's some corner of a foreign field That is for ever England."*? Well, I still don't feel like that, and I don't imagine any of the other chaps in my company do, either. All the same, we do feel *something*. We feel that this is our chance to prove ourselves to ourselves. To show that even for an average fellow like myself there is more to life than getting up in the morning, going to work, and being driven like a machine till you are pensioned off.

'You know, the other day I was talking to some air-gunners and asking them why the devil they had volunteered for what's considered the most dicey number of all. Oh, they had their answer pat enough. They swore it was the one-and-six a day extra pay. But they were only kidding themselves. Because I bet the real reason was that they wanted to prove to themselves that they had the guts to do a job like theirs. None of us feel like heroes, or want to be treated as such. But we do want to feel like men, and this is our chance.'

No, none of us wanted to be treated like heroes, only to prove ourselves, I repeated to myself, as the sky began to darken over the sea and the night to creep up behind me, touching me with a cold hand. I had a long slog back from the coast ahead of me, to Esher, where I knew, whatever the hour, I would find my mother, in her sitting-room defiantly full of flowers from the garden, listening beside the wireless for the last B.B.C. bulletin and hoping that it would be read by someone who was actually of Swedish descent, Alvar Liddell, whose voice, after that of Churchill, was to give her more reassurance than any other during the war years. It must have been the same for a multitude of other women fenced in on the home front, since there was some thing so completely unruffled about his tones. My own journey that night might have been a less lonely one had I already read Alice Duer Miller's *The White Cliffs*, with its incantation:

> *'I am American bred,*
> *I have seen much to hate here – much to forgive,*
> *But in a world where England is finished and dead*
> *I do not wish to live.'*

My mother, fired by her American blood and encouraged by her histrionic successes as a young woman, learnt the poem off by heart and recited it to the local branch of the Women's Institute, while overhead the Battle of Britain was fought and won. If that display of mingled trust and defiance seems a little laughable now, it is surely no more so than the story I was to hear that summer in a fighter squadron's mess, of the wife, living as close to the airfield as possible, who was awakened by the knocking of the local policeman with the warning that he was seriously considering running-in her squadron-leader husband for a disturbance of the peace. There had been more than one complaint in that sleepy Kentish village of his having made a supercharger din when he drove his car into his garage late at night, and slammed the doors.

It was another world up there in the skies, far away from the plodding feet on the beat; a world that caught at our imagination but that we could not translate into reality, since there were no excursion trips for the many, only solo voyages of exploration for the few. Those who were claiming that the certainly remarkably calm waters of the Channel during the crucial days of the evacuation was nothing less than a miracle sent from on high, now insisted on calling the Hurricane and Spitfire pilots 'miracle men', deifying them as 'knights of the sky', in cliché phrases and banner headings that they themselves found embarrassing and alien to their innate modesty. In consequence, when I was given official permission by the Air Ministry to visit stations like Hornchurch in the thick of the battle, and

Getting brown for leave 'up the smoke'

A mine goes up on the Dover Patrol

Trawler fishermen from Aberdeen. They said I was lucky for them; but I only remember how sick I was

Captain Piper of the *Royal Archer*

spend a few days there so that I could try to paint a more truthful portrait in words, I found them at first, not surprisingly, wary and shy of the outsider, though in the end I was to become unexpectedly close to one of them.

In all branches of living there is the accepted type, with orthodox characteristics, and the particular person with his own individuality. At the period of the see-saw struggle for aerial supremacy, almost all the pilots in action were peacetime volunteers who had seen in the Service an escape from having their feet anchored to the ground in Civvy Street. Few of them had reached School Certificate standard or, for that matter, got their colours for conventional games. That kind of discipline had irked them. They were, mostly, loners who had the war not happened would have probably drifted from one occupation to another which needed no formal educational qualifications, ending up, as likely as not, tinkering with cars in a garage. When I discovered that their remuneration for shooting Messerschmitts out of the sky was only fourteen shillings a day, which seemed a hardly adequate sum for saving the civilian population from invasion, I challenged several of them in turn as to what they thought of their pay, and recorded at the time that only one of them had a single complaint. And that wasn't strictly concerned with the money itself. He merely suggested that as he had become a non-stop smoker between sorties it would be a great help if in the mess they could get a duty-free issue of cigarettes, such as the Navy had.

This comment came from someone who already had the mauve D.F.C. ribbon on his tunic, looking very clean in contrast with a deliberate and disdainful shabbiness of his attire. In any case, his uniform had had a ducking that could scarcely be expected to improve its appearance. He had been on his way back from patrol, in his Spitfire, when his kite had suddenly burst into flames. The last that was heard of him on the R.T. was that he had sighted a destroyer beneath and was going to bail out, somehow. Actually, he turned the machine over, and fell out. Twenty-four hours later, he had turned up in the mess wearing a petty officer's uniform, which had caused much ribald comment. On his tunic he now wore a naval button, and in exchange he had sent one of his own, when he returned the borrowed clothes.

I noticed that he preferred telling me anecdotes of a kind that would not cause him to be accused, even remotely, of shooting a line. Like most of his companions he owned a dog, and I came upon him giving it a bath. 'You see,' he explained, 'as I had a bath myself in the Channel earlier in the week, I decided it was Wimpey's turn today.'

I had a dog, too, and when he told me the name of his and I volunteered the name of mine, I think that was the moment when the first of the barriers came down. Anyway, that evening, when a whole crowd of them bundled into an old jalopy to make for the nearest pub, they asked me to come with them and it was like being in the Lion d'Or again.

They all seemed to have very thin wrists and very white teeth, and startling blue eyes. But perhaps it was simply the sky reflected in their eyes during their shorter and shorter sojourns on earth. Certainly they all wore their hair long, much longer than would have been permitted in the Army or the Navy. If they had wanted to create the style that the Beatles were to launch a quarter of a century later, they would have had sufficient tonsorial material, I imagine, except that in the wind that always seemed to be sweeping across the airfield even on the hottest day – and that summer was a halycon one as far as the weather was concerned – their mostly fair manes seemed exaggerated, because it was taboo to put any grease on your hair. The explanation, I discovered, was simple. They didn't want to mess up their helmets, and, after all, they were more often in their helmets than out of them.

They didn't use the inside of their mess much, except for actual eating, and even then they had the gramophone or wireless on, full blast. The tune that was their favourite at that moment was one of Connie Boswell's numbers called *Martha.* They'd play it a dozen times running. I suppose everyone who lived through that summer and the next and the next has some particular song that was precious to them, so that its words cropping up suddenly in a Television Spectacular – 'I'd like to sing an oldie for you now, which I think with our new backing is absolutely great' – still have the power to turn one momentarily to stone. Because otherwise it would be too painful. You must not allow yourself to think like that any more. Or else, which is even more chilling, you cannot.

The slang can bring it all back, too, digging up the graves of yesteryear. The other day a friend used the expression 'blonde bombshell' and for a moment I was puzzled why that dated phrase should make me feel instinctively apprehensive and forlorn. By the time I realized why, the conversation had moved on round me at the luncheon table, and anyway, who to would be interested now? Even at the time I was careful not use any of their own copyright slang when I was with them, though it was as catching as chickenpox. Still, that would have been trespassing on their territory, and I was only there on sufferance. At least, at first. 'Wizard' was the word which kept on cropping up over and over again. The ultimate term of pleasure and approval. At the same time, they had an equally expressive counterblast, 'Punk'. That went for any shade of disapproval up to what was really beyond the pale. For instance, when I enquired if they had any superstitions – though they could hardly reply that they preferred not to fly on a Friday – they answered instead they had no time for that punk. After all, one of their squadron had got himself written off, driving home on leave in the blackout. He had run into a tree in Epping Forest, after having brought down five ME109s in as many days. Of course, he must have fallen asleep at the wheel. So why not walk under every ladder in sight with your eyes wide open? All the same, many of them did wear a St Christopher medallion on a chain round the neck, together with their identity discs. Challenged in regard to that, they had their alibi ready. It pleased the girl friend who had given it to them.

I saw such a medal round Brian's throat the first night he came back from leave. They had put me in a hut with two beds in it. The other one was empty. Everything was such a scramble, so transitory the overriding atmosphere, that I didn't like to enquire if the other bed was empty because its occupant had gone on leave, or gone for a Burton. It is a long time since I heard that phrase but I can use their slang now that it no longer matters. It was bad enough bothering them with any questions at all, and this was one that you simply did not ask. For that matter, the bed I was sleeping in could just as well have been a dead man's last resting place, I told myself as I examined the only sign of human habitation on the wall. Compared with even a junior officer's cabin in a destroyer, it was as impersonal and uncomfortable as a cell. There were the two small wooden chairs with stiff backs, to put your clothes on, and nothing else. Except that equivalent of a green baize notice-board over the opposite bed. Here, instead of notices of meetings for staff members was a montage of pictures of cuties cut out of magazines, serving as a background for a series of black and white snapshots, all of the same girl, and all with the same expression, smiling into the sun. She was extremely pretty and disturbingly young.

But then he was only twenty-two himself. He had joined the Royal Air Force straight from school. Undressing that first night, he was wearing a pair of bathing shorts, instead of briefs. He explained that he and his girl had meant to have a final bathe that afternoon, and had got all ready to go and then settled for something else.

'It was wizard that June was able to wangle four day's leave at the same time. Not much, but it was the first I've had since the balloon went up. June works as a secretary at the Ministry of Supply. They sound a stuffy lot, and I told her to tell her boss to take his finger out and get us more machines. God knows we need them.'

He had a fresh lot of leave pictures to add to the board, and this meant several of the pin-ups had to be removed. I decided June would be pleased if she was here now. After all, she had an official status. They were engaged, but when I asked if they were planning to be married on his next leave, his face, so sunburnt that the smudges under his eyes and the very fine etched lines were almost hidden, clouded over and went blank. So that I wished I hadn't made the suggestion.

'We both decided this leave that it would be better to wait a bit.' Just as he was about to turn out the light, he added: 'If I were married I would be thinking of June, in the air. She'd be my responsibility. I wouldn't be able to blot her out, as I can now. She knows there won't be any other girl for me, ever. But this way, it isn't that I am free exactly, I just don't want to think of anything when I'm flying, except my machine and my target, and not wasting any of my sixteen seconds' worth of ammunition when the moment comes.'

'Only sixteen seconds?' I echoed.

'Yes. That's all. It's plenty long enough.'

The light switch clicked and the darkness came, but not for

him sleep, except in fits and starts, like a man in a fever. Old battles, new battles, he seemed to fight them all, sometimes crying out in protest during the night, so that it was a relief for us both when the dawn came, serving as his alarm clock, for he was on call at five o'clock.

I imagine he hoped it would be the same as the morning when he had found himself at ten thousand feet over the French coast.

He put it like this:

'It was one of those wizard mornings you prayed for in the summer holidays, when you used to wake up thinking, "Whoopee, it's going to be a scorcher". Actually, it was icy cold, but marvellously clear. I received the message that three Messerschmitts were approaching from the east. I got behind them, they did not see me, I climbed five thousand feet in steep spirals and came down on their tails. The next second I saw glycol fumes pouring out of one of them and then the pilot bailing out below, and a moment later the same thing happening to a second man, clouds of thick black smoke. Afterwards I went on to Calais, and shot down another 109, and when I got back I hadn't used up all my ammo.

But he went on quickly, to make it clear he was simply repeating his report on landing, and that it had nothing to do with his own skill and tenacity. 'Every time I take off, I always feel as though the bottom of my stomach is coming away from the top. But I imagine everyone feels like that.'

Now I knew at last the real answer to the question I had asked so many members of this new, exclusive club. Of course, it was easier for both of us to talk in the half-light and privacy of the hut. For instance, I was not even shy to press him if he ever thought of the other fellow, what he was like as a person, in the middle of the dog fights, and he said: no, never at the time. It was too hectic; but sometimes when he had got back safely and was making for the mess he would wonder what his opponent had been like, and his family, too. But he switched off as soon as he could, with the blare of the gramophone drowning such thoughts, because it wasn't any use. 'And I try not to think of my own family, either,' he said simply.

Only of June, because she, I came to understand more and more clearly, represented the future in his eyes. She had no link with his childhood memories, he was already in uniform when they met for the first time, and so their relationship was without those kinds of roots, and yet in another way they were utterly anchored to each other. With the instinct for self-preservation of the hunter – where the undergrowth was the cumulus clouds utterly out of reach for us ordinary mortals – he would try deliberately to divorce her image from his mind, all through the hours that he spent at the dispersal point or on patrol, or when he was larking about in the mess, his feet still scarcely on the ground, Hermes, with a shiny seat to his trousers and frayed cuffs to his tunic, and a mug of wallop in his hand.

It was only when he was alone again in that uncompromising hut that June became once more the incarnation of all his passionate longings for survival; so warm and real a presence her translated image from the snapshots on the wall that by the end of my stay amongst them I, too, felt that I knew every hair on her head. Since in his heart Brian never expected to see me again, and since, too, there were no witnesses to our communion, he could talk to me without restraint, using me as a kind of confessional. It was with something of a shock that I realized he had never volunteered June's other name, when, at the last moment, as we were saying goodbye, he pushed a piece of paper into my hand with her address written on it, speaking softly so that no one else should hear. 'It looks pretty dicey about any of us getting any more leave at present. Would you explain to her why I don't ring her up. It's too . . .'

Too tantalizing he meant. I understood absolutely. Hornchurch was a million miles away from London at that moment. I sensed it myself strongly on my return. It was as though I had been sharing an oxygen cylinder with them all, and now it was empty. I wrote to June at once, explaining where I had been and suggesting that she should come and lunch with me in my Ebury Street home, giving a date only three days ahead because I could never be sure how swiftly I might be despatched on another mission.

She rang me up the next morning to accept, and I could tell from her voice how pleased she was in her turn at the prospect of being able to speak with complete freedom about her feelings for Brian. My front-door bell rang just as I was tapping out on my typewriter the last paragraph of my portrait in words. Instead of Brian's final aside to me, I had used the actual words of one of the other flying officers of his Wing.

'I'm awfully sorry I haven't been able to tell you much about myself. You see, we live such ordinary, everyday lives here.'

Then the door opened, and she was standing there in a white cotton dress and a black voile scarf tucked in at the neckline. I came towards her eagerly, but I stopped before I reached her or was close enough to take her hand. I am not sure whether it was that unexpected black splash at her throat or something about her manner, but I think I guessed, even before she spoke.

'Brian's mother telephoned me just as I was leaving for the office. I don't know when it happened. She just had the bare news from his station commander.'

'But I was with him on Tuesday,' was all I could say. And this was only Friday. I couldn't take it in any more than she could. It was the first time I had been so personally involved. We went through the motions of lunch, almost without speaking. I tried to persuade her to have some kind of drink, offering whisky, brandy, anything; but she simply shook her head.

'I couldn't bear the idea of staying at home today, or going to Brian's mother, though she asked me. We've only met once.' She turned towards me, imploringly, her food untouched, but no tears on her cheeks. She was too numb still to weep. That would come later. 'I thought there might be something you could tell me, something I didn't already know.'

'He called his Spitfire "The Blonde Bombshell".' My voice trailed away. I could not see my companion's own ash-blonde hair, but instead a news flash picture on a movie screen, a fighter plane spiralling out of control, down, down, sizzling into the sea, a funeral pyre quenched by the engulfing waters. Had there been time in that last second before oblivion came, for him to glimpse her face?

'Brian had an old bicycle he used to pedal across the airfield from the mess to his dispersal post. I don't think he had a pet name for that. He said he hated running at school, and still hated it.'

When she said nothing, I tried again.

'In the mess, they played Connie Boswell's *Martha* over and over again.'

That struck a chord at last, and she was able to control her voice sufficiently to reply.

'On his last leave he bought me a copy of it and we played it all the time on my portable.'

Would she play it again that night, in her bed-sitter in Kensington, or break the record in half? I would never know.

I went on desperately. 'There was something Brian said the last night I slept in his hut, just before he switched off the light. It was meant more for you than for me. "June is my first love and my last." He wasn't being prophetic, because I have never met anyone so marvellously confident for the future, or so tremendously alive. No, he meant, June, that you were the only girl he had ever really cared for, and that you would be married the moment it was all over.'

'And live happily ever after? But don't you see, it *is* all over.' She turned her head away, one hand to mouth as though to stop herself from screaming. 'I am sorry,' she said after a moment, and I marvelled at her control. 'But it's no use. I shouldn't have come. Oh God.'

Then she had got up so swiftly from her chair that I was still seated at the table when she had gone from the room, to be alone with her agony. A moment later, I heard the front door shut with a dead finality. And I went on sitting there, knowing that I would never for the rest of my own life be able to erase from my consciousness her cry of despair that the God whom she believed had blessed her love had, after all, deserted her. So it is not surprising that sometimes still I hear her voice when I drive up the Great North Road, past the derelict airfields, with the summer winds blowing the unkept grass aside to uncover the patches of scarlet poppies, of academic interest to antiquarians. Did it really all happen only thirty years ago? Most of the sheds already looked so seedy, though not quite as forlorn as a ship going to its final rest to be broken up in the knackers' yard. That is surely the saddest sight of all.

So many times I have meant to stop the car at a convenient lay-by and climb over the fence. But somehow one is always in such a hurry to reach the next destination, to sustain a spurious sense of still being in the swim. Certainly it is not because I would be ill-at-ease in the company of the ghosts I might encounter wandering among the poppies. *'Life to be sure is nothing* *much to lose, But young men think it is and we were young.'** For there is a certain comfort in the argument that Brian and all the others, the few who became so many in the end, were luckier in a way than the ones who did survive, only to find no place for themselves in the market place where all the best jobs, the 'cushy numbers', had already gone to those who stayed behind, the 'indispensable' ones in 'reserved occupations'. In any case, what had the years of flying, of killing or being killed, taught a young man fresh from school in regard to the skills and qualities needed for an integrated life in peace time? No wonder that some of them drifted, clinging to their outmoded slang, because they could not come to terms with the commerce of the cities, the small change of an everyday existence.

The man who understood them best was the architect of their victory. By the time that I myself met Air Chief Marshal Lord Dowding, head of Fighter Command during the Battle of Britain, he had already reached the eighties, now living in a house that suitably overlooks the whole Weald of Kent, in whose skies so many of the dog fights were fought. I found him physically frail but still immensely alert when I went to call on him on the Sunday morning that I had taken to be another anniversary of the climax to the battle, the victory point in the battle, September the fifteenth 1940. So that it was with a feeling of considerable surprise that I heard my host declare:

'We always celebrate this day, because it was the one on which our Spitfires and our Hurricanes finally chased their fighters back over the coast, inflicting such damage that they never attacked, on that same scale or the same way, again. In consequence, invasion became an impossibility.

'At the same time, I have always held the view myself that a decision taken on an earlier date really won the Battle. That May, I was summoned to a special meeting of the Cabinet. I had already, on paper, put in an urgent plea that every fighter plane should be brought back from France. As the Germans advanced, you can appreciate that the wastage of the machines left on the ground was an appalling one.

'The French were clearly pulling out of the war. I was determined that we ourselves should still have fighter protection for our shores. However, Churchill could be extremely obstinate.

* A. E. Housman.

He had a tremendous sense of accord with the French and was equally determined that everything possible should be done to aid them, right up to the final moment of their collapse. The argument went to and fro, until I became acutely aware that there was only one thing that could possibly make him change his mind.

'So while the Ministers went on talking, talking, I walked round the table and placed over the Prime Minister's shoulder, bang in front of him, a graph. This was a graph that showed precisely how the loss of our machines had mounted during the previous ten days, and how, if these losses on the ground were allowed to continue, in another ten days we shouldn't have a serviceable machine left with which to carry on the fight over our own coast.

'I have always found it easier to convince through the eyes than the ears. Anyway, my strategy on this occasion worked. The P.M. broke off the discussion, to examine the graph in detail . . . and there and then changed his mind. It was the decision of a big man, torn in half by conflicting loyalties, and I am of the undoubted opinion that because of the vision that Churchill displayed, this proved to be one of the turning points of the war. All that followed during that summer stemmed from that moment in the Cabinet room.'

He himself, as he looked back to those hectic cliff-hanging days when he was working round the clock at his Headquarters at Stanmore, had only one regret. 'I never had a free moment to get out to the actual stations, like Hornchurch where my son himself was stationed, and meet the pilots who were actually flying the sorties. I think I understood their temperament, exactly what they would accept and what they wouldn't, how far we could drive them without breaking them. Nevertheless, I knew so few of them personally at the time.'

There never is sufficient time, I thought, as almost inevitably I enquired what he considered were the qualities that went to the making of a first-class pilot, faced with the challenges of war.

When I arrived, my host had been amusing himself with a jigsaw puzzle spread out on a table in front of him. As he pondered over his reply, he picked up a piece and searched vaguely for its slot. His own life and career had been a little like a jigsaw puzzle, I decided, except that, as a dedicated spiritualist, he was utterly convinced that everything is part of a master plan. At school, at Winchester, because he had such an allergy to studying Greek he begged that he should be transferred to the Army Class, although no member of his family had ever had a career in one of the Services, and almost as soon as he had been commissioned he requested to be transferred again, this time to the Royal Flying Corps.

'In 1914 we had a cruising speed of about forty miles an hour,' he had told me earlier, comparing it with the four hundred miles of which the Spitfire was capable. 'You worked the rudder with your feet. And when you looked down there was a hole between your feet, showing the earth beneath.'

It was then that he had produced a souvenir that was concealed beside the fireplace, so that for a moment I had imagined that it was a poker he was grasping in his hand. Until it was explained that this was the 'joystick' from the biplane in which young Dowding had been flying over the German lines on one occasion in 1916. I did not have to have the gash, half-way down it, pointed out to me. He had kept it as a souvenir, a kind of mascot, too.

'Another quarter of an inch and the spray of shrapnel that struck my plane would have blown it out of my hand, and I would not have been sitting here, answering your questions.'

There was a pause while he searched again for the right place for the piece of the puzzle that he still held in his hand. I wondered if he had forgotten my question, for old men do forget, but the next moment he was replying in precise terms.

'The French have a saying that there are no bad soldiers, only bad officers. You could divide flying material into three groups. The enthusiastic volunteers that would never make the technical grade, the ones who would be all right and not let down the side, if well led, and the heroic ones.'

However, it is the technical grades that take precedence in peace time, I thought a little wryly, as we walked through the hall where on the wall hangs a framed picture of the first annual reunion of those who would rather be classed among the volunteers than labelled the heroic ones, even by the man whom they themselves so greatly revered. He himself was in civilian clothes, with a symbolic bowler in his hand, and gathered round him were a group of the faces that have a special place in the chronicles of those times, bearing names that for many still possess a kind of mystical incantation. Hilary, Malan, Gleed, Deare, Aitken, Stanford-Tuck.

All the same, I had not expected to be quite so stirred the day that I finally crossed over their side of the fence. Because, after all, I was being brought face to face only with a reconstruction of the Battle's background, not the real thing but, instead, a mock-up for a film planned to celebrate the thirtieth anniversary. It was with mixed feelings in consequence that I had accepted the invitation to watch some of the shooting. However, the moment that I arrived on the now lonely Cambridgeshire airfield of Debden, even though the long line of fighter planes wore neat macintosh hoods against the summer's wind and rain, even though I was fully aware, too, that when they eventually left the ground they would be flown by Spanish pilots, who today are trained on the same type of machines, yet to be confronted by the implacable black swastikas painted on their tails filled me with a sense of terror, a waking nightmare.

It's only a film, it's only a film, I kept on repeating to myself as we walked along the lane to where at the end a machine stood, disguised instead as a solitary Heinkel. This discovery made one of my guides comment:

'The first thing I got in the war was a Heinkel, over Whitby of all places. That was in the February of 1940, before the main Battle started. Afterwards a lady who had been walking along the front at the time said it came in so low she could see the swastika on the tail.'

It was Peter Townsend speaking, roped in, like several others, as expert adviser for the film. He wore a dark blue sweater and no jacket, dressed as though for a walk across the Downs. We had never met before, and considering the number of 'gongs' he had acquired, I was surprised at first to find what a quiet, gentle voice he possessed, and how untouched his looks have been by the years. My instant reaction was that if he chose to change out of the casual clothes he was wearing back into uniform, he could have played himself, in the film, without seeming in the least incongruous.

'It's funny what you remember, and what you forget,' he was saying. 'Occasionally I have a nightmare, still, that it's all happening over again. But usually if I lie awake all I hear is the wind, like today, through the soft grass, before it was cut in the summer. It used to serve as an extra brake when you brought your Hurricane in to land.'

Yes, personally he had liked flying Hurricanes best. Moreover, he had a slightly startling theory to propound that if all the students who are for ever demonstrating about this or that could be persuaded to take to the skies instead, there would be no further Battle of the Universities.

His smile is both sweet and ironic, and I was aware at once how carefully one must watch. It had been the conflicts and the hazards of the peace that had taught him to be so wary, I reminded myself as he added, 'Looking back now, I have an idea that joining the R.A.F. in the 'thirties, several years in fact before we sniffed the war in the breezes, was at the time a kind of rebellion for me.'

My two other guides that day, Robert Stanford-Tuck, who does not answer to diminutives like Bob or Tommy, and 'Ginger' Lacey, understood precisely what the third of their triumvirate was seeking to express. They themselves had been accredited with the same winning score of twenty-nine planes, and yet what a contrast they made in appearance: the one with the amiable ginger moustache, who had started the war as a sergeant-pilot, and has only recently retired from the Service with the rank of squadron-leader; and the other, who had commanded a wing of Spitfires, with the sharp line down his cheek like a sabre scar and not an ounce of superfluous flesh on his tall, steely figure.

Superstitious? Even as I made the suggestion, and they shook their heads in unison, I saw again the St Christopher medallion hanging round that other pilot's neck. And instantly wished I had held my tongue. Besides, one sensed that these three had all been utterly certain – yes, but hadn't he? – that they would come through. The one whose fate it was to be seconded as an equerry to the Palace spoke for them all when he said:

'The only time I took up with me a mascot that had been given to me the day before, by a young cousin, I was shot down immediately and had to bail out into the sea.' Again that disarming smile, like a cloak, as he went on, 'I am having a shot at writing a book myself, starting with the inception of the

Royal Air Force at the end of the First World War, and ending with the climax of the Battle of Britain. I have just succeeded in tracing one of the pilots I shot down. I am going to visit him as soon as they don't need me for the film any more.'

Again he spoke for them all when he emphasized what a disgrace they all felt it was that 'Stuffy' Dowding, as they alone had the right to call their former Chief, had never been given the full credit he deserved. 'Surely it's not too late for him to be more fully honoured now?' they exclaimed in chorus, looking at me as though I had the power to arrange such things. It was they who had been the gods, I thought, not I. Alas, their leader died before he could be given the final accolade.

'Do you remember the frightful names we got called?' they reminded one another. 'Like Knights of the Sky,' I suggested, hoping this way to exonerate myself. At once Townsend capped it with his own favourite, 'Intrepid Birdmen', as we strolled back to the cars that would take us to Duxford Aerodrome where the main shooting of the film was being done that day.

I rode with Stanford-Tuck in his dashing MG sports model. A young man's car, but then he is still a young man, in vitality and lust for living. Today he has made a success of growing mushrooms, in Kent, his feet firmly rooted to the earth, an example to all the others. I was amazed to discover that he had brought a shooting stick with him, which he opened and leant on the moment that our gyrations came to a standstill. It was part of his philosophy of adaptation to circumstances. Nevertheless, I had a sharp intimation of what his mood, his attitude must have been like, leading his wing into battle, when we found ourselves marooned behind a lorry which refused to budge.

As we squeezed by at last, he volunteered, in his clipped, very English voice, 'I think some of the fellows in the mess used to imagine that I had no feelings because I kept such a grip on myself, that summer. You had to. If you began to think of the losses, and started counting your own friends who had gone . . . well, you simply couldn't . . . or else. . . .'

'Did it make you feel very bitter? I mean, after it was all over.'

'My dear fellow, every summer I go off shooting stags in Hungary with one of the most celebrated of the Luftwaffe commanders, Adolf Galland. When I was shot down and shoved away in a prisoner-of-war camp, he did the interrogating. That's how it goes.

'Today we are good friends. Though we are still rivals over a different kind of "bag". It's marvellously wild country into which we disappear. We stalk all day and loll in front of a log fire in our hunting lodge in the evenings. Sometimes you can hear the stags fighting each other, the crunch of their horns out there in the darkness.'

It was almost as though he were talking of the other battle, Spitfire or Hurricane against ME109s, I thought, curious to hear which of all the aerodromes from which he had operated he liked the most.

He knew at once. 'Biggin Hill. Everyone and everything was bang-on there, all the time. You had a tremendous sense of being right in the thick of things, but never at panic stations.'

They had transformed part of Duxford Aerodrome into Biggin Hill. We arrived just in time to see one of the hangars going up in smoke, after a daylight bombing raid by the enemy. The thick, black funeral pyre made us cough and choke. Most sensibly the W.A.A.F. personnel had taken to the slit trenches at the double. One of them was Susannah York, but somehow that didn't seem absurd because, like the other actors, such as Kenneth More, playing yet another Air Force veteran, she had lost her contemporary identity. It was the battle scene itself which had taken over the occasion.

I joined the co-producer, Ben Fisz, whose idea it had originally been to make the film and who had himself served with the Polish Air Force, standing beside the director of the picture, Guy Hamilton, who in his turn had spent most of his war at sea. To their visitor the latter explained that all the actors playing pilots were intended to be composite portraits.

'I suppose you could say that the character of Skipper is based on "Sailor" Malan, and that of Susannah York on Dame Felicity Peake, as she now is, who ended up as the queen bee of the W.A.A.F. but was a young officer at Biggin Hill on the days we are reconstructing.

'She described to me herself how magnificently the girls behaved, explaining it this way: they were so afraid of the men thinking they were afraid that they simply had to show them. She herself had just lit a cigarette afterwards, with trembling fingers, when a sergeant yelled at her, "Put that out, you silly bitch, a gas main has burst".'

In one of the hangars, transformed into a canteen for the extras, Peter Townsend was compelled to hold court, as though it were an anteroom in the Palace. A motley throng in a bizarre collection of clothes to face the rigours of a peaceful English summer had descended from all over the globe, to report on the progress of the film, and now were boggle-eyed to find themselves face to face with one of the most decorated of pilots but also a man whose name in the post-war era was to achieve a totally different kind of fame.

However, he displayed no irritation at their persistent questioning but remained the polite and charming courtier, who was clearly far more glamorous in their eyes than any of the assembled film stars. I wondered if he was recounting again the story he had told me over lunch of those other days when he was so close to the Throne.

'On one occasion I had to entertain a Persian official of some kind. He enquired what I had done in the war. I tried to explain to him, briefly. Understanding shone on his face. "Ah, you were a big arse," he exclaimed.'

Whilst I was having a cup of tea myself, 'Ginger' Lacey brought up the youngest of his three daughters, clutching her autograph book. 'Would you mind?' I decided that with his modest, self-deprecatory manner that hid so much strength, he was the prototype of all the sergeant-pilots, to me the salt of the earth. But then hadn't my life been saved by another such ginger-haired sergeant, over Stavanger?

'Ginger' Lacey had an anecdote to relate, too. 'The last time I went to my squadron's reunion dinner, my daughters demanded I should get them Douglas Bader's autograph. I was not too keen to have to ask for it, but they made me promise. When I brought it back on the menu, I did just mention he had done a swop for mine, for his nephew. "Why on earth?" was the answer I got to that.'

His unfading grin pierced me. Would the generation that had not been born when the Battle of Britain was being fought, react to the film simply as yet another fictitious yarn on the big screen? Immersed in writing a chronicle largely of those times, I had a proprietary interest in that question-mark which coloured

The *Royal Archer,* typical of scores of small cargo boats that never counted the cost

The tug *Freebooter* tows a giant floating dock through the Irish Sea

My messmates on board H.M.S. *Arabis,* first of the flower-class corvettes. What a misnomer

The Duke and Duchess of Windsor

all our conversation that evening at dinner in the Newmarket hotel where we were staying. I noticed that the other two 'big arses' automatically left it to Peter Townsend to choose what we should drink. Living outside Paris now, on the farm he has recently acquired for his attractive Belgian wife and their three small children, and speaking the language like a native, he had no trouble with the wine list.

'I wish we could give the students who spend the time they should be studying in demonstrating for anything from Biafra to legalizing pot, the sense of national pride that the Battle of Britain gave us,' said Stanford-Tuck. 'Perhaps this film will do the trick.'

He himself is more fortunate than some parents. His own children are not the protesting kind. One of his two sons had just taken his Law Finals, he was able to announce with pride, the other was at Sandhurst. I could understand why they had accepted the yoke of self-discipline so early in their own development, since their father, I discovered, gets up to start work at five o'clock every morning, winter and summer alike. He was clearly being utterly honest when he assured me that he found it no hardship at all. Moreover, when I asked him how he had managed to survive the three years he had spent in captivity, for that has always seemed to me the severest test of all, he replied laconically that he had been too busy to notice if the days dragged. 'Too busy?' I echoed, before I realized that my dinner companion was referring obliquely to all the attempts he had made to escape. After each abortive attempt, until he finally got away, his punishment was another dose of solitary confinement.

'Wasn't that absolute hell?' I suggested.

His answer was unexpected.

'No, in a way it was a relief. I was on my own. I had all the time in the world to take stock, to get onto terms with myself. You must do that, you know, to stay the course.'

Even if I hadn't known, he would have made me understand what he meant by the very simplicity with which he expressed himself. It was the same with Peter Townsend when later that evening I found myself having a nightcap with him at the bar. All round us were men with brick-red faces to match the checks of their suits, who had been to the races and were talking about what they fancied for tomorrow. They did not glance in our direction. We were the outsiders.

'They always talk now of the parties in the pubs near the aerodrome. But it's funny, I don't remember any. Certainly not that summer. We were too occupied. And if it doesn't sound pompous, too disciplined and professional. You had to be to survive.'

For a moment I was back at Hornchurch, conscious of all the hours that I had lain awake listening to the stranger in the other bed, now muttering, now crying out in his sleep. Never completely still or at peace with himself. I had not thought of Brian for a long time. It was incredible to realize that June would be fifty now, old enough to be a grandmother. It all depended how long she had waited for the scar to heal, if it ever does really heal.

It was my turn to order another round of drinks. When they came, I asked Peter Townsend, 'Were you married then to your first wife?'

'No, but I did marry, of course, during the war. We had only known each other for six weeks. Ridiculous, wasn't it?'

Later came the period in his life that we could not discuss, the name that we felt we must not mention between us. Though I had often thought how extraordinary it was that he should have said goodbye to the Queen's sister in the same house, in Sussex, where Princess Margaret was destined to meet for the first time the man to whom she is now married. I was there that night at the party when they met. Tony Armstrong-Jones had been taking family photographs. But if you used such a coincidence, such a strange link in a novel, the readers would find it too contrived to accept. Today that house has itself been swallowed up by the tide of post-war development. Incongruously it stands in the centre of a housing estate, conspicuously out of place, empty and unused. A sequel so undramatic as to be almost farcical. Except, of course, to those who were themselves involved.

'I was in Leopoldville, when I decided to spend a year going round the world. I happened to be writing something in my diary and came across a map on the last page. That gave me the idea, though I suppose in my subconsciousness I was already searching for some kind of escape, some sort of therapy, and travel is supposed to provide that. But in my case it was no use. Wherever I went I was recognized. There had been too many photographs in the world's press.'

His face was suddenly drained. For a moment he looked as weary as all his fellow pilots looked at the end of that summer when they had had no leave for so many weeks on end. And so little real sleep, either.

'What was so awful at the moment of the final choice was that I felt so alone, no one came forward to help me.'

Despite, or perhaps even more because of the coarse, indifferent, din surrounding us, his words struck me with a compelling force. For he could have been speaking, too, I thought, of Britain's own isolation during the Battle. Then a moment later his face, like the clouds dark with swastikas, cleared. 'I am married to such a wonderful girl now,' he said.

'I have never heard my husband in all the years we have been married ever once raise his voice.' Now it was the wife of another Hurricane pilot who was speaking to me, a week later and six thousand miles away, in such a different ambience from that Newmarket hotel and those Cambridgeshire airfields that have outlived their purpose, though it is strange what a compulsive pull they can still exert upon the emotions of even casual passers-by on the motorways.

I have a theory that to assess the staying power of any important figure in public life, you must first analyse, at close quarters if possible, what positive impact his marriage makes upon his feelings in private as well as upon his utterances in public. In consequence, I accepted at once the invitation to make a return journey to a country that I had first visited in the days when Northern and Southern Rhodesia were still part of the Federation and Sir Roy Welensky, that monolithic figure, its Prime Minister.

Today the role of Sir Roy is that of an *éminence grise.* On the surface, he seems content to grow his fruit trees, and patiently to assess the current situation for those who remember to visit him, while all the limelight that was once his is centred on the far more imposing house in Salisbury's Chancellor Avenue, occupied, through Prime Ministerial right, by the man with the still fair hair and cold, blue eyes, whose Hurricane crashed into flames in the desert and whose face had to be entirely rebuilt in a Cairo hospital.

When we met in his office for the first time, Mr Ian Smith made an instant and unequivocal pronouncement. Noticing how scorched my face was from the fierce sun shining down on Lake Kariba, where I had been enjoying a week's safari as the guest of Sir Albert Robinson, Rhodesia's High Commissioner in London in happier days, he warned me:

'You must carry a lip-salve in your pocket, as I do. I remember to apply mine every half hour. The sun can be murderous out here for fair skins.'

And black skins? The man whose own skin, because of layer upon layer of graftings, presents a curiously impassive air that is doubtless deceptive, would not be drawn on that subject. And so it was left to his wife to provide an illuminating example of what the power behind the throne can mean in contemporary terms.

Up till our meeting she had been a figure of some mystery to the world at large, beyond Rhodesian frontiers, in that she had refused all interviews in depth, preferring to remain an enigmatic figure in the background. However, I had had a strong presentiment that in her personality, as much as in her openly expressed attitude to existence in a sanction-besieged state, I would find at last the key to the curiously contradictory attitude of her husband, blowing now hot for Independence, now distinctly cooler. And from the moment that – instead of some pink-faced A.D.C. – Mrs Ian Smith herself appeared on the porch to greet me, as informally as though we had met a dozen times before, I had the impression that, for some reason, she had had a change of mind and had decided to use me as her mouthpiece. Her opening words, however, were hardly portentous.

'Come in, everything is a bit Monday-morning-ish,' she said briskly.

Actually I scarcely noticed my surroundings, the bowls of white arum lilies, the massed sweet peas that my hostess had arranged herself. I was completely absorbed, since my first – and lasting – impression was that this woman who majored in History and Geology at Cape Town University, where she also read Philosophy, is far more vital and vivacious in real life than any impression conveyed by her pictures.

I had been prepared for her decisive jawline, but when Janet Smith smiles – and she smiled often during our time together – she is an extremely attractive woman, with a skin untarnished by the heat, compelling eyes and very clean-looking hair.

Indeed, had I found myself seated opposite her in a train, I would have hazarded a guess that she was a woman doctor. She has the calm, contained look of someone accustomed to dealing with crises and herself possessed of the positive skills to do so. In fact, I discovered that she was the daughter of a doctor who had emigrated from Aberdeenshire to South Africa, and that her grandfather had been a doctor, too. While, of her own generation, her brother is a surgeon.

When I enquired how and where she and her husband had first met, she answered promptly, 'In the street'. At my reaction, she threw back her head and laughed. 'Oh don't worry. I was with my sister, who had known his family for years. It was soon after I had been widowed. My first husband was a doctor. I had come up from the Cape to the small Rhodesian town of Selukwe, where my sister lived, to . . .' she hesitated a moment, and then continued evenly, 'to re-fill my reservoirs of strength.'

'Was he already in politics?'

'No, he was farming, but it was in his mind. When later he asked me what I thought of the idea, I had to admit I wasn't in the least interested in party politics. However, as soon as he explained that he wasn't interested in party politics either, but that he *was* interested in sound government, I agreed at once, for I shared his view.

'Of course,' she added, 'neither of us had the faintest idea that politics would make any difference to our marriage.'

There was a pause while we both looked back across those twenty years in Central Africa, and its upheavals. However, there was no sign of flinching, of dismay, in her face at any of the memories. It made me curious to ask:

'Has all that was to follow, especially the challenges of recent events, changed you a great deal?'

'Do you mean, as a human being? I am sure it hasn't changed either of us. In any case, the family wouldn't allow my husband to change. That is what is so amazing about him. He will come home after a packed morning of meetings, and immediately throw himself into family affairs, joining in any discussion. Like the eternal argument over the length of our son's hair. I've managed to get two inches off it, but I wish it could be more. But sixteen is a very independent milestone in any child's life.

'As for myself,' she continued, 'it's very difficult to be one's own judge. Still, last week an old school-friend came up from the Cape, whom I hadn't seen for thirty-seven years, and almost as soon as she had settled in she confessed that she had taken two tranquillizers, because she had felt so nervous. That I would be different. That everything would be different.'

'But it wasn't?'

'No, she assured me I was exactly the same. So I made her promise to take no more tranquillizers. Neither my husband nor myself has ever taken a tranquillizer, or a pep pill, in our lives. His secret is that he can go to sleep for ten minutes, completely to sleep, wherever he is, at any time of the day or night.'

'What we used to call in the Navy a cat-nap,' I said, thinking not so much of Napoleon or Winston Churchill, who were both addicts of this form of refreshment, as of the skipper of the *Freebooter*. 'And what do you do yourself for therapy, for releasing the tensions?' I asked.

'Well, I used to love window shopping, like so many women do. Imagining all the things I would buy if I had the money. Alas, now that's impossible. Not because of sanctions, but because I would be recognized in a moment, and surrounded. So I weed. If you had called, unannounced, this morning, you might easily have found me in my gardening clothes. In the same way, it means a lot to my husband to be able to escape to the farm, even for a couple of days. Thank goodness, we know we shall always have that,' she added.

'Would you mind very much if you could never visit Britain again?'

'Of course I would mind if I could never visit Britain, especially Scotland where I have many relatives. But if it had to be, I should accept it. One must never waste time or emotion on what one can't have, or what is gone. Mind you, Mr Winn, I believe that you can achieve almost anything in the world if you really want it enough. And also if you stick to your principles through thick and thin. You must never, never yield over what you know in your heart to be right.'

It was all her Presbyterian ancestors speaking in unison, I decided. Nevertheless, the woman at my side, in the long, unimaginatively-furnished, echoing drawing-room, didn't sound in the least either smug or hectoring. Merely unshakeable.

What about her children? The two by her first marriage to the husband who had tragically lost his life on the rugger field, the two who adopted the name of their stepfather; the third who was having trouble, as so many other teenagers, in passing his examinations and who, perhaps, was feeling overawed and inhibited by his father's role as a man of destiny. Had they all the same philosophy of living as their mother?

One had the feeling that her influence must be as strong upon her children as upon her husband. It made me ask, 'What do you consider are the three most important tenets to teach the young?'

'A sense of humour is tremendously important.'

'But isn't that something that is inborn?' I queried.

'Yes, to some extent, but I still think it can be greatly increased inside a close-knit family like ours. Often my husband and I catch each other's eye at some function and can scarcely stop from bursting out laughing. There is always laughter when the family is together.

'Then, "Do unto others as you would be done by". That covers surely almost every situation in life, and as a creed of living it is so simple and yet so all-embracing. Thirdly, I consider that self-discipline is enormously important. Because only through a real measure of self-discipline can you achieve freedom.'

'Do you think the young all over the world have too much freedom today?'

She answered slowly and with careful consideration of my question. 'I think they should only be given as much as they can absorb at the time.'

'Has that been your own family system?'

'Well, my daughter is married now, and has the freedom and the responsibilities of a married status, while my elder son has been away from home, working for a time in Europe, where he told me sadly how he used to hear foreigners mocking such phrases as "safe as the Bank of England".'

Her tone did not alter as she delivered that thrust; all the same, it seemed politic to change the bowling, seeking safer ground, seeking the answer to what I had come all that way to discover; something that so many other people, watching the crisis in Rhodesia reaching its climax and beyond, must also have longed to know. Exactly how much and how constantly did the Prime Minister of the new régime consult her?

She herself put it this way.

'Yes, I do believe most emphatically in the value of a woman's

Recognise the face? Ralph Richardson transforms himself into a Fleet Air Arm pilot

The crew of a Sunderland Flying Boat setting out on a ten hour patrol

'Tail End Charlie'

Airmen in training

'Thanks, Ginger, but I shan't want this now'

Sergeant 'Ginger' Bailey and his wife go to Buckingham Palace to collect his D.F.M.

instinct. I consider it is both more perceptive and more highly developed than that of a man. Often, for instance, I have warned my husband not to trust a certain person, and he has asked me for positive reasons and I cannot give them. So I fall back upon some such absurd excuse as that I don't like the way he parts his hair! The last time, I remember I said that he wore suède shoes. To which my husband replied, "Good heavens, Janet, I have a pair of suède shoes myself".'

'All the same you were right in your hunch?'

'Yes, I was right in my hunch,' she said quietly.

The blown-up image of a certain public figure swam before my eyes. Was it the same one as was in her own mind at that moment, I wondered, as she continued with a sudden new, unguarded vehemence in her voice.

'I shall never forget the night my husband was packing to go to the first meeting, the one on the *Tiger*. It was four o'clock in the morning. He could not, of course, tell me where he was going. But for me what was far worse was that he could not take me with him. I guessed however, that it must be somewhere like Gibraltar or Malta, from the clothes that he was putting in his case.

'Of course, I didn't really imagine that they would kidnap him, but all the same, I had a horrible premonition that no good would come of the meeting. Men are like small boys playing at Red Injuns.'

It was a deflating judgment. My companion rose and I followed her into the hall. Here another galling memory regurgitated itself. 'When Mr Wilson came here, he brought so many people with him they filled the house. What did he imagine we were going to do to him? The odious little man.'

Here was the answer; the answer, too, to that slight when inadvisedly on Television our own Prime Minister had referred to his intransigent opponent as 'a poor frightened man'. It was hardly an accurate description, and certainly not a tactful one from an opponent who had spent his own war in the corridors of Whitehall. Those who are proved to be valorous in battle can afford to be magnanimous about such sneers; it is their women folk who rise up in anger, plotting vengeance, and my companion was suddenly transformed. Her self-control had vanished, passion possessed her. I had a sudden vision of Lady Macbeth as I had seen her on the stage at the Chichester Festival, handling the dagger.

At that moment the urbane Director of Information, who had brought me to my rendezvous in Chancellor Avenue, and was now hovering to take me away again, broke in soothingly.

'The last time Mr Wilson was here, his final words as he came through that door to Mr Smith were, "Well, Prime Minister, we may differ over some things and agree over others, but one thing we both agree unanimously about is that Colin Bland is the greatest fielder in the world".'

Only that morning the front page of the local papers had been filled with the account of how this celebrated cricketer had been stopped at London Airport, refused an entry permit to play in a match for which he was an obvious choice. To what ridiculously vindictive lengths could the disagreement be stretched? We were all three smiling again, if a trifle wryly, as we moved out into the brilliant sunshine.

Here my hostess, her serenity restored, lifted her head happily towards the burnished blue sky, as if somehow it was an omen for the future.

'Rhodesia has the finest climate in the world,' she pronounced, and as I took my leave, once again I was aware of how that flowing smile masked the obdurate line to her jaw.

Later, I found myself wishing that I could introduce Ian Smith's partner to a lady I was to meet in the new township of Kariba. For clearly they would have much in common. I had flown, with the Robinsons, down from the capital on the first stage of our safari, to discover on the walls of the airport lounge warning posters, reminiscent of our own wartime ones about careless talk costing lives. Outside, the temperature had risen by so many degrees that my first port of call was 'The Little Shop' which lies close to the circular glass-walled church, – this last building of beauty and splendour that was created specially for the army of Italian labourers who had worked on the Dam.

It was with some surprise that I found the interior of the small emporium reminiscent of a gift shop in an English cathedral town, and as I searched for my bearings among the bric-a-brac, the cool dim light refreshed and reassured me. Over the desk presided an elderly lady with her neat grey hair parted down the centre, wearing a modish two-piece suit.

Her name, I discovered, was Mrs Dixon, and she introduced her two enthusiastic handmaidens as Miss Ellis and Viola Browne. In the end they all gave me their autographs on the back of a coloured photograph of Mr Smith, which they clubbed together to buy for ninepence. There was a variety of poses on show.

After they had kitted me up, with little bird cries, against the blazing heat outside, Mrs Dixon exclaimed, 'And now I must show you my storeroom, Mr Winn'. At the back of the shop there was a large space packed tightly with dresses, hats, handbags, shoes. 'I keep my shop open specially on Sunday morning to help the people from across the border,' she confided. 'You see, they are allowed over from Zambia for two hours. Just time to strip off their shabby clothes here and to go away looking so different, and feeling so different, poor things.

'All my stock is made in Rhodesia,' she added proudly. 'Life is very difficult for the white people left in Zambia.'

Her pale cheeks filled with colour as she continued, 'Every Monday morning I collect my foreign currency and take it to the bank, and I have the satisfaction of knowing I am doing my bit for our economic war.'

'Did your family come originally from Britain?' I asked.

Mrs Dixon shook her head with some emphasis. 'I am a Rhodesian.'

When I had enquired a few minutes before whether she and her helpers were not nervous about the terrorists, since the river that provides today a visual frontier between the two opposing countries flows only a few hundred yards from her shop, I had received the same vigorous shake of the head, this time from them all.

However, when you stand beside the Dam – one of the engineering marvels of our era, its power-house interior like some fantasy from a James Bond thriller – and gaze down from the bridge that crosses the Zambesi at those close-covered, wooded banks on either side, you are instantly aware how easy it must be for the 'freedom fighters' to cross under cloak of darkness, as a climax to the journey which began with their training in Moscow, Cuba or Algeria.

'Of the last lot,' my guide was saying, 'what is interesting is not the ones who were killed but the ones who were captured. By the Africans. These guerrillas receive no support from our own Africans. Why? Because they do not want trouble in their villages. So, although they have the reputation of being most hospitable, they lock up the stranger and walk many miles, if necessary, to fetch the white police.'

Mrs Ian Smith herself had declared to me, 'We would not be succeeding so well without the support of the Africans.' And her husband when he received me on my return from Kariba echoed that, with more confidence in his voice than aggression. He simply intended it as a statement of fact. And certainly on the surface Rhodesia seemed in better shape than on my previous visit, despite the increasing pressure of sanctions. There were more cars on the main streets, and out in the country at weekends, and the shops in the capital were full of goods to buy, if inevitably some luxuries were lacking. The Europeans I encountered on the pavements had neither a shabby nor a defeated air; while again, the Africans themselves assured me how much quieter and more peaceful their townships were, now that the more violent of the agitators had been locked away for an indefinite period.

I took the trouble to visit several farmers. One, who had seen service in the Royal Navy during the Second World War and is, with his wife, completely opposed politically to the present régime, has the reputation of being a model employer. All the same, he had a disturbing story to tell.

A Television unit – not, I am glad to say, an English one – asked permission to take shots of his farm including his herd of Herefordshire cattle. No harm there. At the end of the shooting session, the visitors produced a case of champagne which they proffered as a gesture of gratitude. Naturally, a bottle or two were opened on the spot, and more celebratory shots were then taken in a relaxed atmosphere of mutual goodwill.

However, later, the 'champagne swiggers' were used in close juxtaposition with pictures of 'piccaninnies' with their noses deep in rubbish bins, searching, it was implied, for a crust of bread. In actual fact, sixpences had first been hidden, as a bait, among the garbage.

A far more accurate documentary could have been made of the afternoon I spent at Harare Hospital, in Salisbury, which is given over entirely to African patients and is far better equipped, I was assured, than the European one, for it has the very latest of X-ray equipment and a kidney machine that the other hospital does not possess. All the staff, apart from the Matron herself and a few of her senior sisters, are African, and there is no doubt that both goodwill and mutual trust prevail; indeed, to meet in each ward the nurses, neat and smiling and demure, filled one with a sense of optimism for the future, only dented when it was explained to me how when these ambassadors for their race go on leave, most of them journey into the wilds to join their families in a mud hut, discarding not only their clean uniforms but also their conscientious appreciation of their new status. In a moment they have slipped back a thousand years, often failing to return to duty on the right day or in the right frame of mind. So that the whole conditioning process has to start all over again.

This, of course, is the kind of discovery one only makes at first hand. Even so, however probing one seeks to be, however long one's apprenticeship, as an observer, it is still possible to be deceived or lulled into a false sense of security. As I was made to realize with a sharp awakening on my last night beside Lake Kariba.

It had been for me such an exciting experience, such a refreshment of the spirit to be shown not only the workings of the Dam itself, thanks to the privileged position in the country of my host, Sir Albert Robinson, but to watch through field-glasses with the restored delight of a child, the elephants coming down to the water in the evening to drink, and to spot the hippos disporting themselves as unconsciously as though our high-powered launch chugging across the lake didn't exist.

All sense of time, of place, of personal identity vanished. I was a member of any fishing party on the lake, laughing at our private jokes, elated when someone landed another tiger fish, dozing under the canopy after a splendid lunch. All the half-dozen members of our party were equally relaxed and at peace until returning to our base for the last time, the isolated hotel on Bumi Hills, that had once been the hideout of Mr Hubbard, the founder of Scientology, the proprietor greeted us with the news, received over the radio, that at that very moment the Russian tanks were rumbling into Prague.

Not again! We gazed at each other with sick dismay. It seemed incredible that the pattern should be repeating itself. That evening, after dinner, we sat on the wide terrace, and the splendour of the landscape with the lake spread out below us, now assumed a mocking air. It seemed too untouched, too secure. Down by the water's edge, the silhouettes of the untamed animals could be glimpsed, revelling in their freedom, their natural habitat, while above our heads the arch of velvet sky was extravagantly full of stars, all so much brighter, somehow, than they ever appeared to be at home.

Then unexpectedly, unannounced across the heavens, there moved into our orbit an even more brilliant constellation. A shooting star? No, a Russian Sputnik, Colonel Rogers, one of the members of our party, announced, adding laconically, 'We often get a glimpse of them.' But *this* night of all nights? Was it there above us, deliberately signalling a triumph? Was it a portent? All my ingrown fears of Russia's implacable political philosophy, all the signposts that I had tried to erase from my personal recollection, came flooding back. Despite the tropical heat, I found myself turning cold and making an excuse about our early start in the morning, for our return to the other shore, I slipped away to bed.

On the other shore, and in other clothes, I dined with Charles Rogers and his attractive wife, Doreen, on almost my last night in Salisbury. As on the occasion of the luxurious hospitality that I had received at the Robinsons' own home, Rumbaru Park, all the outdoor and indoor staff lined up in the drive with brimming smiles to greet our return from the wilds. Could such a welcome be faked? There was no sign of short-commons, no outward indication as we drank our dry Martinis that a lethal economic war was in progress. Both the Rogers and the Robinsons, typical members of the upper hierarchy, were openly opposed to any form of apartheid, unwavering in their desire for an honourable settlement with the home country; all the same, while I detected little sign of any pro-Smith upsurge, there was an uneasiness such as you experience sometimes in the twilight, a sense of increasing erosion everywhere I went. And was it to be wondered, I thought, as I listened at the dinner table to yet another example of the manner in which the just as well as the unjust are equally affected by the crazy anomalies in the present official attitude of the British Government towards the 'rebels'.

The daughter of two of my fellow guests had been married earlier that summer in England. Her mother had naturally been eager to give her daughter a traditional wedding with all the trimmings. However, when she arrived in London and visited her bank, she was obdurately warned that she could not draw on a penny of her capital, even to buy a wedding dress. Her funds were officially frozen; and yet she must pay English income tax on the interest from assets of no more use to her than if they had been finally confiscated. Ironically, both she and her husband still possessed British passports, and had both volunteered at once for the Services at the outbreak of the last war in Europe.

It was not difficult to appreciate what resentment this kind of treatment had caused. Yet on dropping me at Meikles Hotel, where I had found the food and service compared favourably with the Savoy, when my fellow guests at the dinner party discovered I was due to sign the book and pay my respects at Government House the next day, they uttered as their last words, 'Remember us to Milly Gibbs tomorrow. She and the Governor are wonderful people and have set a wonderful example.'

The previous occasion on which I had driven up that drive was already eight years ago, I recalled a few hours later with something of a shock. It had been evening, and the sprawling white house had been blazing with light. For the last Governor-General of the Federation had been giving a large dinner party. By a misdirection I had arrived late, and an anxious A.D.C., peering into the driveway, had pulled me across a flowerbed and through some french windows to push me into place, just before Lord and Lady Dalhousie came down the line to greet their guests, with the ladies sweeping the floor in their curtseys, like corn before the wind.

Now it was the even brighter light of morning, and how the wind had changed, I thought, remembering that I had been placed pointedly next to an African lady. Unfortunately, this propaganda had gone awry since she did not speak a word of English and so I could only speculate silently as to whether she had taken down the curtains to make the long evening dress –

yellow sunflowers on a scarlet background – that was, in those days, a Government House edict.

Now my African driver was equally uncommunicative, though, perhaps, for other reasons, as he came to a standstill in front of the wide steps. As uncertainly I stood there, deliberately ahead of my appointment this time, I could glimpse through the open doorway leading into the drawing-room a pleasant-faced, middle-aged lady, in an overall, dusting. Very conscious that the Governor and his wife were managing on a skeleton staff, as well as being shackled in a self-imposed imprisonment, I wondered for a moment whether this could be Lady Gibbs herself. Then the helper smiled and said, 'I'll fetch someone,' and soon the Governor's Comptroller arrived on the scene.

John Pestell had held a high position in the Rhodesian Police Force until, from a sense of altruistic loyalty that can only be admired, he opted to come to Government House to support the lonely symbol of the Throne, who with such steadfastness had accepted an incarceration almost as absolute as that imposed by an enclosed Order.

Sir Humphrey, I decided at once, was an impressive figure. The moment that I came into his study I had the feeling that I was in the presence of someone very much out of the ordinary world. It was nothing to do with the background of Government House. I should have had exactly the same impression in a dentist's waiting room. His hollow cheeks and piercing eyes gave him an ascetic air that, together with his resonant voice, suggested a Calvinist preacher. This impression was increased by the very black suit he was wearing, though it was such a hot day, that his wife had put on a summer cotton dress. I wondered, for a moment, if he was in mourning for the sudden passing of Princess Marina, but I was assured by those who knew him well that he had taken to dressing always in dark, sombre clothes.

Yet most of his active life, until overnight he found himself the innocent centre of a constitutional crisis, had been spent out of doors. As his wife reminded me, 'I married a farmer, and look where it has landed me.' However, a moment later, she was adding with quiet pride and without fear of contradiction, 'My husband is a saint'.

A saint who, on Friday evenings, made his only sortie out of the prison gates at that time to visit the Salisbury Club, so that he could enjoy a game of snooker. He would have liked, of course, to visit his farm near Bulawayo, but he had been warned by his supporters that should he venture so far afield, and sleep away from Government House, he might return to find the gates barred to him and the residence requisitioned for his own use by Mr Clifford Dupont, once a solicitor and now called by the grand title of Officer Administering the Government.

Mr Dupont, who summoned me to his presence during this the second of my visits to Rhodesia, equally likes his game of billiards at the Club. Tactfully, it had been arranged that the two men should never meet, which perhaps was just as well, since Mr Dupont was riding round the town in the vintage Rolls-Royce that once had stood in the garages at Government House.

I did not have to wait long to discover the reason for my summons. I was to leave the country with no false impression as to where Rhodesia's future lay. When I returned to England and gave as my opinion that the two most powerful influences in Rhodesia were Mrs Ian Smith and Mr Clifford Dupont, and that each was implacably opposed to a settlement with Britain, my views both in my newspaper office and elsewhere were received with considerable scepticism. In vain did I point out that were there to be a settlement, all Mr Dupont's powers would vanish in a second. In vain did I try to conjure up the absolute conviction in his light, legal voice when he assured me, so quietly that I could scarcely believe my ears, that the Republic had virtually already come into being when the Privy Council's rulings over the hangings of the Africans, condemned on capital charges, were summarily rejected. He also reminded me, in the same emotionless, yet strangely menacing tone, that Rhodesia under the Smith régime, unlike Britain and America, had had no balance of payments problem in their last budget.

All through our interview, I kept on glancing away across the room towards the coloured lithograph in its golden frame of Her Majesty Queen Elizabeth. Painted in formal clothes with the sitter's corsage flaming with jewels and orders, the picture still hung on the day of my visit on the further wall of Mr Dupont's office. Were other callers as conscious of this anomaly as I was myself?

For the Governor, in contrast, the revitalizing highlight of his day was when, with his family gathered round him – the Gibbs had relations staying with them from England at that moment – he gave the Loyal Toast at dinner, to synchronize with the hidden spotlight that focussed on the Royal portraits in the smaller dining-room which they were now using. And every day, too, there was a comforting stream of callers; both strangers – like a bishop from the United States shepherding a group round 'Darkest Africa', who had signed the book just above my own signature – and friends bringing news and gifts from the outside world.

The considerable expanse of gardens appeared surprisingly well kept, considering that not a penny was any longer provided for them by the Rhodesian Government; underneath the windows of the Governor's study we came upon daffodils in full bloom. 'The bulbs were a present from kind friends,' Lady Gibbs explained. 'I planted them there, so that he could see them.'

I thought of the drifts of gold in my own wild garden in Sussex, dismissing and finishing another winter I had always considered these harbingers of spring to be the most English of flowers, just as Wordsworth who immortalized them is the most English of poets, but now beside the flaming bougainvillaea and poinsettias they seemed even more so.

On the porch itself were tubs of a luxuriant bush I did not recognize. It had delicate flowers of pale violet, white, and dark violet, all mixed together and springing from the same roots. 'The Africans call it yesterday, today and tomorrow,' I was told.

Yesterday and today we knew. The worst about them and the best. But what of tomorrow? The question-mark hung between us, and as we shook hands the tall, handsome woman at my side, who had refused to surrender her work for such good causes as the Red Cross and who had assured me, with some emphasis, that the beleaguered days so far from dragging were much too short for all she wanted to do, made her own comment which was partly a postscript, partly a prophecy.

'I always say that you have to live with your conscience a long time on earth, and probably for quite a time afterwards.'

Today, the Gibbs, their incarceration over at last, are thankfully back on their farm outside Bulawayo, private citizens again, supported not only by their consciences but by the respect of all Rhodesians, black and white. While Mr Dupont has acquired the Governor's Residence, as well as his Rolls-Royce. And I turn over the page, having added another small footnote to the history of these times.

It may have been my imagination, but it seemed to me that the face of the airport official at Heathrow, examining my passport on my return, tightened suspiciously and that he gave me a more searching second scrutiny as he came to the latest endorsement. 'I have been to Salisbury on a writing assignment for my newspaper,' I announced shortly, only too aware what it must have been like to be Colin Bland, and all the others, too, turned away at the gates. What I did not volunteer was that on my arrival at Salisbury the immigration officer had explained, most courteously, that I need not have the name that is at present anathema to my own Government entered into my passport unless I wished. 'If you do,' he warned me, 'you cannot return to Britain via Kenya.'

'I do wish,' I replied firmly. After all, wasn't the endorsement, with its date, a kind of receipt in advance for further knowledge and experience gained at first hand, another experience for me to recall when the last of my global journeyings were over and I would have the leisure to dream and gaze back beside the fire. My conscience, too, was involved. Certainly I would have felt uncomfortably like a cheat, if not a coward, had I sidestepped that official stamp.

Besides, I had already visited Kenya, in other times. Indeed, I had spent several weeks there, ostensibly to report on the aftermath of Mau Mau, though I had finished up by spending the most extraordinary night of my life, not exactly in the arms of a lioness but with a magnificent specimen of the tribe sleeping as tamely as a hearthrug cat on top of a Land-Rover, twenty yards from my tent. At that time, the lion of Kenya, Jomo Kenyatta, was still under close arrest and hidden away somewhere near the Abyssinian border. Instead, into my dispatches concerning my interview both with the white settlers, wondering what Independence Day just over the horizon was to bring, and with the more reputable African leaders, such as James Gichuru, I was able to interpolate a long description of my meeting with Elsa. This brought me a telegram from Lord Beaverbrook, which

I stuck in my scrapbook next to the record of my printed pieces. *'Godfrey, you are a great journalist.'*

Alas, I am afraid the generosity of my boss's praise was undeserved. For not only had it never occurred to me to visualize myself in the role of a lion-tamer, but I had only fallen by chance upon the story. A week-end tennis playing friend of long standing, Billy Collins, happened to tell me just before I was due to leave England that he was about to publish a remarkable book, called *Born Free*, by an equally remarkable woman, Joy Adamson, concerning a lioness that had been her close companion since the day that she had come upon it, a motherless cub.

'Mrs Adamson doesn't like anyone to come near to her encampment, which is beside a small river in the wilds,' the distinguished head of the publishing firm that bears his name explained to me. 'I know that she has said "no" to all kinds of people who were longing to make the trip in the hope of even catching a glimpse of Elsa. But I will send a cable to her husband, George, who is equally remarkable himself and knows everything there is to know about the wild life of the bush. He has been a Senior Game Warden for many years. I will suggest that he fixes a visit for you and himself accompanies you. That should do the trick.'

It did, though at first I seemed to be up against a blank wall. Those in official circles at Nairobi who were aware of Elsa's existence were highly sceptical as to whether I would even be permitted within photographing distance. They were convinced I was wasting my time. While the majority of those to whom I mentioned my proposed project reacted as though I had expressed a desire to meet some African chieftainess, who had gone underground and was given to mysterious hoodoo ceremonies. I was not sure at the time whether it was the lioness's name or that of her Garboesque protectress which most strongly aroused such reactions. Inevitably the more resistance I received, the more fascinated I became by the possibilities of this unusual extra working assignment. And I was not to be disappointed.

In the end, Mrs Adamson's husband got in touch directly with me on the telephone at my hotel in Nairobi. 'Can you rustle up a private plane?' he enquired. I could. 'Then tell your pilot to fly you to the airstrip at Garba Tula. It is the nearest point to the camp. I will take you in my Land-Rover from there.'

Garba Tula. It was double-dutch to me. And as my Polish pilot flew me in the chartered plane that seemed so minute and so vulnerable to the winds of chance, over the dense carpet of forest that stretched endlessly beneath us, I tried not to envisage what would happen were we to crash or run out of fuel. Anyway, this was infinitely better than having three Messerschmitts 110s on our tail, I reminded myself, and immediately the jungle-hopping exercise lost any possible menace. Moreover, the moment that we eventually landed on that handkerchief-sized airfield and my guide for the next forty-eight hours came towards me across the clearing in the scrub, I had an instantaneous, overflowing sensation that I was in good and safe hands. A feeling that was never to leave me. There was not any time wasted in polite, preliminary conversation by the wiry-looking man in safari clothes with the goatee beard flecked with grey, and the startlingly blue eyes that explorers or those who spend their lives in remote parts of the world so often seem to possess. Five minutes after landing, our bags transferred to his Land-Rover, we were on our way.

'How long will it take to reach the camp?' I inevitably asked.

'About four or five hours, though it depends on the state of the track after the rains, or what we may meet on the way,' my companion replied cryptically.

I did not consider that it was the right moment to ask for any further elucidation. I was too excited and thankful to be there at all, and my companion's quiet, and yet authoritative, manner gave me both a sense of confidence and respect. It is always a rewarding pleasure to be in the company of someone who is an expert in his field; and this was no exception.

After a few miles the track became very rough, the scrub on each side pressing in on us much more thickly, and now the wild life of every kind began to be abundant. The herds of giraffes and zebras, whose backs looked as though they had been freshly painted with stripes that morning, took little notice of us, but two ostriches, whom we surprised on the track itself, fled ahead of us with indignant fluttering, like outraged spinsters.

'What wild animals are really dangerous? Or should I say the most dangerous?' I asked my companion, who had spent his whole life studying the forest inhabitants of this part of Africa.

'Wild animals are never dangerous,' was the unexpected

answer I received. Though the Game Warden did add this proviso: 'Unless they are hungry or frightened'.

And there was an exception, too, I was to discover, to that proviso.

'The one really intractable inhabitant in these parts is the rhino. All the other animals, when something unexpected or unusual, like our Land-Rover, appears in sight, give way, obeying their own highway code. Even the elephants allow one peacefully to pass on one's way. Only the rhinos refuse to budge, and automatically turn to bay, insisting on a head-on collision.'

'And what happens then?'

'Oh, they charge the Land-Rover and I have to shoot at point-blank range.' He spoke with the matter-of-fact calm of someone discussing whether it was quicker to go by bus or tube. At that moment our vehicle was navigating the shallow bed of a stream, heaving itself up on the other side with a protesting shake. My own body was being shaken to bits, too; it was a rough ride; but I had no fear. My companion was so clearly and completely in command of the situation.

We relapsed into a friendly silence and did not speak again until we arrived opposite a large rocky eminence, tawny-coloured like a lion's coat, smooth and flat on top. The driver brought his chariot to a standstill. We got out. The relief from the vibration was overwhelming and equally so was the sense of isolation of which I was suddenly conscious.

'That is where Elsa had her cubs three months ago,' he explained, pointing towards the summit of the giant rock. 'Joy and I watched from where we are now.'

'You did not dare go any closer?'

'There was no question of that. We knew that Elsa would wish for a certain degree of privacy at that moment. After that she disappeared with her cubs into the scrub.'

I was to understand the full implication of his words, and to hear the rest of the story, later. Already I had read the precise notice of warning, signed 'Senior Game Warden'.

'The lioness Elsa with her cubs has her lair near the crossing of the Uru River on the Kinna-Tharame track. In order to avoid possible incidents you are requested not to camp or hunt within three miles of the river crossing.'

Just as we were getting back into our seats, a native runner arrived with a letter, from our destination now not far ahead. A frown crossed the face of Joy Adamson's husband as he read the contents. There was a certain dryness in his voice as he explained that his wife was worried because Elsa had not visited the camp for several nights running, and she herself was afraid that the presence of strangers on the scene would keep her beloved one away once again.

I was filled with dismay at the thought of having come so far, and to be turned back. But it was not for me to make a decision; so I remained silent, not liking even to ask how any wild animal could scent one out from such a distance. A moment later, what a relief it was to receive absolution.

'Don't worry. Your presence will make no difference one way or the other. If Elsa is hungry she will visit us this evening. If she isn't, that is to say if she has managed to kill on her own, she will stay away. It is as simple as that. I must explain that Joy always slaughters a fresh goat and tethers its body to a rock in a gulley, near the river bank.'

When we arrived, I took care to stay in the background while Mr Adamson went forward to the clearing in front of the cluster of tents to greet his wife, who was clearly in a very agitated condition. As she talked excitedly, with much gesticulation, I studied her appearance, which was utterly remote from the picture I had created in my mind of a woman living a solitary life in the wilds. Dressed in well-cut khaki shorts, freshly pressed and laundered, with a matching tunic cut very low in a V-shape, she had her shapely back turned towards me. At first sight, she looked much more like an elegant member of the smart set of some Mediterranean holiday resort than the fearless lover of wild animals with an amazing power of control over them that she had already proved herself to possess. Indeed, I was about to be given an extraordinary demonstration, that I would never have believed to have really taken place had I not seen it happen at close quarters with my own eyes.

My fate for the night still seemed to be in the balance, though the other khaki-clad figure was maintaining his customary *sang-froid*, when I was rescued by a whinnying sound from somewhere near the river, that was hidden by a bank of trees. To me it sounded like something softer than a lion's roar, but instantly Mrs Adamson's monologue was arrested in full spate. With an echoing cry of welcome, she started to run down the hill through the knee-length grass, while we followed more slowly. The crisis was over. Elsa was hungry and had announced her arrival and pleasure at finding the feast hopefully and lovingly prepared each evening.

'You're in luck,' George Adamson remarked in his gentle voice.

A few minutes later, I wasn't so sure. At the other end of the gully we came upon Elsa silhouetted in the suffused evening light, with her three cubs crouching on the rock above her, while she tore open the entrails of the goat, taking what she wanted for herself. Later it would be the turn of the cubs to gnaw at the carcass.

Having till that time only had the chance to watch cats of the forest in a circus ring, blinking lethargically at the brilliant glare of the accusing lamps, their fur often having a mangy look, Elsa, unseparated from us by the protective bars of the Big Top, seemed doubly huge, doubly magnificent, in her natural surroundings. I was spellbound, as one is in a dream, playing an unexpected part, hypnotized, unable to escape.

'She likes her vitamins very much.' Was it the lioness's devoted human friends speaking? The caressing voice bore no resemblance to the one I had previously heard protesting at the disobedience to her commands. Now instead it was full of happiness and delight. In my own turn, I was too enthralled to answer, though extremely grateful that I had now been accepted within the privileged circle. It was only when Elsa, having gorged herself, raised her head and after giving me a long – or was it a longing – scrutiny, started to move slowly across the twenty yards between us that instinctively I turned for emergency instructions, only to find that Elsa's interpreter had vanished, as had both my escort from Garba Tula, and my pilot. I was utterly alone. With a stranger.

It was true that I had come a very long way to meet that stranger, but now I was acutely aware that I was wearing the wrong-coloured shirt for this kind of introduction. A bright pink one. Why hadn't someone reminded me that dun-coloured clothes are correct wear for the bush? After all, there was that expression 'like a red rag to a bull'. Surely bright colours must be even worse in the case of a lioness protecting her three month-old cubs. Well, I was about to find out. From somewhere deep in my consciousness, there swam to the surface a piece of advice I had once read about one's best chance when unexpectedly confronted by a man-eating wild animal was to stand one's ground. Turn your back and you'd had it. But I could not turn my back. I was staked to the earth by a combination of astonishment and a sense of total unreality.

The lioness whose story*, so vividly told from birth till death, was subsequently to capture the imagination of the whole world, could not have been more than a leap away from me when abruptly she stopped. What had given me my split-second respite? Before the question could flash through my mind, the correctly-coloured figure of Mrs Adamson came past me, like a handmaiden carrying not a golden vessel but the large aluminium tin that I was to shave from the next morning. Now it contained cool drinking water for Elsa, and as she drank thirstily, and as I watched her, my heart thumping uncomfortably against the side of my chest, it was explained that this was part of the ritual; first the meal, and then the libation, and finally the embrace of mutual love and satisfaction. For now Mrs Adamson knelt down on her knees and put her arms round the other's head, and from their entwined bodies emerged crooning sounds. If only I had a camera, I thought, to capture this moment for ever. Indeed, when I am sometimes asked what is the most fantastic sight that has ever come my way, I always describe that tableau and what was to follow in the course of the evening.

Eventually Elsa retraced her steps to discover if the cubs had left anything on the carcass of the goat, while we went up the hill again for our own supper. After having cleaned myself up as best I could, and dumped my bag in the tent allotted me – where I was warned by my host that I must remember later not only to close the flaps but first erect a barrier of branches, as a special kind of burglar alarum against midnight marauders – I rejoined the others outside the tent that the Adamsons used as their dining-room.

The African night had crept up from the river with a suddenness that never ceases to surprise me. A dark blue velvet curtain

* *Born Free* by Joy Adamson.
Living Free by Joy Adamson.

now stretched between us and the gully. But was it really there at all? I began to wonder as we sat down to our meal on a table made from a packing case, and lit by a hurricane lamp. The Land-Rover in which we had made our Walt Disney journey was drawn up a few feet in front of us. Naturally, at first all the conversation was about Elsa, with my hostess volunteering her own explanation about the goat; how with her cubs to look after, Elsa had little opportunity to hunt on her own, and might easily starve were it not for the provision of these home comforts. At the same time, Elsa's self-appointed protectress warned me not to be alarmed if during the night I heard Elsa's mate calling to her.

'Have you met the father of the cubs?' I asked this extremely youthful-looking woman, who had come from Austria to Kenya, where she had met her husband.

'No, but he often comes near to the camp at night, when Elsa is here. One night in fact, George went out of our tent and found him only a few steps away, while Elsa lay asleep on top of the Land-Rover, her favourite perch.'

At that moment, as though in answer to a cue, there was a swishing and a swirling in the darkness of the scrub, and then Elsa was literally on top of us. There was no time to stand up, to shout out, even to be afraid. Just when it seemed inevitable that she would knock over the supper table and send everything flying, with all of us under foot, she swerved sideways, like a rugger player avoiding a tackle, and leapt on to the top of the Land-Rover. Whereupon, almost as a continuation of the same movement, she settled down with her head between her front paws, in the immemorial pose of a domesticated cat on its favourite hearthrug. For the rest of the evening, she stayed there, unstirring.

Neither George nor Joy Adamson took any apparent notice of this interruption, except to change the subject of the conversation, as though Elsa might be made self-conscious if we continued to discuss her within her hearing. Instead Mrs Adamson spoke now of her other love, which was painting, and of the series of pictures of Kenya's tribal chieftains in their distinguishing robes, that she had contributed to a Nairobi gallery. I was to see reproductions of them in due course, and to be deeply impressed by her professional skill. Equally I was fascinated when she began to speak of Paris; but, instead of its painters, her subject was the night life of Maxim's, where she liked to dine, dressed up for that kind of occasion in such a different style, but with the same instinctive chic as that in which she was attired for this. As she spoke, with a vivacity that was communicative, I conjured up a portrait of her in a very plain white satin dress, to suit her fair hair, with emeralds at her throat. The fantasy did not seem in the least incongruous. For transformed by her mood of enchantment at Elsa's arrival, so that all was forgotten and forgiven, had she not succeeded in turning our alfresco supper into a celebration party, such as one might enjoy, after a first night, at the Savoy Grill?

After a time she got up and walked towards the Land-Rover, bidding me to follow her. 'Elsa has got used to your presence and your smell by now, Mr Winn. You may touch her,' she added imperiously. I put up one hand with a certain trepidation towards the great shoulders stretched above me. From that angle, one's head upturned, Elsa seemed even more gargantuan, and in the light of the tent lamp her coat, that I was to find luxuriously soft to stroke, possessed an incandescent sheen. What a contrast was the glossiness of her fur to that of all the captive lions I had ever seen and suffered for, as a spectator of their listless, unnatural antics. I had always imagined that at close quarters there would be a strong odour, but I sniffed nothing but the scent that Mrs Adamson herself was wearing.

The moment that I touched this superb creature and she remained quiescent, all fear left me. So, becoming more daring, I was soon stroking her paw, and from that it was a short step to nuzzle her under the chin, as I would have done in the case of the only cats I know at all intimately, the Siamese ones that belonged to Vivien Leigh. Elsa neither purred nor repelled my advances, until the adoring human being at my side leant up towards the foundling she had nurtured and guarded to maturity. Then something very startling happened. Elsa began to quiver as though a strong current of electricity had passed through her body, while these two unitedly feminine creatures caressed each other's mouths in an intense communion.

Leaving my hostess still drooling over her loved one, I eventually went to my tent. Here I fell instantly into a deep slumber, exhausted by all the tensions and dramas of the last twenty-four hours, from which I was awakened in the dawn by the cries of a thousand weaver birds, like crickets, overhead. Only half-conscious as to my whereabouts, I put my head outside the flap of my tent and there, her coat gleaming more brightly than ever in the washed, early-morning light, was Elsa contemplating me from the top of her nocturnal perch.

She gave me a long scrutiny, as though she was thinking, 'Now I am going back to my life, and you to yours'. Then she loped down off the roof, leaving what was now a permanent dent behind her, and collecting her cubs from the edge of the scrub, slipped silently away.

We breakfasted ourselves on the river bank, at the spot where only a month before Elsa had suddenly appeared on the other bank, swimming across three times and carrying in her mouth each time one of her cubs by the scruff of its neck.

'I had waited two months for that moment,' Joy Adamson confessed. 'Elsa came and placed the cubs one by one at my feet. At first she seemed puzzled and then hurt that I would not touch them or play with them. They were irresistible but I had to resist them.'

'But why?' I asked, though unsurprised by this time at any apparent contradiction or paradox.

'Because,' she continued with great emphasis, 'they must grow up wild and free. I am determined about that. Elsa came into my life, as you know, when she was only four days old, after her mother had been shot. George and I cared for her till she was fully grown, and then, at the age of three, from this very camp we set her free again. Or rather, *forced* her to be free again, because we both felt that that was where her chances of ultimate happiness lay, in fending for herself and finding a mate. I doubt whether when her cubs, too, are big and strong enough to fend for themselves, she will come back to me any more.'

There was a kind of mingled sadness and pride in her voice, which made me exclaim, 'But I still don't know how you can resist the cubs. I am sure I wouldn't be able to, if I had your amazing gift for winning the affection of wild animals.'

'But I must, I must,' she repeated vehemently. 'It is the same really with Elsa. It is so tremendously important that she should not be turned into a kind of peep-show. That was why I was so nervous that your arrival might upset her.'

I glanced at my host. This was where we had come in. It was time to express my thanks for a fantastic interlude, and to leave. Just before I climbed back into the Land-Rover, I examined the deep indentation on the roof. Only twenty-four hours before, when my driver had made a reference to it, at the same time explaining the reason, I had looked at him warily as though I were listening to a traveller's tale. Now I knew that it was true, all of it was true, and impossible to exaggerate however tempted I was when I held the table at the farewell dinner given for me by the owners of the New Stanley Hotel, in Nairobi.

At the end of my saga, a White hunter who had spent his life in conducting parties of European and American tourists through the bush, leant across the table and in the sudden pool of silence threw a stone that created eddies that are still in my mind.

'You say that George Adamson called you lucky, because Elsa came into the camp the night you were there, whereas you might so easily have drawn a blank. You *were* lucky, but not in the manner that he meant. Do you realize that when you were leaning up towards her, on the roof of the Land-Rover, one playful push of her paw, not necessarily with all her strength, and you would have been dead.'

Before I could say anything, or even smile incredulously, he gave his final verdict, with the confidence of a lifetime spent assessing this particular brand of odds. 'Make no mistake. That is what will happen to Elsa's playmate one day.'

It didn't, because Elsa was destined to die soon afterwards, not from a bullet through the heart, like her mother, but from natural causes. Found desperately ill in the wilds, she was brought back to the camp and nursed with expert care and tenderness by George Adamson, whom I suspect has more knowledge of animals in his little finger than his wife, despite her unique gift for communication and engendering affection. However, it was too late. They were unable to save Elsa.

It must have been about the same time that I read, almost with a sense of personal loss, of Elsa's death that I came across another paragraph of news from Kenya. A woman, who kept a lioness as a pet in a field behind her house a few miles from Nairobi, had driven into the city to replenish supplies, and on her return her first thought was to rush into the paddock to give her own

Elsa some titbits that she particularly fancied. In its gratitude, not appreciating its own strength, the animal had slapped its mistress with such joyful abandon that she had been fatally injured.

It was not surprising then that I should have recalled the words of the White hunter, and have viewed my own interlude with Elsa from a fresh angle.

Was it possible in life that fear and anxiety, just as much as caution, largely came from pre-knowledge of all the possibilities, all the odds? If that theory were accurate, it would account for my own reaction to some of the adventures, especially in the last war, which have come my way, during which I appeared to the onlookers to be much less apprehensive than might have been expected in the circumstances. In consequence, I acquired in some quarters a reputation that was wholly unmerited. It was simply that there was so seldom sufficient time for me to be briefed, or to appreciate, in cold terms, what I was letting myself in for, through my unquenchable desire to describe everything at first hand.

For instance, there was my day-trip to Norway.

That must have been in the late autumn of 1940. I had been chafing ever since my return from the Maginot Line to be allowed to fly on genuine operational trips with the Royal Air Force, in the same way and on a similarly authentic level as the Admiralty were encouraging me to spend some time, now in a minesweeper, now in a merchantman, on an east coast convoy, now either in one of the destroyers guarding them, or again, in an escort patrolling this time the channel ports.

On these occasions I had a feeling, extremely satisfying, of being right in the centre of things, though, of course, I only did one voyage in each ship and then had to say goodbye to the new friends I had made, like the rating who stood apart from the rest of the crew, since he had already received a savage baptism, having been sunk in H.M.S. *Courageous*. With four other fellows he had been in the dark room, developing a film, when the torpedo struck the ship. They had placed the key on a ledge, having locked the door so that no one should interrupt them and let in the daylight. Not surprisingly the explosion dislodged the key, all lights had fused, and it took them five frantic minutes in the darkness to find it in its new resting place, where it had slid into a corner against the wall. Four of those five were rescued, and came safely to shore, but I have often wondered since how many of them finally survived till VJ Day and beyond.

Whenever I was told of such an escape, always in a matter-of-fact voice, I would try to visualize what it must be like to be enveloped in this helpless sensation of going down into the great dark abyss of the sucking whirlpool. I also happened at that time to meet the Commander of the *Courageous*, who was standing on the bridge beside the Captain as the aircraft carrier sank. I had hoped that Commander Abel Smith, as he then was, would be able to fill out the graphic description of his fellow member of the crew, but all that he had to add was, 'My one thought was to keep my mouth shut'. I noted his advice for use on a future possible occasion. Whereupon, as though he could sense what was in my own mind, he summed up, 'I find it best not to think about anything except the job in hand'.

Surely as sensible a philosophy for the exigencies of peace as those of war, and his words have often come back to me when I have found myself about to engage in that most unprofitable of pastimes, jobbing back or indulging in fruitless post-mortems. If the war taught me nothing else, it forced me to take each day and each new challenge as it came, and to be surprised by nothing. The Captain of the Hunt Class destroyer, whose guest I was for one convoy, had concocted a novel mixture for keeping warm taking the watch and staying on all night on the bridge. Having played cricket for the Navy, in less disruptive times, it comforted his spirit, and at the same time his circulation, to wear a pair of old white flannel bags, and over them black corduroys, with a monk's hood over his head. As we peered together into the wall of fog and mist, he asked me suddenly if I knew Housman, who had written so hauntingly of his native Shropshire pastures. As it happened, *A Shropshire Lad* had been one of my bedside books ever since I left school, and I was able to quote:

'In summertime on Bredon
The bells they sound so clear;
Round both the shires they ring them

In steeples far and near,
A happy noise to hear.
'Here of a Sunday morning
My love and I would lie,
And see the coloured counties,
And hear the larks so high
About us in the sky.'

Somehow, it brought the future near; or rather, made another kind of future appear less remote. My host that night, Deric Holland-Martin, was to progress so far in his career that he was to end up as Second Sea Lord, and whenever in later years I would stay with other members of his family in the shires, and we would ourselves meet again in such altered circumstances, it caused me to give thanks that we both should have survived so much, and still have the energy and the desire to climb Bredon on the kind of June day that surely only happens in England. The kind of day that it was my good fortune to enjoy on another of my destroyer trips. The Germans were shelling us intermittently from the captured French ports, but it did not seem to matter. In contrast to the inimical storms in the Atlantic and the North Sea, the English Channel was like a mill pond, exactly the right weather for a test match at Lord's, or for one of those seaside tennis tournaments, at Minehead, say, or Burnham-on-Sea, which had provided me with the most satisfying kind of holiday of all once upon a time.

Having been given the freedom of the ship, with the proviso that I must count fifty and then duck whenever there was an angry flash from the other shore, I wandered happily about the decks. My ignorant state of unreal euphoria was only increased when one of the runners on the bridge, a tall, dark young man, with very much a public school manner, announced that he had an idea I knew his mother. I most certainly did, for this turned out to be Sir Robert Peel, the only son of Beatrice Lillie.

Later, Bobby was to be reported 'missing' out east, after the fall of Singapore. When some months had passed, his mother, consumed by the anxiety and grief that she tried to hide under her unceasing flow of wisecracks (such as her now classic dialogue on the telephone, 'Qui parle? C'est Lady Parle qui peel.') rang me up to ask me to supper that I might endeavour to recall for her every tiny, precious detail of that brief encounter on board her son's ship.

I could only repeat over and over again, 'He was in wonderful spirits. There's a Naval expression, "getting brown for leave". It was that kind of weather. Like a peace-time voyage. And when we came into Portsmouth they played the record of "D'ye Ken John Peel?" over the loudspeaker. It was an affectionate joke, in his honour.'

His mother listened, first eagerly, then politely, for I spoke of another world from which, like so many other parents and loved ones, she had been excluded at the last. I have never felt more inadequate, more aghast at the agony of loss. Her frozen dignity, infinitely more moving than an abandonment to tears, never deserted her, but this was *Pagliacci* transported into another setting. This was the other side of the footlights that the public never see when the curtain comes down. True, the curtain goes up on another production; but in this case from the life of this star comedienne something is always missing, for which no amount of loyal applause can ever provide compensation or comfort.

When eventually I returned myself to Civvy Street, rather battered and momentarily out of step I joined a bridge club, as a kind of therapy. Among the motley assortment of players, whose faces if not their names gradually became familiar to me, there was a woman who seemed to play every afternoon, though she was a very uncertain partner. She reminded me in appearance of a character from a Wilde comedy staged in modern clothes. Always impeccably turned out, she had rather a grand though pleasant enough manner that was something of a contrast to the volcanic outbursts which often occurred when a contract that could have been made was lost. Half the time this particular player appeared to be in a kind of trance, and after one session, after a surprisingly silly mistake, I found myself joining in the complaining chorus. Later, when I was having a drink at the bar, another player from our table during that particular rubber joined me and made some comment about the play.

By this time I had simmered down. I was more puzzled than angry. 'What I cannot understand,' I said, 'is why her game never improves. After all, she gets enough practice. But why does she play so often if she is as indifferent to the results as she appears to be?'

'I'll tell you exactly why,' my companion explained, modulating her voice so that it would merge with all the chatter going on round us about the coups that had been brought off, and the chances thrown away. 'She came here first a few days after the fall of Singapore. She had received a telegram from the War Office that her son was missing. While she was waiting for further news, still allowing herself to hope against hope that he would turn up, after all, as a prisoner of war, she had to have somewhere where she could hide from the sympathy and enquiries of her friends. She was a widow, and her boy had been her whole life. A bridge club seemed the perfect refuge. No one knew her. No one came here from her world. Everyone was too preoccupied with their fortunes at the table to be interested in the reason for her rather strange manner. She just played her cards mechanically and it was a drug, which little by little became a habit that she could not give up. Today it fills in the time, till she is reunited with her son. She is quite certain that will happen. For she is deeply religious, a very good Christian, if a very bad bridge player.'

At the dispersal points of the fighter stations I had visited, such as Hornchurch and Biggin Hill, the pilots, while waiting in readiness to take off again, would play a card game called 'Nines'. You could lose, at the maximum, threepence a hand, and the only firm rule that no one argued about was that if they were interrupted in the middle of a game they'd finish it when they got back. Or scrub it, if . . .

How I had itched to join in, but my instinct warned me that I had no right to do so. I was always scrupulously careful not to overstep my status. In any case, a fighter machine was built for a single occupant. How then could I be expected to be given a ride. Of course, bombers were larger, but even so there was usually only room for the crew. A ship was altogether a different set-up, the Air Ministry explained to me patiently, fobbing off my requests for more active participation so that I could describe the battles of the skies, from eye level, with tame visits to something like H.M.S. *Raven*, the Fleet Air Arm base, where, marking time, Larry Olivier and Ralph Richardson were rusticating their talents while toeing the conventional patriotic line.

In the pilots' changing room, where they strapped me into borrowed harness, there hung from the ceiling, I remember, the twisted bracket of an old-fashioned lamp-post. Someone had suitably christened it Richardson's Folly, and they all called the new boy, whose machine had recently come to a full-stop against it, Rich. It had seemed rather a good idea as material for my Sunday newspaper to be taken for a flip over the playing fields of Winchester by a pilot so renowned in another sphere, but now I wasn't so sure.

However, our hedge-hopping tour went off without incident. All the same, the curiosity value of being shown the cathedral and the school, the frozen river and the snow-painted fields from a new angle, did not lessen my growing feeling of frustration, of being, somehow – unreasonable though it was to think this – cheated. I had a curious premonition that there was a big war-in-the-air story waiting for me over the horizon, if only I could get at it. Pressing on, I persuaded the powers-that-be to allow me to do one of the regular patrols over the Atlantic in a Sunderland flying boat, which was certainly more than large enough to accommodate a passenger, since its length was twice that of a cricket pitch. Alas it turned out in the end to be a monotonous nurse-minding operation of thirteen hours, with the convoy we were helping to guard spread out below us, like baby toy models fashioned upon a sea of plasticine. I tried to assuage my boredom by humming over and over again the chorus of the *Whiffin Poof Song*, which was the theme song of the squadron, dating back to a record-winning pre-war flight to Australia. They had sung it the night before at the party they had given for me after a concert, when the officers and their wives, and the sergeants and their wives, had all linked arms together, in that classless unity which ironically only seems to happen in an emergency on a giant scale. Ironically too, although the places named had no meaning for me then or now, the refrain has stayed in my consciousness.

'To the tables down at Mornays,
To the place where Louis dwells,
To the dear old Temple Bar we love so well,
Sing the Whiffin Poof Assemble,
With their glasses raised on high.
And the magic of their singing casts its spell.'

Does it still for someone, somewhere? Are those of us foolish who want to remember similar jingles? Again, is it sentiment or superstition that makes me still carry in my wallet, every time I make a journey, a pair of Air Force wings, faded from the sun and the wind of so many operation trips, with the words *Happy Landings, Ginger Bailey*, scrawled on the back.

'It looks as though you'd better have something to keep you safe for the rest of this lot,' he had announced in his gravel voice, renowned for its under-statement, during the celebration that night in the sergeants' mess at Leuchars, when it was all over and we were safely back, though too late for 'Ginger' to bicycle home to his wife. So as he had missed his tea, they very decently decided to open a barrel of beer instead, and what followed turned out to be rather a more hectic affair than the gathering in the Sunderland mess. But this time I really felt I had deserved this party. I had been myself properly blooded at last.

Leuchars was a Hudson bomber station not far from Edinburgh. Its C.O. was Group Captain 'Poppy' Pope, with whom I had made friends in the early days of the war out at Rheims. I don't suppose I should ever have received my invitation if he had not intervened personally with the Air Ministry. I considered myself the luckiest reporter in the Street when my passes and permits came through and I caught the train north. 'But your real luck,' my host explained to me afterwards, 'was that I gave you the best sergeant-pilot I had on the station. I doubt if you would have got back with anyone else, in the circumstances.'

'Ginger' Bailey, who had acquired his nickname because of his flaming, scarlet hair, was the boxing champion of the station, and he had wrists of iron. He needed them that day over Stavanger. We met for the first time on the tarmac, in the dawn. I had arrived the evening before, and had had to take quite a bit of ribbing from the brash members of an Australian squadron also quartered at Leuchars. I must have seemed an odd sort of figure to them, not dressed in any uniform. They ganged up to try and make my blood run cold by suggesting all kinds of terrible possibilities ahead of me. The real joke was that they themselves regarded the recce trips over the Norwegian coast, especially when they were in a formation of three, as a 'piece of cake', and no one was more surprised than they were when all their prophecies to the unplaceable Pommy briefly in their midst should have come only too abundantly true. It was amusing to register the way they changed their tune, their attitude towards me, twenty-four hours later. And yet what had I done in between, except hold my breath, and keep my mouth shut?

It turned out that we were scheduled for a patrol – an offensive patrol they called it – on our own.

'Visit beauty spots in Scandinavia. Daily service by best modern armoured liners. Stavanger a speciality. Six hours of romantic, sparkling North Sea at an all-inclusive charge. Special tours can be arranged by consultation with the pilot.'

Perhaps I ought to have had more regard for other notices displayed on the walls in the operations room, such as 'Beware of the Hun in the sun'. Because ours turned out in the end to be a very special tour, and there were moments during it when I was forced to the conclusion that the invitation, prominently stuck up in the cockpit of 'Ginger's' favourite machine, was not as funny as it had seemed when I was being introduced to the other passengers before setting off.

Except for 'Ginger', I only knew them for such a short time, and by their nicknames. The navigator was 'Lanky', whose home town was Luton – does he live there still? – and who had grown a most luxurious moustache as his answer to 'Ginger's' mop. He spent the first part of the trip in the nose of the machine, working out our course. Just behind the pilot sat the wireless operator, a Manchester boy who had just celebrated his twenty-first birthday. It was very nearly Gilly's last one, though neither of us suspected that, as we grinned shyly at each other. And then far away in the rear turret I could just see the legs of the gunner whom everyone, including the ground staff, called 'Dumpy'. He was already in his flight position when I arrived on the scene, and I never saw the rest of those legs till our trip was almost over. Encased in their black flying boots, unyielding, immovable, they became a symbol of some importance to me, later on. Like the Rock of Ages, Queen Victoria, anyone's personal image of stability and staying power.

The pilot of the Hudson bomber was revving up his engines. Rather to my surprise, he wore silk gloves for the trip; very thin grey gloves that he more usually wore under his gauntlets. He asked me to fetch them for him out of the pocket of his greatcoat, just before we set out. In return, he handed me a little brown paper packet. 'You may find this useful on the other side,' he announced cryptically.

'What do you think of just before you take off?' Once again I asked the tag question, having already been put into the picture of how he had spent the whole of his war on this station, and of how, after joining the Service at the age of sixteen, he had served his apprenticeship flying hundreds of hours over the North Sea.

'Oh, I wonder if my tea will be cold before I get back.'

I left it at that. I was buoyant and excited, and not to be warned. After all, we had our packets of sandwiches and thermos flasks, as for a picnic. The one they lent me was bright blue, very suitable for an excursion. It was to get a bit dented, but that can happen on any holiday. Also handed up into the machine by one of the mechanics was something that I mistook at a first glance for a brown picnic-basket, until I suddenly heard a series of soft cooing noises emerging from it; whereupon I discovered that it contained the pigeons, which all the Hudsons carried as an emergency gadget for sending out S.O.S. messages. But how these messengers were expected to reach friendly territory in time to be of any use was not explained to me.

The weather was pretty dirty when we took off. I looked over my shoulder from the seat beside 'Ginger' and saw that the wireless operator was writing in his log book. Two or three times the same entry. *All quiet.* Each time he made a shrugging gesture with his two hands, as much as to say, what else could he put down?

I had put the same entry into my own diary of the day. For it certainly was deceptively quiet. After a couple of hours, I hopefully imagined that I could spy land, but the pilot shook his head. It was only a low bank of cloud on the horizon. 'I hope we'll still find it there, when we want to go in off the coast,' he said with a grunt. I could appreciate that it was rather heavy-going for him, with a head wind against us. We were only making 110 knots. We are all munching gum, I scribbled.

It was only when we at last came in sight of the Norwegian coast that I was conscious of feeling hungry. You know how it is on a summer picnic, the moment that you get your first glimpse of your final objective, like Stonehenge, your instinctive reaction is to want to get the luncheon basket out and stop beside the verge. So I scrambled back amidships to fetch my rations. There were four sandwiches, and I devoured three on the spot. Ham had never tasted like this before. 'Gilly', I noticed, was munching an apple. And he was blowing on his hands, as though the wind sweeping off the Norwegian mountains had reached him inside the fuselage.

Now the two sergeants were staring at the approaching land through their binoculars. We were coming in at Lister Light. Heavens, what a coastline, I thought. There were deep violet shadows in the gorges of the mountains, and the sun, shining brilliantly on the fjords, transformed them until they reminded me of the colour of crushed butterflies' wings, such as are sold at the seaside as souvenir brooches. It was all so peaceful, so incredibly lovely. I must come back here one day for a real visit, and stay longer, I told myself, as I munched away till 'Ginger', offering me his glasses, brought me back to the reality of the moment. 'I take it this is the first time you have been over enemy territory,' he remarked dryly. Had he sensed my thoughts? I nodded and took the binoculars, focussing them on Stavanger. Behind that barricade of mountains lay the aerodrome. Stavanger. Murmur the name to oneself and it sounded as romantic as Budapest, of which I had taken my farewell the last summer of the peace. However, I decided I would not make the comparison to 'Ginger'. He was clearly not the romantic kind.

3.30. *All quiet.*

'Gilly' had just written that down in his log book and gone back amidships himself to have a look out of the astra-navigation dome. I followed him, to stretch my legs. It was a way, too, of killing time. He was still rubbing his hands, in a restless movement, and I remember that I had a spare pair of gloves in my coat. Kid ones for wearing in Fleet Street. I can see 'Gilly' now, pulling them on, gratefully unaware how incongruous they looked with his uniform, as he stared out through the skylight in the centre of the machine.

Then, suddenly, in a whirlwind movement, he had left me, hurtling forward to his wireless table to tap out a message. Attacked . . . Attacked . . .

And then nothing. For this was the last message received from our plane, as we broke radio silence. In the *mêlée* that

Myself with three veterans of the Battle of Britain who were reliving their memories on a Cambridgeshire airfield. 'Ginger' Lacey, Peter Townsend, and Robert Stanford-Tuck

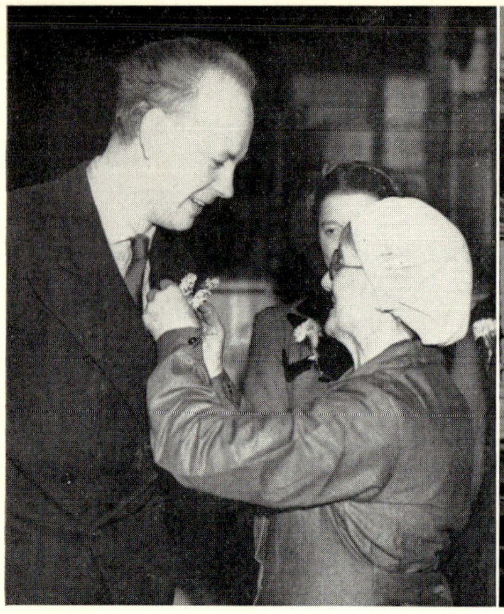

From the oldest munitions worker at the Hercules cycle factory, a sprig of white heather for luck

Choosing the ideal N.A.A.F.I. gi
Miss Eileen Bishop

The Mull of Kintyre lighthouse

followed, the wireless went out of action and so, in consequence, those on home territory back at Leuchars were forced to draw their own, inevitable conclusions. Someone telephoned to someone at the Air Ministry, who in turn rang my editor in the glass-house. Fortunately, John Gordon, being a dour Scot himself, and completely unflappable in any emergency, wisely decided not to inform my mother yet that the machine in which her son had been a passenger had disappeared into limbo over Stavanger. Thus she was saved this false alarm. Which was a merciful thing, as at a later date she was to have a considerably sterner ordeal.

Of course, I knew nothing about this till I returned to London. All I knew at the time was that the machine gave a tremendous lurch that sent me staggering half on the floor, half against the side. A second later, past me came 'Lanky', flopping down opposite me, to man the gun midships. Then 'Gilly' fell past me, too, on to the floor at my feet, leaning full length to unscrew the wheel that slid back the hole, and an unpleasantly large one, too, for the focussing of the belly gun. How he did it and kept any kind of balance I shall never understand. Meanwhile, the blue thermos flask rocketed round and round, hitting us all in turn, as did the basket of pigeons until I managed to get it jammed against the side. While as for the last of my ham sandwiches, it got so tossed about during the next forty minutes that it ended up in crumbs, coming down on our heads like confetti.

My head took a crack against something and I was out for a minute or two. Finding I was not yet dead coincided with the moment that 'Lanky' got a drum of ammunition fixed on to the gun. I don't know what happened to my notebook, but it was extraordinary how my reporter's mind continued to register. I kept on thinking: as long as that red pencil stays behind 'Lanky's' ear, we've got another chance. It was the sort of red pencil you see behind the assistant's ear in your local grocer's. 'Lanky's' navigating pencil.

It doesn't do to hoard anything in life. And now I shan't use my butter ration this week. And I kept on registering, too, the contrast between the legs of the rear gunner, strapped in his turret, solid and unmovable, with the legs of 'Gilly' on the floor beside me, which kept on prancing up over his head, like the young man on the flying trapeze, each time that 'Ginger' brought off another fantastic right-hand turn, or a stomach-destroying spiral twist. However, nothing could dislodge 'Gilly' from his gun, and in his kid gloves he was determined to give back what we were getting. And with dividends.

That evening in the mess, 'Ginger' explained to me that after having succeeded in obtaining the information Coastal Command wanted, he was just turning away from the coast when he came face to face with three ME109s, the nearest only two hundred yards away, opening fire with tracers. Apparently the cloud in which we had been sheltering up till then had, with unpleasant suddenness, vanished. What's more, it took him a whole ten minutes to achieve a semblance of cover again. Actually the first attack lasted from 3.40 until 4 o'clock, and all that time he was pounding his engines at 200 knots, and his panel registered 43 boost.

The technical jargon meant no more to me then than it does now. But I dutifully noted down the figures, in due course, as the proof for those who did appreciate such statistics of how amazingly the machine had stood up to the demands made upon it, as well as upon the arms and skill of the pilot himself, when at one moment in a desperate evading action he nose-dived his machine and only flattened out just above the water's surface. 'What did you think you were flying? A ruddy Spitfire?' his mates chorused round him that evening in the sergeants' mess, and I had the feeling that our private battle, and 'Ginger's' handling of it would be talked about on the station as long as it remained in active use.

It was really two battles. For just when things seemed to be smoothing down a bit, alarmingly there was another terrifying jerk, and the whole bag of tricks started over again. What happened was that after twenty minutes, 'Ginger', believing that he had shaken off our pursuers, came down through the clouds to find one of the enemy politely waiting for us. Fortunately he received such a peppering from 'Gilly' and the implacable occupant of the rear gun turret that he gave up the chase.

There followed a moment of communion which I have often re-lived since. I looked over my shoulder and there was 'Ginger' trying to catch my eye round the corner of the cockpit, grinning at me broadly, with his thumbs up in the familiar gesture of his Service. I had been assured the night before that he was a flaming terror in the ring, but at that moment he appeared like the Archangel Gabriel to me, and there passed between us a look of silent recognition that was to set the seal on a lifelong friendship.

I scrambled forward and he shouted in my ear, as though I had become the fifth member of the crew, 'Go up in the dome and see if we are really clear this time.' So proudly I climbed upon the step, and there was the whole universe spread out before me. Sunlight and brilliant blue sky, with tufted, scurrying white clouds beneath. A perfect Hollywood skyscape. Indeed, the whole panorama gave such an impression of having been freshly painted by a master artist, for my own special delight, that for a few moments I completely forgot why I was there. It was a day excursion once again. And then with remembrance flooding back, I had time at last to feel the reaction, to be really frightened.

When I came down and reported to the skipper that I could see nothing but sky, he lost height once again through the clouds, and relaxing momentarily, shifted his back, rubbing it like a cat, against the seat. From the expression in his eyes, I could imagine how stiff and aching he must be, from having somehow hung on to the controls through all those extraordinary gyrations, but he determinedly gave no outward sign of what he had been through, what he had achieved in bringing his plane back, to fight himself another day. All he asked for was his thermos. Fortunately it had got itself jammed in a corner by the now useless wireless. 'I think I'll have some coffee, Godfrey,' he said.

As I handed it over to him and unscrewed the top, aware that this was the first time he had used my Christian name, the sweet, hot smell rising into my nostrils overwhelmed me. I just got out of reach in time to spew up all the ham sandwiches. Then I felt much better. So much better that I really enjoyed it when 'Ginger' dived steeply again, this time in his version of the 'victory roll', to show how pleased he was that we were back again over our own coast.

It was almost dark when we reached our own aerodrome, and because the wireless had packed up we couldn't announce our arrival. In consequence, 'Ginger' had to make a very tricky landing indeed. It would have been ironic, to say the least of it, if we had ended up in a funeral pyre, after all. Not that there was much petrol left to catch fire, in the tanks. Just thirty gallons. Another ten minutes of flying time. Apparently in the first attack alone, our skipper had had to use up an extra fifty gallons. As for the holes and tears in the fuselage, from the enemy's efforts to bring us down, I doubt if I would have enjoyed the party so much if it had been still light enough to examine all the damage. In the sober light next morning, when 'Ginger' and I were photographed beside his machine, at the station commander's suggestion, my overriding reaction was one of astonishment that we hadn't finally come apart, in mid-ocean.

'Hi, Ginger, I owe you something,' I said, fishing in the pocket of my Mae West which I had put on again, to please the station photographer.

He gave me a cautious glance. I suspected what was in his mind: I was about to embark upon a panegyric of praise and thankfulness for his incredible aerial gymnastics, which he had already dismissed himself as 'a little bit of weaving'. He might have realized that I had served sufficient of my own apprenticeship not to do that.

Instead, I handed him back the small packet he had given me before we set out, which contained fifty kroner. A routine issue, just in case we'd all had to bale out over Stavanger. 'I shan't need it after all now, Ginger.'

'No, you won't. My back wasn't half sore last night. But not half as sore as my wife, Dot. You see, she had kept my tea and my supper hot, and then I had to wake her up to explain why I had got back so late. After all, I said, it seemed a shame to take you all that way, and not show you something at the end of the trip. Though strictly between you and me, we're not supposed to go in so far unless there are three of us on patrol together. But don't put that in your piece, or I'll get a strip torn off me. And none of that Brylcreem lark, either.'

'No, Ginger,' I said meekly. We shook hands, and I was just turning away when he called me back. 'Oh, I forgot something. Dot says she'd like to meet you next time we come down to London, on leave. Is that okay by you? She told me to give you a message, too. We've got a baby girl, Barbara, but we're hoping for another kid later to round off the Bailey clan, and if next time it's a boy, Dot says she would like to call it Godfrey. After what I told her, she hopes he may turn out half as lucky in life as you undoubtedly are. My crew say they'll adopt you any time you like.'

So in the end it was he who had made the speech; and gave me his wings. There was also a sequel to follow, and unlike some sequels, it turned out the best part of the saga. 'Ginger' was awarded the Distinguished Flying Medal for having brought his machine back against considerable odds, the climax to all his other patrols, and when he went to the Palace to collect his 'gong' he invited me to accompany his wife and himself. Barbara was too young to use the other ticket. Her turn would come later when her father, promoted to the rank of Squadron Leader, was to be awarded the D.F.C. for his continued devotion to duty in the Mediterranean.

They stayed with me the night before the ceremony, and in the morning we drove to Buckingham Palace. 'Ginger' was keen to pilot my car, but Dot, whom I had soon discovered was in complete control, though in a very tactful way, said 'No', firmly. She didn't mind what he chose to do in the air, but she was adamant about what he did on the ground.

When we reached the Palace we were allowed to park in the inside courtyard, next to an air raid casualty car, with its stretchers on the roof, from St Pancras. 'Ginger' left us as soon as we reached the main entrance, and we followed the throng up the red-carpeted stairs to the long Picture Gallery and its rows and rows of little gold chairs facing the centre dais, with its two fluted columns on either side, where the King would stand. While we waited, a band of the Guards softly played a selection of nostalgic, timeless tunes like *The Count of Luxemburg* waltz.

Every now and again, one of the participants, relieved of his hat and gas mask, walked past the assembled guests, grinned sheepishly at his lot, and then disappeared, again to be marshalled and formed up according to his decoration. We ourselves were supposed to be in our seats at a quarter past ten, but I noticed that some of the spectators were still arriving twenty minutes after that. The occupant of the seat on the other side of 'Ginger's' wife smiled as she remarked, 'Whatever time you held it you'd never get my sex to be punctual.'

I noticed something else about her sex. For once, not one of them during the long wait took out her vanity case and powdered her nose or fidgeted with her hair. They were too rapt. Even three small boys, who had been placed by the ushers on a centuries-old chest at one side, were as still, with their bare knees and their legs dangling, as the marble statues standing in niches and the portraits on the walls of royal soldiers in scarlet uniforms.

The only touch of scarlet that day was at the throats of some of the Civil Defence workers who were to be decorated for their gallantry. Most of the women themselves wore black, 'Ginger's' wife among them, and the wife on the other side of me, too, although on her black bag was a butterfly picked out in brilliants. As we waited, I kept on looking down at that and thinking of the contrast with her husband's machine, for she had confided that he was the pilot of a Beaufort, who had taken part in a daylight raid over Bremen, and had bombed the two German battleships which in the language of those times were known as 'Salmon and Gluckstein'.

His name was John Becket. The reason it comes back to me is because, through one of those coincidences which are always happening in times of war, we had ourselves already met. I had visited his training station at the moment he was passing out, so naturally I was interested to learn now what had happened to him since. So soon to be decorated. So soon to grow old before his time, I thought.

His wife was saying, 'Do you remember how you wrote that when they sew their first wings on their tunic, they always leave a space for the D.F.M.? My husband told me to do that, jokingly of course, when I sewed his wings on for him. And now . . .'

At that moment the chattering all round us died away, and there was a sudden hush before the band broke into the National Anthem. Through the dark doors, thrown open, came the King dressed in Naval uniform; and immediately, with a minimum of pomp and ceremony, the long line went slowly towards him to receive their battle awards.

First the Senior Service, headed by a boy on crutches who was receiving the Albert Medal. Each name was read out and the name of the ship, but not their deeds of valour. Sometimes a name struck a bell for me. H.M.S. *Aubretia*, for instance, because I recognized at once that that was a corvette, as all the first batch of corvettes were named most unsuitably after flowers.

Immediately I was back in the corvette in which I had sailed from Londonderry, H.M.S. *Arabis*, holding communion with 'Tanky', the ship's butcher, who when the ship was standing up on end far out in the Atlantic used to keep up our spirits by talking about his missus. Although she had been blitzed out of two London homes, she could still write cheerful letters. '*He'll* never beat the ladies, will he?' 'Tanky' always finished up.

It had meant something very important, very real to me, at the time. Would the day come when such simple declarations of faith would seem as old-fashioned and meaningless as the catch-phrases in one of Tommy Handley's *ITMA* shows? It did not seem possible, though there is a fashion in everything, I reminded myself, looking round at all the ladies present, the wives and mothers united in pride, relishing their interlude of reflected glory. It was at that moment that 'Ginger's' wife nudged me, whispering, 'I am sure Ginger is more nervous now than when he was over Stavanger.'

He was just going up to the dais, the first of his Air Force comrades, and the anonymous voice was reading out his name. Flight Sergeant Hugh Bailey. I felt a sharp contraction of my stomach, as though I really belonged to his family and to the son as yet unborn who could bear my Christian name. The light from the hanging lamp lit up his undefeatably fiery hair, which for once was neatly brushed down. Instead of the flying clothes in which I would always visualize him, he had acquired a brand-new uniform for the occasion.

Now the King was shaking his hand and speaking to him. Dot wanted to know, of course, as soon as her husband joined us by the car, exactly what His Majesty had said. What had bowled 'Ginger' over most of all was that after, as directed, he had bowed to the King, the King gave a little bow back to him. He had done it to them all, and it struck 'Ginger' dumb. Or perhaps he only dropped the subject abruptly because he was shy, lest I might explain that it was out of a kind of respect for their valour, for the reason which had brought them all there, that day.

Instead, the moment we had emerged from the gates and left the Palace behind, he asked, 'Can I drive *now*?' Dot and I looked at each other with resignation, and I left it to her to strike a bargain. 'Yes, if you'll let us see the medal,' she said.

So there it lay in her hand, heavy and shining, with his name inscribed upon the rim, and the ribbon matching the mauve strip on his tunic below his wings. In my inside pocket was the complementary pair. The last time I brought them out to show anyone it was for Alan Godfrey Bailey to hold in his own hand for luck, at a rather more sedate evening party (than the one in the sergeants' mess at Leuchars) which I gave for his coming-of-age. The younger Bailey had really quite a lot to celebrate, for wasn't he already a fully-fledged pilot, and soon to join BEA where his father is today a very senior member of the organization, still keeping his hand in on the super jets, and in between much in demand for lecturing learnedly about the skills of navigation?

However, I wasn't fully aware of just how much the clock had come full cycle, until I was invited to the wedding breakfast feast of this godson in a private suite at the Carlton Towers Hotel. I suppose each generation has its own prejudices, and is inevitably biased. Anyway, I decided that although this Godfrey's bride, Patricia, was a very pretty and vivacious girl, and together they made an extremely handsome couple posing for their nuptial pictures, undoubtedly the best-looking woman in the room was Ginger's wife, in her brilliant, peacock-coloured silk coat.

How happily the parents' partnership had withstood the long littleness of peace, I thought, as I lifted my glass in a succession of toasts. Surely the young couple who had just exchanged their own vows would achieve the same degree of happiness if they always remembered that good manners towards each other, in private, were far more important than a patina of universal politeness in public. It is true, too, that all human beings need moments when they belong entirely to themselves, and any marriage will only survive with genuine harmony if each partner is prepared to take the other one on trust as to how their time has been spent apart and do not demean their relationship by ever setting traps. For a degree of personal privacy is imperative for us all, and indeed I am most aware of that myself whenever I attend a wedding.

Naturally, I did not give such advice to my godson or his bride. It would hardly have been an appropriate moment to do so. Instead, I gave myself a sharp reminder. Hadn't I made a vow that I would go back to Norway one day? Wasn't that the real end of the story as far as I was concerned?

I left the wedding reception with the resolve so strongly renewed in my mind that before the afternoon was over I had got in touch with the London offices of the Bergen Line. At last I would explore that coast which had seemed so incredibly beautiful from the air, but this time in a gentle steamer providing a shuttle service between each tiny port, which would take me in easy stages as far as the North Cape and even beyond, to Kirkenses, the most northerly tip of Norwegian territory. In this way I would also be able to stroll ashore at many of the larger places, like Trondheim and Tromso, which as bases and targets had received much mention on the nine o'clock news on those blacked-out nights, with the eternal threat of bombers overhead, for them, for us.

'I am afraid by the date in August that you are free to go, Mr Winn, you'll be too late to catch the midnight sun at its best,' the polite voice at the other end of the line felt it correct to warn me.

'That is all right,' I reassured him. 'I have had my fill of the midnight sun.'

'But I understood you to say that you had never been to Norway before, Mr Winn.'

Here, inevitably our conversation became a little confused, as though we were speaking on a crossed line, as indeed the whole trip was to turn out to be. Though it is only fair to put on record that my twelve days voyage meandering up the fjords, starting and ending at Bergen, to which I flew direct on the Scandinavian Airways line, was one of the most agreeable respites from the increasing pressures of post-war life that has yet come my way. Indeed, I can most warmly recommend it as an escape for anyone who is as allergic as I am to more expensive, regimented cruises.

What a relief it was to discover that there was no bar on board the *Harald Jarl*, no orchestra or sports deck, when I went on board that evening, in Bergen. We were to sail at midnight, with all the lights of the city still mirrored in the waters at the quayside, and from the moment that I stepped across the gangway of this unpretentious, sturdy boat, I had a lightness of heart which never left me till we berthed again.

I had been met at the airport by a young lady with a mass of auburn hair, who introduced herself as a member of the shipping-line staff. 'Was there anything that I would particularly like to see?' Indeed there was. Might we visit Grieg's house? Of course, and off we drove briskly in her car, which clearly knew its way almost without steering to the outskirts of the city, where on a little hill beside a lake the family home and studio in the garden are kept exactly as they were in the days when musicians from all over Europe came to pay tribute to Norway's most celebrated composer.

In the dining-room the table is set for a meal, but I had the impression, even more overwhelmingly in the wooden hut among the trees, that the creator of the music for *Peer Gynt* had left his desk only a moment before and would be returning almost immediately to greet a fresh batch of his admirers. On the long, low table in front of the window, the manuscript score is open at an unfinished page. The candles in their sockets are half burnt down. On the wall hangs the violin, which had been his talisman to fame in the beginning, and in latter years served as the instrument for the flow of musical motifs in his mind; a means, too, no doubt, for keeping at bay the loneliness which consumes all artists at times.

It was for me an evocative prelude to my own brief escape from the equally spartan, cell-sized room in my Sussex writing retreat, where I spend an average of seven hours every day at my own desk. The measure of my release was even more apparent when later we soared to the top of the ski-lift which is an even more popular attraction for Bergen's visitors. This was Kirsten's suggestion, for by now I had discovered that my young guide had been named after Norway's most famous soprano, Kirsten Flagstad, whom I had had the good fortune to hear sing *Isolde* on her final appearance at Covent Garden. I made an effort to describe what it had been like, the emotion and the sense of the occasion which had united and enveloped the audience when she sang the *Liebestod*, in the third act, for the last time. How inadequate my phrases sounded in my own ears. There are some experiences which are sublime, and one should leave it at that.

Standing side by side on the high plateau, Kirsten started to point out with pride the landmarks below. Bergen is a very fair city. Clean and shining, with delightful houses, mostly wood-frontaged, that are a mixture of Hans Andersen and New

England, some excellent stores, and one particularly inviting new hotel, the 'Norge' – where I stayed for a night at the end of my pilgrimage – that matches in comfort and service anything that we possess in London.

In fact, Norway's second largest town was altogether a revelation to me. As was Kirsten herself. She was so composed, with such a flow of idiomatic English. It was not until we were sitting at dinner, before she handed me over to the tour conductor on board, that all was made clear. Kirsten explained how she had spent a year in England, working in the city office of the Bergen Line, and been housed during that period in a Y.W.C.A. hostel in Finsbury Park. The other lodgers had been so friendly and helpful, she assured me, she hadn't felt homesick at all, and I could not help comparing her reactions with those of some of our own girls from the north who find London a most unwelcoming place, especially when they have to spend their evenings alone in a Kensington bed-sitter. Kirsten's one desire, she kept on repeating, was to return to England, and it was moving for me to find this admiration for Britain, and everything British, repeated and mirrored wherever I went, and to discover, too, that English was the second language which all Norwegian children study from the age of eleven, in every school.

With a certain pride, Kirsten announced her final piece of personal information; she had been born on that day in May when peace had officially been declared in Europe. In consequence, the names of coastal towns in her own country, such as Narvik and Stavanger, must have such completely different connotations for her from those they had for me, stranger though I was to these shores. Had I made a mistake, after all, to come? I looked at the young, carefree face across the table. I do not often feel my age, but I did at that moment.

'They will give you a certificate for crossing the Arctic Circle,' she announced, on an encouraging note, aware, I suppose, of the cloud that had crossed my face.

But I have one already. I have one already, though we called ours on board H.M.S. *Cumberland* the certificate of the Blue Nose. I couldn't start explaining all that now, and it was a relief when my hostess said that it was time for me to go on board. You should always sail at night; you awake to a new world, yourself reborn, in the same way as Molde, which is known as the Town of Roses, and which we reached on our first afternoon, has been completely rebuilt and given a new life, after having been razed to rubble, totally destroyed in the war.

I have never encountered, except in Regent's Park perhaps, such a superb array of roses in massed ranks, as we came upon in an extremely original setting. For they were planted on top of the wide flat roof of the strikingly modernistic Town Hall. When one pauses for a moment to recall the monstrous eyesores that most of our own provincial town halls are, it is easy to understand why our group of sightseers off the boat, French, German, Dutch, Canadian, Australian, and of course a leavening of English, were suddenly drawn closer together by their mutual reactions to this unexpected panorama. All shutters came down, and how the cameras clicked.

There was one particularly delectable scarlet floribunda to which I could not put a name, so in curiosity I asked our courier, Liv, half hoping that I could stump her. Liv, the same age as Kirsten, was herself studying at Oslo University. This was her way of earning some pocket money during her summer vacation, and her second year at being the guide and good counsellor on board the *Harald Jarl*. Liv – which in Norwegian means Life – was efficient without being bossy and in consequence was an equal success with all nations, and of course she knew all about the rose, which she explained was named after the town itself.

Apparently there had been a Molde rose before the war, but in the utter obliteration from the skies, not surprisingly the rose had almost completely vanished. Until a few years ago a German horticulturist, making the same trip as we were making, saddened to hear the reason why the rose had faded away, went back to his own country and set about the repropagation of the Molde rose. In due course, he presented the first bushes to the town as a gesture of reconciliation, a kind of resurrection.

Certainly his gesture had not fallen on barren ground, and the symbolism contained in it, together with the exuberance of the roses, created such a strong impression on me that for the rest of the excursion over the mountains, till we reached the ferry that would take us on our way to Kristiansund, I found myself instinctively sitting next to one of the German passengers whom I had previously avoided.

Matheus, our driver on this occasion, was something of a character. He did not speak such good English as Liv, who carried on the official commentary through a microphone. All the same, Matheus relished adding his interpolations. As when, passing through an ancient Viking village, he reminded the company of the other raids, before bombs or aeroplanes had been invented, which his ancestors used to make on the east coast of England. Their ships would return, triumphantly loaded not only with booty but with brides. 'That is why we have such pretty girls here in Norway,' he added gallantly, bursting into song, as a climax, with his rendering of *My bonnie lies over the ocean.* Matheus had such a success with this that he insisted on giving us, as an encore, of all things, *It's a long way to Tipperary*, in which rather to my surprise our varied collection of nationalities all seemed to be equally word-perfect.

I glanced over my shoulder and there were the other Germans, especially the three elderly sea-dogs in their blue blazers and nautical caps, whom I had already classified as ex-submarine personnel, revisiting their war-time bases, singing loudest of all. How quickly you would change your tune to *The Watch on the Rhine* and *Heil Hitler*, the successor, if you had half a chance, I thought sourly, until with a sense of guilt I saw again the fluorescence of roses on the town hall roof. On my return home, in contrition I wrote something about the Molde rose. Whereupon from Germany I received an anonymous package containing three of the bushes, which I have planted in a sheltered spot at the end of the iris walk, and christened them Hans, Ernst and Joseph, after my three fellow passengers with their bristly, now grey thatch of hair, and jowly-cheeked faces which became floribunda-hued in the evening, from an excess of fresh air coupled with the bottle of red wine they used to consume in their own corner of the sun lounge, lifting their glasses to each other in private, jovial toasts. Private, since they never spoke to anyone else on board. They did not need to do so. Their interdependent triumvirate was utterly absorbed in its special mission, reliving *Der Tag.* The day when it looked, in their eyes, as though Germany, not Britain, was soon to rule the waves.

Was this an annual return? Were they refighting old battles, still gloating over the amount of tonnage they had sent to the bottom of those northern waters? In the evenings, when the rest of us played cards in a desultory fashion, or sat on the upper deck in the milky, sea-scented, generous twilight, with the primeval rocks on either side of the fjords, like evocations of Valhalla, they pored industriously over elaborate maps that showed every tiny inlet of the coastline, pointing now here, now there, with grunts of guttural satisfaction. I tried to take an unprejudiced view. They had just as much right to relive their war service as anyone else. The only time when my gorge rose and almost choked me was when I came upon the three sea-salts striding down the aisle of Trondheim Cathedral, in martial step, as though it had been their kings and queens who had been crowned there and would be one day again. Had they, during the Occupation, attended services there of thanksgiving and rejoicing for their victories, and to have each fresh flotilla blessed? I know I was being unreasonable – after all, hadn't we had similar services in our own churches? – but I turned on my heel and left the church. As I came out into the sunlight again, I felt giddy and sick and had to close my eyes for a moment. Nevertheless, that did not prevent me from seeing once again the rafts, with their frozen bundles in the duffle coats, while the rescue ships hove to, so that they could haul in their nets with the drowning catch of bodies – themselves becoming, through the inevitably, agonizingly slow manoeuvre, a sitting target for U-Boats, who were having a field day, indeed.

Yes, but I was soon safe again. For I have never had a more positive sense of security in any ship than I had on board the *Harald Jarl.* Even when we rounded the North Cape, a name with so many war-time echoes, and encountered our only day of poor weather. On landing we were enveloped in a thick sea mist, which made us fearful of being separated from the rest of the party, as it swirled mysteriously round the marble bust of a previous visitor, Louis-Philippe, Duke of Orleans, later King of France. It was an unexpected confrontation. Had he really been here, and over a hundred and fifty years ago? It put everything in a completely new perspective; it gave us all a neutral talking point. As usual, the Germans in the party were far better informed, I noticed, than the rest of us, even about French history.

On the return journey to Bergen, I made a private expedition on my own. This was the suggestion of Liv, who invited me to visit a family with whom she had been in communication, in Tromso. We had not moored along the quayside till eleven o'clock in the evening, and were leaving again at half-past one. Surely they will have gone to bed, I suggested doubtfully. No one goes to bed at this time of the year, it was explained. Because of the long imprisoning winter ahead, Liv's countrymen are greedy for the final traces of the twilight, the lingering after-glow, when even at midnight the skies are often still a kaleidoscope of gold and a strange, unearthly shade of ceradon green. That evening provided something for which I had unconsciously been searching, and the moment that we drove over the post-war bridge garlanded with lights, I had the sensation, such as occasionally comes to one in life, that an experience of lasting significance was waiting just ahead of me.

Liv hadn't the address but was full of resource. 'The name is Marienborg, he is an electrician,' she told the taxi driver, and immediately his face lit up. 'Marienborg the electrician,' he echoed, and I thought: everyone knows where the electrician lives, just as you are aware, in any close-knit community, where the plumber has his habitat, and the carpenter and the joiner.

Olaf and Betty Marienborg were, indeed, very much wide-awake, for they were in the middle of a birthday party for Betty's sister, who at midnight would be crossing a barrier far more dramatic – and once upon a time for her sex far more quelling – than the Arctic Circle. She would be forty.

As we all fell upon the chocolate cake and toasted each other in schnaps, I discovered that my host had built his own house with the help of two friends who were themselves fellow craftsmen. The surprisingly spacious, sweet wood-scented sitting-room he had painted all-white, adding built-in bookcases and colourful, carved ornaments.

In one corner there stood a radiogram and television set, commonplace features in the living space of the civilized world. But my host and hostess explained with a certain pride that they had had their television set for only six months. Moreover, it had been the very first privately-owned model in Tromso.

'On the first evening when it worked, all our neighbours crowded into this room to have a look.'

They did not need to say anything more. You could sense from the look on their faces that it had been their great night. A *première* of *premières*. And a little of the lustre's aftermath rubbed off on us chance, transitory visitors.

I had been enthusing about Bergen and how much I was looking forward to renewing my acquaintanceship with the city and to do some more exploring, when Betty Marienborg broke across my polite chatter to exclaim:

'We have never been to Bergen, or to Oslo. I doubt if we will ever go. We could not afford the journey. It does not matter,' she added with a natural dignity which I found extremely impressive. 'We have our television set now, for the coming winter darkness which keeps us indoors so much of the daytime, too. And best of all, we have our home, which means so much to Olaf and myself, for it is here that our children will grow up, happily, in peace.'

This was the true reality of life as these parents saw it, stripped down to its fundamentals. Their words were not intended as a set-piece, a kind of testament, any more than the spontaneous outburst of the mother of my godson, William, had been at the moment that she was waiting for him to be born, and the war-clouds were ominously blotting out that summer's sun; nor again was the tableau of the sleeping children presented to their visitor as a deliberate declaration of faith. Nevertheless, I, the incurable spectator, could not help feeling strangely involved. And for this evening alone, my journey would have been a rewarding one, tidying up, as I did, much unfinished business.

On our return to the living-room, the television set had acquired a solitary, hypnotized spectator in the person of Kim, the huge, slobbering wolf-hound with his tongue hanging out, off duty now that his daytime charges were once again tucked up in their cots. Now I was able to push away that other tableau which it had been only too easy to conjure up; those other midnight rendezvous when Tromso neighbours would slip, like silent shadows, into the house of the one among them who dared to possess the prized radio set which could pick up the ghostly news bulletins from England. I almost expected to hear Big Ben striking now. But the Marienborgs and their neighbours did not hear it. That was the comforting thought; they did not hear it. It was not simply a case of never seeing Oslo or Bergen in their country, they would never see London either, to which in its blacked-out, beleaguered state so many of their compatriots, like Aarl, the pilot of H.M.S. *Leda*, had managed to make their way to enrol in the Free Norwegian Forces. The freedom of the Marienborgs, and all the countless families like them, was of a different substance from escaping across the North Sea in a fishing smack, as Aarl had done, or buying an air ticket nowadays to the sunshine of the Costa Brava. Another long winter's darkness ahead of them was bearable, because that other kind of blackness of eternal night, when your country is occupied by a foreign dictator, was behind them. What mattered now was that the house they had built with their own hands needed no barricades; above all, the future belonged to their children, who were still hostages but surely in a world no longer implacably bent on self-destruction.

On my return journey from Bergen my plane, to my surprise, landed at Stavanger. I had not asked specifically to be put on this route, and in a way it was more tantalizing than a direct flight back to Heathrow. For inevitably there was only a brief time on the ground which gave the travellers no opportunity to explore the town. Instead, we were herded into the transit lounge where the usual duty-free counter of scent and spirits enticingly met our eyes. Fishing in my pocket, I discovered that I had exactly fifty kroner left. Surely the notes should have been in a small brown packet? In any case, the coincidence was altogether too perfect a rounding off to my return journey. I shall never dare to put it into my autobiography, I told myself, and now with full official approval I spent the equivalent of the undercover allowance, doled out to me at boarding time that morning at Leuchars, for my day excursion to Norway.

Delighted with my windfall, though it meant yet another package to carry, I joined the queue of transit passengers at the door of the lounge, to follow them on board for the rest of our comfortable but uneventful flight. I could hardly have wished it to be as crowded with incident as my previous trip back from Stavanger. I suppose I had expected to find myself making comparisons all along the route, but instead, as so often happens, my mind went off on quite a different tack. I suspect this may have been because of my still-lingering sense of gratitude for the cloak which had enveloped me each evening when, in a mood of recurring relief, I had made a rendezvous with the twilight on the upper deck of the *Harald Jarl*. It was a kind of quietude which grows increasingly rare. Inevitably I could not help setting our pleasant form of delivery service up and down that coastline, working to a time-table that was leisurely but never late, against the unreliability and general scruffiness of our trains at home, and the nightmarish overcrowding of the roads, especially at week-ends, which made one thankful to be able to stay put on one's own territory.

I wonder if Frank Willis is still making the journey from London to Bradford and back in his lorry five times a week? I was astonished how there should come back to me the name of a companion on a certain night of the war, considering that I had scarcely thought of our journey together for a quarter of a century. Perhaps it was that my voyage in the *Harald Jarl* had had the effect of ridding the storehouse of my mind of so much rubbish, that now it was possible for me to see with a clearer vision the mementoes that rightfully belonged there. In consequence, I was suddenly aware that my day trip to Norway though dramatic and thrilling in retrospect, hadn't really been the most arduous and demanding twelve hours that I had spent as a war reporter.

It has often been stated – and as often glossed over – that in the Second World War the civilian population had a thinner time than the Armed Forces. Certainly as far as rations were concerned, I fed better as an ordinary seaman in the last two years of the conflict in Europe than I did when I was still in a position to cross the street from my newspaper office, and eat at the Savoy or Simpson's in the Strand. Again, those who for one reason or another found themselves fighting on the home front had the dreary burden of carrying a gas-mask everywhere with them, though they were denied the support and the smart turn-out of an official uniform of some kind. By day the Home

Guard, and the roof-watchers by night, had to wear their increasingly shabby pre-war clothes. It is true that no hysterical females presented city workers with white feathers; but no one presented them with clothes coupons, either, or extra petrol coupons such as I was always able to scrounge with ease each time I visited a battle training area. Those left behind had so little to sustain them; no promotion in Service rank, no change in scene; while, nervous of becoming bomb bores, they came to dread even more the hampered, uncertain trek home each evening into the suburbs, one ear always alerted for the first sound of the wailing sirens, cut off from the freemasonry of an army unit, deprived of the comradeship of a ship's company, and yet just as much in danger of each day being their last.

I suppose I was in a position to evaluate the contrast with some preciseness, since I had a foot in both camps. Where the writing of my two weekly articles was concerned, and my broadcasting sessions, it was easy enough both to feel and create enthusiasm when I was describing the Station life of the young men training to be pilots or rear gunners, or again the spirit of an isolated gun site where members of the A.T.S. had become members of the team. Their jokes, their mascots, even their superstitions, everything that coloured their lives made excellent copy; the descriptions wrote themselves. Whereas seeking to make my readers appreciate what it was like being on a winter night-shift in a Midlands factory was an infinitely harder task. Who was interested in this other vast army, necessary though they were, of munition workers in grubby overalls – except other munition workers? Or those who were curious to discover what difference there was in factory pay and, say, that of a corporal in the Pioneer Corps.

Well, Frank Willis took home five guineas each week, and I think you may well decide that he earned every penny when I tell you what he did for it. I write of him now, and the night that I was his passenger, as a tribute not only to him but to all those others whom I should like to feel will include themselves – whatever their niche on the home front happened to be – if they chance upon this page.

It is curious how there is often some trivial detail that sticks in the mind when much else of greater importance is forgotten. The driver of the twelve-ton lorry that took me, and a cargo of foodstuff from the east side of London to Leeds City Square, driving through the night, did not wear an overcoat. Nor a tin hat either, but that I could understand. However, considering it was the coldest adventure I myself had in the whole war, and in some ways the most nerve-ridden one, too, I should have expected my companion to have acquired a duffle coat from somewhere.

'You get used to it,' he said, as we were introduced in the depot where the grouped lorries, parked side by side under the mercury vapour lights, were like automata in some futuristic underworld. I was not sure whether he was explaining his own point of view or issuing a warning to me. My host for the night did not speak again while the cargoes were sorted out. The vehicles of the huge fleet going out that night were lined up in a row, each open at the back against the loading bay.

'You always start on time, whatever it's like?' I persisted.

He nodded quietly as he climbed into the driver's seat, and I hauled myself up beside him. Some of his mates were booked for the south, for places like Bournemouth and Southampton, but most of them had the longer ride up the Great North Road, for Sheffield and Liverpool and Manchester. We were the only crew bound for Leeds, a loner; but later, in the small hours, Frank was to assure me that he preferred it that way.

As we came out into the yard another raid had started and there was a sudden crescendo in the barrage close at hand. So close that beyond the open gates the whole length of the walls of the buildings opposite were lit as brilliantly as though film studio arc lamps were being trained on them. Fortunately, already the din from the concourse of running engines was so embracing that it was impossible to tell how near to us the bombs themselves were dropping.

At this moment my companion decided to get out again and I wondered what he had forgotten. But, in fact, he wanted to adjust the one headlamp permitted to him. 'The engineers have been at it today,' he explained, 'and it's a bit too bright.' Considering the illumination to which, against our will, we were at the moment reduced, I controlled a desire to laugh, realizing that the joke would not seem funny to my companion, who had made such journeys too many times through every kind of danger and discomfort.

It was quite another sort of joke, easier to share, when he told me about the soldier stranded on the road, to whom he had given a lift. 'I always stop for anyone in uniform,' Frank explained, 'but after a mile this fellow asked to be put down. He said my cab was too slow for him.'

Actually it surprised me very much what an impression of speed you can achieve in a lorry travelling at twenty miles an hour; much more than in an aeroplane travelling at two hundred. I suppose it was the intense vibration which deluded me into believing we were achieving at least three times the speed we really were. That and the unyielding blackness, which made me wonder how Frank drove at any pace at all.

And yet as we advanced through wall after wall of darkness, he seemed to know exactly what was there ahead and what we were approaching round the bend. Right from the start he encouraged such confidence that I trusted him absolutely, even when I could feel the weight of the cargo shifting from side to side, as we crossed the camber of the road. Ever since, I have understood why lorries do not always pull back on to their side of the road after passing a slower vehicle as quickly as you yourself, edging impatiently forward in their rear, would like them to do.

A long time after the night journey I am describing, I happened to ask John Surtees, the year he was crowned world champion, what he considered was the hallmark of a first-class driver, not on a racing track but on ordinary roads, and he replied without hesitation, 'Oh, someone who never has to use his horn'. And I noticed that Frank never used his horn once the whole journey, nor his single headlamp either, except at a blind corner as a warning to show that we were on the way round.

Our first stop was at the café, three miles beyond Stevenage, which is the Savoy Grill of night-time lorry drivers. It would take us an hour and three-quarters to get there, Frank announced, and no express train with a reputation to maintain could have been more punctual. For having started off at seven-thirty, it was exactly a quarter past nine when we drew up. Once as we came to a roundabout, Frank jerked his head. 'The lorries which are going to Birmingham, Manchester and Liverpool carry straight on here.' 'What's it called?' I shouted above the vibration. 'Bignall's Corner, South Mimms.' What a place to make your date with destiny, I thought, as we ourselves swung away to the right. They were going one way, we were going the other, and who would have better fortune before journey's end?

It wasn't such a redundant, melodramatic question mark either. Because the next day I was to hear that twenty minutes after we had passed another roundabout, a stick of bombs had been dropped on that very spot where we would have been had we lingered at Jack's Hill, Graveley.

Here Frank had a bacon sandwich and a cup of tea, and I had two helpings of sausages, I distinctly remember, because they were so satisfying for my civilian stomach. I was thankful for the opportunity to stand up and stretch myself, though I looked longingly at the fire around which had already gathered a privileged circle. But there was none of the camp-followers, the lorry-jumping dames, that I had expected to come upon. The war had quite cleared them out, Frank assured me, and went on to tell me about his own family and how he had been driving for the last thirteen years.

He might have been anything between forty and fifty, and I was to watch him age visibly during the night. Actually, he was thirty-seven, and his elder son was fourteen and the younger one ten. His face lit up when he told me how the older boy had just left school and was apprenticed to be an electrician. It was clear that he considered that a cut above his own life, with infinite possibilities which I would like to think have been realized. It's strange to reflect that Kenneth will be older now than his dad was when we met, with no doubt children of his own growing up, whose ambitions will be checked at every point by unceasing rises in the cost-of-living index. Today it is like coming upon a sheet from a store's old catalogue to hear the voice of Kenneth's father saying to me:

'In Bradford, we pay eleven and six a week rent, wherea when we lived in London for four years we couldn't get ar accommodation under twenty-five shillings a week. And none of our neighbours would talk to us either.'

I have heard that accusation so many times, that I am forced unwillingly to believe it. When I lectured across America after the war, at the end of every meeting the Luncheon Club ladies, in their extraordinary hats, would come up to me to thank me for the way that their G.I. sons had been made welcome by complete strangers when awaiting their embarkation orders before D-Day. And always the name of the town where they had been treated as a member of the family, given a hot bath and a place beside the hearth, was somewhere in the north. There were more wartime American camps in the north? Is that the answer? I wonder.

Certainly that night on the road, everyone was equally friendly. There was Lofty, for instance, who came to our assistance at once when our engine wouldn't start, standing on the handle while Frank swung. I never knew his real name, because Frank didn't know it either, though they had been meeting night after night for years, two lorries drawing up at the same café.

But there was a variation, a considerable difference in Lofty's itinerary from ours. He drove his seven-ton lorry up to Stamford and back every night. Except one evening each week when, in his own words, he had a gala. 'I go right on up to York. It varies the monotony.'

As we ourselves set off again, he shouted after us, 'You'll know when you reach Baldock, because there's a bump just before you come round the corner. When it's too dark to see anything, because of the blackout, I can still get round by that bump.'

In the end, I didn't notice the lorry-driver's landmark because I was too engrossed trying to carry on a conversation above the unceasing din. 'Ever been to Baghdad?' Frank shouted, just outside Grantham, as we came down Spittlegate Hill. Looking back now, through the other end of the telescope, I understand why he threw that unexpected question at me at that moment. It was because the drivers, making their way north at night, wrestling with the implacability of the total blackout, hated that hill most of all. It was so easy to lose control there and have your six wheels skidding and sliding over the kerb. Whereas, as soon as they had manoeuvred their cabs safely through Grantham, and were out on the other side, these night-riders felt they had passed a kind of milestone; for them the worst of the journey was once again over and their spirits would soar, as Frank's did, so that he was back again in Baghdad, in the army, a lad of twenty instead of edging forty, and with rupees in his pocket to burn.

And yet perversely, when I challenged him as to what made him choose to become a lorry driver, he knew the reason at once. 'I always fancied the life somehow, and I wouldn't want to be back in the army now, though it would be a cushier life, I reckon, even as things are. Here in my cab I feel in my glory.'

Not for the first time then I decided that few writers are able to put into the mouths of their characters words which as genuinely express their feelings as those that in actual life spontaneously emerge.

At our second stop, our only other stop during the night, Frank left the engine of his lorry running, though we stayed inside the café for almost an hour. Two miles from Newark this pull-up for drivers was situated, and it was so popular in those days, and no doubt still is (though this is one of the names that hasn't come back to me) that there was no place left for us in the parking ground, since so many other vehicles, dark and sombre with their secret cargoes, were there before us.

How good it was to edge oneself into the warmth. Like coming off the middle watch, mercifully released from the cage of the port director, that I was to come to know so well, down, down the companion ways into the heavenly fug of the mess-decks and the temporary oblivion of one's bunk. All that comes later in this story, but now that I am trying to put all the pieces into place it occurs to me that without doubt the port director of H.M.S. *Cumberland*, patrolling the Denmark Straits between Iceland and Greenland, with the wind cutting you in half as it appears to blow in both directions at once, and the passenger seat of Frank Willis's lorry on a February night, were the two most exposed positions in which I found myself during those six topsy-turvy years. For Frank's cab had no glass in the side windows; only two cloth blinds, such as you will find in a railway carriage, which my host politely pulled down, though they were precious little protection. Perched high up as we were, the east wind seemed to attack us from every quarter, seeping up through the floorboards, thrusting through the innumerable cracks, pursuing us from behind. And not only the wind. As we came into the light, I looked at Frank and he looked at me, and he announced, 'You're almost as black as me.' There was a certain satisfaction in his tone as though he had half-expected me to stay whiter than white, but instead the transformation had happened and now I was truly one of them.

All the other blackamoors grinned a welcome at us, their teeth in contrast with their complexions shining like the capped mouths of film stars in Hollywood, while 'old Bill' behind the counter, who I imagine is presiding elsewhere now, had his big moment when he was in a position to announce with a great show of crustiness: 'No eggs.' All the same, it was quite obvious that underneath his fierce exterior there was a seam of tenderness for his regulars, whom he hated letting down. After all, hadn't he once upon a time served seventy dozen eggs a week? We discussed with nostalgic relish such gastronomic memories of the past, while Frank satisfied himself with chips and peas, and I had a rasher of bacon and some very sweet coffee, so warming that it might have been laced with brandy. We lingered here much longer than at the other stop. I could see that Frank was very tired; he leant back in his chair and did not speak much, just sitting with his feet up against the fire, steaming.

There was a juke-box in one corner. Hopefully, before I discovered it was out of order, I looked at the selection on offer, and there were two Bing Crosby's among the titles. '*Sail Along, Silver Moon*,' and '*I Cried for You*'; and of course, almost inevitably, '*Ah, Sweet Mystery of Life*'. However, perhaps it was just as well that I was not able to have my pick, because as I was scanning the titles a huge fellow in belted corduroys came past me, with black alleys running down the sides of his face, and shoved threepence down on the counter from his giant's hand. Tuppence for a cup of tea, and the other penny was for two aspirins. It was then that I noticed there were more packets of aspirins piled up on the counter than cigarettes.

'Thawed out?' asks Frank. I nod. It's a quarter past three. We move towards the last lap. Sixty-eight miles seems considerably less than a hundred and ninety. All the same, when we reach the final twenty I begin to wonder if the journey will ever be over. I have been dozing fitfully, and then I wake up to the sight of a host of will-of-the-wisp lanterns in front of us. For a moment I am confused, imagining we must be back on Markham Moor, where on the road near Retford Frank had three punctures on his previous journey, and been impaled for eight hours. Instead, the tiny lanterns of the Moor fairies turn out to be bicycle lamps of the first shift of the day, though it is difficult to realize that the dawn is just over the hill, since the darkness is still so absolute and it has been a long time since we have encountered any traffic. Not since Stamford, in fact, where the lorries going south passed us, and Frank shouted, 'That's one of ours, with Harry in the cab,' at which, peering out and seeing only a vague, untranslatable, shape, I queried, 'But how on earth can you know it *is* Harry?' But Frank did know, and that was one thing I'd learnt in the war; never to argue with the man on the spot.

Now we are coming into the city at last, and the trams are starting, and my host makes his last effort at conversation, bawling above the engine and the incessant rattling, 'I will say it's a good city for trams, Leeds. At this hour in the morning you can go for two miles for a halfpenny.' Which was a fair enough tribute from a Bradford man, though I don't imagine it could be repeated about any other place in our isles today, where such a workers' tariff still exists.

A halfpenny, a hundred pounds. By this time I am too stiff and numb to care about or understand the difference. What I can appreciate is the sudden intense stillness, the complete cessation of all sound, as Frank brings his cab to a standstill in City Square, delivering me, as in a taxi, to the door of the Queen's Hotel, where I have booked a room. In five minutes I shall be in a hot bath, and then I shall be able to sleep for ever, I remind myself with a sense of overwhelming relief. But even such a glorious prospect ahead of me cannot cure my temporary paralysis. I am utterly unable even to fall out of the cab on my side. In the end, Frank has to climb down himself and pull me out, as later the oncoming watch would do, reaching out from the top deck of the ship beside the port director. Now there is no ice or snow upon my cheeks, only the light from Frank's torch which flickering to and fro illuminates his own features too, so that in the act of shaking hands, and wishing each other luck for the rest of the run, I discover with dismay that it is not so much the face of a blackamoor at which I am gazing, as of an old man.

I slept the sleep of utter exhaustion in my hotel room and it was evening again before I woke, having dreamt that I was standing on the stage of the *Grand* at Leeds, in the middle of a music hall performance, naked and unprotected except by the coon make-up on my face. A bizarre prolongation of the moment when I had paused in that state in front of the mirror of the bathroom, before soaking gratefully in the steaming water, astonished by the black and white contrast of the dirt and grime of my journey and my pale body stripped of its layer upon layer of protective jerseys.

Who was this figure sleep-walking without his pyjamas in the dawn, in a northern hotel? It was not surprising that I did not recognize myself, for it was a period in my life when I was striving to do so many different things, and in the process becoming so many different people in turn. I found myself getting used to writing in railway trains, in the corner of a N.A.A.F.I. canteen, in a theatre dressing-room, waiting my turn to go on in a concert, with a message to the 'Folk at Home' from those 'Out there'. This was considered to have instant impact, and so I was roped in to give my services, whenever available. Of course, I wasn't available when I was away at sea or being taken for a ride by an enthusiastic tank commander, rehearsing for the Libyan desert, on Salisbury Plain, or even travelling by night lorry to Leeds. I had to fit in all the expeditions, all the invitations, as best I could, always with the proviso, 'circumstances permitting,' hoping I would not have to opt out at the last minute from a date to open a Special Savings week in some town, or a speaking tour arranged for me by the Ministry of Information. This would consist of at least three talks a day, some massed meetings of Women's Institute members, but others in settings rather less conventional, such as an aeroplane hangar, or the dockside at Liverpool. Or again, I would find myself perched high beside a crane in some such spot as Smith's Dockyard on the north-east coast, gazing down at a sea of cloth caps belonging to the men who were building the ships in which I briefly sailed. I don't know what they thought of my haranguing. I thought a lot of them, even of the young commando in a scarlet beret who, on another occasion, gratefully resting his feet on the grass, slept all through the hour which I spent in describing in some detail what exactly it was like being on board a corvette guarding a convoy far out in the Atlantic.

It was a hot afternoon, and the parade took place in a glade in Sherwood Forest, of all places. Their colonel introduced me, and while he was doing so I remembered how a friend of mine, who was adept at this sort of thing, being a Member of Parliament and a member of the Cabinet besides, had strongly urged me to adopt the same technique as he himself had come to find so effective. 'Fasten one fella with your eyes and never let him go,' Jay Llewellin admonished me. 'That way you'll have the whole lot with you.' So I picked on someone in the third row, who looked intelligent material for my experiment, and who was at that moment giving his commanding officer his whole attention. However, the second that the military figure at my side handed over to me, I watched my victim take off his beret, loll his head on the shoulder of his next-door chum, and go off to sleep. It was not that my gaze was hypnotizing him; it was my voice that was lulling him to slumber. All through he never stirred, but I refused to surrender. At him, at him alone, I pointed every joke, every gesture that I made was in his direction. No use. He was out for the count. Until I sat down and the colonel rose again to give a vote of thanks. Instantly, my guinea-pig without being shaken was awake, wide awake once more. The familiar sound of his colonel's own voice, carrying such dangerous overtones so often in its wake, was like a douche of cold water in his face. He was straightening his battle-dress, putting on his beret again at the right angle, before he started to applaud more enthusiastically than anyone in his row.

What a baptism it all was, though inevitably some of the captive audiences I was given, or who had me thrust upon them, have stayed more clearly in my memory than others. For instance, there was the week-end that I was invited to launch the Warship Week that Stockton-on-Tees were holding. I arranged to stay with friends at Richmond and to drive over from there. Gratifyingly there was a large turn-out, though it was a Sunday evening; but this may partly have been because the local Member of Parliament was there to introduce me. I had had no single break of any kind since that first Christmas at Brighton, and not surprisingly I was beginning to feel completely drained so that everything, especially pouring myself out on a public platform, was becoming increasingly an effort. However, my chairman's vote of thanks was couched in such spontaneously moving language afterwards that I felt my journey really had been necessary and my tiredness temporarily left me. We drove back to St Nicholas in, as far as I was concerned, a state of thankfulness. All the same, I was sufficiently curious to cut across the congratulations of my companions to ask the name of the M.P. that had escaped me, since it was not on the official programme; he had found himself able to join the party of welcome at the last moment. 'Oh, don't you know each other? His name is Harold Macmillan, he's a back-bencher who's married to one of Eddie Devonshire's sisters, Dorothy.'

Many years later – in fact, only last year – I happened to be a guest of honour at one of the monthly Dorchester luncheons so unflaggingly and skilfully arranged by Christina Foyle. On this occasion the object of the exercise was to celebrate the publication of the autobiography of Lord Egremont, who had been the private secretary to Mr Macmillan during his period of office as Prime Minister. The chemistry of the luncheon did not ignite until Mr Macmillan, again not on the printed list of speakers, was persuaded to rise to his feet. Instantly he had the whole audience, well-fed though they had been, eating out of his hand. It was a masterly performance, and after the party broke up, and the eager autograph hunters were swirling round the author of the day, I found myself momentarily standing next to the back-bencher of long ago. 'I hope you won't think I'm being impertinent if I thank you for the treat you have given us, and the lesson in professionalism.' The elder statesman smiled as he replied, 'It was not nearly as good as the speech you made in my constituency one Sunday night during the war.' We had never spoken to each other since that brief meeting. I was dumbfounded, until someone to whom I described this encounter, and who is closer to the political world than I am, commented, 'The big people always remember. It is something they learn on their way to the top.'

In reverse, I felt a very small person the night that I spoke in the Town Hall, at Bolton. It was the climax to a tour for the

Ministry of Information, throughout Lancashire. The week before I had been in Scotland, addressing audiences in places such as Dunoon, Fort William and Oban, and trying not to be too glib or automatic in my delivery, from constant repetition, like a music-hall performer with his patter. After all, hadn't I done variety performances, too, being sandwiched by Jack Hylton – whenever I could manage to be a free agent for twenty-four hours – between a plump little girl with a big voice and a squeeze-box, called Mary Naylor, and an extremely modest shrimp with a disarming line in adolescent humour, named Ernie Wise? They were part of a bill touring England, which took its title from a B.B.C. programme, *Youth Takes a Bow*, most expertly compèred by a genial giant with red hair. This was Bryan Michie, later to be Controller of Television for the West, who possessed the gift of making all his 'discoveries' already seem like the stars of tomorrow he assured his audiences they were going to be, and actually became in the case of Ernie Wise and another lanky youth, Johnny Lockwood. Not surprisingly these youngsters didn't welcome the night I turned up in Leeds or Manchester or Cardiff, or wherever they were performing that week, because in order to allow me ten minutes quick-fire talking time a minute had to be lopped off each of their acts. However, Jack Hylton, who was an extremely shrewd assessor of public taste, was insistent that this was providing a far more effective opportunity for reaching the hearts and the minds of the average citizen than any amount of sponsored official appearances in Town Halls or Assembly Rooms. 'If you can go on cold on to a music hall stage,' he assured me, 'telling stories about the war effort, when the audience is really there to laugh and momentarily forget the blackout waiting for them, that's the most effective kind of propaganda. It's also the best training for you,' he added, 'if you decide to enter politics when it's all over.'

How right he was about the training part. I have never been really nervous of any audience since, and that evening at Bolton, though I could hear my voice beginning to grow hoarse after two factory meetings earlier in the day, I could sense from the lack of rustling and coughing from the packed rows in front of me that my audience was completely with me. Once again I tried to vary my material, and at the same time prevent myself from sounding stale by describing my latest visit to a training station of the Royal Air Force, in the Cotswolds, where the bomber pilots of tomorrow were being turned out, and in juxtaposition, as a contrast, adding a description of what it was like to be in a minelayer off the Irish coast, at that moment of sweating, increasing tension, before the cargo of 'eggs', as the crew called them, each weighing half a ton, were released over the ship's side.

If anything should touch us now you wouldn't have time to grab a harp, the fellow pressed beside me at the unrailed stern whispered, while we waited stiffly in the choking blackness for the operation to commence. As, my back to the sea, I gazed away into the indeterminable cavern where the cargo in four rows, two on the starboard side, two on the port, was housed against this moment, it was impossible for me to distinguish which shapes were the men at their action stations, which the mines attached to their sinkers. Indeed, one might have imagined there was nothing animate there at all, had there not come from somewhere at the end of the tunnel the first snatch of the song this crew always chose to sing as they waited for the light to flash its signal, when the captain was satisfied that we were over the exact spot in the minefield that was being laid.

'Bless 'em all, bless 'em all,
The long and the short and the tall,
You'll get no promotion this side of the ocean,
So cheer up my lads . . . bless 'em all.'

Plonk, swish, a sigh. The last of the load had disappeared over the side, the men had surged below to have their kye, and my companion, the torpedo gunner, had taken off his gardening gloves and disappeared in the darkness towards the ward-room. Only I myself had lingered behind, alone in the hollow tunnel where a few minutes before human beings, and the implacable instruments for destruction for other human beings, had been intermingled.

Even now I can still experience again in all its intensity the moment of disembodied isolation; of horror and revolt against the whole impersonal exercise. In a flash of revelation I was made acutely aware of what I had tried not to admit, to acknowledge, the utter futility of any kind of war, of every kind of war. They laid mines for us, at sea, on land, we laid mines for them. What was the use? Where did it all lead? What was to be the end? A cancelling out. An utter negation.

I tried to push the treasonable thoughts behind me, and I took care not to voice my doubts in the ward-room, or upon the platform that evening at Bolton. That was not why I or the audience were there, but for exactly the opposite reason, for mutual reassurance. Carefully I pointed out that the more efficiently and enthusiastically the jobs, even the distasteful ones like laying mines and dropping bombs were performed, the sooner the just and lasting victory for which we were all striving could be attained.

'They want to be bomber pilots because that is the quickest way to end the war. They may look younger than their average age of twenty, they may not be allowed to keep a motor-bike, but when one of them in the mess reads out the latest casualty figures from the Russian front, you see the same look in their eyes. And you have only to fly with them and watch them at bombing practice to realize the intensity and singleheartedness of their feeling.'

I was reaching my peroration. I had interpolated the reference to our 'brave allies', the Russians, which the Ministry official had suggested, and now I was taking out my wallet and holding up for all to see the wings that 'Ginger' had given me, as I described in turn my last evening at the Air Force station at Little Rissington; how I went into one of the huts on the camp and found the boy with hair black as tar in a cauldron, and the thick eyebrows, to match, with whom I had been flying that week and whom I had chosen as the prototype for my portrait. I was able to tell him that his Flight Commander's report, which he had personally shown to me, stated: 'A keen type. Quick to learn. No special faults.' Encouraged by that, the keen type went to his cupboard because he had something, in his turn, to show me. His best tunic and there on the left breast was a pair of wings, not like the ones I myself carried everywhere with me, but shining new.

He would have to wait another week before he could actually appear in the tunic on the day that he passed out from the Training School. Meanwhile, he could only gaze at this insignia

A souvenir I treasure. General McNaughton, Commander-in-Chief of the Canadian Expeditionary Force, with our wartime Prime Minister

Farewell to Dunkirk

St Paul's defies the flames

The morning after a blitz in my street

which he had coveted so passionately in the secrecy of his sleeping quarters.

'I sewed them on myself. It took me hours. I've never used a needle in my life before because my mother always did all my mending. But I was told it would bring me luck if I did it myself.'

The words now were rushing out.

'I bought them in Burford. They only had the two-shillings sort. I believe you can pay as much as six shillings, when they are really silvered up. But I reckon these are good enough to be going on with.'

What could I add to that, in recounting the dialogue, on that Town Hall stage, except to suggest that there were still some things in life that could not be bought, only earned, like freedom for the civilized world. I may be kidding myself, but it didn't sound so corny and meretricious as it does now. Anyway, it was all over and another evening of exhortation concluded with the chairman's polite platitudes, and then the audience were reaching for their gas masks, making for the exits, except for those who crowded round me for autographs, which I signed with the flourish of a film star.

At the end of the queue there was a little woman in a brown coat, with a small piece of beaver at her throat, and she was wearing – I can see her still as though it were yesterday – a black felt hat. She put out her hand and timidly plucked at my arm. She was very shy and deliberately had waited till the last.

'Thank you for what you said just now about our boy.' She spoke so softly I could scarcely hear her. 'Of course I recognized it was him from what you wrote in the paper.' I looked from her to the man standing solidly beside her, who seemed very intent on lighting his pipe, while his wife fumbled in her bag. From it she took out a crumpled copy of the page in which I had described my visit to Little Rissington Aerodrome and my flight over the rich, red Cotswold earth in the company of her son, whose picture with myself and his instructor was at the top of the column. That picture and what I had written below I had intended as a composite portrait of them all, but for her it was clear that there was only one member of the Flight.

'How is your son getting on? Does he like his new station? What Group has he gone to? His C.O. picked him out as being the best of that particular batch. You must feel very proud of him.'

It was then that my already hoarse voice trailed into silence. For there was a look in the mother's eyes which stopped me in mid-sentence. It was all that I could do not to put my hands over my ears, as relentlessly she went on:

'We have the picture from the paper cut out and framed on our kitchen wall, so that I can look at it all the time. He promised us that he would write and ask you for the original, if you could possibly spare it. But there wasn't time . . .'

'You see, Mr Winn, your picture is the only one we have of him in his proper flying kit.' The father now spoke for the first time.

'His plane didn't return from his very first trip over Germany. They tell us there's no hope.'

Consumed by a feeling of self-horror, as though in some complicated way it was my fault, I gazed down at them, unable even to protest – *but it can't be true; why, it's only a few weeks since he was showing me the wings on his tunic* – while she in her turn shook my hand, pressing it between both of hers as though it was I who needed the comforting, not she or her husband. 'We thank you with both our hearts for what you wrote, and what you said tonight. We shall have that to keep, to remember always.'

They were putting the lights out at the end of the hall. We were the only people left, except my driver from the Ministry who was waiting to take me back to my hotel at Manchester, and the slices of spam and ersatz coffee awaiting me for my supper.

It was a cold and austere supper, in every sense, for which I had no appetite, and afterwards going to my room, so clearly indifferent to my occupancy, I was only too well aware that however many sheep I counted, sleep would elude me. Instead, I kept on wondering – as though it made any difference – over what target that particular plane had been swallowed up in flames, and spiralled downwards to oblivion. Was it in the obliteration raid on Cologne? As a deliberate boost to morale on the home front, a thousand bombers had been deployed, for the first time. A landmark in the switch-over from the defensive to the offensive. All the newspapers carried huge banner headlines, and my own editor, John Gordon, possessed of the sharpest news sense in the Street, considered it something of a scoop when the Chief of Bomber Command, Air Marshal Harris, agreed to receive me in his sécret Headquarters, hidden away in a grove of beech trees near High Wycombe.

Brought into his sanctum by his P.A. I found him poring with marked satisfaction over a batch of huge blown-up photographs taken in daylight twenty-four hours after the raid. 'Come and look at these, Winn,' he greeted me with exultation in his voice. I stood beside him and peered down through the stereopticon, a toy that was new to me, with the power to give a third-dimensional look to the black and white markings beneath it. Thus what had once been buildings and shops, and were now whole streets of ruined shells, stood up startlingly from the prints, damning or divine evidence – according to what point of view you adopted, on whose side you believed was the God of hosts.

From any angle, Cologne, naked beneath the stereopticon, looked like a ghost city, evacuated overnight, for there was no sign of human occupation, only of fleeing footsteps in the streets and roadways, footsteps in the snow. Snow in May? I myself felt less elation than puzzlement, as turning to the commanding figure with the sandy hair and moustache at my side I queried, 'Is that snow?' 'Snow?' he echoed. 'Of course not. That's the ashes from the still burning buildings. In some places it's reckoned to be six inches deep.' I thought of the cathedral arches and of the beech trees outside, their fresh verdure to triumphant a proof of the spring's resurrection. Instead, ashes. And now the ashes in the mouth of the mother who had lost her only son, even before he had had time to come of age, to marry and have children of his own. What comfort to her were those blown-up pictures and all the others like them that, in the end, placed side by side, would doubtless stretch from Land's End to John O'Groats? What comfort indeed, however dazzling the skill with which they had been taken at high altitude by a member of the special unit, or however positive their evidence of damage and destruction and death to the enemy.

METHOD MAY TAKE TIME, BUT IT IS BETTER TO BE LATE, MR AIRMAN, THAN THE LATE MR AIRMAN.

Over and over again, as I sought in bed the embrace that was denied me, this cute slogan, written up in capitals on the wall of their squadron commander's office, repeated itself and repeated itself again, till in the end it was being shouted accusingly from the end of that long black corridor where the mines were stacked, ready to go over the side, mingling now with the macabre chorus of '*Bless 'em all*', now with the bowdlerized version of Rudyard Kipling's '*IF*', which was recited with optimistic pride by the latest batch of volunteers at yet another training station I visited, this time for rear-gunners:

'If you cotton to tracer
And harmonize your gun,
Systematically sky search
Especially in the sun.
If you're good at recognition
Of aircraft friend or foe,
Can estimate four hundred yards
And think you really know
The sighting that's required,
A long but steady burst,
If you can do all that, my lad,
Then Fritz will come down first.'

Soon after the phase of the phoney war had come to an abrupt end with the realities of the retreat from Dunkirk, I had paid a visit, on an overriding impulse, to Air Commodore Peake, then head of the Public Relations Department at the Air Ministry (and later to be Chairman of Lloyds' Bank) who was inclined to lend a sympathetic ear towards my frustrated efforts to become airborne, though at first he could not do much about it. On this occasion I was eager for other help, off on a different tangent. Would he use his influence to persuade the recruiting wallahs of his Service to accept me as training material for a rear-gunner's seat? I was doubtful if I had the capabilities necessary to handle the controls of any plane, but surely, impractical though I was by nature, I could acquire the 'gen' necessary to become elected to the exclusive club of Tail End Charlies. However, the father confessor I consulted on this occasion, having agreed to put forward my application, was clearly unenthusiastic. Although too polite to say so in actual words, I suspected that he considered I was a proper Charlie even to contemplate the idea, and he pointed out at some length that he considered I was being of far more use with my pen than I would ever be with a turret gun, even if I ever managed to get on target. I went away from my confessional not wholly convinced. However, as the months passed, and I was allowed to have a day trip to Norway, and to fly over enemy territory on other occasions, too, I became less restless and dissatisfied with the role that had been allotted to me. Until tonight, as I lay huddled in my bed in that Manchester hotel, all my own doubts came flooding back, consuming me once more.

It wasn't the responsibility of getting the score right on each occasion which worried me so much, as the increasing danger of self-glorification. No one else had accused me of it, but now in the candid hour before the dawn I was accusing myself. Hadn't I stood on that platform and all the other platforms, and relished the applause? Was anything so wrong with that? After all, it was more a tribute to the people I spoke about, than to myself. In the beginning, that had been my own attitude, but tonight that encounter with the mother of the pilot whom I had used as calculated material to play upon the emotions of my audience had filled me with a revulsion not only against myself but against all the cunning processes of the propaganda machine of which I was merely a cog. I was fast turning into a music hall performer, with a whole stream of stories 'grave and gay about our brave boys and girls'. Soon they would be putting that on the bills beneath my name. It wasn't their fault, it was mine. I was beginning to relish the public appearances, the broadcasting dates – 'Here is Godfrey Winn just back from a trip in a corvette, to tell you at first hand about these sheepdogs of the Atlantic' – and the pictures, at the top of my magazine and newspaper pages, taken with the men and women who were actually doing the job, almost as much as I relished each new challenge to provide fresh ingredients for the propaganda pot. It was legitimate for a writer to seek his copy where he could find it, but wasn't I beginning to dramatize my own self unconsciously as the spectator of, and sometimes the participant in, so many curious if not undangerous adventures? Now that my mood of self-criticism was in full spate, I even compared myself with a profiteer who, discovering a shortage in wartime and the means to assuage it, turns his discovery to his own account and ends up with a fortune. After all, I reminded myself relentlessly, I was still receiving the same large sums of money as in peacetime, while thousands of others, like Angie's husband, Robin Fox, had surrendered their professional careers, at a most important stage, to exist and keep their families as best they could on a soldier's meagre wartime pay.

I can't go on like this, I can't, I told myself savagely, in a crescendo of self-reproach, and suddenly, as I lay there exhausted and tormented, it became absolutely clear to me what I must do. In retrospect, even my abortive plan to become a rear-gunner had something theatrical about it, but if, instead, I joined the Navy as an ordinary seaman, and stayed for the duration on the lower deck, refusing to be drafted into the Intelligence or any other chairborne branch after my initial training, then surely that could not be regarded by anyone as savouring of a stunt. I could sink into anonymity until it was all over; that was the consuming thought now uppermost in my mind. No longer would I have to strive to keep up other people's spirits, or my own, in public. No more eternal arguments with the censors about what could go in, and what could give information to the enemy. Or about the ethics of war, the unquestioning demands of patriotism, as when, for instance, I had dared to suggest that the behaviour of genuine conscientious objectors, pilloried and ostracized for turning their backs on public opinion and approval, might one day be considered to be the bravest conduct of all. Certainly had I shared their beliefs I would not have had the courage openly to martyr myself. It is so easy, so fatally easy to go with the swim. From now on, all I would have to worry about would not be questions of conscience, but simply keeping my boots clean and jumping to attention and saluting every officer in sight. What a relief it would be to shed the load. What a holiday it would be, floating with the tide, and I fell asleep resolved and at peace at last.

Nor did I have any doubts the next day, or the day after, even when I made myself consider what it would be like to exchange my comfortable bed in the captain's day cabin for the crowded messdecks. If I had been sick before, how sick would I be now? I brushed such unpleasant comparisons aside; this time my mind was genuinely made up, and the first person I wanted to know of my decision, even before my own family, or the editors who had me under contract, was the captain of the ship, H.M.S. *Pozarica*, which more than any other had made me feel completely at home, on board.

Captain Lawford wrote back: 'I am sure you will be very happy in our Service, if you remember always to ask the advice of a Stripey. They know everything, and together with the petty officers are the backbone of any ship.'

I accepted his advice, and never forgot it; just as I accepted with equal gratitude his invitation to come and spend a week as a guest on board my favourite ship before the naval training establishment, H.M.S. *Ganges*, swallowed me up, in August. This would be my third time on board, though the first visit had been little more than an introduction, a mutual appraisal, that afternoon in the Irish Sea when the '*Pozy*' had seemed like a 'Battle wagon' compared with the tug, the *Freebooter*, whose guest I was during the towing operation that took a floating dock from Plymouth to Greenock. Of course, she wasn't a battleship, she had been a banana boat in peace time, carrying cargo and a few passengers between Tilbury and Spain. Nor had there been anything spectacular about her war record to date; she had been on the 'milk run', as she described it derisively herself, looking after convoys on the last lap of their journey between Canada and England, or back again, operating now from Milford Haven, now from Belfast. I had fallen in love with her. not for her pedigree, not for the splendour of her three-thousand tons of armoured plating, or the strength of her four-inch guns, but in the same way that you will often love a mongrel rather than all the pedigree dogs on show at Cruft's.

And of course, there was her crew, every man Jack of them, with whom I had made friends on my second trip on board, and now would be meeting again for these last few days of freedom. Like P.O. Hynes, who was at the station to greet me, looking every inch a pop-eye sailor, deputising for Sandy, the gunner's mate, who had been too busy to get ashore. I ought to have guessed there was some significance attached to that. As it was, did I gaze at Sandy's deputy with a slightly more wary eye than on my previous trip, when at sea he had welcomed me to share his searchlight platform? A P.O. was a god to a mere sprog, I reminded myself, and that's what I would be in a fortnight's time. Meanwhile, let's have one for the voyage, at Bunker Hyne's chosen port of call, in Milford.

Handing round his duty-free cigarettes with a lordly air, he remarked, 'Do you want to know the latest buzz, Goff?'

'We're not going to Bangor and back, but to Murmansk this time,' I suggested, grinning. 'Instead of the 'milk run' it's to be the suicide run, from now on, for the dear old *Pozy*.'

'No, don't say anything like that. It'll turn my water green,' broke in my companion, ordering a second round. 'No, we're going to victual you in our mess while you're on board. That way you'll be able to draw.'

'Draw?' I echoed, never having even tried to make marks with a pencil since the wet afternoons in the nursery, donkeys' years ago.

'Draw your ration of rum, I mean. Your *tot*.' He made it sound like all the sacred waters of the East, flowing from one spring.

'You'll be grubbing, of course, with the pigs.' This was the lower-deck term for all wardroom officers, whether popular or otherwise on board. There was no disparagement intended; he was simply underlining – unconsciously, perhaps – the traditional difference between 'them' and 'us', that I was about to learn to appreciate at closer hand, and in more practical terms.

Meanwhile the officer of the watch was at the top of the gangway to greet me, as though I were someone of importance, and when I had been conducted to the captain's cabin there was Mulley, more Jeeves-like than ever, waiting with a pink gin poured out for me; and already in his sea-going kit, my host with that faint quizzical smile at the corner of his lips, that was to come to mean so much to me. I took in appreciatively the comfortable contents of the cabin, the family photograph frames on every table, and then my gaze came back to the carved profile, and the two wings of greying hair. He looked thinner than when I had last seen him, and I had the feeling that he was sleeping badly, which was not surprising, considering that the loss of his son, Peter, was still so close behind him. He greeted me, however, with the same warmth, though with a question. 'You are coming with us, Godfrey?'

'Of course I am coming with you. I am going to have my first real holiday of the war, before. . . .'

Somewhere in the distance a bugle sounded, summoning the off-going watch to their midday meal – in a few months' time I would be answering the summons myself – and in the remoteness of the captain's cabin there was a stillness, though I really was only aware of it in retrospect, after all the explanations and the arrangements had been made.

'I mean, you are coming with us to *Russia*?' This must be a joke. On the first of August I was due to report at Shotley. That was why I was here, to share his cabin for the last time. He knew all this as well as I did, and he couldn't be aware of the joke I had had with Bunker Hynes, in the pub on shore. And, of course, it was a joke, wasn't it?

My host was leaning forward, holding the glass of pink gin in his hand that he only pretended ever to drink for hospitality's sake. Mulley had retreated to his pantry, preparatory to dishing up. But what was my host himself dishing up? In growing astonishment, I heard him say:

'Yes, Russia. Murmansk or Archangel. It's all laid on. First we take the convoy as usual and deliver it to the goods yards. Then we move on to Belfast to take on extra ammunition and stores, and I shall have to have an adjustment made to our tanks to carry more oil. These ships aren't meant for such long sea-time, but the trouble is, Godfrey, we are so hard-pressed for escorts of any kind. As you know, Godfrey, things aren't very clever at the moment . . .'

He was the clever one. What he wanted for his ship, and his ship's company, he always somehow acquired in the end. He wanted nothing for himself, only for them. Of his own volition he had decided that to have me on board, as a kind of diversion, would please everyone, though, of course, he could have had no inkling of what lay ahead, in his original invitation, because, after all, he had pointedly suggested that I leave my pen and note-pad behind. There was irony with a vengeance, since in the end I was scrounging spare 'bumff' from all over the ship, because there was so much to record.

Actually, right up till the last moment I never imagined that

I would be allowed to sail. My body belonged now to their Lords of the Admiralty. However, as usual, my captain – as I always think of him, more than of any of the others with whom I sailed – got his way. I shall always believe that he succeeded partly by a ruse, playing on natural human vanity, that I have employed myself on occasion since. He upgraded all the officers at the Mad House, as he always called it, with whom he had to speak from Belfast. On the closed line to London I would hear him saying to the Commander with whom I had dealt in the Public Relations Department at the Admiralty, 'Oh, *Captain* So-and-So, may I borrow Winn for a month or six weeks? I am sure we shall be back by then and the experience will do him good. It might serve as part of his sea time.'

To my utter amazement, the next day he was rung back with the required permission; I would not be regarded as a deserter. All the same, I was not to elect myself as the first official war correspondent on one of these Murmansk convoys, because that might cause repercussions. Especially with the Russians, who were touchy and suspicious and did not care officially to be observed.

Thus in the most courteous and gentlemanly manner I was shanghai'd. Not that I minded, at the time. Who would have, in such circumstances? I was jubilant at the prospect. After all, I would be at sea, sharing their life on active service, and so were banished all guilty feelings about not reporting on the right day, even when it became a kind of ritualistic chant on board. '*You'll be late now for the Ganges* . . .' interposed with the mocking variation of '*You'd be far better off at the Ganges*'. I could take this joke against myself and toss it back with relish, as long as the battles and the excursions were in full spate. It was only when week after week we were idly marooned against the wood piles of Ekonomia, and, bereft of victuals alike for our guns and for our stomachs, the date of our return became daily vaguer and more remote, that – in reaction, I suppose, from all the effort I had consciously made to live up to and deserve my reputation as the ship's mascot – I found it increasingly difficult to hide the weight of melancholy that pressed down on me. I felt so utterly useless. I wasn't even keeping my boots clean. What would be the verdict about my non-appearance at the barracks? Six weeks at the latest, my captain had promised the powers-that-be. Would they be in possession of a full report concerning P.Q.17. or be as ignorant of what had happened to us as we were of news from home? In any case, could that be accepted as a sufficient excuse for me? I even began to have traitorous thoughts about ever having allowed myself to be enticed on board; it would have been better if I had just cleared my Fleet Street desk and spent my precious last few days at Esher, mowing the lawn for my mother, and attacking the weeds. That would have been a far more positive contribution. I was so utterly used up, in such a cave of depression underneath the surface, that I was even beginning to talk to myself on these lines, unable to appreciate how much harder it must be for my mother, counting the weeks, too, with the silence widening out; too proud to ask my elder brother, in charge of the submarine room at the Admiralty if he could give her any inkling of what had happened to the ship whose address was at the top of the last letter she had received from me, with a Belfast postmark; even having to endure her photograph being taken with my dog in the garden, by a central photographic agency whose cameraman, in parting, innocently let fall that there was a strong rumour in the Street that her younger son was missing . . .

So many rumours at home, so many buzzes on board the *Pozy*. There was nothing else for the crew to do in the dog watches, except play solo-whist and exchange mouth-watering descriptions of what their first run ashore back home was going to be like, and what a certain blonde party could expect from them.

There was even a buzz about myself that I first heard in the P.O.'s mess, where I was made so welcome every night as an engrossed spectator of the solo school. Teach them even the rudiments of bridge, and in no time I decided, as I watched Mac, the quartermaster, with the huge arms, playing a hand in masterly style, they would be teaching the high room, at Crockford's, a thing or two.

Percy Price, who prided himself that his overalls, with the judicious addition to the washing water of his own chemical solution, were a nearer shade to Mediterranean blue than anyone's on board, came into the mess, having washed his smalls, and his singlet and scrubbed his face for the night.

'I hear they're sending a Catalina for you,' he said, starting the ball rolling, so that even Sandy, poring over his stamp collection, and gloating over the additions he had managed to buy in Archangel post office, looked up expectantly.

What a hope! 'They're sending a Catalina for Admiral Bevan, not for me,' I patiently explained about the visitor who had made a brief visit on his way back to London from Moscow, to report on many things.

However, the buzz had started, the buzz continued, and grew to such proportions that I sincerely believe, today, writing so long afterwards, that in the end it made itself come true. An example of wish-fulfilment in excelsis.

Members of the crew, whose names I didn't even know, would stop me in the companionways and wish me luck for the return voyage. Mr Smith, the chief engineer, even offered me his lucky piece of coal, and Tom Brooks, who was pretty 'chocker' now that all the shelves of his shop were bare, managed all the same to produce a piece of 'nutty' he had been hoarding and which was worth more than its weight in cigarettes, a word belonging to the past; while Florrie Ford, Sandy's opposite number, presented me on behalf of the P.O.'s and the C.P.O.'s with two ash-trays fashioned from shell caps and most lovingly polished.

I was deeply touched by this demonstration of mass goodwill towards me. Nothing like it had ever happened to me in my life before. At the same time, I would not allow myself to believe in the authenticity of the buzz which had triggered it off, until the captain himself, one morning at breakfast, greeted me with a letter that he had just finished writing at his desk.

'I don't know where you will be landing, Godfrey. But would you please post this for me to Belfast. There is nothing in it of any importance except to my wife and myself.'

I took the letter and held it in my hand wonderingly. Mrs Lawford was with us in the cabin again, as she had been on the morning before we sailed, in her neat grey flannel coat and skirt, bringing the small bunch of geraniums because she thought they would last longer. And how long ago was it? Two months? Three? A century?

'You mean, it's true, the buzz? I am really going back first? But how? Anyway, I'd much rather wait and be with you all on the return trip.'

Considering how browned-off I had been myself, I was surprised at the instinctive vehemence in my voice.

'Your job is finished here,' the captain said gently. 'You should go back, if it's possible. Things are not very clever at home. All sorts of rumours are flying round about us, I gather. You can make a personal, unofficial report at the Mad House. Not being in the Service, it will be easier for you to speak up.'

'I've promised the crew I'll write the whole story as soon as I get back,' I blurted out.

'If *they* let you,' my host corrected me, dryly.

Mulley emerging from his pantry, to re-fill the teapot with hot water, announced, 'Give my love to the Strand, sir.' When he had gone – I marvelled at the lack of envy in his voice, but that went for all of them – the man opposite me, who was appreciably greyer than when we had set forth, continued in the same gentle voice:

'You're off this afternoon. I haven't told you before in case it fell through. The American cruiser, *Tuscalousa*, is taking back the wounded from the last three convoys. She will be crammed tight with stretcher cases like young Jimmy Campbell. There will be no room on her for anyone else. But M.S.1, who is in charge of the operation from here to Kola, has most kindly offered to try and scrounge a bunk for you on one of the escort destroyers. *Marne, Martin* and *Middleton.* They came through at forty knots, and had no incidents. It's a gamble, of course. But if you don't have too much trouble on the way back, it will be something to tell them at the *Ganges.*' Once again the quizzical smile that was as much part of our relationship now as searching for a fresh subject, a different and safe subject of conversation for each meal. Now he would be left alone with his squirrel's cage of all his *post mortem* thoughts about the convoy. 'Are you coming to Divisions, Godfrey?'

It seemed impossible to believe that this was the last time I would take my place on the woodpiles, with half a dozen ragged children still calling out hopefully for chocolate and cigarettes, and the crew drawn up in ranks, but myself a little apart of them, and yet not of them, while the captain read prayers.

'O Eternal God, who alone spreadest out the Heavens, and rules the raging of the seas . . . preserve us from the dangers of the sea and the violence of the enemy . . .'

Inevitably my mind returned to the first morning of our arrival, when after many nights without sleep, or even time, let alone the surplus energy, to shave, everybody on board the *Pozy*, from the greasers in the engine room to the young officers like Crisford and Brian Place, had cleaned themselves up with meticulous care, and paraded in their No. 1s, in front of the watchful, unyielding gaze of the natives, as though they themselves were back in their native Pompey and a peace-time Review was about to take place in the Solent. Together with the crews of such other ships that had arrived, alongside them, wearing whatever had come handy. It was a bizarre setting and we were a mixed crowd, but the intensity of the feeling engendered could not have been deeper, or more positive, had the service of thanksgiving taken place in St Paul's Cathedral. And after it was over, the captain stood by the gangway exchanging smiling greetings with the complement of his own ship's company, many of whom he had not seen since we left Belfast lough.

As it came to my turn to pass him and go on board again, he had said, on a different note, 'I am afraid I didn't read prayers very well.' And I had heard him, in the same voice, no louder, on the night of the last great attack, speaking down the voice-pipe to Mac, hidden from him in the wheelhouse below, hard to port, hard to starboard, and the ship swinging round in the last split second.

I had not answered then. What could I say now? I was equally without words in our last moments together, when I walked beside him along the quay to where the *Bramble* was berthed. 'I expect we shall be back before you leave for the *Ganges*. But if not . . .' And then, as though to preclude any other possibility, he added, 'In any case, keep in touch. And let me know what happens to you at the Mad House. I hope you are still glad you came with us, Godfrey.'

'Very glad, sir.' I managed to get that out. Later, in M.S.1.'s cabin, I found it easier to gaze at the pile of old *Times* that the

Bramble's captain read to keep up his own morale, each morning at breakfast, in the interlude while my captain handed me over. I was stupidly almost in tears, even though I kept on saying to myself, You're going home, you're going home. 'Here's the body, Crombie. Good luck.'

The body tried to make itself invisible at the ship's rails, and as the distance between the two ships began to lengthen, I saw a slight, fair-haired figure on the *Pozy* run out over the fo'c's'le and wave his arms. It was Sandy, my first friend on board at his end of the ship, and the last. He was shouting something, and as I waved back I faintly picked up the words . . . 'Strand . . . the smoke . . . a tot.'

This I translated into 'going up the smoke', their slang for leave in London. The Strand, which in Sandy's case, unlike Mulley's, represented a visit to his beloved Stanley Gibbon's stamp shop to evaluate on this occasion, no doubt, all the Russian new issues he had acquired, and the tot would be a reunion in my Ebury Street home. We'd talked so much about this on board, and how we'd catch up on the drink we'd never had that morning, at Milford Haven, when Bunker Hynes had acted as his deputy.

With memories of my riotous evening as the guest of the *Fury*'s wardroom in Seidisfjord, on the way out, still fresh in my memory, I had rather hoped for a pink gin or two on board one of the British destroyers, before our miniature convoy reformed itself at Kola and the *Bramble* turned back to Archangel. But in the end, the body was transferred to an American destroyer, the *Rodman*, and there is a strict rule that all American ships are dry. In compensation, however, I found myself accommodated in a cabin as luxurious as a state room in the *Queen Mary*, and had my first meal on tinned peaches, which tasted after our hard tack like crêpes suzette.

It was very ungrateful of me, but somehow I couldn't settle down to such luxury; I wasn't attuned to it; I had forgotten it existed in the world; and I lay awake, wondering jealously who would captain my hockey team, the *Sunday Express* Six, which had challenged all the other ships, and chiding myself, because I had forgotten to ask Mac for his home address, on one of the outer islands in the Hebrides, so that I could have written to his missus, too.

'Och, mon, give me Sauchiehall Street on a Saturday night . . . a nice day to spend a quid ashore . . . if I was at home now, I'd have both me feet up in the bleeding oven . . . Ernie Davison. I'd got his Ma's address . . . and the St Alban's High School for girls, who had adopted the *Hazard* . . . and the wife of the skipper of the *Leda*, that had given the Old Sockites party . . . the best party of all . . . the pilot's wife in Oslo . . . if only I could write to her. . . .'

In that state between sleeping and waking I kept on going over all the many messages to deliver.

The speed of the ship assuaged my impatience to get back, to be of some use again as a reporter and a messenger. We reached Iceland in four days, which must have been almost a record. Certainly the contrast with the delays and hazards of the journey outward was very marked. We had many alarums, but no solid, definite clash materialized. In the middle of one night, summoned to Action Stations, stumbling in the darkness because of the ship's lurching, I stupidly allowed a steel door to swing on to my hand, crushing three fingers. The pain which followed was so intense that it was only by comparing my lot with that of Jimmy Campbell that I kept my sense of proportion.

When we finally berthed at Greenock, my hand had to be set in a Glasgow hospital, where I spent my first night on home soil again. This was something of an anti-climax, and there were more to come. I arrived in London with my arm in a sling, feeling self-conscious and a fraud at being forced to play the part of the wounded hero which I certainly was not. Inevitably, I was hazy from all the drugs I had been given, and suffering from delayed shock. My own doctor took one look at me, and ordered me to bed. From which I was aroused by a summons to report at the Admiralty to the First Lord himself.

This was A. V. Alexander, who had a round, red face, and a jocular, nautical manner, which he had acquired somewhere along the line from his early days before he entered Parliament as a Labour Member, with the backing of the Co-operative Movement. We were on Christian-name terms, and in my distinctly downbeat condition I had expected a rather different welcome from the one I received.

'Sit down and tell us everything that you can remember about the whole voyage out. You are such a valuable witness, because you are a trained observer. It was a stroke of good fortune, indeed, that by chance you should have been a ringside spectator of 'P.Q.17'.

Alas, the conversation didn't go in the least like that. On the desk of the First Lord's room, as I entered, were spread the typewritten sheets that I had hopefully submitted for censorship, for publication in my newspaper. Even upside down I could see how ruthlessly scarred they were with blue pencil, and query marks. My heart sank. I had been through this kind of scene so often during the war, though never before at this level. Or with such a brusque and brutal pay off line. Not a word of my story could come out.

'Not a word,' I repeated dully. 'Not a word.'

'Don't you see, Godfrey, what valuable information it would give to the enemy?'

That old, familiar, face-saving cliché, to avoid anything that might create a springboard for questioning in the House, or in the uncensorable leader columns of the papers. Utterly ludicrous, in this instance, because the Germans had been giving out on the radio, with Lord Haw-Haw having a field day, full and detailed bulletins of their 'glorious victory', day after day. There was nothing that I could write to which they could not have added the most factual of postscripts.

I remembered my promise to Sandy – in fact, to every member of the *Pozy* crew – that the folk at home should have a true, visual account of what it was really like on the Russian Run. What would they think of my promises now? Would they fully understand that the silence wasn't my fault, that I was being officially muzzled?

In an agony of mingled rage and despair, I burst out at last: 'Don't you see, the survivors will soon start trickling home, and their accounts will lose nothing in the telling as they spread from street to street. Later, the families will start writing to the Admiralty, to their Members of Parliament, to their local newspaper, demanding why weren't they told the truth at the time. And it will be worse, far worse, in America. They'll accuse you of hushing it all up, because you are ashamed of American losses added to our own. They will say that we are to blame, whereas I know, from having been there, that whatever criticisms can be made of the overall strategy, our fellows there on the spot did their damnedest to get what was left of the convoy through to Archangel. . . .'

But it was all no use – all my arguments, all my protests. I was finally silenced by a remark which for sheer fatuity entirely summed up the attitude of all those in government departments, at that time, who were eternally nervous that some skeleton might fall out – or be pulled out – of their administrative cupboards, creating a scandal, which in its turn could precipitate their resignation.

'I am completely aware of the conditions on that Run. I have been to Iceland myself, in a cruiser, and we had a submarine alarm.'

Then I was led away by a sympathetic aide, and put back to bed. I would have been far more comfortable in my mother's house at Esher. It would be at least a month before my hand could be taken out of plaster and I would be passed fit enough to report to H.M.S. *Ganges* at last. My doctor kept on suggesting that what I needed was the still comparatively untouched peace and quiet of somewhere like Cornwall, but even when I was on my feet again I stubbornly would not leave London. I must be there, in case the ones to whom I had given my telephone number arrived back, unheralded but safe, and we could have the reunion 'up the smoke' we had promised ourselves so often, fenced in by the woodpiles of Ekonomia.

I did not mind the days so much; it was the long nights I came to dread. I had not been in the metropolis for such a stretch of time since hostilities had begun, and I had the debilitating and unnerving sensation, which I have never experienced since, of feeling an outcast and an exile in my own city. I was sick and tired of telling and retelling my story, with its infuriating, frustrating sequel of obliteration, as though the teller had been a spy, instead of a loyal supporter of his comrades. Even when a close friend, from my previous life, suggested a meal, together, I found myself making excuses. Instead, I hid myself in places where I was unlikely to encounter anyone I knew. The anonymous, indifferent blackness of a cinema was the most likely bet. I would sit through the programme twice round. The Regent Palace Hotel, of all places, became a comforting kind of sanctuary, too. I have never entered its doors since, but I can still recall a bar downstairs, with a great deal of rococo gilt decoration, and round it, in possession, would be Commonwealth airmen, using it as the anteroom to their messes, interspersed with groups of Canadians in battle-dress. No one even glanced in my direction, (I had not been wounded in their war) and after closing time I would hide in a corner of the huge lounge upstairs, ordering a cup of coffee and reading without comprehension the evening paper that someone had left behind. Often I would stay till I was the last person left, before I could force myself to face the trek home, via the now deserted coffee stall at Hyde Park Corner.

Wear something white in the blackout. Wear something white in the blackout. It was a current slogan, and for me it served as the equivalent of counting non-existent sheep through a gate. My sling was white enough, but it didn't prevent other night-walkers from bumping into me, so absolute was the blackout. Whereupon my arm would start to ache intolerably before I reached Ebury Street, and I would make that an excuse for taking a couple of sleeping pills, and hope and pray that I would have the sense not to take any more that night.

In the end, it was not the telephone that brought me the news for which I was waiting so ardently, but a telegram which read:

'THE SWIM WAS RATHER COLD BUT I MADE IT. I WILL GIVE YOU A RING. PILOT LEDA.

He was dressed in a borrowed civvy suit, when he turned up three days later, and it clearly irked him not to be in uniform. For the first thing he said was to tell me that his new uniform would be ready by Saturday. He had already reported to the Admiralty, demanding another ship, and he was clearly not pleased that he had been told he would have to wait for at least a fortnight before being re-posted.

After all, where could he go on leave? What did he want leave for? I reminded myself, as automatically I poured out for him the drink that he had vowed never to accept till it was all over.

Shaking his head, he began without a preamble, his two hands clasped very tightly against his knees. 'They got us in the dawn. You know how it is yourself, those most dangerous hours at sea, the dusk and the dawn. I was asleep in my cabin, and the next thing I remember was being on the quarter-deck, and the ship split in half. Yes, right in half. Afterwards, they said it was a tremendous explosion, but the funny thing is I can't remember any noise at all. I only remember the oil everywhere, and a kind of numbness, as though I was still asleep . . . we tried to launch a whaler . . . the one you went sailing in sometimes, in the dog watches . . . but it was too badly damaged by the explosion . . . so in the end I had to dive into the oil. When I came up, I found myself close to a carley float. Later, we rescued the Sub; – do you remember how he led the scrum on the night of the Old Sockites party? – but he had had a basinful. When he came round at last on board the rescue ship – yes, it was the *Rathlin* that picked up our survivors – he kept on saying, "Please take me out of the Drink, please take me out of the Drink." No one could make him understand that he was O.K., among friends. . . . I was very pleased when just before we parted company, your ship sent Captain Banning a signal. I made a copy for you.' He fished in his pocket, and handed it to me. *'Goodbye and good luck to a gallant ship and a gallant ship's company.'*

I couldn't concentrate on the words on the paper. I couldn't see the *Rathlin*, as she had been in the dawn, after the last great attack on the outward voyage and we had drawn alongside, and the two ships had cheered each other. I could only, with a leaping of my heart, register that my ship had been with them, on the return trip, and survived.

'The *Pozy* was with you?' I reiterated, still half unbelievingly.

'Oh yes, and the *Bramble* and the *Seagull*, too . . .'

'And she's quite all right?' I interrupted my guest.

'Oh yes, quite all right. We lost over a dozen ships, all told. But not yours. The *Pozarica* and the *Palomares* split up and went to Belfast.'

Belfast. So that was the reason why I hadn't heard. Or rather, only heard now. Second hand. What did that matter? She was safely back, and they would have come into harbour joyfully playing *'I've got sixpence, jolly, jolly sixpence,'* over the loudspeaker, alternating with *'She went and lost it at the Astor . . .'*

'Did you save anything, Aarl?' I asked. When he shook his

head, I went on mercilessly, 'Not even the pictures of your wife?' This time he jumped abruptly to his feet, exclaiming, 'What show are we going to? You promised we'd see a show together. *Fine and Dandy*? That's a good title, anyway. Do you know, Godfrey it's the first time I've ever seen a show in London.'

It wasn't till the beauty chorus danced to and fro across the stage, that he began to relax, and to allow his clenched hands to slide off his knees. Gratefully he rubbed his back against the comfortable stall. The lights, the music, the pretty girls. Everything that was contained in the matelot's phrase, 'big eats'. This was the mirage, that was the reality, though, even now, inevitably they were inclined to overlap; so that when there was a topical sketch, with the drollest of comedians, Leslie Henson, attired in full-feathered regalia, as a hen, egg-bound through too much blitzing, my companion's instinctive reaction was to whisper under the cover of the gales of laughter:

'Do you know, Godfrey, the night before we sailed, I managed to scrounge fifty pounds of potatoes. Fifty pounds. I couldn't believe it, after all the times that the Russians had said "No" to us. We planned it out that there would be a potato for every chap, every day, until we got home.'

We managed quite a spread the afternoon the entire Lawford family came to tea. Joyce Lawford was in uniform; her younger sister, Doris, was soon to join her, in the Wrens. I had not met either of the girls before, though I knew their faces almost as well as that of their brother, or for that matter, my own brother, and the father had spoken to me often of them during the long empty hours at Ekonomia, when all the photograph frames could be set out again by Mulley. I was at ease with them at once, as though I really was a member of their family; a distant cousin, perhaps, recently returned from foreign parts. I found myself admiring their typically English looks, and searching for some sign on the elder sister's face of her recent ordeal, plotting her father's convoy, on the walls of the underground room, at Liverpool, removing the discs, each with a ship's name on it, as one by one the numbers grew less and less. The only time Joyce showed any emotion was when she exclaimed, 'I shall burst if I eat another piece of cake'.

My mother had brought the cake up from Esher. It was a rich fruit one, of pre-war ingredients sent by her brother from Canada, which she had hoarded, in a tin, for some very special occasion. This must be it, since she had also denuded her garden of the last of the roses, together with a huge bunch of michaelmas daisies. When she appeared, laden down with her gifts, my heart was very full of love and gratitude that she did not chide me for not having come home, on my return, for more than a few hours. We were suddenly very close again, and as I watched and listened to the two mothers talking on the sofa, I could not help wondering, not for the first time, whether it was not their sex that was the braver one, as well as the more understanding. That afternoon my captain's lady made it aboundingly clear to me that henceforth I was to consider myself a member of their family clan as well as my own. And I have. It was like a second christening party, I decided.

'I hope you will let me come down one day and see your garden,' Mrs Lawford was saying, looking from vase to vase, with my own mother's eyes following appreciatively.

'That's *Ophelia*, and that's *Madame Butterfly*, and that single scarlet one is *Red Letter Day*. The second flowering of *Ophelia* is particularly beautiful, I always think, and *Red Letter Day* often goes on flowering with us almost up to Christmas. My family always tease me, because they say I hate cutting the flowers in my garden, but *you* will understand, being a gardener yourself. Roses particularly die so quickly, indoors. May I give you another cup of tea?'

'Oh, thank you. It's delicious. *Real* Earl Grey, isn't it? I wonder when all these things we once took for granted will come back?' They exchanged the secret, enclosed look that women share. 'You know, David is a great gardener, too. I think that's what we miss most. To be able to get our furniture out of store, and plant things again and watch them growing and increasing, and settle down in our home for good, this time.'

'Of course, I do realize how lucky I am,' she added quickly. 'David is to have a shore command at last.'

Captain Lawford had come straight from the Admiralty that afternoon, and he did not have to tell me that he had spoken his mind. The old familiar Olympian aura surrounded him once more. And he had been given the one shore command he would himself have picked: over-all authority to reorganize the trawler Base, first at Belfast, later at Liverpool, where it fell to his lot to equip all the trawlers that were to play such an important part in the D-Day landings.

Such a feeling of happiness filled my flat that afternoon, now that everyone was full of good news at last. For another of the survivors from the return trip, Commander Wynne-Edwards, turned up, too, in a brand-new uniform and with a brand-new command, looking so pink-faced and healthy that it was impossible to believe that only a fortnight ago he had had such an icy ducking, hanging on precariously to a carley float. *Leda*'s captain had news, too, of his pilot; Aarl had won promotion and would be returning to Russia as the navigating officer of the flotilla's flagship, *Bramble*.

'He's tickled to death. And to be sailing again, so soon.'

'I bet he is,' I exclaimed joyfully.

In such manner did the afternoon pass most pleasantly, in gossip of a new school year about to begin, with its changes and its gaps, inexorably filled, and myself as the newest boy of all. Outside the twilight darkening into night was shut away; there were no sirens yet, no sound of a hostile sea. The *Bramble* was still moored beside a northern quayside, taking on stores, safe and snug. And in the warm, flower-filled atmosphere of this family reunion, I had no premonition – why should I? – that the fate of the *Bramble* was to be even more implacable than that of the *Leda*. For she was destined to be sunk, with all hands, on her very next voyage – there was to be not one single survivor – when she was swallowed up in those greedy waters that we had come to dread.

Surely such single-minded devotion as her navigating officer had vouchsafed towards his two loves, his wife and his ship, deserved a better fate?

I ask that question now, but at that moment all I sensed was that one chapter of my own life was ending, even as another was beginning; even as my front door closed behind my guests and we lingered saying our goodbyes on the landing.

'Well, it's been a good party,' my captain summed up. 'When are you off to the *Ganges*?'

'On Monday morning, sir – at nine a.m. Exactly four months late.'

'Four months late? But not four months wasted,' he assured me in the quiet voice that was so seldom raised.

'They haven't allowed me to publish a single word about our trip,' I blurted out. 'The First Lord. . . .'

'I know. I heard all about it this afternoon. But you did your best. And I am sure you will be glad now of a rest from writing. One day, no doubt, many armchair critics will have their say, and then as the only writer on the spot you will be in a unique position to have the last word, and you will be able to make a book from your diaries.' He paused before he added, 'It is very important that people should not be allowed to forget this time as quickly and as easily as they did before.'

He put out his hand and shook my hand as formally as we had done at our first meeting, that calm, beguiling August afternoon, when I had been ferried across from the *Freebooter*, and had my first glimpse of his cabin on board the ship that in the end was to mean more to me than all the others.

'I won't forget what you told me about the Stripeys,' I said quickly, because I knew how much he hated any show of emotion.

He turned with a smile of relief to the others. 'Now where shall we take the girls to dine tonight, Godfrey? The Savoy, or the Ritz Grill? Somewhere without music, don't you think?'

This was the best way, I thought, taking my cue from his. 'Yes, somewhere without music,' I agreed. 'It's been rather noisy these last few nights.'

But as I listened to the muffled footsteps of my guests going down the stairs, with my captain bringing up the rear, I looked at his back disappearing and saw again his figure, in the padded blue jacket that he always wore, descending the companionway from the bridge, for a cup of kye, in that dawn when the final attempt at total destruction by the enemy was over, the last eggs from the Junkers 88s had been dropped, and their bomb racks empty, they had turned away towards their Norwegian bases. And left us, to sleep on our losses.

'Peter is now with Richard. Invincible and invulnerable they will return to succour us.'

I no longer felt alone, when I heard the front door shut. No more had I the compulsion to hide in a movie house, or stand against the wall at the bar of the Regent Palace Hotel. I did not stir from my flat again until my Monday morning summons, and spent my time tearing up the plethora of unused and now unwanted notes that had accumulated during my three years as a war reporter. All my dispatches, in triplicate, for the censor's pleasure. It gave me an empty feeling in the pit of my stomach, just to hold them in my hands. Well, I would keep the original, unpitted copy for the day when I was able to recapture it all again in a completely unexpurgated form. But the rest could go into the waste-paper basket, which filled up and was emptied and filled up again. I found myself wishing with longing that I could have made an actual bonfire of all the 'bumf', a symbolic bonfire of everything that had to do with this phase of my war-time life. Only two things in my eyes remained untouchable in the holocaust that, once begun, grew on appetite. My day-to-day diary on board the *Pozy*, and a scrap of paper that had been given to me, as a farewell offering by M.S.1 when he handed over my body, from the deck of the *Bramble*, to the *Rodman*'s captain.

I was holding it in my hand, when my front door bell rang, and there was Sandy standing on the landing, come post-haste from Stanley Gibbons in the Strand, where he had brought off a splendid swop of the unfranked Russian stamps he had acquired in Archangel, for the precious British colonials which meant so much more to him, in his philatelist's eyes.

When he advanced into my living-room, and I was able to have a good look at him under the light, I found that his pale-gold hair was neatly brushed down, the buttons of his number 1's were shining to match, and he looked as though he had just swallowed the cat's milk. He stood there in the centre of the room, slightly swaying on the balls of his feet, as though the ship was still moving under him, emptying his pocket first of his newly-acquired haul of stamps to show me, and then of more Mars bars than I had got my teeth into on the whole voyage.

'I've brought you a few rabbits,' he announced. 'I know you don't smoke, Goff. And now what about that tot of whisky you promised me?'

'Here's to the ship,' he said, a moment later, swallowing the contents of his glass in one gulp, as though it was his noonday tot of rum on board.

'Yes, here's to your ship,' I echoed.

'She's *your* ship, too, you know, now.'

'Thanks, Sandy.'

'There were quite a few buzzes going round on board about you when we reached Belfast. The strongest one was you had been put in irons by the censors.'

'Not my body, only my mouth, and my writing arm.'

'What bastards they are!'

'They're only obeying orders.'

'Then what fools the bosses are. Because they won't be able to keep your pen in irons for ever. And then you must tell the whole story, from the beginning to the end, not just for the sake of the *Pozy*, because she came through this lot, but for all the others. Especially for the families, who just get a slip of paper, and perhaps a letter afterwards. "Sorry, no more details, missing. . . ." They wouldn't mind that so much if they knew the real truth, they'd have their pride of what it was like on "P.Q.17" to warm them. Mind you, you'd have to leave out nothing. No flannel, no excuses. But you'd tell them, "We fought the enemy, and those who went down, went down still fighting. And what more can you ask of any man?" But when they muffle it all up, you begin to think you've done something to be ashamed of, and that those whose graves are in the bloody Barents Sea perished, poor sods, in vain. But they didn't, Goff, you know they didn't.'

It was then that I looked at him closely a second time, and to my astonishment this time I saw what I had never glimpsed in the Pilot's eyes. So appalled was I by the revelation that I could not speak. I could only sit there, numbly, with the record, our ship's entering-harbour record, playing itself over and over again on the gramophone, while Sandy, who was usually so silent in the dog watches, counting and recounting his stamps, broke into a torrent of words that a couple of tots of whisky had released from the hidden depths of his consciousness.

'It's always the same in the Service when something goes wrong. It always has been since I was a boy. Hush it up. Pipe down. No inquests. At least, not in public. It would do them good to hear the talk on the mess decks, sometimes, when no one from the other end of the ship can hear. You'll be stowing your gear our end of the ship from now on . . .'

He grinned at all that conjured up in his mind, and went on:

'I still can't think of you in the old rig. *You'd be far better off at the Ganges*. I guess you'll remember that, won't you? And mind you give my love to Mess 20 – well, perhaps not my love, but my respectful salutations. That's going far enough, I reckon. I can't believe I went there close on twenty years ago, and the boy who slung his hammock next to me had come all the way from Birmingham to join the Navy, and we used to take a rise out of him, because he'd never actually seen the sea in his whole blooming life. I've often wondered what happened to him and if he still likes the look of it – the sea, I mean – today.'

Now I found my voice again. 'I come from Birmingham, too. I believe it's supposed to be the place that is furthest from the sea in the whole of England. But I may have got it wrong.'

'I bet you hope your first ship as an O/D* won't give you another bellyful of the Barents Sea. You want something like the Milk Run, if you can wangle it. And beware of anyone who calls you "Jack" when you join your first ship, Goff. He's probably only been in the Service a month longer than you have. . . . It'll seem funny for you drawing an O/D's pay, but all the pay in the world isn't any use to you, or me, if we end up on a raft somewhere out there.' He got up and stood in front of the fire, as if to reassure himself. 'You'll see, what'll happen again when this little lot is tidied up. Now we're a band of bleeding heroes. It's "jolly Jack" and "good old Jack" and "Bravo and Brave Boys at sea". But tomorrow? What'll it be like then? Goff, I've known the Service in peace-time before. No one looked twice at our uniform then. We were just a necessity, and a bit of a bore at that, like coppers or pillar-boxes. Is it going to be like that again?' he ended vehemently.

When I didn't answer, comparing what he had been saying with the outburst to me of the unknown soldier in the café at Arras, just before the fall of France, that seemed already like a century away, Sandy mistook my silence, my feeling of impotence, for dismissal. As though I could ever have enough of his company, or that of any of the others. And now there was only one

* Ordinary Seaman.

thought in my mind: would I never set eyes on any of them again, once the *Pozy* had sailed under her new captain?

'Don't go yet, Sandy,' I implored him. 'Have another tot of whisky.'

But he shook his head, and handed me his gas mask to help him on. 'I must be getting back. You see, my missus really worries about me when I'm on shore. Never when I'm at sea. Women are funny, aren't they? Do you know what she said to me, when I turned up on this leave? She said, "If anything happens to you, I'm going to pack up from Sanderstead and go and live at Pompey. I shall feel nearer you, in sight of the sea." You'd have thought she'd have never wanted to look at the sea again, wouldn't you?'

'You would have thought so,' I agreed, and now I was glad that he was making a move to the door, otherwise I might have cried out a warning, and what good would that have done?

We all go to our personal destiny, I told myself, as I looked out of the window to catch a last glimpse of his trim figure passing the gaping, blitzed gap that has now been rebuilt as a block of flats. Everyone in the street pronounces it to be a great improvement, a sort of social uplift for us all. Later, when I drew the curtains and put on the light, and started clearing up our glasses and the bottles, I found that the piece of paper that Captain Crombie had given me was lying on the table. I had meant to show it to Sandy, and now it was too late. Still, that didn't matter. Because he knew so much more about it already than I would ever know.

'We have in the Navy a unique expression. We talk about a ship being in good order. It means discipline of the right sort, it means giving of service which comes more from the heart than the head, it means happiness, it means integrity, it means modesty, it means courage and selflessness.'

And as I read once more the words that were to become like a page of the New Testament to me, in the months ahead, I heard Sandy's voice again, exclaiming:

'Mind you, there were some good things about the *Andrew*, in the old days. Plenty. You could leave your pay on the table, in your mess, if you were an O/D, when you went to clean yourself up in the wash-house and you'd find it there when you got back. And blokes didn't become killicks overnight, and officers in six months.'

Well, that wouldn't happen to me, I exclaimed aloud. And indeed, it didn't. As for the rest, no doubt it would all come out in the wash. And it did.

Part Two
Ordinary Seaman

Ian Smith, the
·er behind a
troversial throne

At breakfast with
the Adamsons
beside the riverbank

Adamson tells
.bout Elsa's

Ordinary Seaman G. H. Winn

'When a ship that is tired returneth
With the signs of the sea showing plain
Men place her in dock for a season,
And her speed she reneweth again.
So shalt thou, lest perchance thou grow weary,
In the uttermost parts of the sea,
Pray for leave for the good of the Service
As much and as oft as may be.

BUT COME BACK TO IT.'

The exhortation was written in letters of faded gold on the shadowy side of the vast drill shed in Chatham Barracks. I imagine it is still there today, though I have never been back to look. For my own part, these lines by an unknown hand came to have a strange fascination for me as day after day, waiting for a draft to my first ship as an O/D, I crossed and re-crossed that No Man's Land. It was filled with an eddying concourse of sprogs like myself, fresh from their initial training at H.M.S. *Ganges,* mixed up with transit ratings, drafted back to base from one ship and soon to be despatched to another, and survivors, whose bizarre attire would have made them stand out even had their faces not had the grey look of sapless old men, compared with those of us who had so obviously only been dressed in bell-bottoms for a few weeks.

I don't think I have ever felt quite so forlorn as on that Friday evening in January 1943, when yet another wartime draft from H.M.S. *Ganges* was discharged into the murky twilight of the drill shed, and suddenly, with a hopeless sinking sensation in one's stomach, one became hideously aware that from this moment one was completely on one's own. The hand-picked petty officers who had nurse-maided us with such patience through our initiation into the Service, had vanished for ever from our ken; so apparently had our class-mates in the navigation school, and our companions in Hut 46, which had been our home for the last three months. And how snug and safe with its tiers of bunks that hut now seemed in comparison with this gaunt, impersonal shunting yard, I thought, as I peered again at the slip of paper with my name on it, that I was supposed to hand over to the mess caterer, GG6 Anson. But that meant as much or as little to me as a street in Peking written in Chinese lettering. How should I ever find my way in this labyrinthine cluster of buildings?

I visualized myself lugging my kitbag, now seeming as heavy as a sack of coals, together with my newly allotted hammock, in which for the first time that night I was hoping to get some sleep, along endless passages leading nowhere. To such a pitch did my panic mount that I almost considered jettisoning my kit and making a bolt into the blackout of the streets, pursued by the voice of authority barking over the loudspeakers. *Take your kit-bags to your mess, and your hammock to the Tunnel where you will sleep tonight.* But where was the Tunnel? And what was the Tunnel? And why did everyone have to sleep there, newcomers and old hands alike?

I have often wondered since what would have been my ultimate fate that night had I not suddenly been confronted, from amid the sea of anonymous bods swirling round me, by the smiling face of an ex-policeman, used to dealing with flotsam of one kind and another, until, like myself, he had volunteered to join the Royal Navee. Charlie and I had on one or two occasions found ourselves side by side cleaning up the fag-ends, in the dawn, off the parade ground at the *Ganges.* Having already been in Chatham Barracks for a week, he was delighted now with the opportunity to display his knowledge. When I called out, with rekindled hope in my voice, 'Do you know where Anson is?' he volunteered at once to translate and be my guide.

Even in my very short time in the Service I had learnt that the most likely way of obtaining either essential knowledge or assistance of any kind was to look dumb and helpless. Even the toughest Stripeys would usually surrender to such tactics. It was the cocky ones, who imagined they knew all the answers, that came a cropper.

'Anson Block. That's bang facing you as you come up from the steps from the parade ground,' Charlie was explaining. 'GG6. That's on the same staircase as I am.' When I continued to look blankly and beseechingly at him like a lost dog, he clearly decided that action was the best form of defence, and to my eternal gratitude stooped down, picked up my kitbag and put it over his shoulder. 'Here, take your hammock and follow me.' As my hammock was about a tenth of the weight of my kitbag, I obeyed with alacrity. 'What watch are you?' he asked over his shoulder. 'Blue. Oh, bad luck. You won't get out of barracks till Monday night.'

'They told us we'd get a week's leave on arriving here,' I protested.

'Oh, that's a carefully distilled buzz to lure us all here. Otherwise, you might have gone absent without leave, in transit.'

I thought wistfully of the train that had brought this Friday's draft here from Shotley, and the carriageful of my chums from Hut 46: Ron Ewington and Ted Dowsett, the two eighteen-year-old inseparables who had worked on the roads, before they enlisted; and the boy nick-named Enoch, after a radio favourite of the period; and young Alan, the massive miner's son from Durham, who was for ever boasting with just pride that his Ma was the best cook in their street. Where were they this minute? Already separated and departed from my ken. It was my first abrupt awareness of how transitory were most relationships in the Service; together today, gone tomorrow.

'Do you know what ship you've got yet, Charlie?'

'Yes, I'm going to a newly-commissioned frigate.'

'Oh, I hope I get something bigger myself. I am always so frightfully sick in small ships.'

At this self-reminder – especially of the time I had found myself coughing up blood, since there was nothing else left in my stomach, when I was out as a reporter in a rescue tug, operating from Campbeltown – the drill shed, which we were temporarily leaving behind, didn't seem quite such a dungeon. At least, there was a firm deck beneath my feet, and no shaking and rolling, no stench of machine oil, no backwash from the galleys.

However, the barometer of my spirits was again registering a deep depression when we eventually reached GG6. The lair of the Artful Dodger in *Oliver Twist* seemed like an anteroom in Buckingham Palace, in comparison. After the imposed orderliness of our hut at the *Ganges*, where we were for ever being lectured on how pussar the Navy was, it was something of a shock to discover the sprawling heaps of baggage, some of which was being used as seats by groups of ratings in various states of undress, smoking round the antediluvian fireplace. The burning coals were the only relief to the sombreness of the scene. We had been warned by the captain of the *Ganges* in his farewell address that we should find things very different at Chatham, but I don't think any of us were prepared for exactly what we did find, though, superficially, the layout was the same as on the mess deck of a battleship.

Rows of mess tables divided the long room diagonally. A partition separated the two sides. On the top of the partition was a mass of hammocks; along one wall, a mass of kitbags; in one corner a mass of pegs; in fact, it was a mass invasion, as I was to discover at breakfast next morning, when I waited in vain for a plate, a knife and fork, a cup. There just wasn't sufficient cutlery to go round. If you were lucky, an early bird allowed you to have the loan of his plate and cup after he'd finished, but more often than not by then the grub had given out.

At the moment, supper was my immediate and urgent objective. 'Your best hope,' Charlie was advising, 'is the canteen. I'll take you across. What they serve's excellent when you can get it, especially the ham-and-egg. But there's the usual stampede. Your only hope is to say you're a survivor, just come ashore. You are one, anyway, when you've been in this place a week. Mind you,' he added, with the judicial fairness of someone once connected with the forces of law and order, 'I don't think you can really blame the authorities. It's simply that, owing to the war, about six times as many men are passing through here all the time, as in peace. They just can't cope. Though some chaps say they don't make any effort to improve things, so that almost everyone welcomes a draft to sea.'

I dumped my kit a little apart from the rest of the mountainous pile, so that I would be able to recognize it again easily after supper, and was about to hang up my oilskins and overcoat on one of the empty pegs, when my companion stopped me in my tracks. 'You'll never see them again.' When I looked at him with the innocent surprise of a sprog, he continued cheerfully, 'Everything is liable to be "borrowed" here. You'll be lucky if someone doesn't cut the bottom out of your kitbag. That's a favourite trick. I've heard half a dozen fellows moaning about it, even in the short time I've been here. There's no loyalty to your mess, or messmates, because you don't know who they are. Many of them you never see twice. This is like a waiting room at a station, and everyone for himself. Another common trick is to pinch your blankets out of your hammock, and then lash it up again. You can't carry your hammock around with you all day, but I should certainly advise you to stick to your coats, till you get a locker. And you'll be very fortunate to get a locker,' he ended his depressing recital, 'unless you have the luck to catch someone just going on draft. But you'll have to be nippy to get to the head of that queue.'

'But all our gear is marked, Charlie,' I remarked, with an ingenuousness which often came back to mock me later, at sea, when in swift succession I 'mislaid' four balaclavas, three scarves, two hats, two pairs of seaboot stockings (most desperate loss of all), a collar, writing case, and a gas mask that I, in my turn, had had to replace, borrow, or else be in the rattle. I was always hearing echoes of confirmation by the stripeys on board of what Sandy had told me on his farewell visit to Ebury Street; of how, in peace-time in the *Andrew* any rating could leave his pay on his mess table, go away on watch, and still find it there four hours later. These stripeys were very bitter sometimes about the gradual erosion of the honourable standards that once upon a time had ruled the mess deck; very fierce, too, in their protective maintaining of other immemorial rites and customs. As I found to my cost one evening, months later, on board H.M.S. *Cumberland*, when, lured from my mess bench to the next-door one a yard or so away, by the drooling noises of admiration for a fresh lot of pin-ups about to adorn the bulkhead, I precipitately found myself sprawling on the deck with a furious three-badge stripey louring over me and demanding in a rum-nurtured voice: 'Would you keep your hat on your bloody head if you was visiting a neighbour's home?'

It seemed hardly tactful to counter in my defence that I had to keep my hat on my head, even in the Heads* let alone when I was in my own mess, because if I put it down for five minutes, I might never see it again. Such replacements of kit were scanty in those Arctic waters in which I was soon to find myself once again.

Charlie was leading the way to the canteen, where the scene reminded me irresistibly of the Bateman cartoon suggesting what might happen if every member decided unexpectedly to visit the London Club of the R.A.C. for luncheon on the same day. Swiftly (I was learning fast) I grabbed two just-vacated seats while Charlie fought his way through the scrum to the counter. 'Got a light, chum?' asked one of my neighbours. As I felt for the matchbox in my pocket, I had a contrasting vision of myself lighting the twin candles in their Queen Anne sconces in the dining-room at home. I saw my mother taking her place opposite me, and the sheen of the freshly-picked roses between us on the dark, polished mahogany table. . . . No, Sponge, you've had your dinner, that's quite enough for you . . . and my Sealyham staring up at me with his eternally moist, hungry eyes. Was he missing his master? Not as much as his master was missing the civilized order of the home life he had once taken a great deal too much for granted.

Glancing round me, I wondered idly what my companions were themselves thinking, as they fought for their suppers. Were they remembering their homes, too? Longing to be back in Civvy Street, even if their particular street had had its baptism of bombs? Had they realized, when they joined up, that war meant this, just this, so much more than the drama and excitement of battles?

'Only sausages left,' Charlie was saying in the kind of resigned voice that everyone seemed to acquire, civilians and service folk alike, from the boredom of standing in too many queues with too little success.

'*Only sausages left*. It would make a splendid title for a book about the long littleness of war, instead of the long littleness of life,' I suggested.

'Will you write it? A lot of the fellows at the *Ganges* said you'd only joined to get material for your writings. Copy, isn't that what you call it?'

Despite the curiosity, rather than hostility, in his voice, there

* lavatories

was still a touch of the bobby with his notebook. However, I did not mind answering him frankly, especially after his rescue operation.

'No, I joined for exactly the opposite reason. To be able with a clear conscience and much relief to put away my pen for the duration. Afterwards? Well, I simply don't know.'

The future, and what it might contain for Ordinary Seaman JX 377610, seemed at that moment far too remote and unreal a prospect to attempt any kind of confident prediction. At the note of uncertainty in my voice, my companion who like myself was older than the average age of the *Ganges* intakes, and himself already married and a father, spoke with a surprisingly articulate urgency, reminding me of the unknown foot-slogger who had addressed me with similar passion in the café at Arras.

'You *must* write it all down one day. If you don't, who will? Not the historians, they'll be producing learned tomes about the strategy, and handing out sarcastic bottles from the sidelines, while the generals and the admirals will be equally busy explaining away the disasters and the losses as never being *their* fault, and taking all the credit for any victories, which God knows have been precious few so far. But you are seeing it from such a different angle. That is, if you stay on the lower deck, and don't become a C.W. candidate*.'

I shook my head decisively about that last proviso. My mind was completely made up and remained so, never wavering. I was very conscious of my deficiencies and the power of command was one of them. 'I'd make a lousy officer,' I admitted candidly. 'I hate giving orders to anyone, even in Civvy Street. All the responsibility I desire now is centred round keeping my boots clean. By the way, Charlie, I learnt a marvellous tip from another ex-bobby at the *Ganges*. He advised me that a little spit on the toecaps works miracles. And it does.'

Maybe. But my saviour that night, whose fair halo of hair had made him seem like the Archangel Gabriel when I had come upon him in the encircling gloom of the drill shed, was not to be diverted from his thesis.

'After all, a professional reporter like you is trained – just as they trained me to pick out suspects and skates, and sense when something funny was going on, when I was on the beat. Of

* candidate for a commission

course, I know that a lot of newspapers exaggerate their stories, and the public lap it up, but you won't have to try your hand at fiction at all. Just describe what it's really like being dumped in Chatham Barracks. If you consider your temporary mess is a muckhole, you wait till you see the Tunnel. No one could exaggerate what sleeping in the Tunnel is like. There ought to be questions asked about it in Parliament, and I bet there would be if prisoners of war, or conchies, had to sleep there.'

'Why, what's so terrible about it?' I asked, my stomach, which had been temporarily assuaged by a lashing of sausages and a mug of hot, over-sweet tea, now succumbing to a fresh wave of apprehension.

'You come and see for yourself, chum.'

And I did. In any case, it was compulsory for every rating housed inside Chatham Barracks and not the fortunate possessor of a night ashore pass, to sling his hammock in the Tunnel. This Tunnel, I understand, had been built originally at the time of the Munich scare, for the safe custody of important documents, not for the accommodation of a horde of human beings. But when the air raids commenced in savage earnest, it was appreciated that live bodies were more important for the war effort than dusty files. So sirens wailing or no sirens, down you go, boys.

In the days when I really was a boy, I used to find it difficult to hide my *ennui* when old soldiers, encountering each other by chance, would swop over my head their reminiscences of the mud of the Somme. It was only when I saw that small masterpiece of a film, *Oh What a Lovely War*, that the Battle of the Somme assumed an entirely new and permanent significance in my consciousness.

Just as with the former gun-fodder of that terrible campaign of attrition in Flanders, so, not surprisingly, do those of us who came to Chatham, equally unfledged and unbaptised, find in the Tunnel, whenever we meet, a source of unending anecdote. Yet it is a sobering thought that a new generation (of matelots, too, for I imagine that the Tunnel has long since passed into antiquity) may find our old sailors' tales equally divorced from contemporary interest.

I have to admit, too, that there was no mud. Everywhere the cement was scrupulously dry, and everywhere there were ventilation shafts, but nevertheless, you were forcibly aware of a curiously disembodied atmosphere (despite the living bodies hung like hams in a storage vault all round you) as you penetrated further and further down the incline, and came to the crossroads. Here you were faced with the decision, whether to turn right or keep straight on in search of a gash billet for your hammock, and as you hesitated, and began to breathe in more deeply the filtered air that was neither fresh nor foul, you had an extraordinary sensation of having become a disincarnate spirit about to enter hell on earth.

I have earlier described my trip in a Sunderland flying boat, when the vibration was so great that you could only speak to the pilot through a voice-tube, but throughout the fourteen hours we were airborne I had no sense of claustrophobia such as I had now. Indeed, had not Charlie been with me that first night, I doubt if I would have had the will-power to continue to push my way right to the end of the Tunnel, past the early comers who had already slung their hammocks from the low roof, and were industriously employed tying the laces of their boots together, and hanging them next to their heads, not unlike the child who refuses to be parted from his favourite toy, even in sleep. The boots smelt rather more like boots than usual, and monotonously banged your head as you passed. Now thanks to my initiation at Charlie's hands, I did not have to ask yet another stupid question as to why they were hung like that, and not placed on the deck. Each owner had a very shrewd idea they would not be there when 'Wakey, wakey, rise and shine' came round once more. Moreover, if you did not make a pillow of your tunic and trousers, they might very easily not be there, either. As for your money, the best place to hide it was inside your socks, underneath the soles of your feet.

Even when we reached the farthest end, it still looked as though I should have to sleep standing up all night. Every hook was already doubly employed, Eventually Charlie spread my hammock on a shelf, one of a series at one side, about a foot above the ground. It reminded me at once of the type of alcove that in a cathedral supports the sleeping effigy of a crusader, though Charlie's own reaction was rather different; he was only concerned as to whether, when I had crawled in, with the roof of the next shelf two inches above my head, the weight of my body would press my hammock down on the deck. And that would be most unseamanlike. He kept on stressing how important it was, even in such an unnaturally confined space, to keep one's hammock taut so that it did not sag in the middle. All my thoughts were on sleep. I hid my watch, put my boots between myself and the outer wall of the Tunnel, which I suppose was about ten feet wide, and crawled between my blankets. At once I felt the clammy coldness of the deck's cement floor against my backside. I was too tired to care.

'Okay, Godfrey?'

'Okay, Charlie. My first night in a hammock. I didn't expect it to be like this, but thanks for everything. Anyway, I bet it's worse in a German concentration camp.'

A couple of shell-backs looked over the edge of their own hammocks and gave me a pulverizing look. A blue light shone down, which exactly matched their scrutiny in its intensity. They clearly took a poor view of such conversational exchanges. And they gave me the same look again the next morning when I reached GG6 again, unwashed, with my mouth feeling like the inside of a parrot's cage. With wistful eyes I searched the plate-rack and found it completely empty. The killick of the mess? The mess caterer? I had become so accustomed to P.O. Ellwood presiding like a benevolent butler over the meal times in Hut 46 that I was hopelessly lost.

The two benches each side of the table were overflowing with strangers in singlets. Compared with my messmates at the *Ganges*, they appeared sea-beaten, like characters from a Conrad novel. Not that they looked any older than I felt at that moment, as gingerly I squeezed my backside on to the extreme edge of one of the benches. 'What do I do about getting a plate and a cup and some grub?' I at last ventured to ask my neighbour. He did not answer, but continued to masticate his own breakfast even more loudly, rubbing a piece of bread round the rim of his plate, with the passion of Popeye.

So this was the mucking-in spirit of the lower deck, of which I had spoken so eloquently on so many propaganda platforms! Of course, later I was to appreciate that it wasn't fair to judge the spirit of a naval barracks, where you were unlikely to have the same neighbour for two consecutive meals, by a comparison with the close-knit comradeship engendered in any ship, pussar or otherwise, that is actually doing sea-time. But at that moment, still cowed by the impact of my introduction to the Tunnel, I relapsed into disillusioned silence, finding for once in my life a situation that was completely beyond me. I just sat there, staring down at the table, as though I expected a miracle to happen and food to appear from nowhere and be placed in front of me. And the extraordinary thing is, that is exactly what did occur. True, the plate had already been used once, and congealed bacon fat rimmed its edge; but what did that matter, if there were a double rasher and two chunks of bread on top of it?

I did not dare touch it at first. I was so certain there must be a catch somewhere. I had usurped someone else's place. I braced my shoulders for the heavy hand that was about to descend upon me. It did descend, but when I looked up fearfully, to my surprise and delight it was to discover another familiar face from the *Ganges* smiling down at me; MacMichael, the young Scot from Edinburgh, who was a dab at knots and splices and had coached me the night before the exams, though he almost despaired of my hands that were all thumbs; Mac, whose pink cheeks and thick curly hair looked doubly fresh in this frowsty gathering.

'I couldn't pinch a knife and fork. We shall have to use our fingers. You make a start. I've got my eye on a cup.' He was off again, and a moment later I saw him snatch a cup from the hand of one of the silent shell-backs, who suddenly got back his voice to demand, 'Do you draw, Jock?' Mac knew that he wasn't referring to art, but he also knew that you had to be twenty-one before you could draw your tot. When he shook his head, the old hand instantly lost interest again. No doubt he had the glimmer of a plan of exchanging cutlery at every meal for sippers, or even 'gulpers', from the sprog, who was now continuing his scrounge, in search of tea. As I watched him depart backstage, it vexed me to have to admit that despite the fact that he had only just left school, whereas I had been earning my living for close on twenty years, he'd shown far more initiative than I had, and far more resilience, too. Not without reason they call the Scots the colonizers of the world, I thought. I have long since lost touch with both Charlie and Mac, who made my first twelve hours at Chatham bearable, and I only wish I could send them a copy of this chronicle so that they will know the years have not dimmed my sense of gratitude.

If I were asked what had been the worst week-end of my life,

I would have no hesitation in declaring that it was that January week-end in 1943, when my second night was, if possible, more dismal than the first, since I found myself marched off to be on sentry, during the middle watch; on guard, for the whole of our floor of Anson block, against home-grown thieves. You were handed out gaiters and an impressive khaki belt to give you an air of authority, but heaven knows what I should have done had I surprised a light-fingered matelot at one of the piles of kit-bags. I have never seen myself in an heroic role, and I only kept awake because I was so scared of being caught nodding at my post.

They believed in keeping you busy, however brief your sojourn among them. In Sunday's dawn, after two nights of little sleep, I found myself in a gang, cleaning the cigarette ends and other litter off the path outside Anson Divisional Office.

With one wary eye cocked for Authority in the form of P.O.s on the prowl, my chance comrades voiced their feelings in a manner with which I was in complete sympathy, though I was as yet not so vociferous as they.

'It's muster here, and muster there, and if you ask a P.O. where you are supposed to be, you are like as not in the rattle for being adrift. But I ask you, how 'yer supposed to know if you dussn't ask?

'The great thing, chum, is to have yer answer all pat and ready. Now supposing you are doing a loaf, and someone catches up on you and asks what you are supposed to be doing of, don't go dumb, or you've had it. If it's an officer, salute smartly and say, "Shall I carry on, sir?" and he'll salute you back and say, "Yes, carry on." You've hypnotized him, see. It's something they say in their sleep. But if it's a bleeding P.O., you have to be more crafty. Before he can start on you, tell him you are on the way to the butcher's.'

'The butcher's?' I echoed, making the perfect stooge.

'Yus. The doc – in the sick bay. He's bound to say carry on, cos, if you was to die, he'd be in the rattle himself. See?

'An oppo of mine was waiting draft to his ship. He'd got his draft, but didn't fancy filling in the time till the day, scavenging, like we're doing. So he has a real bright idea. He goes to the dentist's waiting room up at Collingwood, the library it is, and sits himself down in an empty chair, and goes on blooming well sitting there the whole week. The dental tiffy comes in and shouts out names, but never of yours truly, of course. In fact, they never caught up on him. That is, not till he was tin-fished in the Med.'

I began wondering if I might get a draft to the Med myself. It would be a change from the cold of the Atlantic, the North Sea and the Arctic wastes. I didn't fancy going back on that route at all. Unfortunately, you had no choice unless you tried to do a wangle, or a swop, and I hadn't joined to do that. Better just to wait till your turn came, your name was called, and you picked up another slip of paper from an office in the drill shed, this time with your ship on it. It was a haphazard sort of lottery, but there was a detached remoteness about it which, in a way, at least as far as I was concerned, was a relief. So far I had been able largely to maintain my anonymity. I was desperately anxious to continue like that; to leave my destiny utterly in other hands.

Not that I was exactly delighted when that Sunday afternoon I found myself chosen, for the second time in twenty-four hours, for patrol duties, this time in the town. Two P.O.s and two ratings. The party split, dividing the streets in two, and despite my imposing belt and my gaiters, the January cold seeped through me. I have never known four hours pass more slowly, except in the port director at sea, and I hadn't come to that comparison yet. *Your top button's undone. Put your hat on straight. Take your hands out of your pockets.* My superior companion walked with a stately measure, as befitted his position, but apart from uttering stereotyped rebukes whenever he got a chance, exchanges between ourselves were non-existent. It had already been impressed upon me that you never spoke to a P.O., in ordinary conversation, unless he spoke first to you. At last he did. 'It's as cold as bleeding Russia,' he volunteered.

'As a matter of fact, it wasn't at all cold when we were there. Steamy hot most of the time, and we had a plague of mosquitoes.'

I wasn't deliberately coaxing a positive reaction from the august figure beside me, but I certainly received one. First a cautious glance to port. Was I masquerading as a sprog, in obviously new matelot's clothing? 'When was you there?' he demanded suspiciously. I told him. Six months ago. Was that all it was? It seemed already like another century. How amused I was to see the abrupt change in my companion's demeanour.

He not only unfroze, he actually smiled. For a moment I thought he was about to break all bounds and shake my hand. 'We was on that convoy, too.' 'Were you?' This was more than I had ever expected. 'Yes, we was the Admiral's flagship.'

Now I was released. The words came pouring out.

'But I visited the *London* the night before we sailed from Iceland. I came on board with my captain, after dinner. I was his guest, you see, for the trip. It was the first time I had ever been on board a county-class cruiser. She seemed as big as the Savoy Hotel. When the party was breaking up in the ward-room, a message came for me, asking me down to the Warrant Officers' mess. It was a wonderful excuse to stay on. Flags offered to take me there. There was a gunner with a ukelele. He was terrific. He went on performing for hours. Do you remember? "We are the London boys?" In the end, Flags sent me back to my own ship in the Admiral's barge, but I hardly remember anything about that, except there was the most marvellous dawn I've ever seen. The aftermath of the midnight sun.'

I had made a vow to myself to keep my mouth shut about the past, and I had managed pretty well at the *Ganges*, but here I was breaking it. I couldn't help myself. I was resavouring the emotions of that return across the water, when I felt as though I was the solitary spectator of the first dawn of all.

'It must be a bit of a change, like, for you.'

I am sure he did not mean it unkindly, but of course it brought me back to where I was, and what I was doing now, with a bang.

I looked round me, blinking. We were abreast of one of Chatham's hotels. An urgent thought stuck me. Tonight I would have to sleep again in the accursed Tunnel, but tomorrow I was ashore and, by fair means or foul, was absolutely determined to sleep in a bed. Now my patrol leader had unthawed, dare I risk it? I blurted out my surely harmless request to nip in, and book myself a room. Instantly his expression changed. We were back to square one. The patrol must, at all times, keep to the streets. But supposing all the rooms were booked by the time I got ashore tomorrow? He didn't even deign to answer that one. We were moving off again. *Do up your top buttons. Put your hat on straight. Take your hands out of your pockets.*

When we finally got back to the drill shed, I was so numb

with the January cold that I took refuge, not in the canteen but in the washhouse, which in all naval barracks, and equally in all big ships, too, becomes a communal meeting place, the equivalent of a lower deck club with the heating strength of a Turkish bath. The average British matelot is about the cleanest human being in the world. He is for ever washing either his person or his clothes, scrubbing his mate's back or having his own scrubbed, while passing the latest buzzes along the line.

By chance I found myself standing at the basins next to a stoker, stripped to the waist, with *I love Mother* tattooed on his chest. In no time he had invited me to scrub his back, and in payment for this service proceeded to regale me with a dissertation on the advantages and disadvantages of deserting from the Service. Temporarily depressed though I was by the prospect of the Tunnel ahead of me, I hadn't contemplated quite such a desperate step, enticing as my ablutions neighbour now made it sound. For he described at considerable length how he knew a bloke who had got away with it for months and had had a smashing time.

'Got a job as a lorry driver, he did. Got double pay for driving all night through the blitz. Got himself more beer than he could properly swallow, and some high-class dames, too. Got himself some smashing civvies, and bought himself a stolen identity card into the bargain. And not a runt in his street opened their bleeding mouth. Police kept on coming round, and only got a sore tongue for their pains. Yes, I am telling you it was a bit of all right.'

His enthusiasm enveloped me in a cloud of warm steam. He expanded and glowed as he stood there beside me, drying himself. I had a sudden memory of a crook whose acquaintance I had made at the Roehampton swimming pool. When in due course he came clean with me, he said something that had stayed in the back of my mind ever since. How he always wore plus-fours when he came up West, because surely the police would think twice before picking up someone as a suspect who was dressed in the golfing attire of the day.

The memory, the comparison, was like a far-off preface. It was the postscript I was interested in now. The true life-story I had just been told was surely too full of detail not to be a personal one. I gave the kind of suspicious sideways glance at my new friend that I had been subjected to earlier in the afternoon by my superior on patrol. 'A bit of all right for your mate?' I echoed, with some emphasis on the last part of the question.

'Yus, until they caught up with him.'

'And how did they do that, if the neighbours didn't natter?'

'Well, he was in one of them pull-ups for lorries, having a cup of coffee, and warm when the police raided it. Wanted to check up on all identity cards. That was okay. He had his identity card handy all right. But they weren't satisfied. P'raps they were after stolen jewellery, or some'at. Anyway, they started to search all the customers. Put up your arms and empty your pockets, sweetheart. Then he was properly copped. They found his naval paybook in his pocket.'

'His naval paybook?' I echoed again, and more incredulously this time. 'I simply don't believe that. He wouldn't have been such a fool. Why, that would have been the first piece of direct evidence he would have burnt.'

'You'd have thought so, I agree, chum, but I'm telling you he didn't. So they found it and brought him back to this bleeding dump.'

I turned away. The new boy was being taken for a sucker. No writer would dare use such a plot in a book. It was too improbable. Of course, it was true that it was drummed into you from the day you joined that a sailor without his paybook was a sailor adrift. So you clung to your paybook as though it was your marriage lines. But. . . .

'But you still don't believe me?' I shook my head stubbornly and a bit sulkily, too. *I love Mother*, whom I was never to encounter again, had come up behind me at the door of the wash-house, and hit me exuberantly on the shoulder. 'Well, anyway, thanks, chum for scrubbing my back. No one did that for me in Canterbury.'

Now the emphasis was on his side, and even more marked. Canterbury was Chatham's glasshouse. He could hardly have made his meaning plainer. Twenty-four hours later, having double-checked that my own paybook was in my pocket, I escaped from prison myself for a few hours, and made my way as quickly as I could to the hotel that I had not been allowed to enter as a prospective customer the day before.

An elderly female, more quailing than any jaunty,* was enthroned behind the reception desk. To my enquiry she replied with smug satisfaction, 'We are booked right up'.

'You don't think there's a chance of a cancellation? There isn't a bed in a sitting-room, perhaps?' I continued with desperate politeness.

'We can't make beds. Why don't you try the Sailors' Home or the Sailors' Rest?' She was as much aware as I was that they were always booked up days ahead. Her eyes left me for the group of officers, warming their backsides round the fire at the end of the lounge. How I hated them at that moment, already snugly ensconced, but I hated her even more. I felt myself beginning to tremble, as desperately I raised my voice, not caring who heard my lament. 'But I *must* get a bed.' At that, her expression became even more supercilious, as she put me in my place, once and for ever. 'Beggars can't be choosers,' she said.

Yes, she really made that extraordinary remark, at a time when all barriers were supposed to be down, all class distinctions swallowed up in the universal black-out. But not all rank distinctions and snobberies. They were stronger than ever, as I was learning fast. There are some things one never forgets in one's life. This unedifying verbal exchange was one of them, though to make remembrance doubly sure I repeated it word for word in my next letter home. It was only after my mother's death that I discovered that she had kept all my wartime letters, and I have that particular one beside me as I write.

'Don't worry,' it went on, 'I got a bed all right in the end at a much nicer place called The Prince of Wales. Plus a chop for my supper, what a luxury, and breakfast next morning at half-past six, though they aren't supposed to serve breakfast till eight. All because of Nora who seems to run everything.

'Nora's husband has always been in the Navy and he has been sunk twice, and is now, as a P.O., commissioning a new ship. Let's hope for all their sakes that it will be third time lucky. Because with their two small sons they deserve a bit of luck. Nora treats all her customers, gold braid or O/Ds like myself, exactly the same . . .'

Nora was a beautiful woman: not just beautiful that evening because she found me a bed, but beautiful at all times, and in all

* Naval police.

lights. She had very dark hair, which she wore piled high on her head, carved cheek-bones, and a pale magnolia skin that enhanced her equally dark eyes. She had a graceful figure, too. I came to think that, had she been dressed up and painted by de Lazlo, she would have looked more truly regal than any of his patrician portraits. I can still recapture the shock of surprise I had that first evening when I came upon her at the end of the dining-room, guarding her two small sons as they worked at their prep.

They will both be grown up now, and following, perhaps, in their father's footsteps, in the Senior Service. I do not know. But I would like to think that they may chance upon this and read this tribute to their mother, who treated all the hotel guests, whatever their rank or accent, exactly the same. We all started alike from scratch. Neither of us knew each other's names that first evening. I was simply another prospective customer, and she was serving the suppers, and I was lucky; there was both a bed and a chop left. I suppose to some it doesn't sound such bounty today, but all the same, I wonder just how many ex-servicemen have come to look upon the whole race of women with new eyes and new sense of grateful respect because of a similar welcome and show of spontaneous kindness in some strange town, far from their native heath.

You may have a few pints in the bar, if you are in funds; you may pay visits to other ports of call in the course of the evening, such as, at Chatham, the Long Bar at the Lion, or The Prince of Wales, but all that is only leading up to the supreme moment when you get into bed, after having had a bath, and feel the cool linen against your skin, and it is as though you have never slept between clean sheets before. Alas, only too soon you are crawling out again, in the despairing half light to catch whatever transport there is back to your camp or barracks. You certainly don't imagine you'll be served breakfast at that hour. Yet when I stumbled down the stairs, the sleep still in my eyes, there was Nora at the door of the dining-room. 'You're late,' she said severely, standing over me as she had done with her sons the night before, while I gulped down the glorious fresh coffee and the ration of bacon that I had never expected, even in my eventually euphoric mood of the night before. Not another word was spoken between us. There wasn't any time or breath to spare. Nora simply regarded this extra service, it was plain, as part of her wartime duties, and she never let me down or turned me away once during the weeks I was waiting for my first draft chit to sea.

Even if occasionally Nora took a morning off duty, she always provided an understudy in the person of Joyce, who in contrast was plump and coltish, and served behind the bar with a slightly wary look. You suspected that men in uniform had little glamour for her; she had coped with too many of them. Whereas Nora was somewhere about my age, Joyce was only seventeen. One morning when I arrived in the dining-room, Joyce was already there, sitting at a table, reading a book. She was wearing no make-up at that early hour, and without it her protective mask had vanished. 'What are you reading at half-past six in the morning?' I asked her with some curiosity. She looked up with the kind of smile I had never intercepted across the counter. '*Gone With The Wind*. It's such a lovely story. I am reading it for the third time,' she said.

Towards the end of the war, when my acquaintanceship with the screen Scarlet O'Hara was to blossom unexpectedly into a close friendship which was to last till the end of her life, and was to come to mean a great deal to me, I told Vivien Leigh all about Joyce's taste in reading, and about Nora and The Prince of Wales at Chatham, and how fortunate I had been. It delighted her as much as my account, at a later date, of my return trip to the *Ganges* to pick up a bus load of post-war recruits so that they could have a night out in Ipswich, with 'big eats' thrown in, seeing my own film, *Holiday Camp*, which was showing that week.

Ranks, who had made the picture and a small fortune out of it, decided that it would be a nice publicity gimmick if the author of the original script was photographed for the local paper with a group of latter-day sprogs. I concurred, hoping that our guests would not notice the unconscious irony of the film's title when applied to their present occupation of Hut 46 and all the others in the Covered Way. What I myself secretly registered was that somehow they looked so baby-faced and physically undeveloped compared with our draft. Or was it simply my imagination at play, in the same manner as policemen on point duty appear to grow younger, sometimes impertinently so, every year? I suppose it should have occurred to me that I myself was already six years older than on those wintry mornings when I had cleaned and polished the outsize spittoons in the P.O.s' mess, as the favourite, as far as I was concerned, on the list of unskippable pre-breakfast chores. True, there was a monumental fug compounded of the fumes of stale baccy and stale beer, but that surely was infinitely preferable to cleaning-up the parade ground at that hour, with a bitter wind off the North Sea blowing all the dust in your face. Instead, I used to take heart the moment I was faced again with the convivial signs of last night's solo school, the tables laid out, the seats still warm with the imprint of their occupants, massive as battle-wagons and equally as reassuring.

I am not one for going back in life, ever. Whether the journey is likely to prove a sentimental or unsentimental return, it is equally over and done with before it has started, as far as I am concerned. I have never, for instance, been back to Chatham, because I am sure that Nora has long since left The Prince of Wales, and it would all be so different, even the tailor's shop in the High Street where we had our streamlined No. 1s made for us, distinctly unregulation in cut, to wear with a buccaneer's swagger each time we went 'up the Smoke'. Usually, yesterday's memories, tinted by Time, are so much more pleasurable than today's reality.

Sharply I learned that lesson for all time when I was foolish enough to revisit Madeira after the war, and found the atmosphere changed out of all recognition since my almost annual holiday on the island in the 'thirties. In those days, to spend Christmas at Reid's, with Gandolfo presiding over the hotel with the benign air of a high prelate, and to sunbathe on the rocks on New Year's Day, below the sloping gardens, full of hibiscus trees in bloom, after watching the firework display in the harbour the night before, exuded the kind of glamour which staying at The Mandarin in Hong Kong now possesses in all seasons of the year, in this age of jet travel.

Nevertheless, invited by the *Ganges*' newly-appointed captain, an ex-submariner, to 'come back and inspect the ship', I should have been less than human had I refused the invitation, of which the climax, as far as I was concerned, was undoubtedly the moment when we reached the petty officers' mess, just before lunch. An informal visit, beautifully timed. With an alacrity it was pleasing for an 'old boy' to watch, they all leapt out of their chairs in the presence of their commanding officer, and proceeded to shake hands in turn with the civilian at his side. A confrontation that could have been a source of awkward embarrassment, at least for me, had not the instinctive patina of Service manners prevailed. All shyness vanished the instant the genuine warmth of their all-embracing smiles was proved by their offer of a lethal tot of rum for the guest, who during the period that he had been passing through their ship-shape hands had not been allowed to draw his own daily ration. We were back on familiar ground and honours were easy.

In the faces, lined and pitted like a map of a thousand voyages, of the veterans gathered round, I looked eagerly but in vain for that of the father-figure who had wet-nursed me through the initial stages of our training, and whose responsibility it had been to preside over each fresh batch apportioned to the hut in his charge. Had he become 'chocker' over a shorebase job, and asked to go back to sea again? Or were his Service days over and gone for ever, and his anchor down permanently on shore? His name had been P.O. Ellwood, and I often think still how lucky our lot were to have him as our guide and mentor during that traumatic transition of civilian into Serviceman, when for the duration I myself became G. H. Winn, using once again a second initial discarded since the days when my mother sewed Cash's tags on to my clothes before despatching me back to my preparatory school at Hunstanton.

At one time P.O. Ellwood had been the Navy Boxing Champion at his weight, which impressed even the toughest of the Liverpool-Irish contingent, and even, too, the fellow with the greasy black hair and engaging smile, who had been in my carriage from Liverpool Street to Ipswich in the first short stage of the long, long journey ahead. Automatically he had elected himself the Life and Soul of the Party, handing round his most precious possession, brought with him into captivity – a book for each of us to have a dekko at, which he assured us, in triumph, was 'good and dirty'. My last sight of him at the *Ganges*, true to form, was running round the parade ground, with a dummy rifle over his shoulder and sweat pouring off him, doing punishment drill. Nevertheless, he never bore any resentment towards our own P.O., however much he might choose to rail at authority in general for its determination to crop his hair and make him conform until he was indistinguishable from the rest of the products of the sausage machine.

What impressed me most myself about P.O. Ellwood was that although he had a very hoarse voice, presumably from all the years of having to bellow out orders above a gale at sea, he never once shouted at us sadistically, just for the pleasure of watching us panic. Nor did he boast of all the seatime he had put in himself, though it had ingrained in him the habit of perpetually moving from the ball of one foot to the other, swaying a little in the process as though there were a moving deck beneath him instead of merely the utility floor of our hut. Under his unrelenting scrutiny – though I admit that those who fancied their imitations of such popular performers as Hutch were permitted to croon a selection of the songs of the day – this floor was scrubbed and scrubbed again each morning before we were allowed any breakfast. In his eyes, we were only too clearly a ragged and ignorant lot – why, we didn't even know that our black silks adorning our jumpers were not introduced as mourning for Nelson, as I had always imagined myself, but as a sweat-rag for sailor with pigtails – but all the same, he never threatened us with dreadful yarns, as some of the old salts delighted to do, about the fate that lay ahead of us when we finally got to sea.

On only one occasion did I hear our keeper's roughened voice take on a red-hot evangelical note. This was when Ginger, who had volunteered already for the Patrol Service – no pussar's flannel, no Divisions, no standing to attention when you came in and out of harbour – had the temerity to suggest that the then Chief of Combined Operations would never have had such swift promotion had it not been for his hereditary title and position. 'Look, Chief, if he hadn't started out as *Lord Louis* . . .'

Ginger, a not very bright but cheerful and harmless cockney youth, got no further. He had succeeded in dropping the naval brick to end all brick-dropping on the toe of someone who became for the next few minutes the spokesman of the whole Navy – not rag-tag wartime intakes like us, but the R.N. proper – and with a full-calibre shoot P.O. Ellwood went into the attack. As I revelled in the flow of expletives, and marvelled at the passionate loyalty displayed towards one of the heroes, if not the leading hero of the for'ard end of ship, I hugged to myself the feeling of exhilaration that had come my way on the morning that the appointment had been announced. On the urging of Lady Louis Mountbatten, who was increasingly to take me under her wing, her husband had most generously given me his first and only interview at his secret headquarters. During this, he had made a comment which, at such a low ebb in our fortunes, seemed like a draught of champagne in contrast to the ginger ale that he himself drank before lunch. 'From now on,' announced the ex-destroyer captain, who had his own scores to settle not only against the enemy who had succeeded in sinking him three times, but against those who had so stupidly forced his father to resign as First Sea Lord at the beginning of the First World War, simply because of the German name, Battenberg. 'From now on,' quietly repeated the son who through sheer ability and force of personality was destined to reclaim his father's chair in due course, '*the word impossible will not exist in our vocabulary. . . .*'

I tried to make myself believe that it didn't exist in my own vocabulary either, during my time at the *Ganges*, but there were some very doubtful and taut moments. We were down for seamanship and gunnery instruction on alternate days, and hopelessly clumsy with my hands, I despaired of ever mastering the intricate art of bends and hitches. Indeed, I never did; and ended up with appalling marks in that particular exam, though my shame was to some degree tempered by the hundred out of a hundred I received for Boat Work.

I have never been any use at making things with my hands, but I was born with a facility for memorizing almost anything at sight. In consequence, during all the hundreds of interviews I have had in the course of my journalistic work, I have never had to make a single note. I suppose some people would contemptuously refer to this as learning things off like a parrot; others, kinder, would refer to it as the gift of total recall. Anyway, when I was asked by the Lieut.-Commander examining us for the contents of a sea-boat's emergency stores, I was able to rattle off the list, without missing anything out. I still can, so here it is:

'A sea-boat should contain one compass, one tin of biscuits (the seams of the tin are soldered over and the tins enclosed in wooden boxes before being stowed in the boat as they are liable to become damaged by exposure and rough treatment). Two jerrycans filled with fresh water. One sea-boat's box containing four Short lights, one Very pistol, twelve signal cartridges (six green and six red) one boat's bag, one carpenter's bag, lead and line, lantern and candles, one life-belt for each of the crew. . . .'

I was astonished to learn that eighty per cent of my fellow-passengers at *Ganges* could not swim. It seemed incredible, but this was the official figure given out when we were lectured on the subject of learning, and learning fast. I myself had no need to have such a warning instilled into me, having an acute vision of the grey wastes of the Atlantic, and there in the foreground one solitary lifeboat, its pale scrubbed planks the colour of men's bones dried in the sun – drifting helplessly and hopelessly because it was empty. Empty. So what use were all the emergency stores so carefully packed in the tuck-box?

How grateful I was now that I had been thrown into the cold waters of the Wash and forced to learn to swim, as a small shrimp at my first boarding school. Now that I was forced to endure four doses of P.T. every week, how thankful I was, too, for all the training I had spontaneously done in the days when my chief ambition in life was to play at Wimbledon. Our instructors had decided that to make us all a little more lively, we should strip to the waist. Up and down the long room we ran, now on tip-toe, now imitating the loping strides of a cross-country runner. Press-ups and knee-bending was thrown in as a jolly bonus. In the first week or two I used to watch the clock on the wall with an ever-increasing fear in my heart that I wouldn't be able to stick it, or keep pace with my companions, most of whom were not much more than half my age. Actually, I soon discovered to my relief that in many cases I was in better shape than they were, because few of them had ever done P.T. before in their lives. So they puffed and blew down my neck. It was a great comfort, and soon instead of staring beseechingly at the clock I was re-reading for the hundredth time the inscription written in letters of black upon the opposite wall.

'If you can meet with triumph and disaster,
And treat those two impostors just the same . . .'

As it happens, that same over-familiar Kipling quotation is also inscribed over the Players' entrance to the centre court at Wimbledon, probably the last thing they record before they pass through the gate to meet the challenge, not only of their opponents but of the critical gaze of the serried ranks of spectators. I have stood there at the bottom of the staircase, after one more championship meeting has been over, alone with my reverie of unfulfilled ambition of playing there myself, speculating as to what is in the players' minds at that implacable moment of no escape. Obviously I shall never know now, from personal experience. But as for the other challenge of being pitchforked into all the rigours of square-bashing service life at a time in my life when I was contemplating giving up singles on the tennis court, somehow I survived, though I was for ever making a fool of myself, as, for example, on the very first day that I wore a naval cap. After being kitted up by a posse of Wrens, whose own smart turn-out shamed our scruffy assortment of civilian attire, I found myself making a hopeless mess of the simple manoeuvre of 'Hats off', which we should have to perform at our first church parade. I still shiver when I think of myself standing there, dropping my cap and the P.O. in charge looking at me as though I were something the cat had produced.

After all, to him it was a simple manoeuvre. You lifted your right hand across your face, grasped firmly the left side of the cap's peak and removed it, in one smart movement, behind your back, where you held it, standing at ease, till the command of 'Hats on' again. Then in one swift movement – didn't I tell you *one*, not *six* – you reproduced your cap, like a conjuror, still holding the left extremity of the peak with the thumb and first finger of your right hand and somehow you had it on your head so that it stayed put till the next order (stand at ease, stand *easy*) when it was permitted to raise *both* hands to your head, remove your hat, swivel it round so that H.M.S. on the cap ribbon was dead front, and replace it properly. A simple enough manoeuvre? . . . Perhaps I am prejudiced, because I am overwhelmingly left-handed, and this was very much a right-handed affair, but at least, it was something of a relief that mine was by no means the only hat that fell at our instructor's feet, nor my arm the only right arm that got itself twisted in a contortionist's grip round my neck. Didn't I tell you *one* movement? Yes, sir. Then let me see you do it properly this time. Yes, sir. Hats *off*. Hats on. Hats off. Hats ON.

By the end of our first week that particular hurdle had been more or less mastered. But then we left the comparative security of the annexe, and were marched across to the main buildings to start all over again, eyeing the masthead at the end of the parade ground with a fresh outburst of terror, because hadn't we been assured that every draft had to climb right over it before passing out? Certainly 'passing out' was exactly the right expression to use. A hundred feet high. It looked a thousand at first sight. Of course it was only a mythical buzz, the first of the many that we were to hear during our time in the Service, but inevitably we arrived in Hut 46 in a very disturbed state of mind. There we found a self-possessed, stocky youth on guard against the tiers of beds that comprised the starboard side of the mess, already occupied by some members of the draft that had arrived a week ahead of us.

He strolled over, watching us stow our new kit-bags, try the beds. It was easy to sense how aware he was of his vast superiority. Didn't he know all the answers to what the grub was like, the instructors, the canteen, the officers? The Delphic Oracle was never more feverishly consulted. Suddenly he broke off from his lurid discourse to eye me sharply. 'Haven't I seen your face before, chum?' he demanded. Reluctantly I told him my name. Just the surname.

'You mean you're *Godfrey* Winn?'

'Yes,' G. H. Winn admitted with even greater reluctance.

'Fuck me. I used to empty your waste-paper basket.'

It transpired that seven years before he had been an office boy at Geraldine House, which was in those days the London headquarters of the *Daily Mirror*, before it moved into its present palatial offices in High Holborn.

The office boy and the paper's columnist occupying the same hut, I had visions of the mickey being taken out of me, good and proper, in the weeks ahead. However, I need not have had any such premonitions. For the situation that seemed fearful took a most unexpected turn. 'That was a smashing blue job you had,' he continued.

'A smashing blue job?' I echoed. I had already acquired sufficient Service slang to appreciate that any female of the species who didn't actually squint was a 'smashing party', but surely he wasn't speaking in equal enthusiasm of the daily page I turned out in those days under the title of '*Personality Parade*'?

Suddenly it dawned on me. He was referring to the blue sports coupé which the lorry drivers graciously used to allow me to park beside their own cabs in the forecourt. 'The Blue Boudoir', as some of my less privileged colleagues called it.

'It was a Renault,' I explained.

However, I could see that he had swiftly lost interest in the past. It was the present which mattered. He was examining my appearance critically, and once again I was uneasy till he said with friendly patronage, 'You want a tiddley bow to your hat, chum. I'll make you one if you like.'

'They told us when we were kitted up in the annexe that whatever we did, we mustn't alter our bows.'

How prim and B.B.C. my voice sounded even to myself.

'Of course they did. They told us, too. Look.' He produced his own cap lying on his bed, and stuck it on the back of his head in a manner that would have horrified our Divisional Officer, Lieut-Commander Rogerson, who was for ever delivering the same homily: 'For heaven's sake, don't try to look like the advertisement of the Jolly Jack Tar who uses Brylcreem. I don't know where this idea came from of wearing your hat on the back of your head, but you will never see a proper sailor doing it. It's only the fellows who go into Ipswich on leave, and try to impress the population that they are old salts. All they succeed in doing is looking like a lot of chorus boys in a musical comedy.'

Such admonitions and comparisons had clearly had no effect on my erstwhile colleague. For there was the bow, dead on the front – the ribbon must have been slashed to achieve that position – and as skilfully pressed flat as a four-leafed clover. My particular chums, Ted and Ron and Alan – the last the Durham miner's son – were absolutely overcome, while I found myself eyeing the tempting model held out in front of us with considerably more awe than he had ever shown towards my car. I could feel my own stock going up in leaps and bounds at the prospect of a whole stream of tiddley bows changing hands, but that was nothing to the night when an even more tiddley collar to match most unexpectedly fell upon my bed.

In the relaxed half hour before 'Lights Out', when we all lay sprawling on our beds, either trying to catch each other out with questions from our Manuals – *The Headlead line is marked . . . at two fathoms, two strips of leather . . . at five fathoms . . . at five fathoms* ... wait a jiffy, I've got it ... *a piece of white bunting*, whatever the hell that is ... *at ten fathoms* ... – or more pleasurably discussing for the hundredth time what we intended to cram into our Christmas leave, into this mutually protective, enclosed Order of noviciates, down the length of the hut, swaggered the collar's wearer, until he reached me and stopped. I was his port of call.

I looked at the intruder's face with puzzlement, since I did not recognize my visitor. I looked again, this time at his collar, and my eyes lit up with longing. You could sense at once that this was the authentic article. It hadn't been artificially bleached in soda to attain that coveted shade of Mediterranean blue, but had faded gradually from long service in the sun. A real matelot's collar, legitimately worn by someone who, having been sunk in the Med., had been allotted a quiet number for a spell, as a signaller at the *Ganges*.

The stranger's presence in our hut that evening was soon explained. One of my trips as a war correspondent had been on board his destroyer, and though we had never spoken on that occasion, having heard now that I was 'inside' he had come along to cheer me up. For when, with spontaneous enthusiasm, I admired his collar – though I would scarcely have noticed it in the days when I was still dressed as a civilian myself, even at sea – this dialogue took place.

'Do you like it?'

'Like it? It's the best I've ever seen.'

'Would you like it, mate, is what I said. . . .'

'You mean. . . .'

'I've got several others. If you'd like it. . . .'

'Oh, I couldn't.'

'It's yours,' he said, cutting short my half-hearted protests, and a moment later there it was, lying on my bed. I still couldn't believe it, even when he had taken his departure, and all my mates, who had tactfully turned their backs, now gathered round me in a circle which generated mass excitement.

'Look what Goff's visitor left behind ... isn't it a smasher! What did you pay for it, Goff . . . a quid? Ten bob? . . . nothing?'

Slowly it began to dawn on them. This was a present from a former 'shippie', an insignia of a club membership that cannot be bought but has to be earned.

'All the same, you must have given him something in exchange,' they persisted.

'Well he did ask for my autograph,' I was forced to admit at last.

'Your *autograph*?'

A gale of incredulous laughter was followed by an equally astonished silence. They gazed at me as though they were seeing me for the first time, as though it was I who was the Olympian stranger, not my visitor. There really must be something in this writing lark, after all. I might be an absolute clot at bends and hitches, no earthly use as an oar in a whaler, have a high-brow forehead and a voice like a B.B.C. announcer, but oh boy, it was a beautiful collar, the sort they'd give a whole week's pay, at three bob a day, to be able to sport in their local dance hall, on leave, and all I had apparently done to acquire it was to write my name on a piece of paper. Yes, there surely must be more to me than they'd imagined, and though they'd been friendly enough before now, they treated me almost with respect, and certainly with grateful affection when I loaned them, in turn, the collar for a try-out, when I wasn't going ashore in Ipswich myself.

However, the real climax in the life of this particular collar came on Christmas Day, when I wore it for dinner at Claridges. Jay Llewellyn was my host and his other guest was another war-time sailor, Alan Lennox-Boyd,* who despite his height and gait of a loping Labrador had shown a preference for squeezing himself into those small, swift greyhounds of the sea, torpedo motor boats. He had, in fact, only that morning come up from the flotilla base where he was commanding one of the latest class. Like the majority of the younger Members on his side of the House, Alan had instinctively refused to regard his parliamentary duties as sufficient war service, but insisted instead in participating as actively as our host had done as a soldier in the previous world conflict. In due course, Alan was to be promoted to Cabinet rank himself, and will be regarded by the unprejudiced as, perhaps, the best Colonial Secretary of the post-war era. In both his public and his private life he is someone whom it would be difficult to dislike. In marked contrast to the majority of professional politicians, there was nothing devious

* Viscount Boyd of Merton.

or self-seeking in his behaviour; and his readiness to smile on all the world is in no way a front but the true reflection of his character. Moreover, like our host on this occasion, who was to end his distinguished career as the first Governor-General of the Rhodesian Federation, and to die in harness, despite repeated warnings that his heart was giving out, there was not then, and there isn't now a trace of pomposity in his make-up.

So often Members of Parliament, even those who are within one's own intimate circle of friends, cannot help talking at you, instead of to you; but these two I exempt absolutely from that charge. That evening we were all in tremendous spirits, and eager to rope in another member of the Cabinet who happened to be at the next table with his family. After I had had to parry some good-natured chaff about my collar, it was the turn of our neighbour to be teased with a reference to the contents of Woolton Pie and the expression of our relief that it was for once missing from the menu. Such sallies were easily parried by the calm confidence of the man who had genuinely achieved a fair share for all of what rations there were, with the consequence that there was no doubt that at that time Lord Woolton was the most popular of all Churchill's Ministers.

Spartan though that Christmas dinner was, when judged by peace-time standards, it is not surprising that it should still stand out so vividly in my memory. All the square-bashing was over; now there was only the final hurdle of the passing-out examinations early in the New Year, and I would be a fully-fledged, ordinary seaman. Rather to my surprise, I found that I was less self-conscious about wearing my newly-acquired uniform in London than I had expected. I certainly no longer felt or talked like a civilian, and perhaps, again, my absurd pride in my collar helped. Alan, either tactfully, since he was an officer, or thankfully, had chosen to be in mufti for our reunion. This was to be my night; and then for the rest of my week's leave, which I spent peacefully at Esher, I could resort again to slacks, or one of the winter suits which I had worn the previous Christmas. This I had spent in an hotel at Torquay, no longer as once upon a time full of guests discussing each other's clothes, manners and morals, but instead taken over for the duration as a recuperative and convalescent centre for the pilots and air crew of the Royal Air Force.

Nowadays, Christmas has rather lost its magic for me. It has become so blatantly commercial. There seems to be too much feasting, too much food heaped on the table, too much drinking, and too many unnecessarily expensive presents for the very young, who surely would be just as content with something less elaborate than the replica of a space ship that can only be handled – and enjoyed – by a mechanically-minded parent. I had always imagined that Christmas belonged to the children, not to the multiple stores, and it is perhaps because I have no children of my own, and inevitably feel the loss particularly at Christmas, that I am becoming increasingly allergic to the blatantly material yuletide pressures. Or perhaps it is that I shall never be able to obliterate from my mind that Christmas morning at Torquay, and the party to greet Father Christmas which assembled in the ballroom.

The only traditional prop was the figure in the red robe and the long beard and sideburns of cotton wool. Out of his sack he produced a pretty meagre selection of gifts for all the men in their blue uniforms, surrounded by the nurses who did so much to make their life more tolerable. A packet of razor blades, a single handkerchief, a Service tie, a couple of *Mars* bars. Yet as the name of each recipient was called out from a list and he went forward to receive his package, he succeeded in grinning as enthusiastically as a schoolboy. There was one fellow who could not walk so upright as the others, but it was utterly impossible to tell from the expression on his face that, like Group Captain Douglas Bader, he had lost both his legs in a crash. His smile was immaculately controlled at the moment when Father Christmas, in his gruffest voice greeted him: 'I don't think we've met before. Are you a new boy?'

At that, a great roar of laughter went up from the other patients, who now recognized behind all that fuzz the figure of their medical C.O., and at the same time appreciated the irony behind his greeting, since they were only too aware of just how long their fellow voyager had been there, mending. Afterwards, when I got to know this patient, I marvelled at the way he could still make a joke of it all, boasting to me not of his battle exploits but of being the only man who has ever wooed the planet of Venus with a signalling lamp from his kite – 'I gave her everything I'd got' – mistaking her lustre for the recognition lights of a fellow aeronaut. Just as another pilot could make a joke of the narrowness of his own escape after his plane had crashed. One heard so many fantastic stories at that time, but this one has stayed in my memory because there was a certain originality about it. Thrown a hundred and fifty yards, he had landed up to his neck in a sewage farm, where he was found by a farmer eight hours later. 'But the nurses wouldn't come near me for eight days after that, and I don't blame them,' he added.

That was the only way; always make a joke of everything. When they first came to this rest-house half-way to recovery, they were still in the condition that they could not bear to hear a telephone ringing – they would be certain it must have a message for them. They could not sit in the same room for more than five minutes. They could not read a book. They could do nothing except think of their squadron, their friends; put out their hands even in their sleep, to touch the cockpits of their machines.

Galsworthy has written somewhere of the crisis which comes into a man's fortune, when he may crack beneath the weight of overwhelming circumstances, and then recover and return to life, never the same man again, because something has died, something has fled, but grown in stature and resilence and finerhewed, having attained his second wind. There was a guest at The Palace who in a small way I was able to help towards that state.

On an earlier visit to Torquay, I had knocked on the door of one of the single rooms at The Palace, to find a young man sitting up in bed with a dreadfully mauled face, and claws instead of hands clutching the counterpane. This was one of Archie McIndoe's guineapigs, from East Grinstead, having a respite and a breathing space. Soon he would return for another series of operations at the supremely accomplished hands of the greatest plastic surgeon of his time, who had made the King Edward Hospital at East Grinstead his wartime base.

Bill Simpson had only just returned from his honeymoon when he was despatched with the first British squadron to France. It wasn't the 'phoney' war for him. Shot down, with his plane blazing like a funeral pyre, he was so brutally burnt that apart altogether from the damage to his face and limbs, the odds were dead against his survival, in his seemingly endless sojourn in

Frank Willis – lorry driver by night. 'Many would say that in this war civilians had the hardest time'

Author Maurice Levinson drive
me home in his own cab

Ivor Novello with Vanessa Lee

John Winant, wartime
American ambassador t
the Court of St James

various poorly-equipped hospitals in Occupied France. Finally mercy was vouchsafed and he was repatriated via Spain. None of the authorities concerned had the compassion or even the common sense to warn his wife, when she went to meet him on his arrival, just what to expect when she saw her husband again for the first time since their honeymoon. She knew, of course, that he had been crossed off as a total casualty, but somehow, holding on to hope, she had imagined that he had been patched up like a piece of china that has fallen off a mantelpiece into the ashes of a fire. All the time of their separation she had desperately held on to the picture of him as he had looked on his honeymoon; the same picture of himself as a handsome, unscarred young flying officer that he still carried in his own pocket book.

And because no one had warned her, the shock of the confrontation was overwhelming. On the other hand, I had been warned and, besides, I was uncommitted, except as one of the voluntary band of Archie's supporters. I had been privileged to watch him operate,* and had marvelled at his surgical skill; but I had come equally to respect and admire his flair as a psychiatrist. Indeed, I was to experience it personally before the war was over. Meanwhile, I came as a kind of messenger, with the words of Bill Simpson's saviour echoing in my mind.

'Bill has a tremendous story to tell which would have a message and a meaning for all sorts of people, if he could only somehow get it down on paper, and out of his system. Even if it was never published, I believe it would help his ultimate recovery enormously, to spew it all up. See what you can do to encourage him.'

Even after an initial encounter at Torquay with this guinea pig, I was instantly convinced that McIndoe, so implacably tough and even ruthless one moment, so gentle the next, had once again hit upon the exactly right kind of therapy. For the patient, with the curtains drawn against the light which burnt against his reconstructed eyelids, was so articulate, and so enthralling in all that he had to relate, even when he did not, at this first meeting, reveal his inmost feelings, that I found myself wishing that I had not neglected to learn shorthand. In any case, I was too committed in other ways to act as his 'ghost' writer. Un-

* See the author's *The Infirm Glory*, page 41.

fortunately, it was only too obvious that his hands were quite incapable, at that period in his recovery, of holding a pen. It was then that I made the suggestion that he should work, on his own, in bed, with a tape recorder at his side as the go-between; and to encourage him to conquer both his natural reticence and his initial awkwardness at having to use such an artificial gadget for self-expression, I repeated to him what Somerset Maugham, my own mentor in the early days of my literary apprenticeship had once said to me, in exhortation:

'Writing is the supreme solace. You go into a room by yourself; it does not matter how small it is so long as there is room for a desk; you shut the door, and within half an hour you have completely forgotten all the petty vexations that were previously occupying your thoughts and weighing you down. Now you are immersed in something so much bigger and more important, at any rate to yourself. All your most passionate convictions and longings are little by little released, and this is at once a relief and a revelation. You are a free man again, and whatever the ultimate fate of your work, no one else in the world could have made a precisely similar pattern of words upon the page. It is yours and yours alone.'

The first Sunday that I was at the *Ganges* I bought from habit a copy of the *Sunday Express*, and there to my delight was a whole page given over to a glowing review of Squadron Leader Simpson's '*One of our pilots is missing*'. There have been many war odysseys published since, but none that has been written with a more arresting narrative force, and to prove that this first effort in authorship was no mere flash in the pan, Bill followed it up later with an equally compelling account of his ultimate repatriation, and his second marriage, this time to one of the nurses who succoured him at East Grinstead. His surgeon was able to build for him a new face, and to give him back his confidence in living, but only he could build up for himself a fresh career still close to the world of flying, which was for ever part of his being. Today Bill is the head of the public relations department of B.E.A. and held in esteem by everyone in his orbit. But I sometimes wonder how many of those who come in contact with him, puffing away at his pipe, have any real inkling of his own personal victory; just as I wonder sometimes if his saga which is there for ever, in print, would ever have been translated stage by stage to paper, had I not by chance being visiting Torquay, to open the town's National Savings Week.

I am often asked what I consider is the most vital attribute in attaining success as a professional writer, and I have no hesitation in replying that I consider the first essential is to be completely natural, and utterly oneself on paper in the same way as one should be in real life, if one is not to set up barriers of uneasiness between oneself and the rest of the community. I keep regular working hours every day, and each morning, when the process of communication commences once more, I pretend to myself that I am talking to an old friend, who has been ill, and is now recuperating but still shut away indoors, as Bill Simpson was on the first time that we met. I set myself the test that I am seeking to bring the world outside the windows close to this person, listless and fractious from too long an incarceration. Would this bore them? Would that?

Something that I cannot believe would bore anyone with sensibility is the artlessly devised letter I received during that Christmas leave, from one of my messmates in Hut 46, with whom, and his own particular oppo, Ted Dowsett, I established a working partnership, a kind of balance of power arrangement. They provided their hands, I my wits.

It was headed: '25 12 42.

Ron,
6 Winnington Road,
Enfield West, Middlesex.

'Dear Goff,

'Thanks very much for your letter. I was pleased to receive it. So far Ted and I have had a very nice leave, plenty of drinks and just as many girls. Ted and I have finished our courting. We will tell you more about it when we are back on the Ganges. I don't suppose this will reach you until after Christmas but I hope you had a nice time and didn't get too drunk.

'My pop came home Wednesday night and will be home until Monday so all we need now is my brother Jack (in the Navy and out in the Med. at that time) *to be home for the first time in 18 months, and we would have a complete family, but I suppose we are lucky to other families, only having one of our*

family away. Well, Goff, I thank you once again for your letter, and will close with, give my regard to your mother, your girls and the rest of your family.

'Your old pal,

'Ron.

'P.S. Ted sends his regards to all.'

In the train that was bearing us once again from Liverpool Street to Ipswich, I soon discovered the reason why Ron and Ted had finished with their first efforts at serious courting. Their girls had been too determined to clutch them all to themselves, while the boys had not surprisingly wanted to be out and about, with the gang, showing off their uniforms, as I had shown off my collar at Claridge's. But all that was behind us, and we were stripped down to our overalls once again when we got back just in time to find ourselves Duty Division on New Year's Eve. This meant lining up after Evening Divisions, under the masthead, when fatigues were served out haphazardly by a pointing finger: 'You, you and you'.

'Ward-room party, left turn, carry on.' Picking up our heels and saluting the quarter deck, we set off gloomily in the vague direction of the officers' quarters. The moment we were safely round the corner and out of sight of the Duty Officer, we stopped dead. 'Where the bleeding hell is the ward-room, Goff?' I wasn't sure. 'I think it's that building over there,' I replied doubtfully, recalling that I had seen our D.O.* on the steps, exercising his Dachshund. So we slouched in that direction. Just as we reached the steps, the door opened and one of the dentists came out. I saluted smartly. 'Excuse me, sir, but is this the entrance to the ward-room?' He took one look at us, and answered in the voice of someone who had served on the staff of Jellicoe at the Battle of Jutland. 'The entrance *you* want is round at the back.'

The skivvies entrance, and that's what we were for the rest of the evening. At first we imagined, poor sods, that we were going to get off lightly with the tea-things, piled in heaps, from the other side of the hatch. A Wren P.O., very neat and workmanlike in an apron over her uniform, was in charge. Wisely, she said nothing, and gave us no hint of what lay ahead of us.

* Divisional Officer.

It was left to a corporal in the Marines to enlighten us. Putting his head round the door, he demanded, 'Got all the gash hands you need?' Why *extra* hands . . . and then suddenly it dawned on me, the reason for all the other pile of plates of sandwiches and cakes and sardines on toast, placed side by side with the washing-up. Of course, it was New Year's Eve and there was to be a party in the ward-room; we were there as extra waiters and washers-up. We shouldn't get away for hours, and there would be no time left to study our Manuals. In my fury and disgust, I dropped the teapot I was drying. As the Wren prepared to scold, I had my excuse ready, the echo of so many domestic crises in my childhood. 'I am very sorry, ma'am, but it came apart in my hands. . . .' 'Don't . . .' she started, but never finished her retort to that ancient bromide, because at that moment there was a loud commotion outside, in the passage. And no wonder. One of our lot, mild little Enoch, had excelled himself. He'd had a ball on his own. Directed to carry some of the supplies of liquor into the wine pantry, he had succeeded in dropping the most precious bottle of all. Whisky. Worth its weight in gold, at that time of acute shortage, and destined on this occasion to serve as the foundation for the Cup. One of the doctors had offered to concoct this for the purpose of assuaging the thirst of the dancers, and who knows, at the same time to loosen the inhibitions of the Wrens.

We all crowded into the passage, and surveyed the disaster. What a mess, what a waste. Momentarily I had forgotten that not for nothing were the Marines referred to as the Navy's sheet anchor. The corporal was completely unperturbed. 'Get a pail, you, and you get a cloth, and mop it up, and squeeze it all into the pail, and don't suck your fingers as you're doing it, see; and you' – that was me – 'don't stand there doing nothing, get the french chalk and sprinkle it over the ward-room floor.'

I was longing to watch just how much mud from our boots went into the pail, and equally just how clean the cloth was for the mopping-up process; at the same time, I was as eager as any member of any kitchen staff to discover what was going on the other side of the hatch. They were certainly bent on having a gala, I decided. The holly had been kept up round the pictures from Christmas, a special stand for the band had been set up, and all the wives were temporarily ignoring the difference of their husband's ranks, as they pooled their artistic talents in arranging more evergreens and an assortment of balloons. The atmosphere was congenial and colourful; no hint of disharmony here until the Commander's wife arrived in the doorway; whereupon, owing to my over-enthusiastic ministrations to the floor she skidded and, unable to recover herself, ended up flat on her back in front of the grand piano. There she lay like a cow in a field, while all the others gasped at the spectacle of her skirt pulled up above her knees. Because she was senior to them all, no one dared touch her; her person was sacrosanct. I sometimes think she would have been lying there till today had not I, the culprit, the undesiring cause of her downfall, felt it was my duty to advance to her help and lift her to her feet. Not that I received any thanks, or expected any. A gash hand in overalls. I was invisible to the company, though not they to me. As once again I bent my head, discreetly sprinkling further seed in a distant corner of the room, I heard the discussion begin to re-kindle as to exactly what height the balloons were to be hung. 'No, not *too* high . . . you know *he* always likes to prick a balloon at midnight. . . .'

At midnight my duties long since over, I was woken by the sirens of the ships in the river heralding a new year. For once I had no anxieties as to what the next twelve months had in store for me. I would float with the tide. It was an extraordinary relief not to have to make any decisions and resolutions for myself. Instead, sleepily I speculated as to how the party in the ward-room had gone, and whether the ship's captain (if he was 'he') was about to prick his balloon (without over-reaching himself, one hoped) in the ritualistic gesture which apparently gave him such pleasure. How appalling if at that very moment he, too, was landing on his backside! Had a succession of the dashing dancers commented upon the smoothness of the floor? – 'It's like parquet, I've never known it as good as this before.' Had others been already affected by the aphrodisiac qualities of the cup – a drink that always seems so innocuous in comparison with hard liquor? Of course, it depended on the ingredients. Especially on this occasion. A blur of voices sounded in my ears, and one of them, the commander's wife, was exclaiming, 'What absolutely delicious cup. Yes, I would like another glass. I wonder what has given it its special flavour this time.'

Smiling happily to myself, I turned over and was instantly asleep again, only to find myself a few hours later once more on my hands and knees, performing what Enoch contemptuously called women's work, this time myself in charge of one of the pails. It was my turn to be a member of the squad that every morning scrubbed the deck of our hut. Having fetched a pail and filled it in the larger wash-house, and snaffled a piece of soap which one tipped into the water, we began the operation. It was more of a token operation, I always felt, than an exercise in hygiene. Because we all were content to swab in the dust and scrub over the dirt ingrained in the very rough wood, our one thought, all our thoughts were achingly pin-pointed on the breakfast that would be dished up at seven o'clock. Meanwhile, we divided ourselves up into pairs; one flooded the surface and afterwards mopped up with a dishcloth that smelt of a million garbage cans and would have been altogether too fruity for last night's cup, while the other scrubbed. Then we changed over, like the front and back legs of a pantomime horse.

Starting at the centre of the hut – with all the beds temporarily telescoped together at the farther end – we worked backwards to the door, which sometimes I thought we would never reach. The black-out shutters had not yet been taken down; the central heating had been turned up; the atmosphere was like a Turkish bath, without any of the amenities. The fumes from the dust and dirt were stifling in one's nostrils, the sweat poured down one's back inside one's overalls, but still my companions, especially the eighteen-year-olds, were vocally undefeated.

'Come round any old time and make yourself at home,
Put your feet up on the mantelshelf,
Open the cupboard and help yourself,
I don't care if your friends have left you all alone,
Rich or poor, just knock at the door
And make yourself at home.'

But that had been last night; the belated return from our ward-room chores had inspired this uproarious greeting from the rest of the hut's occupants, belting out the theme song that we had adopted as our own, though I have never heard it since.

In the morning, with so many of us scattered and delegated

to different jobs, it was inevitable that communal singing should be replaced by solo efforts, though many of these efforts were different versions of the same song which at that moment was all the rage: *Jealousy.* Some of my mates succeeded in giving an uncanny imitation of Hutch, who had made the number his own, while others preferred to strike out on their own. Unable to sing two notes in tune, I at least had the sense not to make any effort at harmonizing. Nevertheless the song entered my consciousness for ever, and when years later I was invited by Roy Plomley to select my Desert Island Discs for his radio programme of that name, it was impossible for me to leave out the particular recording by the coloured singer who, for three decades, was so important a part of the English world of light entertainment. For I was absolutely certain that wherever I was shipwrecked, on whatever distant, deserted shore, to hear it once again would instantly conjure up for me the unconquerable, overwhelmingly physical atmosphere of Hut 46, where I left something of myself for ever, the last lingering exultation of my youth.

I imagine the same ritual continues today, though the songs my *Ganges* messmates crooned can have little meaning or appeal for a generation in thrall to the Rolling Stones and the Beatles. I have as little knowledge of the current 'pop' scene as I had in my deck-scrubbing days. Nevertheless, I found myself one Saturday evening of the autumn of six years ago climbing the stairs of an anonymous building close to Cambridge Circus. At that moment, the West End audiences were crowding into the nearby Shaftesbury Avenue theatres. In the barren, unfurnished room where a rendezvous had been arranged for me, the walls, with their peeling paint, were decorated with posters of such plays as *A Taste of Honey* and *The Miracle Worker.* As I looked at the posters, and decided that there was a certain symbolism, a link here with the intriguing encounter that lay ahead of me, I thought, too, of all the players who had rehearsed in this room for a multitiude of productions of one kind and another; so full of hope that success was this time almost in their grasp, and so often to be reminded in due course once more of the implacable truth that half the members of the Actors' Union, Equity, are permanently out of work. Would it be different for the latest Merseyside group who, already acclaimed in the provinces, were about to have their most important challenge to date, the star spot of the *Sunday Night At The Palladium* television show? So many 'pop' singers blazed like comets for a brief spell across the sky and then vanished into darkness. Eternal darkness. Would it be different for them?

The Beatles, with the hair-style that they made their own, were still not much more than a name to me, though, a few days before, thanks to an introduction from our mutual legal adviser, David Jacobs, I had had a long talk with their manager and discoverer in the lounge of Grosvenor House. Here, with no home yet in London, Brian Epstein was staying. He was dressed in the kind of silk suit that 'pop' groups wore like a uniform, but there all comparison ceased. For at that time he had not yet discarded the solid air of the middle-class Jewish background from which he was sprung. Epstein's tragedy was that in surrendering one background, he became so overwhelmed by the trappings of the world into which the fantastic success of his protégés catapulted him that he was never able to put down roots into reality again.

This son of a prosperous Liverpool store-owner was the classic example of the actor *manqué*. He was nearly thirty when we first met, but as soon as he started talking of the time that he had enlisted as a student at the R.A.D.A. his voice had the eager lilt of a stage-struck youth. A moment later his expression had changed, he was earth-bound once more as he described his return to Liverpool and entry into his father's business.

'Even if I had been any good as an actor, my father would not have liked his elder son on the stage. He believed that my place was in the business. And I could see his point, though anything to do with the theatre will be my first and last love. Fortunately we were able to come to a sort of compromise. My father allowed me to set up record departments in all our shops, and today we have the largest turnover in our part of the country.'

'And you served behind the counter yourself?'

'Certainly. And one day in the lunch hour, a customer came in and asked for a record that I'd never heard of, and which wasn't in any of the lists we had. It had been made in Germany with an orchestral backing by a young unknown group from Merseyside.'

'The Beatles?'

'Yes, the Beatles.'

'If that particular customer hadn't come in when you were serving, and with that particular request, none of it might have happened,' I exclaimed. 'Or do you think the really big talent always comes to the top in the end?'

'I don't know. But I do know that this is the biggest ever in its own line. Though all I knew then was that I was out to prove to my father that I could be as much on the ball in business as he was. So I wrote off to Germany, tracked down the record, and when it came, and I had played it over to myself, I had a sudden hunch – and what a hunch it's turned out to be – to see the group in the flesh.'

'So?'

'So I decided to drop in at the smoky, smelly cellar where they were performing for peanuts. Their act matched the surroundings. It was pretty ragged and their clothes were a mess, and yet . . . I sensed instinctively that there was something dynamic here, if only it could be harnessed and left at the same time untamed. . . .'

The hotel lounge was full of rich travellers, sorting out their baggage, longing for a bath, asking the reception desk clerks what theatre they could recommend for that evening. It was all so cosseted, so far removed from the atmosphere of Liverpool's now defunct Tavern. I blinked and turned again towards the smooth young man at my side, whose butter-soft skin concealed, as I was to find later, steel beneath. He was saying in his classless voice:

'I think you will find the contrast even more remarkable when I tell you that their latest recording has sold half a million copies in ten days. But less than a year ago when I took their tapes to two different London recording companies, they weren't in the least interested. I was pretty desperate. I had taken French leave from the store to act as a different sort of salesman, and my father kept on telephoning me, asking when the hell I was coming back.

'On the Friday morning, I promised I would catch the afternoon train. I thought I'd had it. I went into the H.M.V. gramophone shop in Oxford Street, where you can have tapes transferred to discs, and the attendant who was looking after me said suddenly, "There's one of the E.M.I. executives upstairs this morning. Would you mind if I asked him to listen to this?" "Mind?" I echoed. Why, I would have gone down on my knees.'

'And what happened?' I echoed in my turn.

'Why, the executive broke off from the meeting, and I shall always be eternally grateful that he did. He rang up George Martin, the king-pin at the E.M.I. head office, and . . .'

'And you telephoned your father to say you'd be returning on a later train?'

'That's exactly what I did do. And do you know, that tape,

that very first record, *Love me, do,* sold a hundred thousand records. We were in.'

As I was in, the only spectator at their private rehearsal for tomorrow night's show. Or rather, myself plus the tailor who had brought with him the four new suits, black like a matador's, that Epstein had ordered for them to wear, replicas of his own. They put them on and pranced round the rehearsal room, bowing to an imaginary audience, tomorrow's audience of fourteen million viewers.

'Ladies and Gentlemen: we are very pleased to be here at The Palladium.'

Suddenly, uncontrollable excitement possessed them. The Palladium. The Palladium, they shouted out, screaming like their own fans, as other pilgrims have cried across the centuries. Jerusalem on high.

It was the youngest who spoke the introduction. He wasn't satisfied till he had taken them through it a dozen times. 'It's the moment before the curtain opens,' Paul commented with the air of a veteran. 'You finger your guitar and hope they won't start throwing things.'

The moment they started to tune their guitars they seemed to fill the shadows of the lonely rehearsal room, darkening into twilight, and at the same time to grow in stature themselves. When they weren't actually performing, my first and last reaction that afternoon was that they were four pleasant, polite and unassuming young men; though it is true that had I not known who they were, I might have mistaken them for the grandsons of the Marx Brothers. Especially Ringo, who possessed the mournful look of all comics.

'They always think I am unhappy,' he admitted, 'because I don't smile much. But you see, I am the serious one.'

He was reading a paper-back on how to do without sleep. It gave me a chance to examine at close quarters his basinful of hair, which seemed so extraordinary a style at the time, but today, in comparison with current tonsorial fantasies, is almost humdrum.

'It's cheaper to wear it this way,' George assured me. 'No perming, no styling, like most of the 'pop' singers go in for. This way it only costs four-and-six, and the tip.'

They had arrived an hour late, after a long drive down from

the North and a series of one-night stands, culminating in Stoke-on-Trent.

'Aren't you very tired by the end of the week?' I suggested.

'We sleep in the car. It takes us all day to wake up, and then we are ready for the next show,' John Lennon told me, the only one of the group who was married at that time. When I asked him if his wife was with them, he shook his head, explaining that she would watch *The Palladium* show at home, in Liverpool. 'I've quite enough to look after myself,' he said.

Now they have all gone their own ways, but what struck me immediately at our first meeting was their complete harmony with each other the instant the actual rehearsal commenced. There were no arguments, only professional discussion, in which Ringo alone, as the drummer, did not participate. Instinctively he seemed to hang back, so that, the session over, I had to push him forward or else he would have been out of focus when the photographer from the newspaper which had me under contract at that time came to take some pictures. It seems rather ironic, now, that I should have had to coax him into camera range, since he has subsequently shown himself to be the member of the quartette most capable of coping with all the complications from the aftermath of the riches and the fame which have engulfed them.

Ringo Starr has succeeded in settling peacefully into a private domestic life of his own, as husband and father, while he has conquered his shyness in front of the cameras to become a straight film actor of considerable range. Whereas during the same week that John Lennon, the one who invented the name of 'The Beatles' – 'It's nothing to do with beetles in a cellar, but beat, man, beat' – chose to give a public exhibition on his honeymoon with his present Japanese wife, in an Amsterdam hotel, George Harrison and his wife were fined heavily for possessing a huge haul of cannabis discovered in their Esher bungalow.

I hated reading the newspaper reports. How unspoilt they were, how charged with their own vitality, raring to go, they had been that night I had met them in that gloomy tomb of a rehearsal room. How they had filled it with their own fluorescence. There had been no need of any artificial stimulants then. And remembering, too, the ambience of Esher, regarded as a commuters' paradise, where I had shared a house with my mother for twenty years, it seemed such a strange metamorphosis, a disharmony made sadder still by this Beatle's bitter comment as he left the court.

'It's only in Britain that people don't like the Beatles.'

That, of course, was petulant nonsense. The Beatles will always be held in high regard for what they have achieved by the unique sound of their music. Having been among the first to recognize their talent in print, I feel I am in a position to suggest now that what has gone wrong somewhere along the line has been their inability, especially in the case of George Harrison and John Lennon, to pour back sufficient of the bounty that has fallen into their lap. They demand the fruits of their success and the adulation, without being prepared to assume any of the responsibilities of adult citizenship. Perhaps it has been part of their appeal for the adolescents that they themselves have not grown up in the full meaning of the phrase, any more than Brian Epstein was able to do, who right up till his unnecessary, wanton death went on referring to his discoveries as his 'boys', seeing himself as the fifth member of the hierarchy, the eldest Beatle. Then, when the group ceased performing together, except for recording sessions, though he was still their manager – 'the boss' as they called him with affection and gratitude – to the end, he could not help feeling to some extent excluded. So in order to try and prove that he was someone big, in the theatrical firmament, in his own right, he started producing and putting on plays, with dire results. He had all the money in the world to squander, but too little productive talent of his own. Depressed and disappointed, though he would not admit it, he finally turned to pep pills by day, and sleeping pills by night, a diet that was ultimately to destroy him.

Once he proclaimed to me, standing outside The Palladium, 'All that matters is to have your name in lights'. And I could not persuade him otherwise, though I had persuaded him to spend the Sunday before the Whitsun holiday on a journey all the way to Bolton in Lancashire, to hear an unknown singer in a pub, who had been recommended to me with such persistence and such enthusiasm by one of my readers, Mrs Simpson of Russell Street, that in the end I felt it would be churlish of me not to do something about it. His name was Michael Haslam, he was married and worked by day in a local tannery, and he specialized in singing ballads, such as *It's all over now.*

As it happened, Epstein was looking at that moment for a ballad singer, as a contrast on his touring bills to such of his properties as Billy J. Kramer and Gerry & The Pacemakers. Otherwise, I doubt whether he would have ever listened to my suggestion, and in a way now I wish I hadn't been persuaded myself to make the effort. Because to have done nothing might have been kinder in the long run to the dark, tall young man, with the sort of looks which Elvis Presley first made fashionable, and the physique of a miner, who packed them in at week-ends at The White Hart. Except that if the Beatles' impresario had not turned up that Sunday evening in Bolton, yet another pub singer might still be imagining he was only there because the luck of being discovered had just never happened to come his way.

Certainly the audience reaction that evening was tremendous and entirely spontaneous. I can hear it, smell it now. Even so, I was not entirely convinced myself. Was he not simply a handsomer edition, in a shiny dinner jacket, of my *Ganges* mates performing as they used to scrub the decks, an imitation of an imitation of an imitation? Undoubtedly there was a voice of some lyrical power, but did he also possess sufficient personality? And how would he stand up to another environment, bereft of his regular admirers, alone on a stage, or in front of a T.V. camera?

Epstein brushed aside my doubts. On the spot he decided to sign Haslam up with the arrogant impetuosity of a czar. After the entertainer had finished his performance, we stood in a little group in the passage behind the saloon bar. There was the singer and his blonde wife, Helen, heavy with child, and Mr Harrison, the proprietor of The White Hart, who was paying Haslam three pounds a night, and would not try to persuade him one way or the other, and my correspondent, Joan Simpson, who had made it all possible. Such a moment of drama and decision, in various versions and against a varied assortment of backcloths, has been played out in a hundred movies.

'As long as I work in the tannery, we have our own house, and here I am singing in my own home town,' Haslam volunteered, in the broad Lancashire accent that he seemed to lose the moment that he gave his interpretation of someone else's song.

It was as though for a moment he was secretly afraid, assessing the odds, arguing himself against the break from the daily routine he knew and could take in his stride.

I turned to his wife, half hoping to hear confirmation of his doubts from her, but all she would stubbornly repeat was, 'Mike can't sing often enough for me. I know he can be a star'.

I reminded Mrs Haslam of the points her husband had made. As soon as the process of grooming commenced, it would mean giving up their free living quarters, his safe job and pension, uprooting themselves and travelling south to London, which can be an inhospitable city for those who have previously spent all their life in the north. Would it not be better to stay where he was, a big pebble in a small pond? But she herself had no doubts, no doubts at all, and in the end it is the woman who decides. 'I know Mike can be a star,' she kept on reiterating again and again. The die was cast.

Two or three evenings later, Epstein and I met again, this time in my London home. We had arranged that he should pick me up and have a drink, *en route* for The Palladium. He was eager for me to see perform another of his protégées, this time the girl, also from Liverpool, who through his astute judgment had with surprising speed reached what used to be the Mecca of all music-hall artists. Cilla Black.

In the fervent hope that one day Mike Haslam, equally skilfully projected, would reach the same goal, I accepted, though Miss Black's nasal voice with its Liverpudlian vowels screaming at me over the radio at breakfast time had not created in my mind the most enticing of images. However, none of that was my affair. I could switch off the knob. Whereas the other artist, uprooted and disorientated, was to some extent my responsibility. In the forty-eight hours which had intervened, my initial doubts had only grown.

'After all, Brian, if I hadn't dragged you to Bolton, you would never have heard of him.' Even to myself, it sounded like a self-accusation, but my guest again brushed aside my fears.

'Don't worry,' he replied, with a rajah-like wave of his hand.

'But I *do* worry,' I protested anxiously.

'You shouldn't. Don't you realize, it's nothing to do with you any more. Mike Haslam belongs to *me* now. From this moment he is *my* discovery, and I shall look after him completely, change him, mould him, fit him into my set-up. All the credit, all his future success will be entirely *my* doing. You merely introduced him to me. Anyone might have done that.'

I was flabbergasted, rather than relieved, by this lofty declaration. In an instant he had assumed the air of the great, international impresario slapping down a small-time sleazy agent who had dared to suggest that he should have a slice in the property value of the unknown name about to be groomed for stardom. Of course, I wanted no financial stake in the young man's future. I was not in show business in any shape or form. At the same time, I surely had an ethical stake. A moral stake if you like. Anyway, something quite different and rather more binding.

But I was meeting the real Brian Epstein for the first time. Gone was the mask of mock humility, worn by the apparently modest young man fresh from the provinces, who in his original talk with me in that incongruous set-up of a hotel lounge had praised and congratulated everyone except himself. For the first time I glimpsed the strong hubristic streak in his nature which was swiftly to grow into a kind of sickness. Not surprisingly, I was dismayed and we had an uncomfortable evening, saved, as far as I was concerned, by the affectionate welcome I received in the dressing-room of Frankie Vaughan, who was the real star of the show. He and the boys in the band were in a poker session, but the occupant of the coveted number 1 room broke off without a trace of annoyance and jumped up from his seat to offer us drinks. How different had been my reception in the number 2 dressing-room. Miss Black was seated in an ungainly position, her legs sprawled out in front of a portable television set, and did not trouble to get out of her chair, or to make any attempt at conversation. After a few embarrassed moments, I backed out into the passage again, and it was then, at my suggestion that surely his new girl needed a matronly, experienced woman in attendance, to help and advise her back-stage, that Epstein made the comment that having your name in lights was the only thing which mattered. I suspect he thought my suggestion was an impertinent one, though it was only intended to be constructive.

Unfortunately, I had already promised to have supper with him afterwards, and then to see his new house, and Miss Black, dressed in a black leather coat, more suitable for the back of a motor-cycle, came along, too. Not wishing to lie openly about my reactions to her performance, and searching for some topic of conversation which would be of mutual interest, I asked my host if he was contemplating adding any other female singers to the troupe of artists under his banner. I am still surprised when I recall the reply I received, uttered with absolute and final conviction.

'No, I do not need any other women artists. Cilla is the Edith Piaff of England.'

Whatever she was or has become – and Miss Black has undoubtedly achieved a large and loyal following among her contemporaries – she is not another Edith Piaff. How could she be? Nor, for that matter, can she be compared, vocally, with the latest discovery to come out of France, Mireille Mathieu.

As for Mike Haslam, I spoke to him the other day after a long silence. He told me he had decided to stay on in the South, and was still singing whenever the opportunity occurs. No doubt he still hopes one day to see his name in lights and I wish him nothing but good fortune in his quest.

As for his powerful protector, he cannot answer any more questions. Even while he was still alive I never talked with him alone again, after that evening at The Palladium, when in the small hours I found myself standing in a room dominated by a row of telephones of different colours on a long desk. Nothing else about the house, the modernistic innovations of which suited his temperament, left any mark upon my memory. Of the furniture, the fabrics, the pictures on the wall – though we made an elaborate tour – I have but the vaguest recollection now; they were the stereotyped professional decorator's blueprint for a star. Only the telephones, those inanimate props of a tycoon existence, stare at me like a blown-up photograph on my desk. The symbols and instruments of a certain kind of power.

'I lift one receiver,' he told me exultantly, 'and say to the operator: Get me a Hollywood number. I book in that call, and five minutes later I am talking to New York. Hardly have I rung off, then it is Australia on the line. Everyone wants me, everyone wants the Beatles. Everyone wants all my boys.'

'What about the time-factor?' I asked. 'For instance, when it is midday here, and perhaps three o'clock in the morning there, or *vice-versa*?'

'I don't mind about that. I am ready to take calls all round the clock. I like it best sitting here by myself through the night, doing business. Big business.'

His usually deceptive quiet voice rose to a crescendo; he was playing the big scene in the third act from all the stage and screen dramas of which he had been cheated by his inability to make the grade as an actor in the legitimate theatre. But I had no desire to play in turn the part of the stage stooge, and fled from that house in Kinnerton Street to walk home through Belgrave Square, where at the corner of Chapel Street and Groom Place the nocturnal life of the fifth Beatle was finally to snuff out in the last of his London homes, whose larger rooms he had furnished in even more grandiose style.

Some months before that happened, he had a breakdown, which was hushed up, and then they put him in a private nursing home at Roehampton, which caters particularly for patients whose mind has been temporarily disturbed. After that he was never left without a friendly and considerate bodyguard, who became his shadow night and day. Except on that week-end when, in a sudden change of mood, he decided to drive himself from Sussex back to London, though it was a Bank Holiday week-end – as had been that week-end we ourselves had spent at Bolton.

The Chapel Street house was only a stone's throw from where my elder brother lives, and sometimes, when I was dining with my family, my sister-in-law, more in bewilderment than disapproval, would comment: 'Such strange people hang about Mr Epstein's house. They wear such peculiar clothes. Sometimes on a Sunday afternoon, there is almost a crowd. I suppose they are waiting, hoping that one of the Beatles will come out.'

That Sunday afternoon, when the news broke, and the police cars drove up, the flower boys and girls in their peacock clothes left the King's Road parade and crowded into Chapel Street, as though they were queueing up for a 'pop' concert. But the doors were closed, you had to possess a very special pass even to reach the anteroom, and as far as I was concerned the epitaph was spoken by David Jacobs – not the disc jockey but the show business lawyer, with the looks of a film star – who acted for so many other names in show-business beside the Beatles.

Now that it was all over, the final battle lost, Epstein's

adviser from the start spoke to me with a freedom he could not have done before. Nor would I have felt it right to question him.

'The trouble with Brian was that he had everything, and yet nothing. He had a strong family feeling, right till the end, and his loyalty towards the Beatles and his other properties, like Cilla Black, was fantastic. I suppose you could describe it as a kind of love affair on his side, but nothing stands still in life, and he was conscious that they were inevitably growing away from him, as they matured both as artists and people. This made him more and more restless and unhappy, though he wouldn't admit it except in one of his increasing moods of depression, when all I could do was to remind him how much he was worth, in money and properties of one sort and another. But even that knowledge began to lose its flavour. It was then that he started taking pills to try and recapture the sense of euphoria he had had at the beginning. It was imperative for him to feel that he was still in the swim himself, not just taking a percentage of their earnings.

'I hoped so much that the house at Heathfield would make a difference. I was delighted when he discussed with me, buying it and I kept on telling him what a piece of luck it was for him to find it, for it was really charming and secluded, and yet you could see right to the coast from the garden, and he was planning all sorts of alterations, Hi-Fi in every room, and a room turned into a private cinema. It was a new toy, and I prayed the magic would last.

'He had gone down that week-end for the Bank Holiday. But after dinner on that Friday evening, he suddenly changed his mind and drove himself back to London, alone. I don't blame his bodyguard in the least. How could one? The trouble with Brian was that he simply would not go to bed, and that week his guard had been up at all hours with him. He was dying on his feet for sleep.

'The next afternoon, late, Brian spoke to them at Heathfield. He had just woken up himself, and was having his breakfast, at six o'clock. He had his butler there to look after him, and though he sounded drowsy, that was natural and they didn't worry. What would I have done had I known? It's always so easy to be wise after the event. Sometimes one has a kind of instinct, and can act swiftly, but even then it can be too late, or impossible to protect the person indefinitely against himself, if the seeds of self-destruction are strongly developed in him or her. In this case we shall never know for certain exactly what happened. Except that he went to sleep again that night, and never woke up again.'

'But why, David . . . why does it have to happen like that? And more and more often these days. . . . The empty bottle of sleeping pills beside the bed.'

'I was very close to him, right from the start. I could advise him over many things, and indeed, tied up his business affairs to good advantage. In a way, I was closer to him than anyone. He really unburdened himself to me. Yet there was something in his nature that neither I nor anyone else could reach or alter. He was not so much a loner, as a oncer.

'What do I mean by that? I mean that he was incapable of any lasting physical relationship with anyone. He was incapable of love.'

We were talking in David Jacobs' own home, in Hove. I had watched this transformed from a medium-sized house, with a commonplace red-brick façade, set back a few yards from the sea-front, into an indoors imitation of a star's elaborate showplace in Hollywood. How enormously costly the gutting must have been, though the final result was oddly disappointing. The cold-looking imitation marble floor, the endless pale walls, the vast expanse of glass windows, the three or four smaller rooms turned into one huge living space cried out for the Californian sun all the year round, to light up and fill the emptiness. The house needed, too, the colourful, outsize personalities that are a commonplace in Beverly Hills. Moreover this brilliant lawyer – an extremely wise and compassionate counsellor – who had induced a wary respect for himself in the legal maze, needed no such flamboyant background to set off his personality. I suppose all of us have blank spots in the projection and management of our own lives – even those, if not especially those who do so much for other people – and this was his. Here in this psychadelic setting, so far removed from the conventional atmosphere of the English seaside, and even more remote from the London law courts where he spent much of his time, in a black jacket and striped trousers to match, he could dream that he, too, was in show business like so many of his clients. For had he not admitted to me frankly once that, like Epstein, he was also an actor *manqué*?

Having already usurped so much of the strip of garden at the back, to throw out the walls of his incongruously elaborate party-room, he was for ever obsessedly talking about yet a further extension in the shape of a heated, enclosed, swimming pool – 'it's going to be six feet longer than the Prince Littlers', and theirs you know is bigger than Binkie Beaumont's' – that he was seeking permission from the local authorities to build at that moment when his own life was cut off, like Epstein's, on a Sunday afternoon. The manner of his death was more sensational than any of his cases, often in defence of 'pop' singers found in possession of drugs, and the subject of newspaper headlines.

Of course, I did not visualize the kind of end it was to be, but for months beforehand I became increasingly nervous that the man who looked after all my affairs had lost control of his own destiny, and was no longer aware, cleverly, cold-bloodedly aware, as once upon a time, where each footstep was taking him. I now write about the progression towards the final, disastrous crack-up in the hope that it may cause some of those on the brink to draw back from their utterly false, self-deceiving assumption that 'pep pills are quite harmless, and not habit-forming, it's only hard drugs you have to worry about'. As though there was no connection between the two kinds.

I have no medical qualifications, I am not a trained psychiatrist; but haunted as I am for the rest of my life by the question-mark as to whether there was anything more I could have personally done to arrest the final disaster, it seems to me that the first link in this particular chain was that David, like so many people at the top of their particular profession, refused ever to rest. I would often hear him boast that all his travels, his flying trips to New York or Hollywood, were entirely concerned with his work. He was never really free, and did not want to be, though this enslavement was the beginning of the drug-induced *folie de grandeur* which was first to engulf him and then destroy him. Whenever I implored him to take a proper holiday, he would monotonously reply that without his constant presence his father's family business would collapse. Whereas, in the ultimate analysis, it was his own grave that he was digging.

On Saturdays I had a standing invitation to lunch alone with him and his mother, now in her eighties, severely crippled by arthritis, to whom he was utterly devoted and a very good son. She lived in a nearby flat, and whatever parties he was booming up for such theatrical friends and neighbours as Dora Bryan, they saw each other regularly every week-end. Saturday lunch was sacrosanct. However, when I was there, we were unable to have a quiet family meal together, since the telephone would rarely stop ringing. At first sight it would appear to be extremely inconsiderate of his clients to pursue him to his private residence, over the week-end, but I suspect that subconsciously he encouraged the practice. The sound of the telephone held for him the same kind of excitement and potential drama as it had for Epstein. Someone needed him; someone believed that he alone could sort things out for them. And he would come back to the table to eat up the tinned apricots, his heavy, opaque skin glowing.

Although he was to be seen eating at the Caprice, where he had his own table, with entrepreneurs of one sort or another, he himself was completely indifferent to food, and one did not go to visit him at home in search of a Lucullan banquet. He was attentive in offering you a glass of grocer's hock, but, again, he was unaware of the taste because he never drank anything himself stronger than a Coke. For a long time he did not need any such stimulants. His brain was ice-cold, razor-sharp; too sharp, some of his opponents would remark ruefully and bitterly. Yet he was apparently oblivious of the enemies he made, and was completely without fear in fighting the cause of anyone who had turned to him for help. Unselfseeking, he coveted neither honours nor social aggrandizement, and when he went to the States, in the protective entourage of the Duke of Edinburgh on one of his charity tours, it would have been only human if he had made some mention of it on his return, but he was as silent, even to his close friends, as he was about his multitude of legal involvements. For him, everything was in the cut and thrust of the battles he fought, and for a long time the tide went his way, because he was always able to pinpoint the flaw in his opponent's case and batter away at it. Yet however much involved he was in some *cause célèbre*, such as the Liberace libel case, he was never too busy, at any hour of the day and night, to listen to some small person in a mess, and however unimportant – or sometimes unsavoury – the case might be, he would find time and energy to sort it out, and often no bill would be sent in afterwards. Those who could well afford it paid for the others.

In the beginning, my own relationship was entirely a business one. Recommended to me by Gilbert Harding, whose own career he had sustained in a remarkable fashion, since Gilbert was another of those bent on self-destruction, and his own worst enemy, I myself in the twelve years that David Jacobs looked after my contracts, and all the other complications of my working life, never had cause for a moment's anxiety about my affairs; only for relief and gratitude. Instead my anxiety, increasing and terrifying, was in the end for him.

How much does one ever know about the intimate, emotional details of the life of even a close friend? I have always held that a man or woman's private life, except where it impinges dangerously on the community, is his or her own affair. Like all responsible members of the medical and legal profession, my lawyer was sealed off in a cocoon of reticence. A repository for secrets, how many of them were his own? At week-ends, everyone else poured out their troubles and problems to him, while he just sat there, on the long sofa, in that lonely room, listening. He would ask pointed, ferreting questions which had to be answered truthfully.

Yet in turn, one could never question him directly. In consequence, because I knew that I would only receive an oblique answer, I had to record the small though disturbing signs of a personality change, and impotently accept my inability to intervene. Whereas before he had been a noticeably shy and unobtrusive guest in one's own home, now, whoever was there, he would take the centre of the room and talk, talk, talk, incoherently and by no means always discreetly. He was like a jack-in-a-box, wound up to bursting point. Again, in a restaurant, it became embarrassing to be with him, for he would hold forth to the waiters like the worst kind of Moneybags. This sort of behaviour was utterly alien to the nature of the man who had always had impeccable manners and courtesy in public. And in public again, I became frequently astonished and appalled when he would come out with some such grandiloquent utterance as,

'I am going to break the monopoly of the Grades'. It was, of course, palpably impossible and absurd. Then why did someone who in the past had been so acute in his judgments make such a dangerous and ridiculous remark? Was it because his mind was becoming unhinged?

Overwork, plus what else? I was pondering about it all – was I my lawyer's keeper? – the evening that he came to my flat to change, before we went to a first night together, as we often did. Already myself changed into a dark blue suit, I had been reading the evening paper on my lap. 'Why aren't you wearing a dinner jacket?' he demanded. 'But it isn't that sort of first night,' I protested. 'Nonsense,' he retorted, 'go and put one on at once. They always like to see *me* in a dinner jacket. Where's Bardwell? Ring for him to run my bath.'

It was unheard of him to give orders to my staff. Utterly unlike his character, which I imagined I knew so well. My guest came and stood over me, pointing to the *Evening Standard* on my knees. 'You've seen the coverage they've given me.' 'I read that you were making a plea for mitigation once again in a squalid drug case,' I replied. 'Haven't you an *Evening News*? It gave me a whole column.'

Gave *me* a whole column. I looked at him, aghast. Was it my imagination, or were the pupils of his eyes dilated? They seemed suddenly excessively bright. He had always emphasized to me that, though he had often to assume the role of prisoner's advocate in drug cases, he would never for one instant even toy with the idea of experimenting himself. That was the sliding path to hell. Hadn't he seen the aftermath at close quarters so many times?

A woman friend, whom I had sent to David for advice, had rung up to tell me that two nights ago she and her husband had invited David to dinner, but had been unable to get a word in edgeways about their own affairs, because he had produced a non-stop monologue about all the glittering new clients from the States who were coming to him. 'This morning we had a bread-and-butter letter from David enclosing what do you think . . . a large red pill. "This is the unceasing source of my unquenchable vitality. Take it and see what happens to you." Of course I have despatched it down the loo.'

It had seemed an amusing joke, a harmless idiosyncracy, as

we laughed together over the phone; but soon a sense of uneasiness had flooded in. This was to increase as my companion went on chattering loudly through the performance – again an extraordinary thing for him to do since he had such a respect for the art of actors – and reached its climax the following week-end when we had arranged to go to a party together on the Sunday morning. As this was being given to launch the Brighton Festival by someone whose home I had never been to before, I needed a guide for the car.

That week-end I had as my house-guest my dearest woman friend, Joanna Kelley, who after seven years as Governor of Holloway had recently been promoted to be one of the Assistant Commissioners of Prisons. Inevitably there was little that she did not know about the other side of the track, though to meet her, elegant and at ease at a social occasion, you would never suspect what her life work was, how many excursions it entailed into the darkness of wickedness and despair.

We called for David at midday, and he came dancing out into the garden in his underclothes, and kissed Joanna, whom he was meeting almost for the first time, on both cheeks. In the bright sunshine his hair seemed unnaturally black, and his cheeks were coated with pancake. He was as bizarre as a travesty of Dorian Gray. Tactfully Joanna made no comment but admired the tulips in what was left of the garden, till our guide appeared in a screaming orange shirt he had acquired in Hollywood, and we all got into the car together.

A few minutes later he turned to Joanna and demanded, 'Where are we going?' She looked at him in bewilderment. 'But surely *you* are taking us, Mr Jacobs. Godfrey says that Lady Cohen is an old friend of yours.' 'Oh, we are going to Renie's, are we? All right, I'll take charge.' And did. So much so that at the party itself, such was his unnatural, over-excited state of exuberance, when I introduced him to the wife of the Vice-Chancellor of Sussex University, he took hold of Susan Briggs by the neck, shouting, 'I demand to meet the man who gets more publicity in our local Sussex paper even than I do. Where is your husband? Take me to him.' Whereupon he proceeded almost to frog-march her across the lawns.

That evening, as it happened, the Asa Briggs were dining at The Mill House, and Asa, discussing the morning's very pleasant social gathering commented, but without malice, because he is not that kind of person, 'I must say your lawyer was pretty high, before lunch'.

Joanna and I exchanged glances, with the same thought passing through our mind. 'But David only drinks lime juice or Coke or something like that,' I protested uneasily. 'I've seen him at dozens of parties and he never drinks alcohol in any form. I promise you, whatever it was, he wasn't under the influence of drink at the party.'

There was a momentary pause, and the conversation flowed on. Later, when my guests had gone and Joanna and I were alone, she said quietly:

'This can't go on or it will end in total disintegration. He is very close to a mental breakdown now. I have had so many cases to deal with of people on the border line. There are all the signs that he is most unwisely taking drugs of some kind. Perhaps he imagines they are just pep pills, not lethal pills. That is what they all think. . . .'

She was seated in the armchair opposite me, in front of the fireplace where we have relaxed so often, discussing every subject under the sun. Prison cases, but, deliberately, without a name or a face. The problems and the solutions. But this was different. This was happening to someone close to me, for whom I had both affection and respect.

'You assure me that he is a very kind man and a good family man, and has done a lot professionally for little people at different times. You cannot stand by, and let it happen, without making an effort. All these jokes about red pills aren't amusing, if the whole future of someone you care for is at stake.'

'Of course, I agree. But what am I to do? David's surrounded these days by a clique who flatter him and sponge on him. Increasingly, in every way, he is losing his judgment. It's as though a devil has got inside him.'

'Drugs are notorious for bringing in their train a complete personality change. All the same, the devil of drugs can be exorcized. Certainly in the earlier stages. You must be brutally frank, and repeat to him exactly what the world is saying about his increasingly eccentric behaviour in public.'

'But he wouldn't listen, Joanna. I did try but he brushed it aside. His attitude now is: don't interrupt me, you are in the presence of the greatest lawyer in the world.'

'Then you must write to him. Put it all down implacably on paper. That might shock him into awareness.' She got up from her chair, drawing her stole more closely round her shoulders, though the evening was full of the promise of summer. 'This twilight world of unreality . . . I have encountered it so often in the course of my work,' she exclaimed.

So it was I who was shaken awake. Half that night, after my house guest had herself gone to bed, I sat up in my writing room, drafting and re-drafting a long, imploring letter. I did exactly as my own best friend had bidden me. I was uncompromisingly factual. But at the same time I made it abundantly clear that I was doing this in gratitude for all the times that, as my lawyer, he had allowed me to unburden myself, listening most sympathetically to my own anxieties of one sort and another, and inevitably coming up with a constructive solution.

I realize now that I was simply wasting my time. (But supposing I hadn't tried. What would my feelings be now?) Yet another victim, in chains, had passed on too far along the road leading to purgatory. A week elapsed, and then from his London office came a brief acknowledgement, akin to 'In answer to yours of the nth.' 'Please don't worry about my health. I have never felt better. It is *your* health you should be worrying about. . . .'

A typewritten letter from a stranger. Even so, I still refused to accept defeat. I asked the junior partner of the firm to lunch in the privacy of my London home, and spoke with great frankness to him. He did not deny that something was wrong, but suggested that the explanation was that David had been under great pressure concerning a case where the original evidence had not stood up, and they had had to start again from scratch. Once that was sorted out, all would be well again.

I could not help feeling that this was wishful thinking. It was true that David had acquired an enviable reputation for never losing a case in which the over-all strategy had been worked out by himself. At the same time, I sensed that there was far more to the present situation than one or two defeats in the courts, bitter though they might be to his professional pride. He was a very sick man, but no one wanted to admit it.

I tried once more, inviting myself to dine one evening later in the summer. Could we have a quiet meal alone? I suggested.

On arriving at the house in Hove, I found to my dismay that there were two other guests, plus yet another new houseman, who our host, in one of his bouts of fevered eloquence, assured us was extremely psychic. A tall young man, of quiet demeanour, he sat down with us, after dishing up the meal, for which I had no stomach. And I noticed that our host, too, hardly touched his food. We sat at small separate tables, in the yawning aridness of the long living-room, as though our ill-assorted group were chance fellow-passengers, embarked on a futuristic jet, on a journey into space, final destination unknown.

As far as I was concerned, it was an abortive, uneasy evening. I left early, and as I reached the gate, from behind the front door scarcely shut behind me, I heard a scream of shrill laughter. Now the dreary spoil-sport was gone, they could enjoy themselves. Was that it? But once upon a time it hadn't been like that, and I was desperately sad at the sea-change.

I only saw David once again. The early part of the autumn I was in Canada, fulfilling television engagements, and embarked upon a coast-to-coast tour, as the guest of the Canadian Pacific Company. I spent my birthday in a train crossing the Rockies, and so did not expect to hear from David as I would usually have done. On my return, I rang up the office to be told, briefly, that the senior partner of the firm was ill, and resting in a nursing home. He was not allowed to see visitors, so there was no point in giving the name or address; but of course, anything sent to the office would be re-delivered.

In answer to the flowers I sent, I received another of those brief, typewritten notes on office paper I had come to dread, and how shaky was the signature. It was as though someone had helped him to hold his pen. Later I learned that the nursing home was the same one at Roehampton in which Brian Epstein had been placed, when he was recovering from the first of his breakdowns. But even with that information, and what it implied, (everything always comes out in the end) I was totally unprepared for the change in my friend's appearance and demeanour, when I also heard through the grapevine that he was back in the house in Hove, that once upon a time he had dreamt of transforming into a Hollywood setting.

I found him that Saturday afternoon not in the playroom where he had delighted in giving parties for stars such as Sophie

Tucker and Danny la Rue, but in the small front room, more conventionally furnished, on the other side of the hall. He was sitting hunched upon the sofa, in a pair of old trousers and a sweater, gazing vacantly towards the blacked-out television screen. Like a child given a new toy for Christmas, he kept on pointing at it and repeating the word, 'Television. Television. Something has gone wrong with it, but the man is coming to put it right.'

So that he might sit in front of it, all afternoon and evening, mesmerized by the changing tableaux, so far removed for the most part from life. How many times had I watched The Palladium show with him myself, in happier times. The Beatles, and Judy Garland, and Shirley Bassey. When I tried to lift him out of the dispirited vacuum into which he was now sunk, by discussing the latest development in a personal matter being dealt with by his firm, he continued to look at me with eyes that were blank. It was painfully obvious he could not recall a single detail about the correspondence which he had originally triggered off.

Instead, he drifted into a completely different subject.

'You'll understand,' he said in a confidential whisper, 'I am not sending any Christmas presents this year.' The munificent gifts, the widely-scattered largesse of a potentate. Yes, I understood. He usually spent Christmas in California. 'Are you soon off to Beverly Hills to convalesce?' I asked, clutching at the straw that such a change of scene, away from our depressing winter climate, where in the past he had always felt so much at ease and in his element, might still succeed in bringing about a metamorphosis.

'Oh, I can't,' he protested, in a shocked voice. 'You see, my mother is so ill. She is upstairs. I moved her from her flat. There are two nurses, on duty night and day.' Just for a moment there was a flash of the *folie de grandeur* manner, a stab of colour in his ashen cheeks, and then he slumped again, turning from me to stare glumly once more towards the empty television screen. My throat went dry. The doctors had taken away his unreal state of euphoria, but what were they putting in its place? I remembered the verdict of the eminent psychiatrist, after the death of another friend, who had thrown himself in front of a train at Piccadilly Circus, though he was by nature the gentlest and most unviolent of people: 'He had the bug of self-destruction too deeply embedded in him for anyone to be able to save him.' I could not think of anything more to say. There was nothing more to say, so that, in a torturing kind of way, it was almost a relief when the houseman came back and stood just inside the door. Except that he was not in uniform, but dressed in casual clothes, it was like the signal that a prison visit had to end, I thought.

This time no laughter pursued me down the road to where I had left my car. I did not get in at once, because I could not drive away. I was blinded not by the sea spray, but by the bitter tears stabbing at my cheeks. This was the end. At that moment, I knew with absolute conviction that I would never see again the man who had given so many people a new lease of life, a future without fear, but was unable either to cure himself or to be cured.

On the following Sunday I lunched in a flat suspended high above the sea-front. It was impossible to believe that Christmas was so near. The light off the sea, which always seems to have an extra brilliance at Brighton, was reflected on the walls and the ceiling. Once again I drank in with appreciation the simplicity of the all-white décor, that was as successful as that other far more elaborate and expensive one in the Hove house had failed because it was, somehow, dead. Inevitably we spoke of David's illness; my host had invited him to lunch that day, but he had refused, explaining that he felt he could not leave his mother.

'I am sure he ought still to be in the nursing home, and under constant surveillance,' I said. 'I hear that as soon as he heard that his mother had had a heart attack, he discharged himself, and apparently it is impossible to make anyone stay put anywhere unless it is a case of their being officially certified.'

'I saw David's houseman at a party last night, and when I left, he was still there. Apparently David had rung up himself, and asked if someone would look after the houseman for the evening.'

'I suppose David felt he was becoming so cooped up, in that house of illness . . . or else. . . .'

I did not finish the sentence. Had we not already discussed my own fears *ad nauseam*? Talk. Talk. Where did it get one, where did it lead? I drove home into the country, my own sense of uneasiness increased. All afternoon I could not settle down to reading the Sunday papers. It was as though subconsciously I was waiting all the time for the telephone to ring, and when it did, and the voice was that of a woman to whom David was devoted, I took the words out of Betty's mouth. 'David is dead.' At first we only had to accept the implacable fact, not the means. Both of us assumed that it was an overdose of pills of some sort, as in the usual, ever-increasing pattern, and when the next day I heard what had actually happened, and how David had been found hanging from the roof of the garage which he had had specially enlarged to house his magnificent Bentley, the means for the end seemed so brutally alien to his character, his fastidiousness, and at the same time so monstrously bizarre as to appear even now to me utterly and completely incredible.

A couple of days before the New Year, the telephone in my writing room rang again, and this time it was the voice of the houseman himself, though when my secretary, who was with me, answered the call and told me the name of the caller, it conveyed nothing to me. Why should it?

Puzzled, I got up from my seat to answer, and the voice said:

'Mrs Jacobs has asked me to ring up to say how pleased she was with your letter. . . . How is she? Oh, much better. She has decided to stay on here in Princes Crescent, and seems very comfortable in the suite upstairs.'

There was a pause. I remembered the week-end that Betty had been staying with me. David had shown us all the changes he had made upstairs, telling us we were the first to see them. The luxurious quarters he was providing for a living-in cook and manservant. 'So that from now on I can have every meal at home.' He was so confident, so certain about what lay ahead. Instead, the staff came and went, came and went. At least the staff sitting-room, I decided, was not being wasted after all.

The voice at the other end of the line was speaking again. It had another message to deliver. This time a personal invitation. 'I am asking a few of David's special friends, like Susan Wilding, for a little New Year's Party, tomorrow night. Are you free?'

No, I am not free. And never will be free of the lingering doubts, the weight of my regret. One Sunday last summer, on one of those glorious days when one exults just in being alive, I was giving a tennis party. One of my guests for lunch was Lady Cohen of Brighton, who is so active in Sussex for a multitude of

The Mountbattens at a Palace Investiture. A wartime team

A peacetime visit to Butlin's camp at Filey. Lady Mountbatten talks to band-leader, Ivy Benson

Earl Mountbatten of Burma at Broadlands, September 1968

crusading causes. Through David, we ourselves are now friends. As we walked on the lawn, beside the giant mulberry tree that I am assured is three hundred years old, she suddenly exclaimed:

'I can't believe it's only a year since David brought me here to lunch the first time. It was another wonderful day like this. How do you manage always to have such weather for your parties? And the forecast on the wireless was bad this morning, too, but you can never be sure how it will turn out. Isn't it strange, no one talks of David any more? It's almost as though he had never lived.'

The families of those whose sons and husbands and lovers were annihilated in the war that ended over a quarter of a century ago, must feel sometimes that they, too, are buried beneath the blanket of Time. Their griefs, their souvenirs, their self-torturing evocations of the past. They have had their faded snapshots – *'Life to be sure is nothing much to lose, but young men think it is, and we were young'* – their letters, scribbled in the gregarious din of a N.A.A.F.I. canteen, or sitting on the bed of a Nissen hut, in the half hour before Lights Out – there's a buzz we are moving out of here in a few days, I can't tell you where we're going but I'll write again as soon as I can, and roll on the Victory Parade – but there was no victory for them, if there is any final victory for anyone. The ones who were left behind to go on growing older mourn a fading memory in silence and with the kind of special dignity that the bereaved somehow muster, conscious that their own motions of living must continue in a manner that does not dismay or disturb those who are untouched because they came on the scene afterwards; to whom it is all a story told beside the chimney-piece, on a winter's night.

For my own part, I have never been frightened of death, only of not living fully every day. All the same, I have been unable to grow accustomed to its abrupt finality, even in war. I was still surprised, each time I felt the breath upon my own cheek. Especially that lunch-hour break, in Chatham, when astonishingly a mail orderly appeared out of the blue, with a bag of mail for our transit mess, and among it was a letter readdressed for me in a handwriting I didn't recognize, as we had never corresponded before. It was from Sandy's mother. The gunner's mate of H.M.S. *Pozarica*, the ship's stamp collector, and my last visitor from the ship, on shore. And now . . . what was this? . . . 'missing'...that terror-striking, covering-over, euphemistic term... Could I get her any details from the Admiralty?... as though I still had a telephone at my elbow, which I could lift and be put through to the head of the Press Department at any of the Ministries, instead of sitting squeezed in, at the end of the bench, in my overalls, hoping for a plate when someone else had finished with it. Impossible. Utterly impossible that anything could have happened to my beloved *Pozy* and her crew. To me she had proved herself invincible and invulnerable. Were not these the two demonstrative adjectives used in the telegram that the captain had always carried with him, as a mascot, in the pocket of his duffle coat, on the bridge? But there had been a change of captains. Yes, but she had taken part in the African landings and that operation was safely over. What could have happened to my ship?

It was weeks before I was to receive an eye-witness account of the end of that particular chapter in the story. The *Pozarica* had been helping to escort a convoy along the coast, an operation, compared with 'P.Q.17', regarded as less dangerous even than the Milk Run, when 'down sun' a flight of torpedo bombers had suddenly come in attacking low. There were about fifteen of them, Sandy's opposite number, 'Florrie' Ford, wrote to me later, and the ship altered course to avoid one 'tin fish'; but while she was still swinging another struck on the port side right under the aft gun-deck. Sandy had been exhorting his gun's crew to give of its best, and then – silence. They never found a single trace of his body. Altogether there were about forty casualties – dead, wounded, 'missing' – and the ship itself, assisted by the tugs sent out from Bougie, limped back towards the coast, until in the mouth of the harbour she finally foundered and sank to her rest.

'We had an auction in the mess for Sandy's kit,' 'Florrie' wrote, 'and they fetched a hundred quid to send to his missus. You know how it is, on these occasions. Even a stinking old cap will fetch a quid....'

Ian Mantle, who possessed the same intensely blue eyes as Sandy had had, and who like MacMichael had been a class-leader at *Ganges*, arrived triumphantly with two plates of grub, and gave me one. With the patronage of their resilient youth, they regarded me as the lodger who so often never got served. However, on this occasion, my usual gratitude was missing.

'What's the matter, Godfrey? You look as though you have seen a ghost.'

'I have,' I said. So implacably it was true what I had recognized in Sandy's eyes that evening he had called round to Ebury Street for his promised tot of whisky. Instinctively, as though I were alone in a funeral parlour, choosing a memento to be buried inside the coffin, as I had placed the small bunch of lilies-of-the-valley in my mother's waxen hands, I took out my paybook, shutting out all the faces and the bantering chatter round me, and extracted from it the snapshots that I always carried with me now. Pushing aside the plate of plum duff that Ian had produced as such a prize, I spread them round me. I was searching for my favourite one of Sandy, taken in the *Pozy* mess, a time-exposure which had been regarded by the amateur photographer as something of a feat.

Ian, just off to help commission his first ship, looked over my shoulder curiously.

His arm casually flung round me, I started to shake as though I had an attack of 'flu. 'There she is before she was camouflaged, and there she is on the working-up trials . . . that's before I knew her . . . and there she is lying off Bangor, when she was on the Irish Sea run, that was a piece of cake, and there she is when we got momentarily stuck in the ice . . . and that was taken when we were moored outside Archangel.'

Politely Ian picked up each picture in turn, and put them down again. I glanced sideways at his untouched, eighteen-year-old face, with its pink cheeks and trustful eyes, eager for him to say something complimentary, as one always made an effort to do when one's messmates came out with their pictures of their womenfolk and back gardens.

'I don't think I know her class,' he said at last, almost apologetically, in his polite, public-school voice.

Her class? A converted banana boat on the peace-time Spanish run. 'Don't you?' I echoed defensively. 'They're light ack-ack cruisers, with a complement of over three hundred crew.' I began boasting and exaggerating about the complement of armour and four-inch guns. 'They're packed with pom-poms and oerlikons, too.' As though any of it made any difference now that Sandy had gone. 'I've just heard that my best friend on board is reported missing,' I ended up.

'Oh, is he? I *am* sorry.' All the same, he did not ask to see Sandy's picture, because he was naturally more interested in the ship itself, since he was so soon to be off to sea himself for the first time. A brand-new frigate of the latest class. Now that was something.

'I know she doesn't look very beautiful, but I loved her very much.'

'Was she the ship you went to Russia in?'

'Yes,' I said, and got up off the bench, brushing his arm aside, though, heaven knows, none of it was his fault. Still, they could keep their plum duff. I had no stomach for it, or anything else at that moment. I picked up the photographs, that I could not interpret to anyone except myself, and shoved them back into my paybook. It was over, done with, and useless to try to describe what it had all meant to me. Later, perhaps, I thought, as I stumbled down the staircase, surrounded by a pushing, shoving mob, giving their imitations in a variety of accents of the Chief's parade-ground voice. 'Now then, let's have a good fall in.'

One day, perhaps, there would be a final roll call. Meanwhile Ian would go to his frigate, armoured by his innocence of what the sea itself could do, in some ways the most determined enemy of all, and I would never see him again, until one Sunday morning we could come face to face in Bond Street, by chance, in Civvy Street once more, and he was still looking so cherubically unbaptized, as though one of his ships hadn't been sunk, too, and he himself posted as 'missing'. So sometimes there was a better ending. The luck of the draw; the pieces of paper handed out to you in the drill shed at Chatham, and when in due course I received mine, instead of a lottery number there was H.M.S. *Sheffield* written on it. I read it with a sense of relief that soon now I would belong to a ship's company once more, and smell the sea instead of the stale, dehydrated odour of the Tunnel, even as I heard Sandy's voice saying again:

'Women are funny creatures, aren't they? Do you know what my missus said when I turned up on this leave? She said, "If anything happens to you, I am going to pack up at Sanderstead and go and live at Pompey. I shall feel nearer to you, in sight of the sea." You would have thought she'd have never wanted to look at the sea again, wouldn't you?'

You'd have thought that the same line of reasoning should have influenced me, considering how many ships I'd been sick in already, since my first sortie in a minesweeper of the Dover patrol, and considering what an abortive journey our draft were destined to have a week later from London to Scapa Flow, where, after sitting bolt upright all night in the train, not actually shackled together but with no room, even to move our legs, in the special carriages allotted to us, we discovered to our dismay that our new floating home was nowhere to be seen in that desolate anchorage; someone had boobed once again somewhere along the line; so that there was nothing for it except for us to be dumped, like so many other transit ratings before and after us, on board the depot ship. The *Iron Duke*. At any other time that would have been a name to conjure with, but not after a thirty-six hour non-stop trek, with even my hammock presenting a sorry sight at journey's end. Its lashings had become loose, its centre sagged, it was sopping wet. Didn't they say that in the long run you began to look like your dog? Perhaps it worked that way with your hammock, too. I felt just about as bedraggled, and our general mood of mass depression was scarcely dispersed when for our supper that first evening on board we were doled out a bully-beef sandwich, one to each member of the draft, and then ordered to sort ourselves out on our own and find a spare bunk below.

The only other time I had been on board a battleship had been in the days when I had still been writing my page for the *Daily Mirror*. The gun-room president of the *Ramillies* had written to invite me to a party in Portsmouth. Everyone in the office had warned me that there was a catch in it and that I would end up on the quayside without my trousers. Well, I had always been prepared to try everything once and, actually, the worst that happened to me was in the first five minutes. As I came over the side, it was to find all my hosts, very smart in their mess kit, drawn up on the quarter-deck to greet me. I was so astonished at the honour, I tripped over a rope's length and fell flat on my face. Almost inevitably it had been raining, and my stiff white shirt was neither stiff nor white any longer. At least it broke the ice and perhaps the snotties decided I had had sufficient punishment. Anyway, the evening passed off most amiably; it was my first experience of how well the Senior Service can take its liquor, and not surprisingly I found myself recalling it all now, with a certain wistfulness.

At least, though, the *Iron Duke*, like the *Ramillies*, was at anchor, and as one dreary day followed another while we waited for positive news of H.M.S. *Sheffield*'s whereabouts, we were, in one respect, having an easy baptism. In contrast to the time that, as a war reporter, I had been out in the North Atlantic in the *Arabis*, the first of the flower-class corvettes, so unsuitably named, so top-heavy that it had managed to roll and shake at the same time. One afternoon as the sea and sky merged in grey, sullen spleen, the coxswain tried to divert my thoughts from how cold and queasy and miserable I was by telling me how he'd served as a boy in the *Iron Duke*, in the days when she had been Jellicoe's flagship in the line. In consequence, to be a member of the crew was about the most prized billet in the whole fleet. Jamming himself against a stanchion, pulling the landlubber into the lea of the wind, he started to describe in a voice full of love and pride how the Commander-in-Chief would never allow himself to be piped from one end of the ship to the other, as is the usual Naval tradition. Instead, he would wander about on his own, stopping and talking to anyone he encountered, however attired or lowly that particular member of the crew happened to be. 'He'd ask your name, what your home town was, how old you were, and whether you were happy on board. I can tell you, he was worshipped on board,' the coxswain assured me. And on the day the admiral's barge circled the ship three times in farewell, there wasn't a dry eye on board.

The admiral's dining cabin was now the dentist's waiting room. *Sic transit gloria.* But sometimes the glory can re-establish itself in a totally unexpected fashion. Across the passage from where the dentist now received his victims – on board this dumping ground for matelots, for one reason or another adrift – was the Commander-in-Chief's day cabin. Wandering idly about the ship in one of the dog watches, since there was no cohesion in the existence of a transit rating in the slow, debilitating process of killing time, I turned the handle of the door cautiously one evening. I had been told the cabin was no longer in use, but I was totally unprepared for what I would find there. Everything was bare and scrubbed freshly clean. No furniture, no richness of rank, nothing but one unshielded light to reveal all that was left of the physical presence of that slight, shy figure who, on the one occasion when we had met between the wars, had reminded me irresistibly of the drawings of the figure of Mr Punch.

We had spent a week-end as fellow guests in the same house in Somerset, when he had been a member of the shooting party, attired in old-fashioned knickerbockers. He was so deaf, from too much gun blast in battle, that he sat at dinner unable to hear a word of what the ladies on either side were saying to him. On the Saturday morning, there had been a meet of hounds outside the mullioned windows of Chapel Cleeve, but when the photographer from the local paper appeared in the driveway, the guest of honour could not be found. Firmly he insisted on remaining in the background. This was for him the twilight, and he preferred it that way; he had done his duty and was content.

It had scarcely occurred to me that one day I should find myself in the ship for ever associated with his name, or that I should stand unchallenged on the threshold of his day cabin. The cold light shone down on a glass case in one corner, and in that case someone had had the vision to place his ceremonial sword, and his cocked hat crowned with gold, and something else, to create, as it were, I decided, an armed trilogy; his prayer book bound in green leather.

After my discovery, which I hugged to myself, I would make a secret pilgrimage each evening, and shut the door softly behind me, and stand there, instinctively taking off my cap, as though I were in a chapel. Not a lady chapel, but a seaman's shrine. In this cabin were once taken decisions that concerned the whole Navy and influenced the outcome of great battles at sea. Now only the emblems of the previous power and pomp remained. And they had added the prayer book, to make a trilogy, presumably to remind chance visitors like myself how ephemeral all else is. To me it seemed that the simplicity of the three emblems placed together, represented equally the simplicity of the man himself, as the boy on board the *Iron Duke* in its days of splendour still lovingly remembered him now in his manhood, a simplicity which I had only glimpsed until I had been vouchsafed this further revelation. I was strongly comforted, and learnt a lesson from that unexpected confrontation that has remained with me ever since. For surely to be simple and humble, in the honest sense of the word, as he had clearly been, are qualities that one should seek to cultivate, however stumblingly, in a world too dominated today by plastic standards.

One evening I was invited to attend a concert across the passage. The audience was very small, and in its own way equally select. It consisted of the dentist's tiffy, since he possessed a private wireless set, Petty Officer George Kent, and myself. I was only there because, having encountered this particular petty officer in the writers' office, where he had been ensconced, or incarcerated – it depended on one's attitude of mind – for a whole year now, he had proceeded to take me under his wing. After all, I was a kind of writer, too. And that was one link. But far more important in his eyes, I actually knew all the principals in the cast of *The Dancing Years*, and that evening, on the wireless, there was to be a whole hour, sheer, unadulterated bliss for him, devoted entirely to the melodies of Ivor Novello. George, who had a round, friendly face and air of resigned cheerful imperturbability which I greatly envied, was a passionate devotee. A life and death worshipper. Like many other men and women drafted into one of the Services, in self-protection he had succeeded in establishing two lives for himself. Briskly and competently he went through the motions of doing his allotted work in a manner that satisfied Authority, but all the time, though he hid it from the rest of his mess, there was another existence for him, a life of the imagination, hovering at the back of his mind, colouring his waking consciousness, and making the monotonous routine in this barren anchorage bearable. The second man took complete charge the moment that the B.B.C. orchestra broke into the overture from *Glamorous Night*. Unselfconsciously George squatted on the floor of the cabin, with all the scores of the different Novello musicals spread out round him. As the orchestra switched from one familiar melody to another, so was he able to follow the singers, page by page. He could not read the music, but he knew all the words of every refrain by heart. A song in one's heart. The banal phrase took on a new meaning, as I watched his happiness and allowed its aura gratefully to envelop me.

We had discovered our mutual liking for Novello's music, by chance the Sunday afternoon we went ashore. 'We may as well stretch our legs,' George had suggested encouragingly, 'though you won't find it like Pompey.' That was the understatement of the war, as I was to appreciate almost as soon as we disembarked from the drifter. Scapa Flow is the bleakest and windiest landfall with human habitation upon it that I personally have ever encountered. What is considered a comparatively peaceful day up there would be classed as a sixty-mile-an-hour gale in the south. There was no tree to be seen because presumably no tree would survive, and even the few mountain goats looked thoroughly dispirited.

The pipe of 'Liberty men fall in' represented, for any ship anchored in the bay, one of two alternatives. The tin hut that was a canteen plus cinema, or the Church of Scotland canteen that was situated a couple of miles along the only road. We had come for a constitutional and a constitutional we would have. So we put our heads down against the wind, like forwards in a rugby scrum, and fought our way in silence. Occasionally a sad-looking pongo* would pass us, coming from the other direction, seeming, in his shapeless battle-dress, like an inhabitant of Macbeth's blasted heath. And each fresh visitation out of the damp mist made me recall a comment that one of the first bomber pilots to attack Berlin and get safely back to his base in Yorkshire had made to me. We had been discussing and assessing degrees of courage in the mess at Driffield. I was suggesting that, perhaps, the bravest men of all in wartime were those who volunteered to be members of a submarine crew. He agreed that their courage was absolute, but added, rather to my surprise, 'The men whose guts I admire most are the really isolated searchlight crews.'

At the time I had been puzzled by his remark, but now I was beginning to change my mind. As though he could guess my thoughts, George yelled above the wind, 'The greatest excitement in these parts is to try and scrounge an egg to take back to the ship, from one of the few outlying farms. But this isn't the day for such an expedition.'

'Shall we get an egg for our tea at the canteen?' I shouted back, trying to imagine what it must be like for the crews of ships anchored at last, and the men all night in their hammocks, after the trip to Murmansk and back. With a longing that in the darkness becomes a kind of gnawing pain for the 'bright lights' and the 'big eats' ashore. For a sight of Sauchiehall Street in Glasgow on a Saturday night, or their favourite local in their

* Soldier.

home town, or in Pompey and Devonport, and 'up the smoke'. And then instead, this. What an anti-climax.

Still, I did find inside the canteen door a prodigal display of all the Sunday papers laid out for sale. It was only when I had greedily bought one of each, astonished at such totally unexpected service, that I realized that they were not this Sunday's issue, but a fortnight old. However, when I carted them back to the ship I was rewarded by the welcome I received from my fellow starving exiles.

The lady who had sold me the papers also took our entrance fee for her 'club'. Fivepence. It was hardly excessive for what we received. All afternoon, snug and warm from the gale outside, we could browse through the few ancient books on the shelf, have a game of ping-pong if no one had purloined the ball, and bunk down in one of the battered armchairs in front of one of the two stoves, with a cup of tea and a plate of paste sandwiches thrown in. No egg, but all for fivepence. Miss Coventry who bobbed round us all, irresistibly reminding me of a chirpy robin, looked as though she might lay an egg herself at any moment. As the afternoon wore on, during a lull I asked her if she didn't find the loneliness – and the eternal wind – rather forbidding, but she assured me, with the kind of Scottish accent that always carries conviction in its train, that she was a great deal too occupied ever to be lonely or downcast for a single moment. It wasn't so much a statement of fact as a personal declaration of faith. One felt that running this canteen in this blighted spot was the climax to her whole life, giving it a true Christian meaning, at last. I do not think I am being fanciful when I suggest that there must be literally thousands of ex-servicemen who to this day remember Miss Coventry's welcome and the amenities of her canteen, with the kind of nostalgic emotion that comes to you when you faintly hear the snatch of a tune that was part of your youth, emerging through the open window in a street down which you are passing.

There was a piano of sorts in the canteen. It had a few of its notes out of commission, but no matter. One of our fellow guests, also looking for his ship, Alf Roberts of H.M.S. *Jamaica*, settled himself down on the stool, and ignoring the hazards of the keyboard, soon had a group of us round him, and one more sing-song in full swing.

'I say, chum, can you play any of the music from *The Dancing Years?*'

'*Waltz of my Heart?*'

'*Waltz of my Heart.* Oh, get cracking.'

George Kent shoved me aside and leant over Alf – is he still playing the old, familiar tunes on a Sunday afternoon in his own home in Nelson? – and his face was transformed as he started to hum in harmony, only breaking off to describe each scene, as number followed number. Soon everyone in the hut had gathered round, and George had a hushed audience as he described what was happening on the stage. Unconsciously, whenever Alf struck a wrong note, or the piano momentarily let him, George would raise his voice a little, calling the actors and actresses by their Christian names, as though they were dear and familiar friends.

'This is where Roma comes back from England to Austria, and she seems no longer a little girl, and Ivor plays for her to dance. This is where Muriel goes for her singing lesson, and her teacher – that's Olive Gilbert, she has a wonderful deep voice and plays a famous singer in the show – joins in and Ivor persuades her to come back to the stage. The duet's called *Wings of Sleep.* Oh, do let's have an encore, chum. . . .'

'When shepherds tend their flocks. . . .'

Not on Scapa. No flocks on Scapa. But the hut, and the desolate surrounding terrain had faded. We were all in the Adelphi theatre, where the show was playing at that moment. All the colour and the romance of Ruritania was being coaxed from an out-of-tune piano, translated and evoked by a compère with a singing voice. It was a strange if spontaneous partnership, but against all the odds, it created its own magic.

One final reprise of *Waltz of my Heart*, and the pianist had had enough. It was his turn to make a request: 'Got a cigarette, chum?' The spell was broken, though George's face as he turned towards me was flushed and ardent, as though he had just come from a rendezvous with a lover. 'I've seen the show three times,' I said, and then stopped, lest it sounded like a boast. You had to be so wary, not to sound like a line-shooter. However, I needn't have worried on this occasion. Three times. What was that to George? Hadn't he seen it no less than twenty-seven times himself.

It all came out in a flood. 'I saw it first in Glasgow. That was when the show was on tour, before it came back to London. I was stationed at Greenock. I got ashore every other night, and it's an easy trip into Glasgow, if you've got an overnight pass. And I got a week-end, too, so I could take in both the matinée and evening performance. Now every leave the first thing I do when the train reaches London in the morning, I go to the Adelphi. I am always the first in the queue when the box office opens for the day. Once I arrived on a Monday, and they don't play Monday nights. You can imagine what I felt like then. I had been thinking of nothing else all the way down in the train. I was so excited, I couldn't sleep. Still, I was able to book for three performances in a row, went down to see my mother in Pompey, and came up again for a second burst. One good thing about being based where I am, there's nothing to spend your pay on, you can save it all for leave.

'What I'd like best of all. . . .' I had a hunch he was going to say 'get the autographs of Roma Beaumont and Muriel Barron and Olive Gilbert, and could you help?' But it wasn't that at all. Something far more breathtakingly stupendous. 'What I'd like best of all,' he repeated with a kind of awe in his voice, 'but it would be too wonderful . . . I couldn't possibly expect it to happen . . . would be to be in the audience on Victory Night.'

'You are sure the show will still be running?'

My temporary oppo, who so tactfully ignored the fact that I was only an O/D, looked at me in blank astonishment. I might as well have asked him if he believed that it was our side who would eventually be victorious and dictating the armistice terms. And the way that George had gazed at me with such pitying scorn came back to me on the first night of the recent revival of *The Dancing Years* at the Saville Theatre. Almost subconsciously I began to search the stalls before the lights went down, not for the faces of celebrities, but for the unheroic, homely countenance of my friend the P.O. writer in the *Iron Duke*. Surely he would be there, if he could be there. Or was he in the gods above? And surely he would be looking for me, too. Or wouldn't we recognize each other? The hour-glass changes. There's the rub. The heaviness of middle-age descended upon me, and with it a mood of sadness, in no way assuaged by the actual performance, poorly played and sung in comparison with the original cast, and a cheese-paring production into the bargain. This was a meagre tribute to the memory of an artist, whose own favourite composer was Wagner, and who never made any pretentious claims regarding his own talents, during his lifetime, but whose music nevertheless has achieved its own small stake in immortality.

In the intervals, that night, disappointed and resentful, I stayed in my seat, to find my thoughts returning to Scapa Flow and the Church of Scotland canteen. Did it still open its doors every Sunday afternoon, and who had taken Miss Coventry's place, and had someone donated a newer piano? And were the papers still a fortnight old? And did the wind still blow as mercilessly as it is described in a book I have just finished reading?*

'The real master there was the wind . . . All camp buildings, both our overcrowded Nissen and wooden administration huts, were anchored down by steel hawsers slung over the roof, and attached to deeply-buried stakes. I recall evenings in the canteen when we felt the floor rocking and bucketing under our feet, as the whole hut strained its wires. What was more important, the barrels were rocking, too, so there was no draught beer for us . . .'

There was no draught beer for us, either, when after what seemed like a century of useless inactivity we were remustered, and despatched to the mainland again, to take train for Greenock. We were promised that H.M.S. *Sheffield* would appear at any moment over our fresh horizon. Meanwhile they put us in temporary quarters on the quayside, where no provision had apparently been made for us to sleep overnight or, as it turned out, for several nights together. There were three-tier bedsteads, without a mattress or any bedding, placed uncomfortably close together. We spread out our hammocks on top of what seemed like barbed wire, and tried to get our heads down in an atmosphere that swiftly rivalled the Black Hole of Calcutta. Our quarters in the *Iron Duke* or even the Tunnel began to appear like the hygienic amenities of the Ritz in comparison. Especially after I made the discovery of the crosses on the seats in the Heads.

Small neat red crosses. Needless to say, I hadn't noticed them till I was standing up again. What I had noticed was the long queue waiting outside the sick-bay. Poor so-and-so's, I had registered, more short-arm inspections. But perhaps that hadn't

* *Scapa Flow*, written and compiled by Malcolm Brown and Patricia Meehan. Allen Lane, The Penguin Press.

been the reason for the queue at all. The crosses could only mean one thing. That set of lavatories had been in use – *were still in use*? – for V.D. patients, who had caught the plague and were in the condition of: Stay away: Danger.

When I returned to the thick, soupy fug of much-travelled socks, damp clothes and tobacco smoke, I welcomed it in my nostrils; I felt safe again and wisely held my tongue. They would find out for themselves fast enough. Besides, why spread more gloom and despondency than already enveloped us. 'Got a stamp, Goff? May as well tell my girl I'm still alive. I'll pay you back when....' When we got our back-pay. No one had doled out even a 'sub' since we left Chatham, because no one would accept responsibility for a draft in mid-motion. And when H.M.S. *Sheffield* did eventually come into harbour, and we were shooed on board, it was to be greeted with the only buzz that turned out to be correct during the whole time I was in the *Andrew*. The ship was about to go into dock for a refit, and we had arrived just in time to help with the de-ammunitioning. Just as soon as that dirtiest and most back-breaking of jobs had been completed to the satisfaction of those in command, we would be redundant, and whereas the rest of the already blooded crew would be going on leave, port and starboard watches in turn, we, still awaiting our baptism in seatime, would be returned, like empties to the brewery. In this case, Chatham.

When I look back on this period in my life, the desolate isolation of Scapa Flow, the red crosses, like the signs of the plague, on the lavatory seats, the anti-climax of the journey back to Chatham, followed a few days later by another draft chit, taking us all the way back to the Orkneys for the second time in six weeks, I sometimes can't help wondering how I managed to survive not so much the physical challenges as the mental subduing of my natural buoyancy. I think I did so by hanging-on in my mind, and repeating over and over again to myself the words that the crucified cabin boy of sixteen, Jimmy Campbell, had spontaneously uttered to the stranger bending over his palliasse, in the Archangel hospital: 'We dinna lack anything here, except, maybe, a football to kick around the ward.' That sentence had become like a talisman to me, an unintended exhortation never to be defeated. Moreover, it was extraordinary how, at the very moment that you were convinced that you had truly reached the nadir of your fortunes, someone or something came to your rescue, and the latest crisis, though not perhaps fully resolved, wasn't so utterly hopeless, after all. Like my first night on board H.M.S. *Cumberland*, every inch as impressive as the *Sheffield*, a county-class cruiser of which Ian Mantle would have entirely approved, though on the mess-deck she had been christened, for all time, 'the three-funnelled bastard'.

Not surprisingly, it was a long time since I had used our nickname, which grew in affection the longer one was on board, till a few months ago a snapshot of the ship, taken off Iceland, much thumbed and rather crumpled, was literally thrust under my nose. The ambience was unusual, for it happened not in the bar of any inn frequented by ex-matelots, but in a Bristol store in the middle of a signing session, when I was very fully occupied autographing copies of the paper-back edition of *The Infirm Glory*. There was a mêlée, like a female version of a rugger scrum, round the desk where I was seated, when suddenly down on top of the copy of the book I was about to open and autograph came a huge hand, with tattoo marks on the wrist, and a voice, to match, bellowing, 'Remember her, Goff? The three-funnelled bastard. Eh?'

I can't imagine what the throng of shoppers thought. I was oblivious. For looking up, I found myself having my hand pumped by one of the stokers who'd been on board the *Cumberland*. We had never met since. Had I seen him in a bus, it would be no use to maintain that from a crew of over eight hundred I would have recognized him – any more than I would certainly have recognized George Kent. It did not matter. He had produced the password, just as he was producing his wife to shake my hand, too. 'I always promised the missus I'd bring her to see you one day,' he announced with beaming pride. I longed to get up from my seat and carry him off to the nearest port of call that was licensed to sell rum, to spend a glorious hour yarning with him and having a few tots in gratitude that we had both survived the Arctic wastes and the hideous bleakness of the Denmark Straits, which was all part of the *Cumberland*'s patrol duties. Alas, business was brisk that day at Lewis's, and I was there on show to smile and politely thank the purchasers. 'Do you remember the Sheriff?' he called out like a drowning mariner, as the possessive circle closed in again, obliterating his massive head and shoulders.

Did I remember the Sheriff? How could I ever forget him, I thought, as I wrote his name by mistake on the flyleaf and had to cross it out and put my own name instead, even if he had not christened one of his two sons after his shipmate and we did not still exchange Christmas and holiday cards, and keep in touch with our family news.

The Sheriff alias A. B. Burgess, had received his nickname because he was wont to cram a battered old cowboy hat on to his head, and charge down the mess-deck, in the dog watches, astride his hammock, as though he was on Bronco Bill's steed, after them there Indians. 'The Sheriff rides tonight!' Anything for a belly-laugh. Although he was one of the more phlegmatic members of Mess 15, this was his contribution to maintaining the morale of the ship, his way of letting off steam for us all when we had been closed up for days, which could seem like weeks on end. All in all, he was the ship's best entertainer, though you wouldn't imagine it if you met him today, a master baker, living in a neat council house, the front garden of which is full of colour in the summer, in Breightmet, outside Bolton, where I have visited him and his pretty wife, Jean, with the corn-coloured hair. It gives me a particular pleasure to sense their happiness, because it was through me they met in a rather unexpected way, and married, and I was the best man at their wedding and still have the picture of us taken after the reception in a private room at Bolton Town Hall.

But that comes later in the story, later even than when he said to me, with leave in the air, 'Bring back a picture of your garden for my ditty box.' It wasn't much of a reward for all that he had done for me, not only on that first night on board, when after descending what seemed like innumerable companionways I finally ended up in the right mess, which appeared to be deserted at the moment except for a fellow with a thatch of unruly hair and cheeks burnt sienna colour from the wind.

'Hello,' he said with a friendly smile. 'You the new draft?'

I nodded, sick and tired of being asked that question. First on board the *Sheffield*, and now here. How long did it take until you were considered to be an 'old hand'? Considering my standard of incompetence, probably never, I decided.

'Got a billet for your hammock?'

This time I shook my head. I felt at that moment like the

original orphan of the storm, for had I not searched already all along the surrounding spaces, in vain, for a pair of free hooks. Perhaps because my first acquaintance on the ship was a real orphan, he took pity on the newcomer, or perhaps it was his nature always to be helpful at sight. Both 'Burge' and his brother, I heard later, had been brought up in the Greenwich Naval School for Boys, because their father had been a casualty of the other war and lost his life at Jutland. In consequence, whenever we came back into harbour, and the pipe went out over the loud-speakers for every mess to send its own Mercury to collect the mail, there would never be an envelope, in the subsequent scramble, addressed to A. B. Burgess. I don't know if the others were aware of it, but being a trained reporter I could not help noticing the omission, and feeling, in consequence, almost ashamed because of my own bounty, I'd hand over any newspapers I had been sent, so as to keep his eyes occupied in that period of sudden stillness, almost like that of a cathedral, when instead of an organ, in the distance, there would be soft piped music, and on everyone's face there would be a shared look of beatitude.

'Well, let's see if we can find you a gash billet.'

Gratefully I followed my scruffy saviour along the passages that went aft, already filled with gently-swinging snug cocoons, getting their heads down early, past the forecabin Flat where the cinema was rigged in port and church was held on Sundays; on past the gunroom (don't think of the *Ramillies* now) and the padre's ever-open door, to the keyboard Flat, where in the captain's office the deciphering of the secret signals went on day and night, until finally, outside the officers' bathroom, at last a resting place for my body, at last.

'I'll give you gulpers tomorrow,' I said gratefully, using the kind of language I imagined he would use and understand best. This was the very start of our friendship, and I hadn't begun to realize yet – how could I? – that the Sheriff, though he seemed to enjoy playing the fool, and being the butt of the mess, had another side to him that loved all growing things, as a contrast to the eternal waters of the deep, and that he possessed very gentle manners, despite the fact that whenever he went ashore it was never to sleep in civilized comfort in someone's home, but always at the Y.M.C.A. or the Sailors' Rest.

After that, he was always at hand to help me from the kind of blunder it was all too easy to make on board, outraging the traditions stretching back to Nelson's day. For example, you could use what language you liked – and I soon ceased to be surprised at the lurid increase in my own vocabulary – but the one thing you must never do was to call a shipmate 'a bit of a bastard'. I once made the mistake, having just been called a four-letter word myself by someone else, and was lucky to escape a fight. It took 'Sippers' for several days running to put that right. Again, you must never start eating your portion that had been dished out of the billy-can, however hungry you might be, having just come off watch, until every other fellow in the mess had had his plate filled; exact helpings all round.

My worst blunder of all was when it came to be my turn to be cook of Mess 15. I had asked all the right questions about the collecting-up and dishing-out of the grub, but had omitted to get precise instructions about the rum, of which a fresh barrel had to be opened every third day at sea. It had been explained to me that the official dosage was one-third rum, two-thirds water, but my mentor had failed to add the warning that it was sacrilege to wash up the glasses containing our daily tots, thereby dispersing the accumulative aromas that enveloped the rum trap, where the glasses were stored, and which hung from the hook above the table in each mess. And woe betide anyone who touched it or fetched it down except the official rum-drawer for the week. By the time my week of office came round, I was beginning to get my sea-legs, so that my stomach no longer rebelled at the stale, potent aroma, as it had at first when I was an easy touch for old salts like Jimmy Green. He would watch me craftily with his bloodshot eyes, the only touch of colour in his parchment face, and almost snatch the glass out of my hand, remarking sorrowfully, as in one fell swoop he gulped it down, that it would only have turned my stomach up. On the contrary, warming my innards, it would probably have been as powerful a cure as champagne is supposed to be. Anyway, Jimmy wasn't taking any chances, and with two glasses now empty beside him he'd sit back, belching with contentment, while I was despatched aloft with the gash bucket once again.

It always seemed to be my turn again, but perhaps the lord of the mess, the Killick, a rank equivalent to an army corporal, had long since decided that this was the best cure of all. Kill or cure. The bucket would be slopping over with garbage, the stench of which would envelop you as you stumbled up the companion-way to the upper deck. Here, likely enough, you would be met by a tempest of sleet or snow, the deck itself would be ice-slippery, and the distance between the companion-way and the gash-chute was seldom navigated without either most of the bucket's contents being blown up into your face, or else your falling flat on your backside, with everything spraying out round you. This happened to me on several occasions, and each time I was filled with terror lest the commander, that fearful figure, would be on one of his prowls and come upon this distasteful sight. Captain Goodenough, as he became, who had won his D.S.O. on board the *Prince of Wales*, clearly already regarded me as garbage, for when he handed out jobs every morning I was for ever being allotted the Heads to clean out, or the stanchion rails of the quarter-deck to shine with Bluebell. But the same implacable powers of nature which frosted the stanchions green again so swiftly also came to the aid of myself and my gash bucket. Within five minutes the overflow of the soup we'd had for our dinner became a frozen, brown lake, over which the Buffer*, who could have stood in for Henry VIII, strode carelessly without comment, while I held my breath.

Our first patrol, on leaving Scapa, was in the Denmark Straits, between Greenland and Iceland, where apparently there are always conflicting currents, with the wind blowing one way and the tides another, and, in consequence, such mountainous seas that one of the six-inch guns had been stove-in on a previous trip, with several casualties including a man swept overboard. You were always hearing stories, too, of smaller ships than ours having their backs broken, and never being seen again; a total loss. One afternoon, with the empty gash-bucket beside me, I was leaning over the rail, retching my heart out, when someone did stop beside me, and not pass on, tactfully, as they usually did. It wasn't Jimmy Green, but of the same vintage of shellbacks.

In his own fashion, he tried to console me by telling me how he had served in these same waters in the last war, when the Duke of York, as he then was, had also been on board as a member of the crew of H.M.S. *Collingwood*.

'He was only a snottie, of course, and he was a very poor

* Master-at-Arms.

sailor. Sick as a dog he was, poor sod. I can see him now, like yesterday, leaning over the rails just as you are doing, and coughing up blood.'

'What happened to him?' I asked, not really caring at that moment.

'Oh, we had to put him ashore. He never went to sea again.'

'But I like being at sea,' I protested, half-heartedly.

'Then if you do, you are the only one who does. But don't you worry. Nelson had a bucket on the bridge, they do say, at the Battle of Trafalgar.'

Only a fortnight before I joined her, King George VI, now dressed as an Admiral, had visited the *Cumberland* during one of her brief spells at anchor in Scapa Flow. The royal inspection was a commendation for having set up a record for the most steaming-time of any ship of her class since hostilities had begun. However, it was not the kind of record which greatly pleased the crew, since they all agreed it had gone to the head of our captain, who was clearly determined to break his own record again before the war was over. His living and working quarters were so remote from the mess-decks that during the whole of my time on board I caught a glimpse of him only once, going over the side at Hebburn, with his Scottish terrier at his heels. Whereupon I wondered how good a sailor the latter was, and what he'd feel like squeezed numbly in the port-director in the middle-watch.

This is where I finally ended up, as the communications number, combining this duty, more uncomfortable than onerous, with that of being the telephone operator in Y Gun turret, at action stations. But in the mornings, on patrol, when our domestic duties were allotted to us by the captain of the quarter-deck, I was considerably relieved if I was assigned nothing worse than cleaning the brass stanchions. After all, that was no more complicated a task than dusting the front-stair banisters for a housemaid in a ducal mansion. Except that this was out of doors, of course, and exasperatingly so, since often a sudden blizzard would swiftly wreck one's handiwork. After first squeegeeing the decks in the dawn, to the *sotto voce* accompaniment of *Onward Christian Soldiers, but not too fast in front,* I would hide behind the super-structure of my own gun turret, while the ceremony of Hoisting the Colours was once again being enacted. In this way, I would conceal both myself and my tin of Bluebell, at the ready in one hand, and my wodge of cotton-waste in the other, so as not to offend the eye of the commander, whose voice coming over the loudspeaker, implacably penetrating every corner, every cabouche in the ship, would be implemented, in his fashion, by our own P.O. Craven. 'Now get dug in, lads. One, two, six.'

But why *six*? That was one of the mysteries that were never vouchsafed for me on board. I learnt many things. A non-smoker myself, I learnt that the value of a cigarette was almost beyond price. We received an allotment of twenty a day for sixpence, and as barter I found that for one I could get my hammock slung for me, for two I could get my dhobi-ing* done, for three I could be allowed an off-watch period in someone's cabouche, a word I have never seen written, only spoken, but which represented the ultimate luxury, a secret hiding place, a private dug-out, where you could rest snug and undisturbed. It wouldn't be any larger than the cupboard-space usually allotted in a house for storing the Hoover and a few pots and pails. That didn't matter. There was a light, and you could rest your back against the wall, and read, or just doze till the pipe for the next watch forced you awake and on your feet again. One, two, *six* . . . But why six? That's what they were always shouting at me; 'they' being the ones you had to look out for if you were loafing, or caught red-handed in the act, as I was on one occasion, soliciting the left-overs, the gash from the captain's cook, 'Mickey' Rooney, and another Geordie, my head half-way through the hatch. Even then I was saved by turning round and saluting smartly and in my most innocent voice exclaiming, 'Shall I carry on, sir?' What an effect those mystic words always had, what balm they seldom failed to bring in their train, whatever the rank of the confronter. 'Yes, carry on, carry on.' Thus was honour preserved, and with it the patina of a pussar ship.

Before I'd finished, I had set up a record, too, for the number of tins of Bluebell I had used during my sojourn on board. Not from efficiency, but emptied over the side when all eyes were turned upon the Band of the Marines, the smartest regiment of all. I had soon got wise to the dodge that the moment I was able to show that a tin was used up, I could repair for a fresh supply inside the quarter-deck locker, which was a kind of super-cabouche, and the preserve of Willie Craven. His dark, Geordie

* Washing.

head I had found rather intimidating at first, till I saw him smile. That smile was that of an ordinary seaman who has never grown up, despite the rows of books that adorned his super-cabouche, and all the sea-time he'd put in, including the China Run. But it wasn't a request for the loan of a book that had brought me there, but the hope of getting warm at the minute heater, which I usually found that Bob Malloney and Harry Piper, the latter in my mess, had laid flat on the deck so that they could brew a cup of kye. Fortunately they had a legitimate right to be there, as they were in charge of all the tackle, doling it out to suppliants like myself. And a cup of kye into the bargain, if you were very, very lucky. The best cocoa in the world, without any doubt, and made from slabs of special Navy chocolate. I have never had it since, but I could taste its richness in my mouth once again the day that my telephone rang in my hotel suite in Perth, where I would emigrate tomorrow if I were still a young man, for Western Australia has greater potentialities than any other territory of the globe's surface. And it was to Perth that with his family Harry came as a migrant when his time in the Service was over at last. I had no idea of this, any more than he had any intimation of my own visit till he saw my picture in the local paper. But though it was 110 degrees in the shade outside, and it used to be often twenty degrees below with us, it did not seem in the least incongruous to hear Harry's voice intoning once again, 'Funny how you always turned up just in time for a nice cup of kye.' I forgot the sweat pouring down my back; I was flapping along the curved passage of the superstructure in my sea-boots, polishing not the stanchions but my excuse before I reached the cabouche door. I had just manufactured a brand-new one. 'Someone's "borrowed" my scrubber.' Someone was always borrowing your hat, if you were so green as to leave it unguarded for a moment, or your gloves, or your sea-stockings, or the long blue scarf, sent by some kind Women's Institute knitting party to the 'boys at sea', that in the port-director at night was worth its weight in gold. But I wasn't thinking of any of the things I had already 'lost' since we set sail in those icy waters, but only of the immediate, pleasant possibility of the kye being on the hob.

'How are you getting on, Down Under, Harry?' I asked, thinking now how in the mess I'd never heard him raise his voice once. Like the Sheriff, he had been a man of peace.

'Fine, fine, Goff. Australia's a great country. Tell the Sheriff if you send him a postcard. Of course, it's not always as hot as this, thank goodness, but then it's never so cold neither, as it was on the Run. Do you remember chipping the ice off the quarter-deck and it freezing again before you had time to have your dinner?'

'And do you remember, Harry, the time we forgot to post a look-out, and Willie Craven caught us good and proper and confiscated the jug?'

'Yes, he did an' all, but you had all your alibis pat.' He mimicked the voices, and he was a good mimic, despite all his mildness in the mess, where he spent any free time drawing in chalks. 'I only came to get some soap . . . P.O. Potts sent me for a bucket . . . I want some rope to tie up the life-lines. . . . But you, Goff, we knew what you was going to say before you opened your mouth. . . . Please, I want another tin of Bluebell.'

What was Willie Craven doing now? He was standing there in the doorway of the hotel sitting-room, which was temporarily my cabouche, not really angry, though he always put on a splendid show. Pushing the others out, and keeping the final lash for me. 'What the hell do you do with it? Do you *swallow* it, man? Get cracking the lot of you . . . one two *six*. . . .'

I wanted to question Harry as to whether he knew the answer to that one, but I was late already, I had to get cracking that instant, as I was due to address a mass meeting of the latest intake from Britain. The transit ratings of today, I thought, as I arrived at the hostel and faced them from the stage. This was my own first visit to Australia, and though, rather to my surprise, it had turned into a love affair, it was different for me, I reminded myself, because I could always make tracks for home when I had had enough. It was good to be with my countrymen and women again, though I had been warned that I might get a lot of complaints when question time came. In the end there were fewer than I expected. As soon as the men landed a job, they settled down fast, being accepted at once into the masculine freemasonry of beer-swopping in the midday break. It was more difficult for the women, left all day in the hostel, longing for their own kitchen, missing their favourite shops in the High Street, and their neighbours dropping in for a cup of tea. All the same, the majority seemed to be settling down pretty well, and those who weren't were the ones, I suspect, who always imagine that the grass is greener on the other side of the fence, or over a distant horizon. The ones who wouldn't really be happy anywhere, because they weren't prepared to work – to 'give all you are', as I once heard Toscanini in his broken English exhort his orchestra – or to accept the assessment that in any country, and in any climate, life is ninety per cent monotony, and only ten per cent excitement.

That is what the regulars were for ever telling us at sea, and I didn't like to mention that it had been the other way round in the case of P.Q.17. Now the balance was being readjusted with a vengeance. Instead of the midnight sun, there were unnaturally long hours of darkness, preceded and followed by a strange, nebulous twilight which created its own melancholy, difficult to resist. While the uneventful watches, cooped up in the port director, seemed interminable. Thus the excitement, when it did come, the ominous sound of the rattles summoning everyone to their action stations, for which one always had one ear listening, was almost a relief, and certainly something to natter about for days afterwards, at tot time.

My overriding compulsion on these occasions was not to be the last man inside our turret, before we closed up. It was quite tricky for me when I had made it, because I had to get right across and round the corner into the cabinet, the size of a public telephone box, where three of us were squeezed together. Still, I was getting used to that from the port director, and at least it was warmer here, even if it did stink of stale oil. My role in the team was to pass on the firing orders to the rest of the crew via 'Rosy', so named because he possessed the pink cheeks of a Norfolk farmer's boy. He always had a sweet smile of encouragement for me, as I climbed over the mysterious wealth of machinery that I never properly came to understand, except that one careless step, my sea-boots sliding over the end, and I could be for the big jump below. So I was always thankful when this hazard was over, though it meant that the next one was about to commence. The gunnery officer had had the idea that the one job I couldn't muck-up would be answering the telephone and in a clear voice passing on the 'gen'. What he had left out of account was our variety of accents. The marine, somewhere far away in the bowels of the ship, who was our oracle, had a strong Devonian accent, which became even more pronounced in the heat of battle; mine, as I sought to conceal my nerves, became increasingly an imitation of a B.B.C. announcer; 'Rosy' had a charming bucolic burr. Mix them up, and what a concoction resulted. No wonder that our turret never seemed to be on target or to 'bear', so that there would be endless post-mortems afterwards as to why we hadn't been able to indulge in a 'full calibre shoot'. I am sure I was the major culprit, though my gun captain always loyally defended me and I would promise to try and do better next time.

The battle drill was always the same. Away for-ard the first of the guns in range would make the ship buck and reverberate. With dry mouths we would wait our turn, our big moment, that never seemed to materialize, eager for any scrap of information as to what was happening beyond our blind, steel confines. The *Von Tirpitz* at last? A German cargo runner from Japan, trying to slip through our blockade? It was always an anti-climax, as for instance the occasion when a U-boat broke surface only eight hundred yards away. Another curtain-raiser for the show-down with the enemy skulking in the Norwegian fjords, which most of us professed to long for, if not all as ardently as Harry Marshall, an ex-London fireman, who had volunteered for the Navy because he was so sick of being at the receiving end, so anxious to have the chance to fight back. Yet so far, the highlight of what he'd had to tell his street, when he got leave, was seeing a seal sitting on an iceberg, with its thumb pointed over its shoulder. 'I swear it was,' he announced down the length of the mess-deck. 'He was asking for a lift, I'm telling you, and he didn't half look chocker. . . .'

At least, you didn't feel chocker when you were closed up in your gun turret. Apprehensive, concerned, but never bored. I would try to steady my nerves by comparing just how much more intimidating it must be for those far below; the men sweating in the shell lockers and the magazine, the cooks who must continue the motions of preparing tomorrow's dinner, as though they had been engaged to work in a peace-time hotel – we were the size of the Dorchester – and most of all, the sick-bay tiffies wondering just how soon their services might be needed. Not forgetting the stokers, who during the last of the aerial attacks H.M.S. *Pozarica* had to fend off, beat a tattoo on the engine rails. It was like a jazz band, Mr Ford, the chief engineer, told me afterwards. But at least it drowned the swish of the near misses, if not the knowledge that if a tin fish had your number on it, you were hopelessly trapped.

So personally I didn't complain overmuch about the monotony rather than the excitement. Indeed, I greatly preferred our gun turret in harbour, in Iceland, when it wasn't manned, and Curly, another member of the team, suggested that he and I should commandeer it as our own cabouche, for dealing with our joint correspondence.

Curly, Blondie, Lofty, Tubby, there were such a multitude of descriptive nicknames, and though you lived at close quarters with them all for months, so often you never came to know the owner's real name, unless he happened to be in your part of the ship, or answered to Buster, and then you realized it must be Brown. Curly was a Londoner, so that meant that I was Townie to him, which made things even more confusing, except that we got one thing straight about our bargain from the start, and he never went back on it by a single bar. He would hand over the whole of his nutty ration, every week, if – and here was the crunch – I would write his love letters for him. Not indiscriminate love letters, mind you, but only to one 'smashing party' he'd met in the train, coming back from his last leave when the *Cumberland*, for a change and before my time, was standing off Greenock.

He shook his head when I called her by the favourite descriptive synonym for sex on shore, swinging up on to the lockers beside me. Only a partition separated us from the solo school of the stoker P.O.'s mess, with the steps going down to the drying room on one side of us, and the seamen's wash-house on the other. So that it was against a moving frieze of figures, naked except for a loin cloth or a pair of Wellingtons, passing up and down, or queueing for their dhobi-ing, that Curly, my turret mate, unburdened himself of his love.

First and last, I must get it straight, she wasn't a smashing party. That was the whole point why I was being brought into it. She was something quite different. She was, as the narrative unwound, that old-fashioned expression, a nice girl. A W.A.A.F. In an anonymous uniform like himself, going home on leave to Glasgow, she had invited him to her home, because he had made the others in the compartment shove-up for the all-night journey, thus making room for her to get her head down, as we always called it. 'To sleep a little, perchance to dream.' And when she had woken up, she had said:

'Have you time to come and have breakfast, and a bath if you like? I always think you sailors look so lovely and clean.'

'That was funny, that took the cake,' Curly exclaimed, with the wonder still in his voice. 'You know the kind of muck sweat I'm always in, handling those projies. So I say back, "Maybe your ma wouldn't like you to bring home a wicked matelot". "My mother would wish me to bring home anyone who has been kind to me, so that she can thank him, too." Look what she says in her letter.' He pressed the sheets into my hand, and pointed half-way down the page. I had the feeling he could have recited it all off by heart. '*It was as though somewhere a trumpet sounded.*' 'Now that's poetry, isn't it? How can I answer that? The only trumpet I knows of is the one the feller bashes at Green's Playhouse. But I didn't want to take her there, somehow . . . look what she says in her letter,' he repeated.

I started to read now from the beginning.

'I hope you didn't find it very dull just staying at home each time you came ashore. I am afraid it was very selfish of me, but being in the W.A.A.F. has made me love my home even more, and you made even washing up the supper things seem so pleasant. Mother and Dad said they'd never met anyone so full of fun, and that you were always wagging your tail. That's because we once had a retriever dog called Curly, too. Because of his lovely coat. I love the way your hair grows. It's so full of life. I hope you don't mind being compared to a dog. Curly was very faithful. . . .'

I looked up and there was Curly gazing at me with the moist, dark eyes of a dog. 'Goff, I'll lash you up with my nutty every week. I swear I will. You know how much you like nutty, why, they calls you The Nutty King. I can't write like she does. She's been to a good school and won prizes for her English, she told me so, and I can't spell proper, and it takes me a whole dog-watch to write even a page to my own ma. She told me she'd had a very quiet life till she joined the W.A.A.F., and she hoped it wasn't dull for me. What I want you to tell her is how smashing it was to sit in front of the fire, in a bloody fine armchair, and toast my feet . . . and yarn with her sitting opposite me, sewing, and looking up and smiling at me, as though I were the wag of the ship. Oh, you know. . . .'

Yes, I knew now, in a way I'd never known when I had done my trips at sea, sleeping in the captain's day cabin. No watch to keep in five minutes, no chivvying, no Authority eternally on your back. The curtains drawn against the rain, firelight on her face, the deck firm beneath your feet, no movement, no creakings and groanings. Everything snug and ship-shape, instead of not a notion where your next anchorage would be, and all your past adventures now seeming like good jokes in the rosy glow with a glass of beer in your hand, brought out in the guest's honour. Yes, I knew. I could tell her all that and more, as though I were writing to a love of my own. Curly hadn't even a snapshot of his inamorata, so I couldn't envisage her features. Perhaps that was a good thing. She might have looked quite ordinary to other eyes.

All in all, it was a strange courtship. I had imagined that my share of it was to be one letter, an answer to hers, but the draft I produced went so big with Curly himself that he suggested that we should adjourn to the gun turret, where in peace, and without detection of our conspiracy, he could laboriously transcribe each sentence in his own handwriting, with me at his side, translating my own illegible scrawl, and acting as the Oxford Dictionary into the bargain. Spelling had never been my strong suit. But Curly's abiding worry was lest we should sail again from Reykjavik, where one of the scattered, welcoming cafés on shore had an unexpected notice in its window, FISH AND CHIPS TONIGHT, before he could receive an answer to his amorous bombardment, his tender siege. As I had not tried my hand as a ghost writer since the days when I had written tennis articles under the name of the Wimbledon favourite, Kay Stammers, and shared the proceeds fifty-fifty, I began to get as jittery as the real wooer. Not that my doubts prevented me from accepting the three bars of nutty that were our weekly ration. Nevertheless, my own relief was almost as overwhelming as it would have been if I had heard that the war had come to an abrupt end, the evening that Curly came tearing into the Recco space, where we used to forgather for 'Goffers' from the soda fountain, blowing the froth off the top, as though it were a pint of the best instead of an innocuous lemonade or orange-flavoured concoction. I could see from his face that something tremendous had happened. 'Goff, Goff,' he called out over the clamour, the immense, gregarious friendliness of the aftermood of mail time. 'It's okay. It's okay. I've got her answer.' For once, shy as he usually was, he didn't care a P.O.'s button about the crowd gathered round the mock N.A.A.F.I. bar. He was so exultant, so much over the rim of the world, that he started to read out her letter in front of everyone. I suppose he could have sons now of the same age as he was that night, but whatever has happened to him and his bride, in the long littleness of the peace, nothing for Curly, I imagine, could ever have quite equalled the sublimity of that moment when he declaimed:

'Your letter was lovely, the nicest letter I have ever received. You write just as though you are in the room, talking to me, and I can feel I can put out my hand and touch your hair, my darling. . . .'

'My darling. Oh gosh. . . .'

We stared at each other, smiling, both of us speechless. The furnace of his happiness warmed me, burning my cheeks, and I felt the same joy as that other evening long ago when I heard that my first novel had been accepted, and I ran from the publisher's office down Henrietta Street to the post office at the corner, to send a telegram home. I was twenty and the future belonged to me at that moment, as surely as it belonged to Curly at this one.

The next morning at *Stand Easy*, up came Curly, still looking like a dog that has been given a juicy bone, to press a Mars bar into my hand. A bonus? No, what they call I believe in my brother's legal circles, a refresher. I had not been let off the hook yet, but at least it meant that my locker became so chock-a-block with nutty bars, some in silver paper, some without, some plain, some full of nuts, that one evening when I was opening the locker to stow away my overalls for the night, and the ship chose that moment to give a sudden lurch, there was bounty spilled out on the deck, and in such prodigal profusion that in no time a thieving mob had collected, professing to assist me, and a cry went up like a football spectators' chant, 'The Nutty King, The Nutty King'.

After that, it was no use pretending to anyone asking for the loan of a bar, because he was as hungry as I always was in the middle-watch, that I was skint. Nor did it take long for the story to reach the port director, where I usually rationed myself, on watch, to two bars, one for myself and one for my chums. Up till Curly's bartering proposition, my chief source of supply had been swopping two cigarettes for a bar. I've often wondered since if I've missed my true vocation. Perhaps I ought to have been in Trade.

When I ladled out my nutty in the port director, reaching in the pocket of my oilskin, it would mean a shifting of everyone's positions – rather like 'When Father says "turn" in bed we all turn' – with the G.I., P.O. O'Leary, squeezing his long legs into less space than was the privilege of the director's captain. I used to try and hold back till we were three-quarters through another watch. By that time, ruthlessly exposed in our cage, which hung suspended high up, over the side of the ship, all sense of feeling would be gone from my hands. In our efforts to hasten the dragging minutes, we would have endless arguments as to whether the Malta or the Russian convoy escort trips were the more unpalatable. Never having been on a Malta one, I wisely held my tongue, unlike the Killick, who had served in the support force for the landings on Crete and was not the man ever to allow us to forget it.

'Now see, it was a different kettle altogether with the Junker 88s. The bleeders used to pinpoint us at twelve thousand, then do a mucking glide down to about eight, before they dropped their stuff. See?'

I didn't like to mention that I had been given some opportunity to observe the Junker 88s in action, in these waters, for that wasn't really the crux of the discussion. So I said soothingly, instead, that the Med must be a great deal warmer, of course, if you find yourself pitchforked into it. At the same time, too, the barrage must be more intense, your ship would be an easier target to pick out in that clear atmosphere than in the Arctic waters with such brief hours of daylight for the major part of the year, and visibility most of the time almost down to zero. Therefore our present Run was in one sense less murderous, if rather colder. After all, if the Killick had told us once he had told us a hundred times that in the director of his ship, off Crete, instead of the motley assembly of balaclavas, scarves, mittens and sweaters which now enveloped us, he had worn nothing but a pair of shorts. 'And they bleedingly well stuck to the seat. It was so hot . . . see?'

See. But that was precisely what none of us could do, peering into murky, untrammelled nothingness ahead of us, the sleet freezing on our faces and no room to manoeuvre, even to blow our noses. Was it already weeks ago that the captain's voice had explained to us that from now on it would be part of our duties to gauge with precision just how far our convoys could proceed on a northern curve, without danger from the rim of the ice barrier? Heaven knows, I had had a clear enough view of it in the previous brief summer in these parts, looking at first sight as innocent as the sugar icing on a birthday cake; even so there had been something dauntingly impersonal and implacable about its beauty. Now, in contrast, although it was for ever swallowed up in the snow and mist, its existence seemed far more tangible, an almost living presence to be endlessly plotted and captured by the delicate antennae of instruments, that picked up every 'alien object', be it iceberg or U-boat, even perhaps to be talked to on the telephone receiver that hung at my side. You became as fanciful as that, your thoughts chasing each other over the whole spectrum as you waited for another dawn.

As it would inevitably be a false dawn, there would be endless arguments about that, too, as to which was the most arduous and unwelcome watch to keep. Four hours on, and four hours off. And of course you were hardly in a position to take your pick between the First – (eight to twelve) – the Middle, or the Morning, (four to eight). I was always particularly allergic to the Morning Watch, because I would be drowning in sleep when the warning pipes penetrated the snug security of the Keyboard Flat, which not much more than three hours ago I had reached with such thankfulness. Now it is three-forty, and if I don't show a leg pretty smartly I shall be in the rattle, I remind myself, as I rewind my scarves like bandages, pull on my sea-boots and, still drunk with sleep, flop towards the tarpaulin flaps leading on to the deck. Often enough, I would be shoved through them by a little sardine of a fellow in our mess, whose accent I had much difficulty in interpreting, but, unasked though not unthanked, had made it his task to tip me out of my bunk, if I showed little sign of stirring or of having heard the bugles. Then, as though I were a sheep and he the shepherd, he would guide me out into

Vivien Leigh on the lake at Tickeridge Mill

In the garden of Tickeridge Mill

Vivien Leigh as Lady Macbeth at Stratford

the blackness of the open deck. Here the unchanging wind off the ice gripped you by the throat and doubled you up, so that you choked and gasped as though suddenly immersed in an icy tank. Above the wind, you would hear together the bugles' final warning.

'Get cracking, mate, and look where you are going.' The shaming thing is that I can't remember his name now, only his accent, which has made me grateful ever since to the whole breed of Geordies. His own destination on watch was elsewhere. So I was on my own now, struggling up one companion-way after another, and each one more exposed. Apart from the wind buffeting you, so that in the blackness you felt yourself being thrust sideways against the rails, you could also feel the snow freezing into ice on your face.

It would seem like eternity before I reached the top deck, within hailing distance at last of my destination, suspended diagonally above the port beam swivelling in its mysterious arc above the nothingness below. Now came the part I dreaded most, without any guiding light or support of any kind. The last few steps of my journey never grew, from repetition, less perilous. First one boot on the ship's rails; then as I stretched upwards towards the slanting stanchions that knit the director to the main body of the ship, and was just about to heave up my other leg, invariably for no apparent reason, though it always seemed to be part of a malevolent conspiracy by Nature, the ship would give a tremendous lurch, like a horse outraged that a novice should dare to leap on to its back. This would make me tip forward. so that I was spreadeagled half over the narrow abyss, between the ship's side and the director poised above it. Sometimes, I admit now, I used to feel at this moment that it would be almost better to relinquish my tenuous hold, and be done with it, once and for all. But then from above me, as though it were a beacon of reassuring light, a rescuing voice would call out, 'Whose relief are *you*?' I am somebody. I still matter. At that I felt an extra dose of adrenalin pouring through my frozen arteries. With my last ounce of strength, I heaved myself up so that my head was now level with the director's side. 'The Communications number, sir.'

At last there is a general murmur of greeting from the hooded orchestra dimly silhouetted against the swinging horizon, with one human instrument loud above the rest in a solo of thankfulness. This is my oppo, released now to clamp down the companion-ways I have just surmounted, till with delight he can surrender himself to the embrace of the sweaty warmth of the mess-deck. However, first I have to climb back again off the rails, so that he can clamber out, hoisted on his way by his companions' arms. It is one-way traffic with a vengeance. Moreover, in the course of the watch he has become a cripple, without any volition in his numbed legs. There is no heating in the director, exposed on one side to the elements, as there is in a bomber, nor electrically-warmed gloves, as an aircrew rightly receives as an issue. In consequence, my oppo, having reached the deck, leans on me heavily like an old man, though he is, in actual fact, ten years my junior. We can hear the other reliefs for the watch, for the pom-pom platform, as well as ourselves, the signals deck, and the point fives, rolling like the sound of a funeral march up the last of the companion-ways. 'Good laaad, good laaad,' he proclaims, loud enough for all to hear. 'You were the first again . . .'

How warmly my heart beats again. I am alive. Nothing can ever take away from me that spontaneous tribute. Good laaad indeed . . . how generous of him, too, to ignore that last night I was so late in the procession, that in another second I would have been reported adrift over the telephones. But tonight I am ahead of time for once, and all the aching has momentarily vanished from my bones, and the weight of my thirty-five years from my shoulders. I can even smile, if a little sardonically, as I heave myself up for the second time on to the rail, at the memory of a deceiving summer's afternoon in a southern harbour, when a pretty young thing, being taken on a tour of the ship, was heard to exclaim as though speaking a line in a Noel Coward comedy, 'Why, my dear, it must be like sitting in a box at the theatre.' 'Well, not quite,' replied her proudly possessive swain, nervously looking over his shoulder in the vain hope that the comment would pass unrecorded.

Yet actually there were similarities; especially in size, though in our 'box' three-quarters of the space seemed to be taken up with machinery, which made it more cramping than any rear gun turret. There was also a similarity in that, as at a theatre, we were shut away from the rest of the audience, who on a first night, would be waiting in expectancy for the curtain to go up, just as we waited, in speculation, to discover what lay, each night of the voyage, behind the drop-curtain of fog and blizzard.

From the orchestra pit at the theatre, the occupants of the stalls listen to the sounds of the musicians tuning up, and open their boxes of chocolates. Well, we were doing the same now, on our instruments. The fresh batch of recognition passwords have been checked and counter-checked, and for the next four hours the phones have settled over my ears, while the range-finder has reassured himself that not only the person but the nutty supply of the communications number is present and in good condition. Now it comes: Crete, I think; but to-night there is a variation. For once, before the Killick can get started, the range-finder has a different sort of time-swallowing story to tell, about a shippie of his who used to hoard his nutty.

I never discovered whether it was intended as an indirect warning to me, to avoid a repetition of the episode when my own secret store was scattered over the deck – surely better for each member of our team to have a whole bar to himself every night than such indiscriminate largesse – because I became so swiftly engrossed in the saga of Shiner's own supply of nutty. Apparently he never touched even a single bar of his ration, and I simply couldn't envisage such self-discipline, such forbearance, unless he had made some kind of sacred vow. In retrospect, I suppose it could be called that.

'He collected it all for his girl, see. D'yer know what she said to him on his last leave, just as she was waving him goodbye on the platform. "Don't forget, darling . . . bring back your nutty to me." '

'And did he?' we all chorused.

'Did he, bleeding Jesus? I'm telling you what happened, aren't I?'

We were hushed into silence, but even without the rebuke of the actor who had taken the centre of the stage, the messenger from burning Troy, we would assuredly have been too spellbound to interrupt again. Certainly I would, having such a special interest in the nutty market on any ship.

'Bring back your nutty to me. . . .' Week by week, the pile began to increase steadily in the special tin in Shiner's locker. Sometimes he would be able to augment his weekly supply by

doing a shipmate a service and demanding this coinage as the price. At last, he had notched up his half-century, but he could not let his girl know how positively he was keeping faith with her because his ship – like the *Pozy* for a time – was marooned against a Russian quayside, and there was no communication with the world at home. That did not stop him writing letter after letter, recording the latest score, although he must have been at least half-aware that his ship would probably, in the end, be bringing back its own mail. His messmates saved up their pay for their first run ashore in a more salubrious climate; he continued to hoard his nutty, and however tempted Shiner was by hunger in the night watches, he doubtless comforted himself in his hammock, with endless reveries in which, after he had placed the casket in her hands, she would reward him with total surrender.

'A full calibre shoot was to be his reward.'

At last the day came when the ship reached home waters again. Leave was in the offing. Not one more optimistic, wishful-thinking buzz, but a certainty. Meanwhile, the mail drifter had come alongside, and down the steps from the recco-space leapt Shiner in anticipation, singing *Devotion* at the top of his voice. He insisted on continuing to vocalize, despite his mates pleading with him to pipe down, until the letters for his mess were handed out. He had naturally expected at least a dozen from his girl, after all these months of non-communication between them. Instead there was only one addressed to him and this was from his sister – like the Sheriff he had no parents – who worked in the same factory as the one with the sweet tooth and the key to a certain matelot's heart, and locker.

As he started to read his sister's letter, Shiner stopped singing, in the middle of a bar. His voice trailed away into the universal absorbed silence. It was only when he got up from his bench, so violently as almost to knock the others off their perch, that Shiner's oppo, now the range-finder in the *Cumberland*'s port director, noticed that something was amiss.

'His hand was bloody shaky, he couldn't get his locker key off his chain. He just stood there fumbling. You know how it is, after the mail's been given out, how quiet it is in the mess. Well, somehow, it seemed extra quiet now, like it is up here when summat's just coming into range and we know that all our guns are hanging on for the exact range which they'll get from us, and as soon as we have passed it on, the whole works 'll go up.'

As if to remind me that this could happen, at any performance, any night, an enquiring voice came through from the Control Room, and immediately I was once more the automatic communications number. As soon as the flap was over, I was dying to hear what happened when Shiner finally got the key into the locker. But first it had to be explained that Shiner had met his girl through his sister, who worked on the same bench at the munitions factory, and what was in her letter to make her brother's hand shake so much. More than enough, apparently. His sister had caught her factory friend dancing cheek-to-cheek with a Pongo at the Locarno one Saturday night, and feeling kind of responsible, because of the original introduction, didn't waste many minutes on the Monday morning before she was weighing-in strongly on behalf of the only other member of the family.

But I think it would be only fitting if this part of the denouement was put back into the narrator's mouth.

'As soon as they had clocked in, she says to the party as how she'd seen her on Saturday night, carrying-on all ends up, and what about Shiner? "Well, what about him?" comes back smart from the party. "He's been away four months now, and not so much as a postcard with a picture of Old Joe on it. A lot he cares. So why should I worry? Other girls don't. They have a good time, like I'm going to do and just you try and stop me. You may have an engagement ring on your finger," she says, "but that don't give you no right to come it over me. And I tell you straight I'm not going to stay at home, on Saturday nights, and gaze at your brother's picture. Not me with a war on and all these Americans from the camp, who know how to treat a girl." You know the kind of hand-out, chums.

'Well, just at that moment the foreman comes round, and wants to know what all the shindy is about. So Shiner's sister has to pipe down. Mind you, to be fair, you can see the party's point, in a way. Of course she had asked Shiner to save his nutty for her, but it wasn't as though they were going to be spliced his next leave. There was only an understanding between them, like. And that was the worst bit of the letter, which really puts Shiner down for the count. A week or so afterwards the party arrives to work all smiles, and says to the rest of her mates, "Oh, I do hope you'll all come and drink our health tonight. He's a sergeant, and his family live in New York." And then in front of them all she flashes her ring, which I reckon must have been a much bigger stone than Shiner's sister's, 'cos in the letter, which Shiner made me read afterwards, she said she thought it was wicked and wrong to make a man spend all that dough on the ring. But anyway, a ring she'd got, and you know how the Yanks are lashed up with money, and so what chance had Shiner got?'

No chance at all. But he'd managed to get the key off the ring round his neck, and was opening his locker. At a first glance, in their neat rows, our lockers looked a little like so many small deposit safes, with their aluminium surface, and certainly when Shiner picked out his old coffee tin full of nutty he handled it as though it were a jewel box. They were all watching now, in the mess, as he emptied the contents into a glittering heap on the deck. Some had a pretty patriotic wrapping, like Reeve's ENSIGN, specially packed for Cadbury Bros. The Blue Peter and the Red and White Ensign stared up at him, and he stirred the collection with his toe, like a heap of autumn leaves, till suddenly with a savage movement he stooped down, and scarcely waiting to tear the wrapper off, shoved one into his mouth.

When I consider it now, I am conscious, with a physical pain for all that my own hoard meant to me in those days, how it must have been the first time since they had set sail four months before to an unknown destination that Shiner had tasted the sweetness of chocolate. For when his mates had offered him one of their own ration, he would have refused – matelots are like that – because he couldn't pay them back, in kind. But now he didn't pause to savour the taste, he thrust the bar roughly down his throat, and then another and another, not stopping even to relish the crunch of the nutty ones, only breaking off now and again to call his flighty love by all the names for the frail and the wanton since the world began. Everyone on the mess-deck, absorbed before in their own mail, now looked up and watched what was happening, as though they had never heard such language before. Nor had they, in such a context. No ceremonial sacrifice in a cannibal village, I gathered, would have compared with this. And then at last it was all over, the final curse uttered, the last bar scraped up off the deck and shoved into his mouth; then very quietly, looking neither to left nor right, Shiner went off to the Heads and dropped, groaning, on his knees, until he had spewed up the very last of his love.

'What a cow,' said the Killick. 'Of course, if it had been watch ashore for your chum, and they'd been somewhere a bit nearer civilization than Scapa, he could have gone and got properly canned. Then all that good nutty wouldn't have been wasted, and I am sure he'd have enjoyed himself much more. See?'

Yes, we did see only too vividly, and found ourselves drawing not so much conclusions as comparisons, with our own lives. 'She must have a heart of ice,' said the G.I., tenderly thinking of his wife, who was at that moment awaiting their first-born. Usually during our watch together, we'd all get into the act of suggesting possible names for Master O'Leary. Our chief was so certain it was going to be a boy that any girl's name was rejected out of hand. Roland John Charles Michael Denis Patrick. Whatever variations we offered, it always came back to Charlie. However, the rearranging of all the possible names, the combinations and computations would fill in the rest of the time until the faint blue fingers of a dawn so alien from a poet's conception of anything one had ever glimpsed in Civvy Street, would touch the outer perimeter of the ice wall, though without any warmth or relish for another day.

'One day we'll toast young Charlie in ship's kye,' I said, hearing the ship coming to life again beneath me, and the bugles sounding. 'Wakey, Wakey, rise and shine.' Breakfast. But not yet for us. By the time we came off watch at eight, it was almost more of a struggle to climb out of our cage than into it four hours before. Then we had all the threats that the darkness brought in its train to compete with, now we had the total numbness in our limbs. So that it became the turn of our reliefs to heave us down like sacks, and deposit us on the main-deck again. Only the knowledge that the washroom, hot and steamy as a Turkish bath, awaited us in the depths of the ship, followed by a hot cup of tea for our stomachs, gave us the strength to stumble below.

Gradually deck by deck you would feel the temperature change, until you reached the last companion-way and then, as soon as you were past the refuse-chute for the gash grub, which had so often been my undoing, you were, blessed relief, under cover, and soon after that you were joining the queue of naked figures waiting their turn to get under the showers that alone possessed the power to unfreeze our rigid backs, acting as an anodyne.

What I remember in my warm and peaceful Sussex writing-room, nestling under the Downs, is the freemasonry of that moment. Those who were already unthawed were always so ready to help those, just off watch, who weren't. Someone, without asking, would give me a hand with my oilskin, the buttons on which, stiff and obdurate, refused to function, until sometimes a jack-knife had to be produced. At last, like a shell of iced armour, one's protective covering subsided in a heap in the corner; all except the oilskin itself, which continued to stand upright, a scarecrow in a farmer's field, until gradually the heat melted its frozen exterior and, unnoticed, it slid into a puddle on the stone floor.

How I used to long to be able to do the same; to sleep for ever.

But there was only an hour, to clean up and have our breakfast, before our watch would be summoned to fall-in on the upper deck, for the usual routine of hacking and shovelling away the ice that had formed during the night on the superstructure, and the muzzles of the gun. Only an hour, in which to lie with one's head on the table when the breakfast had been cleared away, and faintly hear all round me the reactions to the latest shipboard gossip. A fellow called Harry Richmond was the great purveyor of buzzes. I used to tell him he'd make his fortune, after the war, if he set up as a clairvoyant. I even offered to recommend him to Butlin's, for a season at their camps. Because, like all astrologers, he was never downhearted if last week's predictions had proved wildly off the mark. He simply covered up with the promise of even more dazzling prospects ahead. Like leave, or a refit. Or even a trip to the Far East for a change from these Northern waters. He was in full blast now, and as ever he had an attentive audience.

'I'm telling you it's a cert. I got it from a supply P.O. who wanted me to make him a photo-frame, in my carpenter's shop, and he got it from the wardroom messman, who got it from the captain's steward. And that's not all. No, not by a long chalk. Because, you see, I got it, too, from a stoker writer P.O., who got it from the second engineer who's been told to make out a list of spare parts wanted. What about that? I also got it from the sickbay tiffy, who's doing my hand, and he heard two of the butchers saying to each other as how they're short of that stuff . . . what's it called, Baron?' – Here he'd give me a nudge, and reluctantly I'd raise my head – 'You know the stuff they give you for a dose . . . no offence meant . . . M and B . . . yes, that's it . . . and he said they have to order some more as soon as we get the anchor down. *The anchor down*,' Harry the carpenter repeated triumphantly. 'So are you muckers satisfied now?'

And for once, Harry was right, in that we did spend several weeks at the yards at Hebburn, for minor repairs, during which time some of those with the longest service on board, like P.O. O'Leary, got leave, while the rest of us were allowed ashore on alternate nights. Those who were left in my mess would make in a body for the same pub, expecting me to join them. So to avoid a charge of unsociability, I had to invent some close and clinging relations in Newcastle, as my excuse for temporary non-fraternization. Actually, I became more than related, almost married to the Station Hotel, where I left a standing order for a single room as near to a bath as possible. Even today when I am quizzed as to what I consider the greatest luxury in the world, I invariably vote for a piping hot bath, and as I cast my vote I gratefully visualize once again the hotel, its exterior grimy from the backlash of the trains and its appearance scarcely an architectural glory. But the water was commendably hot, even in wartime, and the sheets seemed like Buckingham Palace linen, so that as far as I was concerned, any backlog of pay had never been better apportioned.

As regards the hotel dinners, I have no recollection any longer, one way or the other. I think this is partly because I avoided the elaborate dining-room, after having been placed the first night at a table next to the *Cumberland*'s commander. This was enough to choke me off any food. My fear of him had not grown less as the months passed. On the contrary. On one occasion, when we were marooned at Scapa, and any kind of entertainment was regarded as being better than none, I had been roped in to describe over the ship's address system one evening what it was like flying with the Brylcreem boys. This meant my invading the commander's cabin, where the microphone was housed. To my horror I found the cabin's owner at his desk, and an awkward pause ensued, with my growing more and more ill at ease until I finally blurted out that it would be quite impossible for me to utter a word over the air unless he left me in solitary state, as happens in a B.B.C. studio. To soften the blow, or rather to excuse my own idiosyncratic behaviour in his eyes, I explained that that was the rule in Broadcasting House. He departed with a very surprised look on his face, that reappeared again when he looked up from scanning the wine list, to spy an ordinary seaman from his ship being seated with some deference by the head waiter, at the very next table to his family. We did not speak, of course. But I took care to avoid a similar embarrassment for us both a second time.

But there was another, far stronger reason why I have only barren memories of 'big eats' and 'bright lights' during visits to the blacked-out station at Newcastle-upon-Tyne. There just weren't any, as far as I was concerned. I was like a dog, whose instinct makes him hide away in a corner of the garden and chew grass. But even after stewing in a boiling-hot bath for half an hour, there was still no life in my hands and feet. For weeks now I had had a nagging pain, too, in my right side, and when I shaved I hated the sight of my face. It was grey and pinched. I held on to the hope that when I stepped ashore again, without a swaying deck under my feet, and the backlash of stale oil in my nostrils, my colour and appetite would return. But they didn't. I even turned down offers of nutty. But that was the nearest sign I gave to my messmates that all wasn't well with me. I was so utterly determined to stick it out and keep away from the sick-bay, and above all not let down our team in the port director.

I hope they never thought I did. But then I am pretty sure they didn't; for otherwise, in the middle of the evening that I found myself, to my astonishment, the central figure of one of the *This Is Your Life* programmes, the tall figure of P.O. O'Leary, looking so immaculate in his Number 1s compared with the way in which he used to be muffled up during the morning watch, would not have greeted me with such a reassuring grin when called on to the stage by Eamonn Andrews. As though to say, even before we shook each other's hands: Don't worry, Goff. None of the last bit happened, any more than this is really happening, that we should be meeting up again, on the stage of a disused theatre in Shepherd's Bush with a blaze of television lights in our eyes, instead of the unyielding black pall that used to cloak the icewall.

None of it? Not even the scrap of dialogue between us the first night we were on watch again, at sea, all leave over, the patching-up done. I could hardly wait before we had settled in our seats, in the box, to start questioning the G.I. about his leave, and the new baby.

'Did you get back in time, G.I.?'

'Yes,' said the G.I.

'God, that was good timing. You must have been bucked about that.'

'Yes,' said the G.I.

'And was it a boy as you always swore it would be?'

'Yes,' said the G.I.

'Well, what are you going to call it?' It was over a month since we'd played that particular game, and I had forgotten all the different combinations.

'We are not going to call it anything. You see, it was born dead.'

Even at that moment, the supreme good manners of the Service prevailed. I am sure it was as much to rescue us from shocked embarrassment as to cloak his own agony of heart, that he added, as a merciful release, 'Will you go below and brew the kye?' And it was his hands, with the gentleness of the big man he was, which helped me back over the side. We will never toast Charlie O'Leary in kye. We will never toast Charlie O'Leary in kye. Like a line from some traditional Irish lament, I kept on repeating the refrain over and over again, when twenty-four hours later I lay, between waking and sleeping, in a bed in the sick-bay, with an injection of morphia in my arm. Vaguely I could remember collapsing finally on the floor of the wash-house, coming off watch, with what seemed like a thousand knives twisting and turning in my side, and one of the young doctors, fetched from his breakfast, standing over me with a syringe in his hand. After that, for days, while we patrolled the Denmark Straits, my body floated on a sea of morphia, which blotted out the pain and the past, everything except that bitter, mocking refrain, 'We will never toast Charlie O'Leary in kye.'

The ruler of the sick-bay, Chief Petty Officer Swift, had the commanding appearance of a Calvinist preacher. At first I was as shy of him as of the commander, except that it no longer mattered; the morphia blurred all the edges. Uckers did the rest. For to my surprise, I discovered that Chiefie was the uckers champion of the ship, a title not lightly regarded in the Navy, and woe betide anyone on shore who had the temerity to suggest that ludo is a childish game. To those battened down for long stretches, it was so much more than a light-hearted means of passing a dog-watch; instead it was a tremendous test of skill and strategy, besides being an extremely satisfying outlet for pent-up emotions. To throw a double-six at a crucial moment, and then get back on to the board and into the fight again, that would be discussed for days afterwards like the photo-finish of a race. Chiefie was gratified to have such an eager pupil; before long he was sending out a challenge to all comers, all visitors including the padre, whom I was meeting close at hand for the first time. Although he turned out to be a most pleasant person, he was a remote figure to the mess-decks, and that was a pity and surely, too, a mistake. In the equalizing atmosphere of the sick-bay, I could challenge him about that. 'But my door is always open,' he protested. Was that a sufficient answer? If he had been seen more often amongst us, would not that have meant a bigger attendance in his chapel, for Holy Communion, in harbour? Was this not the root of the reason why congregations continued to diminish on shore, and in peace time?

I had not the strength or inclination to argue for long. Chiefie understood more than the padre, I thought sometimes. 'Well, we saw them off again,' he would announce with the nearest he ever got to a smile, as he folded up the board and put it away for the night, and my flagging spirits would revive a little. When the others had gone, including Jock the mournful messman, it would be still and peaceful in the sick-bay. Deceptively so. A sense of unreality, partly due to the morphia, and partly to my increased absorption in a game that inevitably reminded me of my childhood, enveloped and seduced me. Deep down, through the rising and receding bouts of pain, I knew that I must fight against it, and I tried to do so.

'When can I get up, Chiefie?'

'When I tell you.'

'But I don't want to miss anything. I don't want anyone to start thinking I'm skulking, or after a quiet number.'

'When you've been in the Service as long as I have, you'll thank your lucky stars if you do manage to miss anything. Here, give me your arm.'

Although he admitted to being fifty, he had been constantly at sea since the war began. On one occasion, I put forward, as an explanation of my collapse, the suggestion that the general seize-up was not due simply to continuous exposure to the Arctic cold, but to the fact that I had been on the go, without a real break, since the war had begun. And that was four years ago. The next second I could have bitten out my tongue, conscious of what my companion's record had been. For after starting off with the abortive Norwegian campaign, he had tended the wounded at Dunkirk. Later he had been in a ship at Crete, which had sunk with such swiftness on being torpedoed that he had exactly two minutes in which to climb through one of the port-holes for a bathe in the Med. But that was only one more 'incident' to him. It fascinated me that he should show far more animation over our uckers battles and our sick-bay partnership. Or when he was telling me about his children; the boy who had just passed his final medical examinations, the girl who was in an established position in a bank, in their home town of Southport. While his only modest pat on the back for himself was when he admitted that it had been not so easy to accomplish it all, on the pay of a leading hand.

'But I was determined that they should both have a good start in life,' he said, as though for a moment he had become the spokesman for all parents and the sacrifices they make.

When Chiefie was in one of his more expansive moods, I would feel idle and useless lying there in bed. I must get back to duty, and as soon as my gall bladder, or whatever it was that was giving the alarum signals, had quietened down, I badgered the butchers to pass me fit. I might have guessed, though, that Chiefie's forebodings would prove correct; for he possessed that kind of prescience. And this time I wasn't off watch when it happened, but at my place in Y gun turret. As the ship rose to battle against mountainous seas, waves of nausea overcame me. Bitterly ashamed of the mess I had left behind me and the disorientation I had caused, I crawled back to the sick-bay, all fight gone out of me, feeling like a punch-drunk boxer, who has truly had it.

'I am sorry, Chiefie, to be back,' I said, making a considerable effort to stand straight, despite the knives at work again in my side.

He glanced up from his desk beside the rep curtains which partitioned off the cubicles, the suspicious, tight-lipped look he kept for malingerers matching the strong, aseptic atmosphere of that corner of the ship. It comforted me when his face softened, though he pretended to be at his grumpiest.

'Lie down there on the couch, and stay there. I told you it would do no good. Look, I was making out your papers. Orders from the Lieut.-Commander himself. He doesn't want any more responsibility where you're concerned. In twenty-four hours we are briefly touching civilization, if you can call it that, and then we're off, the Lords of the Admiralty alone know where. Your guess is as good as mine. But what I am telling you is that this is your last chance, my boy. So take it and be thankful. You've got to go into hospital, and have some proper X-rays done. We simply haven't the facilities here, and too much morphia could make you an addict,' he added shrewdly.

But I was already an addict. Of the ship itself. Despite the frightening symptoms connected with the crack-up in my health, and the consequent pursed lips of the leading medical officer on board, I went on rebelling against the implacable moment when the drifter with myself and my kit-bag, and one of the lesser 'butchers' as an escort, would draw away from the side of the ship that we on the mess-deck might refer to as 'the three-funnelled bastard', but where I had found a genuine sense of comradeship, spontaneous and generous, such as I had never experienced in my life before. And suspected that I would never know again.

On my last morning on board, just before 'Spirits up', I cleared my locker, and disposed of such of the contents as I clearly would not need in hospital. My motley collection of balaclavas went deservedly to the Geordie who night after night had made it his responsibility to see me on my way, before he went on watch himself. To the end we communicated almost in sign language, but he made it abundantly clear that I had presented him with the Crown Jewels; for my part I was aware, then and now, that I was in his debt for ever.

Everyone wanted a souvenir of some sort. It is not so much that matelots have a large store of sentiment in their make-up, as that their life at sea has taught them, rightly, to be thrifty of resources, alert for 'gash' supplies. In consequence, even a pair of sea-boot stockings, full of holes from being pulled on too quickly at panic stations, must not be discarded. That was sinful. Could they not be dhobied and mended and tucked away, as a reserve? Again, even the departure of such a minor member of the crew was an event in an existence as monotonous as most sea-time usually is.

Now it was the Sheriff, with his weatherbeaten face, hovering at my side. 'Don't forget the picture of your garden for my ditty box,' he reminded me once again, in his hoarse voice. No, I wouldn't forget anything, I thought, as automatically I folded my overalls, and pushed them down to the bottom of my kitbag, and the aroma of stale Bluebell was so strong, I momentarily felt dizzy and disembodied. At the same second, a stoker shovelled his way through the mob round me, holding triumphantly aloft an old chocolate box such as Shiner had cherished. 'We had a whip round in the mess, Goff. Everyone knows how partial you are to nutty.' 'I was, Mike, I was. But I am not allowed to eat any now.' Of course I did not mean to sound ungracious or ungrateful. It was simply that this gesture made me all the more desperately aware of the anchors that had gone from my life. All was change. To be given such bounty, at the end. Somehow, it caused the box in my hand to seem as though it were full of lead. 'It's like an auction, ain't it?' someone called out jovially. I shivered. For an auction at sea means a death in a ship, and I was still shivering when Taffy Wilson, who used to work below the ground in Markham Colliery, and had exchanged that for another kind of blind darkness, came up the companion-way from the wash-house, stripped to the waist and still exuding the warmth of the shower he had just taken. He dropped his dhobiing bucket, and embraced me, in the way that boxers do when the contest is over. I was only too aware that I was the loser.

'We had some good skylarks, didn't we? We shall always think of you as belonging to our end of the ship now. Promise me you won't forget us, mate.'

I could not speak. From a remote corner of the attics of my memory, as I closed the neck of my kitbag, came some words by an author unknown to me. *'If one must leave a home, a ship or a woman, leave should be taken when one is still in love.'* The words were still repeating themselves when, an hour later, already feeling strangely remote, I stared up at the towering hulk above me, instinctively standing to attention as though I were on the quarter-deck, where I could pick out the commander, taking a constitutional, with his spyglass under the arm and a couple of snotties trotting, like devoted puppies, at his heels. Not surprisingly, he seemed impervious to my departure, but further for'ard there was a comforting display of waving arms, and familiar faces which I could still pick out as the waters widened between us, with Curly holding something above his head, that was surely too white for any of the handkerchiefs I had ever seen in his possession. Then suddenly it came to me what the object was; the letter. Well, if I had achieved nothing else of practical substance during my stay on board, I had brought about one union, which looked both promising and permanent. Very promising and very permanent. Whereupon, from this spur to my spirits was born another idea, another matchmaking scheme which I swore to myself I would set in motion just as soon as the censor and the Naval Authorities would allow me to write about my time as a temporary member of the crew of H.M.S. *Cumberland*, long since gone to her rest in the disposal yards.

However, she was to maintain her sea reputation till the end. After several more 'special operations' to the north, at last the most popular of Harry Richmond's buzzes actually came true. The issue of tropical kit all round. For the ship was destined, after all, for eastern waters. Which gave all those who had grumbled so continuously about the cold the chance to complain instead just as vociferously about the heat. And most of all, about how long it was before they reached home waters again, and the mail drifter came alongside.

Every man jack on board, at both ends of the ship, had been dreaming of and relishing that blessed moment when the pipe, from the Jaunty's office, would reverberate like a mating call. But on this occasion there was a variation, an addition to the traditional order for someone to act as a messenger for each mess. 'A.B. Burgess is to collect his own mail.'

A.B. Burgess is to collect his own mail. As the voice died away, a roar went up along the whole length of the mess-decks. Not of unkindly but of incredulous laughter. By this time, everyone knew that 'good old Burge' never received any mail; just as everyone looked forward to the night when the Sheriff rode out across the prairie. It was all part of the laughter, the letting-off of emotion, suppressed so long. But Vic Burgess, who had grown accustomed to obeying an order first and thinking about it afterwards, ever since his days as a lad in the Naval Orphanage at Greenwich, dutifully got up from his seat in No. 15 mess and trotted off in the wake of all the others. If this was yet another variation of a practical joke, *pour amuser les autres*, he would play his part as unresentfully as he always did.

Five minutes later he returned from the mail office, staggering under the weight of a sack that was over-flowing to the brim. At that spectacle, everyone's laughter, of course, instantly increased. What a superb hoax. But that is exactly what it wasn't. And the last laugh would have been for the Sheriff, except that for a long time he was too bewildered and overcome, even to produce his usual sheepish grin. Instead of sitting there quietly and unobtrusively while everyone read their letters, how changed the situation was. He simply did not know which envelope, which package, to open first. For apart from all the magazines and papers, and coloured pictures of the English countryside in more peaceful times, there were literally dozens of invitations from unknown friends, suggesting that he should visit or stay with them on his next leave.

This was the spontaneous reaction from the public at large, after reading his story in print. There had been no need to falsify the story to make up for the lack of a picture of its leading character, as some writers might have done. It seemed to me that the facts spoke for themselves; indeed, so overwhelmingly, that long after his messmates had had their fill of their own correspondence, they were still so greatly relishing the Sheriff's astonishing good fortune that they formed themselves into a self-appointed committee to decide which offer of hospitality he should accept first. The Sheriff himself, I am told, hardly entered into the discussion flowing round him. He just sat there, reading and re-reading all the letters, too full of wonder and joy to speak his inmost thoughts aloud. Until the day came when someone lolling against the hot pipes that run behind the messes happened to put his hand down at the back, and felt his fingers close on an envelope. One more as yet unopened letter, which in the spilling out of the avalanche over the table had been swept into this hiding place.

This invitation was from the youngest of the daughters of a Bolton baker. The Sheriff still can't explain exactly why he preferred it to all the others. Perhaps because it came last and made the final impact. Perhaps because he felt there might be an omen, a special meaning, in its belated arrival. Anyway, he wrote off, accepting happily, and in due course, almost unrecognizable to his shipmates in his Number 1s, arrived on the platform of Bolton station.

Here again, I imagine a script writer would streamline the sequel to speed up the climax. But though I started off my literary career as a novelist, I have long since become more interested in stories taken from real life. So let me continue with what really happened. Although his invitation came from Kathleen it was to the eldest daughter, Jean, that this seaman of the Royal Navy, who until that time had had little chance to get to know any family, 'nice girls' in their own home, proceeded to offer his heart and lifelong devotion. However, with the flair and instinct of the true matelot for making everything shipshape, the Sheriff suggested that on his next leave he might bring his brother with him, to make a foursome, which he did. At once, he most commendably and suitably paired off with Kathleen.

Thus were two orphans received into the heart of a typical, warm-hearted Lancashire family; and there they have been living in close harmony ever since. I suppose I could congratulate myself on the felicitous end to the story. Except that I was simply a kind of *deus ex machina*, who had no control over the hand that reached down carelessly behind the hot pipes. Who made that happen? Not I. Therefore not for the first time I find myself wondering just how sharply defined in advance for all of us is the shape of our future, and the path through the forest at this very moment awaiting our footsteps.

The hospital in which I eventually found myself lay on the outskirts of Glasgow. Mearnskirk Hospital. Hut Number 10 – does it still stand there in the grounds today? – was a long wooden structure of a haphazard design, with a row of beds on either side down the main length of it, and a single bathroom at one end. I never discovered whether it was because the authorities felt we were more easily contained on our own, or whether it was simply due to wartime overcrowding in the main building.

At first I felt too ill to care. I had little right to feel sorry for myself, considering that I lay next to a submariner, who had been stricken down with a second attack of rheumatic fever. This was such a severe one that he had to try and sleep in a sitting-up position, all night. Naturally they gave him a lot of dope, and sometimes, when we were awakened by the trolley of mugs of tea at half-past five in the morning – but no warning bugles, no watch to keep – Johnny imagined he was still on board the *Talisman* among the other 'dead-end kids', as they called the stokers in subs. At least he was safe now for the duration, having been shifted to another ship just before the *Talisman* went on her last patrol.

I found I had something in common with the occupants of the beds on both sides of me. Two years before, when still a war correspondent, I had spent a few days as the guest of a submarine depot ship in the Clyde. Invited on board the *Talisman*, moored alongside, it was to record that each mess was hardly larger than the cubicles of a woman's hair-dressing saloon. I had tried to envisage just what it must feel like, living at such close quarters for weeks on end, bracing oneself endlessly for the hazard of depth charges exploding and shattering the stillness of the waters above one's head. What self-discipline must be required by each member of the crew to avoid all signs of panic during such pressures, I reminded myself, as one evening at dusk we watched the *Talisman* slip her moorings, with a few figures in thick white Naval sweaters standing to attention on the narrow deck. The departure was one of silent speculation. There would be cheers from those crowding the rails of the depot ship, for the return. If there was a return. Then the last light faded from the loch, and another loner was on her way.

'I bet, Johnny, you'd like to serve with a crowd like that again,' I'd keep on repeating, in the hope that it would cheer him up.

'You're telling, Tony,' which was his answer to everything, a catchphrase, I imagine, from a current radio programme. 'Now, suckers, what about a game of solo?'

That afternoon, and every afternoon, those who were well enough would crowd round Johnny's bed and have a game, for the love of the game and the memories it evoked of other solo schools at sea.

The patient on the port-side of me, John Causier, with the everlasting sweat on his forehead, like stale dew, and the dark eyes that always seemed to be open, staring at the ceiling, received a stream of parcels from his home in Castleford. He was for ever offering me goodies that I wasn't allowed, even had I had the appetite, but apart from his friendly generosity towards me we had already an established link. A bond for the rest of our days.

John had been a member of the crew of H.M.S. *Keppel*, that was part of the covering force for the P.Q.17 convoy, when its captain, Commander 'Jackie' Broome, the senior officer of the destroyer flotilla, had to make the agonizing decision, later upheld in senior Naval circles, to turn back to guard the cruisers, when it seemed that a show-down with the *Von Tirpitz* and her own attendant forces was finally imminent.

From the bridge of H.M.S. *Pozarica*, we had watched the destroyers disappear in a cloud of smoke over the retreating horizon. I make no apology now for repeating what I heard my own captain remark, with a wry shake of his head, 'Godfrey, you and I would be better off pulling up groundsel in our back gardens.'

I guess that was how John Causier felt now, though unlike Johnny, on the other side of me, he was extremely reticent.

'You know, it makes me want to vomit to read all that flannel in the newspapers about how we hold sweepstakes when they're depth-charging us. It's bloody nonsense. Of course, we are much too scared.'

What frightened him now was something very different. The future. He tried very hard to make jokes about it.

'You know, Goff, what I am going to do when I get my ticket. I am going to get a pitch, when I can squat cross-legged on the pavement, and I am going to sell your bloody newspaper. You see if I don't. After all, that's what they did after the last war.'

Yes, that's what they did after the last war, I had to agree, wondering selfishly what would happen to me, too, if they gave me my ticket. Most days I had a session in the physiotherapy department, where a masseuse tried to pummel some life back into my mummified body, and where I heard a creaking old shellback, as he lowered himself on to the next couch, remind the world at large, 'I reckon, laddie, that death is the matelot's holiday.'

He'd scored his point, and didn't expect a reply. And anyway, John Causier wasn't the one to get involved in any arguments. But when I got back to Hut Number 10, I found myself staring again at John's hands, for ever holding on tightly to the top of his sheet, the hands that were unlike anyone else's in the ward because of the curious, ingrained blue markings on their knuckles, standing out now against the sickened flesh. A legacy from the coal mines in which he had spent underground the years of the botched peace. In the First World War to end all wars, he had only been a boy at sea, and in retrospect now it seemed a picnic compared with the last four years, when, recalled to the colours at the age of forty, it had meant for him one long grinding succession of convoys. The Atlantic, Russia, the Med., and back to the Atlantic. In endless succession. He'd had the lot. So why did I complain to myself, or worry about finding the strength to face Civvy Street again?

When the doctors on their rounds brought a specialist in their trail, I heard him comment as he read John's case card, 'I see they wanted to keep you in hospital, on the other side . . . but you want to get home. Was that it?'

'Yes, sir,' said John, answering once again in monosyllables. Home to Hut Number 10.

Mind you, they did their best to make it a home, if with rather uncompromising materials. After breakfast each morning, Sister Knight, who was my favourite because she reminded me irresistibly of Zasu Pitts, used to push two trolleys down the centre of the ward. One contained nothing but bottles, the other housed a different kind of medicine. Vases of flowers, not very well arranged, but that was unimportant. Even the ferns picked from the hospital rockery, when outside contributions dwindled, were in themselves a tonic, worth more than doses of iron. For were they not something living and green, and therefore very acceptable to eyes grown too accustomed to the endless greyness of northern waters.

I noticed that the only time that John Causier shifted his gaze from the ceiling it was to stare at the flowers, and one morning he called out to the little plump nurse who was always smiling, except when Sister was on the war-path. It was the one occasion I heard John raise his voice or make a request all the weeks we were there together. 'Hi, Ginger, could we have the flowers our end of the ward today? It does me rare good just to look at 'em.' 'Of course you can,' she answered, 'if you stop calling me Ginger.'

'Okay, Ginger. Thanks.'

The flowers were our end of the ward the morning there was a sudden, all-embracing hush, which usually only happened when Vera Lynn's signature tune came over the air. This time the silence was of a more official nature. Down the hut came a uniform we had not seen before. The Matron of Mearnskirk was paying us a visit, with our usual assignment of nurses hovering round her like a screen of destroyers. Instead of any flags flying from her mast, the battle-wagon was carrying a large golf umbrella. It was, to say the least of it, an unexpected appendage to her authoritative appearance. However, when she reached the end of my bed, all preconceived ideas about comparing the head of a nursing hospital to a battleship, or a battleaxe, swiftly disappeared, for there was a distinct hint of laughter in the eyes that shrewdly examined me, lying there sullen and depressed, with the endless rain beating a tattoo on the roof of the hut.

When I had the temerity to ask about the umbrella, to sidestep any searching questions about myself, there was a twinkle, too, in the voice that answered me.

'For eleven months of the year, I need an umbrella like this to shield me on my rounds. Then for a whole month, I exchange it for a parasol.'

'A parasol?' I echoed.

'Yes, I put away my uniform, and I go south. For years now, I have visited, in turn, all the inviting spots in the travel agency posters. That was in peace-time, of course. Last summer, I had to be content with Oban.'

'But that has a beautiful view out to sea,' I ventured.

'It certainly has when it is not obscured. No wonder we Scottish folk have a reputation for being dour. It is our climate, not our character, which causes it.'

'I expect you yourself know the South of France,' she continued in her refreshing voice, with the optimistic lilt to it. 'And Monte Carlo, too. That's the real McKoy. For the duration of my leave, I used to become the complete lady of fashion, and I often used to wonder, in the grand hotels for which I had to save up for the whole of the rest of the year, whether the other guests were deceived by my garden-party parasol.

'I used to catch them sometimes looking at me with a puzzled air, as much as to say, "Now what does *she* do the rest of the year?" Of course, I never satisfied their curiosity. That is half the fun of a holiday, being incognito from your working self. But how I used to smile to myself. Gibraltar. Have you been there in one of your ships? Now that's the place for souvenirs. Though Monte Carlo will always be my favourite. One day we shall *all* be able to travel again. You must say that to yourself. I still have my limbs, my home. My health *will* return.'

Would it? I was in a mood of utter despondency, and the mumbo-jumbo talk of the doctors did nothing to restore my confidence. So much so that I found it difficult to respond even when someone who had been next to me in the gymnasium at the *Ganges*, during P.T. sessions, came and stood beside my bed. I did not recognize him at first, with a bandage round his head and dressed, like so many others, in hospital blue. It was only when he smiled in welcome that I realized that his name was Jack Hempsell, and that I had last seen him in the drill hall at Chatham, with that same shining look upon his face because of the chit in his hand. His first ship. A destroyer. And that was what he had wanted above all else. A greyhound of the sea, though it wasn't quite as he imagined it, the night far out in the Atlantic that H.M.S. *Harvester*, guarding a convoy, ran into a pack of U-boats. His ship – as this nineteen-year-old lad no doubt still refers to it – succeeded in ramming and destroying one of the enemy, but in doing so damaged her own steering gear, and had to drop out of the convoy, a helpless, sitting target now. Everyone stayed at Action Stations all night, waiting.

'The next morning,' continued the boy who had done his training at my side, 'it must have been about eleven o'clock. I had been sent down to my mess to get a cup of char. I suppose the sudden warmth made me sleepy. I must have put my head down on my arms. Anyway, the next thing I remember, there was an awful explosion, and the ship started to heel. A torpedo had got us.

'Somehow, I got on to the deck. They were trying to launch a whaler, but as we were about to lower it over the side, I shall never know why but something made me hold back. I decided instead to jump for it, and chance climbing on to a Carley float. I was as lucky as hell, because the next moment another tinfish got us, just as they were lowering that whaler, and . . .'

I did not want to hear any more. It was all part of the recurring nightmare that stopped me from sleeping at night. I half turned away my head, willing him to go away, too conscious that his eyes were no longer those of a youth but of a scarred veteran. But he remained standing beside my bed, because he had something still to say to me.

'I am going off on sick-leave soon. I am going home. You can imagine how I am looking forward to that, but all the same, I shall go back to sea, if they let me. At first when I was brought in here, and I had no idea how long I'd been in the water because I lost consciousness, I swore to myself that I never wanted to see a ship, or even look at the sea, ever again. I'd had enough. But I don't feel like that any more. I feel I owe it to all the others to go back, if I can.'

He came to say goodbye to me a few days later. The bandage was gone from his head; he was dressed in uniform again, and he had already been outside the gates, to a party. He brought a welcome whiff of the outside world into the introspective confines of our present existence, as with the smile that I would like to believe has not faded with the years he described the abundance of hospitality he had received. It was not simply the Big Eats, it was the atmosphere of careless freedom and laughter, that was worth more than all the medicine bottles on the trolley. Several other fellows from Hut Number 10 had already been to one of Mrs Edwards' 'Sundays at Home', and, like Jack, had been equally amazed at their hostess's understanding of their needs at this moment when they were slowly and painfully returning to life.

'I simply don't know how she does it,' Jack exclaimed.

'You mean providing so much wonderful grub each week?'

He shook his head. Whereupon I discovered that he meant

something entirely different. Once again the look came into his eyes which had been there when he was describing the fate of *his* ship, as he explained that the woman who kept open house for the Navy had lost both her son and her husband at sea.

'You might have expected her after that to be bitter, surely,' he went on, 'to hate the sight of all of us who have been ourselves saved from the sea. But she is just the opposite. Always with a lovely welcome that stops anyone feeling shy at once. And there's always a sing-song to end up. She's got a smashing voice herself. The boys yesterday asked her to sing a solo.'

'And what did she sing?' I asked, curious about the woman who could so easily have pulled down the blinds of her own house, but instead, insisted on going out into the garden to pick flowers for the living.

'She sang *Bless This House*. You must go one Sunday, when you are better.'

But I did not go, because it was a long time before I began to feel any better. With a sense of bewildered impotence I watched my nails break off, and refuse to grow again, so that whereas my friend in the next bed had kept his hands above the counterpane, I instinctively began to hide mine underneath. And it was only with a considerable effort that I dragged myself that few yards from our hut to the next one, where I received heat and sunlight treatment for my sluggish circulation, especially in my legs and feet.

It seems to me from this distance, though it is rather like looking through a telescope from the wrong end, that it was my spirit as much as the extremities of my body that had been touched by frost-bite; and that the infection of my gall bladder had poisoned my mind even more than my blood stream. After the last round of the night sister I would lie awake, welcoming the darkness, because it hid the flow of weak tears down my cheeks, but dreading the restless, yawning hours ahead, when a succession of incidents from the past four years would concertina themselves together and frenziedly beat, with their accompanying sounds and voices, at my brain until I wanted to cry out aloud. Stop, oh please stop.

Instead it was the night sister who stopped beside my bed, and quietly ordered me to get up and follow her down the length of the ward. My first reaction was that I was about to be reprimanded, since I was the one who was always encouraging Hannah to sing *The Road to the Isles* after Lights Out. Once upon a time Hannah had been a deer-stalker in his native Skye, and he was for ever enthusing about the grandeur of the Coolins. Does Hannah still go stalking? And does he remember Hut Number 10 as well as Number 10 Downing Street, which at the beginning of the war was the residence of his most celebrated pupil, Neville Chamberlain?

I promised Hannah faithfully that one day I would visit Skye, but when the day came, it was to find the Coolins hidden from me by mist and rain during the whole of my sojourn on the island, while I searched in vain for my friend with the soft, lilting voice, who sounded like a different person when he was warning us that you must always aim at the throat of the stag.

Would I get off with a warning now?

'I am very sorry, Sister. It's my fault, not Hannah's,' I began. 'I always ask him to sing.'

She brushed aside my excuses, and pointed to the door of the bathroom. 'I thought you might like a bath,' she said. 'It may help you to sleep. You can have one every night, if you like.'

I looked at her with grateful relief. All the same, I felt that there was something else to come. Some other palliative or stimulant. And I was right. There was. Sister was still there in her cubby-hole, when I emerged again. She had something she had decided to tell me about another Naval patient, who had been brought to Mearnskirk Hospital after he had been blinded in battle, at an earlier stage of the war, when the ship in which he was serving, the battleship *Hood*, had been sunk. An actor turned sailor, and this is how Esmond Knight played what was surely his most difficult challenge.

'He was here only for a short time, before he went to St Dunstan's,' the night sister told me. 'He was in a private room. It was wonderful for those of us who looked after him to witness the control that he had already succeeded in achieving. He never spoke of his blindness, of his helplessness, of all that it appeared that he had lost at that time, his success, his source of earning a living, his independence.

'Yet only one thing seemed to worry him. He kept on asking where each piece of furniture was in the room. We imagined that it was because he was afraid of falling over and hurting himself. But he wasn't thinking of himself at all. We only guessed the real reason for his anxiety when his wife arrived from London.

'Someone opened the door for her, and she was there on the threshold, herself uncertain what to do. But he stood up, facing in the direction of our voices, very straight, and taller, too, he somehow seemed at that moment. Then he started to walk towards her, erect and smiling, without stumbling against anything, without hesitating, as though he were making an entrance on the stage, not playing a part for the first time, but instead, one that he knew by heart. That he could play blindfold.'

Whenever from my seat in the stalls on a first night I watch Teddy Knight playing a normal part, his victory now complete, or hear his musical, virile voice over the air, I think of that other evening again, when someone who had dedicated her own life to nursing the sick and the frightened, and those who had temporarily lost their balance, used a tableau as a parable. Adding only her own eloquence, and compassionate understanding. I can't say now that it did the trick, but it helped, of course. Just as Matron herself had helped, and the boy of nineteen, who despite his own brutal baptism was so determined to go back to sea again. What finally put everything into perspective for me, and roused me out of my resentful lethargy, was a letter I received from a woman who had herself found in the exigencies and demands of war a self-realization that was to transform not only her attitude to life, but equally her own personality.

In her letter there was one sentence that has stopped me from whining about anything, ever since.

This was the sentence: *'Self-pity is the most odious of all vices.'*

The letter had been written at six o'clock in the morning, for that was the time that she was called, from now on till her death, and the only time that she had during the day to attend to her personal correspondence. As Superintendent-in-Chief of the St John Ambulance Brigade, Lady Louis Mountbatten, as she then was, had come a long way from the coasting years, the locust years of the 'thirties, when she had first almost casually begun to take me under her wing, and had introduced me to a kind of ultimate luxury that previously I had only read about in the novels of writers like Michael Arlen and Stephen McKenna.

In those days, the Mountbattens, when he was home from sea, divided their time between a magnificent penthouse in Park Lane and what used to be called a 'country seat' at Romsey, with the Test running through the grounds, that they lent to Princess Elizabeth and Prince Philip for their honeymoon. I was a raw young man, without as yet a bank balance, very much an onlooker at all the expensive sports – polo, shooting, hunting and fishing – in which I had no prowess. These were the leisure-filling exercises of a small enclosed coterie, with their own private codes of communication, and I was never to master them.

The Mountbattens were the best-matched as well as the best-looking couple I have ever encountered. I used to wonder sometimes how this sailor, with his tremendous drive and expertise on Naval matters, could be bothered with the narrow fields of conversation inside that section of the Establishment. But then I saw a similar paradox in my own passionate hunger for tennis talk, tennis matches and Wimbledon, and then my surprise turned to understanding, and gratitude, in her case, that she should bother with someone as uncouth as myself, and with no links with their world. But our friendship only really burgeoned during the war years and afterwards.

In those early days, when I was simply a party acquaintance, she would wear slim, beaded dresses, so far removed from her dark-blue wartime uniform, and dart from group to group of her guests, lighting each up with a sudden blaze of incandescence in her determination that everyone should enjoy themselves, that no one should be left out in the chilly shadows. With her arresting beauty, that was a mixture of all the different blood in her veins, it was not surprising that she should seem to enjoy the kind of social success that almost any woman would accept with alacrity, if she were truly honest. What was astonishing was that, during that period, she disguised so well her growing dissatisfaction with the emptiness of her life, and the poor use to which her innate organizing abilities were being put. One more party in a penthouse. One more safari trip in Africa. One more tour of duty as a naval wife in Malta.

I am not sure now who first introduced us, but I suspect it was her stepmother, Molly Mount Temple, with whom she had so little in common. So it could have been an inauspicious beginning. However, I think Edwina recognized in me something that was in her own make-up. A longing, denied her by a conventional upbringing, not only to get to know people in a multitude of other worlds than her own, but also to fathom their fundamental motivations. So much of her own life, at that time, was lived on the surface, whereas she longed to dig deep, elsewhere.

'I have English, Scottish, Irish, German, Jewish and Red Indian blood in me,' she once told me, as though to explain the high cheek-bones and brilliance of her colouring, that took on an almost feverish hue towards the end, when her resources were finally consumed by her refusal to spare herself even for an instant.

I knew about the Jewish blood, because it came from her grandfather, Sir Ernest Cassel, who was to leave her a huge fortune, that might have been detrimental to anyone with a less strong and determined character. This first manifested itself when she borrowed a hundred pounds for the second-class fare to India, to pursue there the one man in the world she was utterly bent on marrying. In this aim she succeeded, without benefit of the millions that were later to come to her and her sister. No one guessed then, as they might have done, at the pent-up forces, seeking an outlet, which lay beneath the cool, upper-class exterior she presented to the Hollywood colony where the Mountbattens spent part of their own honeymoon, as the guests of Douglas Fairbanks and Charlie Chaplin – members of a twentieth-century royalty far different from the ancient Red Indian one, whose blood ran in her veins.

When I queried that part of her ancestry, she assured me that she could trace her descent directly back to the Princess Pocohontas, who came to these shores in the seventeenth century and married an Englishman, John Rolfe.

'Their child was affianced – that's the word they used in those days – to a member of my family.'

However, the family she was proudest of in the end was not her own children, for she lacked close maternal feelings and it would, in any case, have been easier – on both sides – if her two daughters had been sons. She was the kind of parent that no small boy would have had any qualms about having in tow on Sports Day at school; but to possess a mother with such a dazzling appearance is scarcely either an asset or a comfort for a girl floundering through adolescence, encased in puppy fat.

It became easier – again on both sides – when Patricia, the elder daughter, could obtain her own badge of freedom by joining the wartime Wrens. I recall a lunch when I was on leave as an ordinary seaman, during which Patricia insisted on trying on my sailor's hat, that was a variation of what so soon would be sitting on her own head. In the ensuing laughter, I was conscious that mother and daughter were more at ease with each other than I had previously seen them. Nevertheless, the family which increasingly came to mean most to her were the refugee children of Europe, for whom she became both champion and accuser, and, of course, the other native family of St John's, both the helpers and the helped.

Soon after Edwina's death, I received a letter from a post-war member of the organization in Huddersfield, describing how their Superintendent-in-Chief had come to inspect them, on a wet and bitterly cold day. The parade could so easily have turned out to be a damp squib, a hollow official nothing. But Edwina, who revolted furiously against ever becoming merely a figure-head, had transformed the day, banishing the weather by bringing her own warmth to the occasion, making each person presented to her seem the only person to whom she wanted to speak during the visit. 'She never hurried. She had time for us all.' Thus my correspondent added her own epitaph.

On the other side of the coin, many women in her own world were transparently envious of Edwina Mountbatten, because she unconsciously made them feel so inadequate. If self-pity, as she wrote to me at that moment of crisis in my fortunes, is the most odious of vices, surely jealousy is the most destructive. Self-destructive.

Her critics accused her of being too prone to cultivate publicity for herself; of enjoying dressing up in uniform, and later, wearing the ceremonial robes of the last of the Vicereines. Who would not be proud of such panoply, if earned? But though I have a photograph on my desk of her thus adorned, wearing a tiara, and the Star of India upon her breast, another picture, this time a newspaper one, from that twilight of the Raj, remains stubbornly in the forefront of my memories of someone who was for me a kind of saviour; the picture of Gandhi, as he went indoors from the lawns of Viceregal Lodge, at his first meeting with the Mountbattens, putting out his hand spontaneously to rest upon his hostess's shoulders. You can sense that he was reaching for the warmth that she instinctively generated, having accepted once and for all that it was completely genuine, her utter lack of demarcation, ever, in her dealings with any other human being, whatever his creed or his standing in the eyes of the world.

Edwina once confessed to me that of all the people she had met in the course of her travels, and her efforts at self-education, the admirals and the generals, the politicians and the princes, the artists and the tycoons, Mahatma Gandhi, that frail-looking prophet ahead of his time, had stood out head and shoulders above all the others, both the leaders and the rank and file. And I thought of her judgment again when I attended the great gathering at the Royal Albert Hall, held to honour the centenary of his birth. After the Prince of Wales had paid his own tribute, with an ease of manner allied to a seriousness of purpose that bode well for the future, at the end of the concert his great-uncle came on to the stage, as though it was the bridge of his ship, so that he was undwarfed by the vast spaces surrounding him. I only wished that his wife could have been at his side to speak, too, for together with a Prime Minister's daughter, Violet

Asquith, and Stella Reading, creator of the W.R.V.S., she was one of the three most eloquent and inspiring orators of her sex to whom I have ever been privileged to listen in public.

In private, unlike the majority of career women, she never sought to dominate the conversation or hold the company in thrall. Great wealth can build prison walls round the freedom of successful men; doubly so is this a danger where an heiress is concerned. But in her case, somehow the opposite happened. Having broken free, she remained free till the end. Although increasingly, through her welfare work, her efforts to clear up the débris, the human flotsam left behind all over Europe and the East by the war, she came in continuous contact with the very poor, sometimes without a single belonging in the world, she managed, without any contrivance, to be on terms of equality with them. I saw this unexpected and remarkable *rapprochement* again and again.

Nehru, who was to become one of her closest friends, warned her husband, in the throes of the impossible task of surrendering India, without rancour or bloodshed, 'Now I know what they mean when they speak of your charm being dangerous.' But his wife's charm was not dangerous, it was contagious. So that without aping masculine authority, or appearing to be implacable, which she could be, she got things done. The right things, too.

In 1926, the year of the great strike, she helped to man the switchboards of the *Daily Express* office. It seems absurd today that this should have been her first opportunity to prove that she could be efficient as well as elegant, and a most excellent mixer to boot. Even so, it was another twelve years, with war just over the horizon, before she found another chance of confirming that she had been a social butterfly by accident, not by design. She enrolled as a St John cadet, and started right from the lowest rung. I have a suspicion that only she herself secretly believed that she could reach the top of the ladder.

Soon after my unheralded return into Civvy Street, discharged from the Navy through ill-health, Edwina invited me to spend the evening with her. I half-expected that I might be subjected to another pep talk on the lines of her letter. I prepared my defences, as in the blackout I walked from my London home to her temporary wartime abode in Chester Street. Life in the pent-

An A.R.P. warden explains what it was like last night to the Queen

e have been
nbed ourselves
v'

The long ordeal is over. V.E. Day

Princess Elizabeth inspecting the Grenadier Guards, May 17th, 1944

The two princesses in pantomime at Windsor Castle

Princess Elizabeth in A.T.S. uniform

house had gone for ever. Instead, with her husband away at sea, and her own time-table strictly a Service one, she lived haphazardly, doing no entertaining, and I swiftly realized that my expectations of some sort of a meal had been over-optimistic. A glass of sherry, and then as though it had been an arranged signal the sirens started and we were on our way.

'I am taking you down to the East End to see the shelters where our girls are in charge. I have to do an inspection.'

'Oh,' I said. It was not my idea of a night out, on an empty stomach. And in the middle of a raid, too. I had begun to feel that it was perhaps safer at sea. At least, there you never had the sensation that there was a bomb with your name on it.

However, the hours till midnight and after passed without incident where we were concerned. In fact, the procession became rather monotonous, although the enthusiasm and the freshness of my companion never wavered. Although she had an accompanying officer with her, she did not once have to check any of the names of the women in the same uniform as herself whom we met, one after another, through the night. Not only did she know their names, without a slip, but equally she knew their home towns, how long they had been enrolled in the Service, and what their occupations and backgrounds had been before they had become full-time St John workers.

Astonished myself at the completeness of her knowledge, I was equally stirred by the effect her presence and her unaffected comradeship had on all with whom we came in contact. The families in the shelters were clearly moved by her presence among them. I had only seen one other female figure able to conjure the same atmosphere round her, when surrounded by unknown, gaping faces, and that was the Queen herself.

It was almost dawn before we got back to Chester Street.

'Would you like whisky or a cup of tea?' she asked.

'Tea, please.'

'I vaguely hoped we might be presented with a sandwich somewhere. I keep on forgetting to eat these days. I'll see if I can find some mousetrap cheese,' she added, pouring herself out a drink before she went off to make the tea.

When she came back into the room, she had taken off her cap, and her short hair was ruffled like that of a boy. The two bright patches of colour in her cheeks, which had been very evident earlier in the evening, had faded. She looked drained now, and completely exhausted.

'Edwina, how did you know all their names?' I blurted out, as I nibbled at the cheese. 'They were all volunteers from out of Town, replacing the regulars so that they could get some well-earned leave, and catch up on their sleep. How could you get every detail right? I simply don't understand.'

'Don't you? It's quite simple. I spent the whole afternoon memorizing it all. You see, I understood exactly what it would mean to them if I could greet them by name, without first referring to a file. They wouldn't feel just one more anonymous person in a uniform, but someone in their own right. This is tremendously important, the crux of all voluntary service. In peace or war. And besides, if they were prepared to leave some comparatively safe area, to come up to London and risk whatever might fall on their heads, I felt that what I did in my turn was the least I could do.'

Not for the first time I was forced to be aware that the conscientiousness of women far outstrips that of men. But equally I was aware that my hostess was in no need of such a confirmation from me. I was tired, too, and longing for my bed, and the All Clear had long since gone. As I pushed away my empty cup, and got to my feet, she put her hand gently on my shoulder.

'What are you going to do now? I am afraid being out of uniform can't be very easy for you, but . . .'

'It's all right,' I interrupted. 'No one gives me a white feather. It's not like the last war. And I carry your letter round in my pocket. The trouble is,' I hurried on, 'I can't unwind, though, any more than you can. I long, naturally, still to be doing something useful. You know, I spent three months at first hiding away, after the doctors gave me my ticket. I know it was absurd of me, but I felt so ashamed. To be beaten at the post. Serena James cosseted me in that lovely house and garden at Richmond. She has got the whole place full of "vacs" from Newcastle, but she takes it all in her stride. And then Bendor Westminster heard about my being a bit of a lame duck, and invited me to convalesce at Eaton, where I spent each morning sawing logs of wood with him, which is what I believe the ex-Kaiser did, in exile. It passes the time, but I wasn't very good at it.'

'But did it do you any good? You look very thin,' she said appraisingly.

'So do you,' I retorted. I had no real appetite, but always felt hungry. Most odd. Was anyone ever interested in the details of other people's ailments, especially in wartime? But not wishing to sound curt or ungrateful, after all her kindness and understanding towards me over the years, I went on:

'My own doctor is threatening to send me to that clinic at Ruthin in North Wales, if I continue to look so jaundiced and refuse to put on weight, and have this beastly pain in my side. He wants some more X-rays done. It's all an awful bore,' I said apologetically. 'I meant to tell you earlier, but there wasn't a chance, that I'm keeping myself busy writing a book* about the life of an ordinary seaman, the training and all that, which I don't suppose anyone will want to read if the war ends before it can come out, and I hope it will. I mean, the war finish. And I do any other jobs that are suggested to me, in the way of propaganda.'

The mention of that increasingly devalued word was sufficient to end any conversation, and I walked home through the quiet streets, washed by the dawn, to sleep, without any bugle call of 'Wakey, Wakey' sounding in my ears. Instead, my housekeeper, Mrs Bone, who seemed to acquire actual bodily sustenance by a mental refusal to be intimidated by any bombing raid, was standing by my bedside with my breakfast and the morning mail, remaining there long enough to describe with gusto how near disaster had come to 115 Ebury Street, during the course of the night.

'There's glass everywhere at the corner of Eccleston Street,' she announced with a certain relish.

I wasn't really listening because there was a letter from the B.B.C., and that probably meant another broadcast to America, on the short-wave programme, or to Canada. Such chores provided the semblance of still being of some use.

I had never been invited to broadcast before the war, and my first attempts at this extremely difficult medium of communication were such a disaster that when I listened to the play-back I shrank away from the sound of my own amplified voice, in a mood of self-disgust. Was this plummy imitation of Noël Coward giving

* *Home From Sea.*

the toast to England in *Cavalcade* really myself? Certainly it wasn't as I imagined myself, and I should have surrendered to defeat there and then had it not been for the belief in my potentialities as a broadcaster of a woman who was later to attain high office in the Corporation. Janet Quigley, who brought to her work as a producer a widely-educated mind allied to a disarmingly feminine personality, made no effort to reassure or comfort me; instead she deliberately crucified me. I appreciate now that therein lay the only hope of future success. She pushed into my hand, and ordered me to take home with me, a recording of half a dozen broadcasts I had given at tea-time. This series was intended to encourage the women compelled to stay at home, by taking them in turn behind the scenes on one after another of the battle centres I had visited. The idea was an admirable one, and there was little wrong with the scripts themselves, as far as the material that I had re-employed. They were full of colour and of anecdotes about their menfolk in their off-duty hours. But they had been written to be read on the page of a newspaper or magazine; not to be spoken aloud, a voice coming into the kitchen of thousands of homes at the moment when, in opposition, the kids just home from school would be hollering for their tea. The voice was the one I used when I was speaking in a canteen to a mass audience. When I made myself listen to the recordings over and over again, in the privacy of my own home, I finally put my hands over my ears, and almost wept in exasperation and dismay.

However, if I was ready to give up, Janet refused to be defeated. I had unique material to offer. It must not be squandered, thrown away. She tried to explain to me that in broadcasting, sincerity is not a virtue in itself, but just as an actor who seeks to move his audience must not appear himself to be visibly moved, so in projection over the air the best effects of naturalness and simplicity were achieved by a carefully contrived artifice. Cut out the purple patches, the literary expressions, pare down to the bone and, above all, imagine that you are talking to one person who is confined to a single room, so that you, and you alone, are bringing news of the outside world to the recluse.

Ironically, the break-through did not come for me until I no longer possessed a passport to the more exciting scenes of action. Without any commission or preliminary discussion, I wrote a script about 'Hut Number 10'. Something impelled me to do so. We had not been in touch for over a year, but I sent it to Janet and waited. What I did not know till later was that she was persuading George Barnes, then God Almighty at the B.B.C., and later to become the first Vice-Chancellor of Keele University, to give me a slot, on a Sunday evening, at peak listening time. In its next issue, the *Sunday Times*, in the person of Desmond Shawe-Taylor, later to become its gifted music critic, gave me the kind of authoritative praise that breaks down all barriers of doubt and prejudice. From that moment, with the rebirth of confidence, by infinite practice, and by at all times accepting the advice of my different producers, especially that of another woman, Lilian Duff, I have sufficiently mastered the technical side of the medium to be invited to broadcast as often as my other working commitments permit.

One of the first breaks I received, after I was in circulation again on the Home front, was an invitation to broadcast a series about the Canadian Expeditionary Force, building up in Britain against D-Day. I talked with them all, from General McNaughton down to those who were still in hospital after the Dieppe raid and other preliminary canters. I visited them in their camps, and joined them on their tank exercises. It was like seeing the same film again after three years, but dubbed by actors speaking with different accents. It also meant, because of the time lag, being at Broadcasting House as late as midnight, so as to go out live, which the authorities preferred, ignoring the fact that this arbitrary rule might often result in a long walk home for those taking part in such programmes. There was never any suggestion of transport being provided. I had sold my Pontiac, which ate up petrol, when I had gone off to the *Ganges*, and now there seemed little point in acquiring another car, with the ration for civilians so rigidly small. However, having been an impotent witness of the funeral pyre that a tanker instantly becomes when it is blown up at sea, I had little stomach for excursions on that particular black market.

Equally, however, I did not relish the stroll at one in the morning from Portland Place to Victoria. In consequence, I was mightily relieved when one bitter night at the top of Regent Street I caught sight of a cruising taxi and ran towards it hopefully, ready to offer double what was on the clock, if necessary.

I did not see the driver's face until he drew up outside my front door. His silhouette was made up of a conglomeration of scarves, such as we had worn in the port director. Underneath, I caught a glimpse of an extremely scruffy leather jacket. I was putting away my wallet, and getting my key out for the front door, when a voice behind hailed me.

'Say, you are Godfrey Winn, aren't you?'

I turned on the top step.

'Look, you've given me twice my fare, and I didn't ask for it. But I'll give you the whole lot back if you'll do something for me. I've written a book, at least, half a book, and I don't know if it's any use my finishing. If it's any good. Will you give me your opinion?'

Instinctively I shook my head at once. How could it be any good? 'What you need is professional advice from a publisher's reader.' It was a lazy, if reasonable, way out.

'This is my own cab,' he continued coaxingly. 'I am on the telephone at home. If I am out, my wife will take any message. I could always come and fetch you, or pick you up, at any place.'

It was very tempting. I could not place the voice. It had cockney overtones, but with something else added to it, something foreign in the way he emphasized his 'Ss'. All the same, it was a better broadcasting voice than mine, I thought.

'All right. Bring me the manuscript here next Sunday afternoon, at four o'clock.'

Nevertheless, there was little enthusiasm in my voice, for despite the attractions of the bargain we were making, it never occurred to me that I was about to become the midwife to an extremely striking literary baby.

Punctually the next Sunday afternoon, my bell rang. At first I did not recognize the neat young man standing on the doorstep. Gone were all the props and paraphernalia against the cold of the night shift, and instead of the commando's jerkin he had been wearing, my visitor was dressed in a well-pressed, well-cut, dark brown suit, which melded with his very black hair, shining with oil and carefully brushed. The only thing that somehow didn't seem to fit the metamorphosis were the purple shadows under the black-pupilled eyes.

The aspirant could not wait till we got upstairs. 'Look, here it is,' he said, thrusting a brown-paper parcel into my hands. All the way as we climbed, he poured out a stream of words, to hide his shyness.

'My wife, Ray, keeps on saying I am wasting my time. You see, I do a bit of carpentry. The first place I got when I left the orphanage was to be apprenticed to a furniture factory. Comes in useful now. I can make anything Ray wants for our home. We're buying a house, out at Kenton, near Harrow. I can promise you a really good dinner. My wife's an excellent cook. Though I never can make myself eat much. Specially now I'm trying to become an author. Sometimes she says, what is the use of dishing up at all?

'Still, I tell her it's a good deal better than the days when we first were married, before the war. We got married on the dole. We had a bed, and a chair. I couldn't seem to get work. The clerk at the Means Test Office sent for me, and asked if I had nothing more to sell. Do you know what he said? Haven't you got a grand piano?'

The mock-refined change of accent, his mimicry, brought the exchange of dialogue with a brutal clarity before my eyes.

'I hope that scene's in the book,' I said. We were seated now on the green sofa that had been a twenty-first birthday present to me from my mother, when, with one book published, I was so confident the moment had come to have my own studio as a fully-baptised, professional writer. It had never occurred to me at that time that the day would come that I would try my amateur hand at being a literary editor, as well.

The student was shaking his head in surprise. 'Why, should I have put it in?'

'Of course, you should have done. The only point in writing about one's life is to hold up a mirror to the rest of the world,' I said as I started to read the manuscript, swiftly realizing that like so many potential writers, he had not yet learnt the most effective way of marshalling his material. An authentic description of his boyhood in the East End, and the Jewish market, where all the dealings took place still in the Hebrew tongue, would be followed by a wild, turgid harangue, such as you might expect from a soap box in Hyde Park, about the iniquities of the class system and the monstrous burdens placed upon the shoulders of those who were poor through no fault of their own. It was like a badly-digested hand-out for Communism, defeating its own object.

I tried to explain that propaganda – and heaven knows I had had enough to do with the subject during the last four or five years – to attain its maximum impact must always be implicit, rather than explicit. The pupil looked rather puzzled at some of the admonitions of his self-appointed schoolmaster, but he was patient with my comments, and uttered no protesting cry of distress when I slashed through whole passages of the manuscript.

After all, if he would only keep to the direct story line, he had more than sufficient to fill up the gaps. I came to appreciate this myself, with quickening interest, as he amplified the text with his own spoken footnotes.

Maurice Levinson, I discovered, had been born in a village in the Caucasus, though he possessed no personal recollections of his early life in Russia; only the direful tales, instead of fairy stories with a happy ending, with which his mother had regaled his childish ears, reaching so deeply into his consciousness that a menacing shadow still dimmed the lamp of his adult existence.

Like a sudden storm on a summer's evening, a pogrom had swept through the village, burning and battering down every door, and culminating in his uncle's body, among the crucified, being strung up on a gibbet at the end of the only street. The survivors fled, on foot, with the flames that had destroyed their patrimony scorching their memory for ever.

Outside the window in my street there were many signs of the devastation of war; with an accusing gap in the row of houses opposite, the result of a direct hit. But what our street had endured, like a multitude of others, I viewed now with a fresh perspective as I read or listened to the account of how one family among the refugees succeeded in making the journey on foot across a whole continent, until they finally reached Paris. From there it was a comparatively short journey across the Channel to the sanctuary of the Commercial Road, where they found so many members of their race speaking so many different tongues with the cockney overtones that the boy himself soon began to acquire. Remembering nothing of the long, lonely, hungry trek, this part of his life was crystallized only by the climax when the waxen body of his father, worn out before his time, lay for a whole week, with lighted candles at the head and feet, in solemn mourning state in the front room of their East End lodgings.

Maurice had followed this in his book with the contrasting description of an utterly different kind of ritual; his weekly scrubbing on a Friday night in the Public Baths. Here everyone would congregate, luxuriating in the hot water, and lying in it for a long time while they exchanged street gossip with their neighbours, in the same way as up West another kind of club member sits in front of the library fire, and rings for a glass of sherry.

'In our case, it was for more soap,' Maurice said, with a tentative smile that banished, for a moment, the innate sadness of his expression, which still persisted, even after we had had several sessions together, and he was beginning to glow with the passion of creation.

'Yes, put that in,' I urged him. 'Put everything in just as it happened, just as you still feel it in your bones. And never worry about tearing up a few pages afterwards. It is far easier to eliminate than to build.' I told him, as amplification, the advice that Somerset Maugham had given me in my own apprentice days. 'When you get to page two each morning, discard page one. You won't notice its disappearance.' It was a suggestion that the most compulsive story-teller of this century assured me he had followed himself on numerous occasions.

'Shall I put in what happened to my little girl, Marion?' he persisted.

'What happened to your little girl Marion?' I echoed. It was like the exchange of a music hall act, I thought. But a moment later I appreciated that it wasn't like that at all.

'This evening, as I was changing to drive over to see you, my little girl comes running home from school. She's crying, and like her brother, it is very rare for her to cry. So I was very surprised, and I hurried down from my room and she ran straight into my arms. "Oh, Daddy, at school why do they shout after me. 'Yid. Yid.' What does it mean? What have I done? I know it means something horrid." '

He looked away from me, unable to meet my eyes, as though he had cause to feel ashamed. Whereas it was I who felt the weight of the degradation as he continued in his gentle, self-deprecating voice.

'Of course, I know we look foreign, the whole family does. Though my wife is a good-looking woman. But we don't look typical English. How could we? But I had hoped that by now, that we've got our own house, and some money in the bank, not from black market transactions, either, that they would leave us alone. And most of the time they do.'

'Who's they, Maurice?' I demanded. 'Children are notoriously little savages. They have to be taught how to be civilized, whatever background they came from. If Marion was deformed, there would be some children who would even point at her for that. I agree it's awful for you and Marion's mother, as it is for her, and if I were you I'd go and have it out with the headmistress. But surely you don't imagine this attitude is universal?'

'I only know about things as they happen to us. I'll get into an argument with a pedestrian at a street crossing, or in the cab shelter, even. And the argument always ends up the same way. I'm a kike. My race is plainly written in my face. I couldn't disguise it even if I wanted to, which I don't.

'But when the cracks and the taunts start, and there's plenty of them, I go weak in my stomach, I feel I want to pack up with my family and start the trek again. But where? And what's it going to be like after the war is over? Shall we be blamed for the aftermath, the disillusionment, as I've heard us blamed for the shortages now? I am haunted still by the pogrom in that village I shall never see. But it is all there in my mind, more vividly in a way because I can't remember any of it directly. Only imagine it.'

When I did not answer, because I could not, he began to speak more rapidly, more urgently.

'Jew baiting is starting again here. *You* don't notice it, because you are safe from it and wouldn't take part in it. But I tell you I am afraid. Afraid for my children in a few years time. After I finish writing, I can't get to sleep. I keep remembering the day I was separated from my mother, after my father's death, and they took me away to the orphanage. And you've read what that was like. I thought having a family now of my own, and bringing home more than sufficient every week, we would be safe.'

'But you *are* safe. You are in England,' I protested. When he didn't answer, I repeated the phrase as though it were some magical abracadabra. And yet a third time. But still the expression of almost primaeval fear did not leave his face, and I tried to think of what I could do to lift the cloud of depression which now enveloped him.

'Have you got a title yet for the book?' I asked, desperately seeking a change of conversation that he would accept, at that moment.

'Yes, I have. I thought of that when I couldn't sleep. *The Trouble With Yesterday.*'

My relief at such an excellent title – and how hard they are to find, as all authors know – was doubly overwhelming. Now I could repeat that aloud, with exaggerated fervour, and I had something else to distract his mind from what seemed the deliberate, implacable persecution of a member of his family.

'I am sure that if we took out a few of the incidents from your book which would stand on their own, to make very short, short stories, some weekly magazine would publish them. Like the account of the day when the American Negro sergeant got into your cab and wanted to buy a pair of boots. The dialogue is so good. And the whole encounter is so funny.'

Funny! I had no inkling as I said that, no faint, apprehensive stirring in my own mind, that the type of racial discrimination that would become the most explosive of all talking points in the post-war years, would not concern the odious propagation of anti-semitism as it still exists quite openly in some capital cities, like New York, but instead deal with the gradual integrating of the vast company of coloured immigrants in our midst. Yet it is because of that heart-felt outburst one evening towards the end of the war in my flat, with its blind windows boarded up with card-board, that I can see so clearly at this moment why the specious arguments of men like Enoch Powell are so insidious and dangerous.

'I'll tell you what we ought to do,' I continued. 'Send a few episodes to the *New Statesman*, and see what their reaction is.'

'The *New Statesman*?' he echoed, in a voice of awe.

'Yes, I'll dictate the letter to enclose with your typescript, but *you* must sign it. They mustn't suspect that I have anything to do with it. The only time my name gets into that weekly is when there's a sneering review of one of my books.'

When the literary editor, who could scarcely believe that Maurice had received no further education of any kind after the age of twelve, accepted two of the pieces for instant publication, the author's own pleasure and astonishment were together so overwhelming that any pangs of envy on my part were instantly swallowed up. At the same time, my own enthusiasm was strengthened to find him a publisher for the whole book. That must be the next step.

Not surprisingly, it did not happen in a week, or until many weeks had passed. After all, Maurice was working at two whole-time jobs at once, and doing his best at the same time to cope with all the distractions of a family round him, who refused to be banished when with a certain self-conscious flourish he would produce his writing materials again after the evening meal was cleared away, because there was nowhere to banish them to, except into the street.

After he had complained, on several occasions, how much his concentration was suffering, I accepted an invitation to Sunday supper, to sample his wife's cooking. That was the ostensible reason for my appearance, but I was really there with a mission to persuade his wife, for the time being at any rate, to accept Maurice's typewriter as being a more important and constructive instrument than his carpentry tools.

The children, I discovered, had two bedrooms. Could they possibly share one until their father's manuscript was completed and retyped for the third time? With the running order at last in a satisfactory sequence, and with, on the one hand, all the inconsequentials cut out, and, on the other, all the essentials enlarged, it would help the final impact.

If Maurice had a small den of his own, I explained, where he could scatter his papers about as he wished, with no fear of interruptions of any kind during these added working hours, it would make such a difference to the pace of his progress.

I had expected resistance, and instead I had two surprises. Ray Levinson was as fair and as comely as Maurice was dark, with a skin that, however much he washed, remained grey and under-nourished. Secondly, she became my ally almost at once.

'You see, I like dancing, and Maurice doesn't,' she explained later. 'I used to wonder if he wasn't just making an excuse of his writing in the evenings, so as not to have to take me out. But if you promise me it won't be wasted, but he really will see his name on a book one day, then of course the children can double up, for a bit anyway. How long do you think it will be?'

Tactfully I didn't like to suggest that, as things were going, it might be for the rest of their married life. Anyway, it was like asking how long a marriage is likely to last, as theirs has, in fact, triumphantly done. Of course, today the children are long since grown up, and Marion is herself married and with a career of her own, while their son has been content to follow in his father's trade.

They share the cab. Maurice's son drives it in the morning, while his father writes. They meet at a café for lunch, in Marylebone High Street, and switch over driving seats. Then in the evening, the junior member of the firm has another session, if he chooses. Maurice has had many subsequent literary successes, including a brilliant account of a cabbie's life that the *Evening Standard* serialized before publication, a play that was produced on the stage of one of the fringe theatres of the West End, and an extremely moving biography of his mother, the matriarch of all Jewish families, which he called *The Woman from Bessarabia.*

Nevertheless, I am thankful that he held on to his taxi and took my final piece of advice about never surrendering his right to ply his trade through the highways of the metropolis. For, as I reiterated to him again and again, if half the members of the theatrical Union, Equity, were permanently out of work, writers of books were in an even more parlous condition. In a recent survey, the figure showed baldly that scarcely ten per cent earn, on an average, in a year, as much as a navvy drilling holes in the road.

There are exceptions, of course, in every career world. Oddly enough, I think Maurice accepted the truth of my argument, unpalatable though, in a sense, it was to him, because I did find him, and at a first shot, a publisher. Therefore I must be right, because here was the proof of an omnipotence I did not possess. It was simply that Nico Davies, the head at that time of the firm Peter Davies, was a friend of old standing, and he agreed at once to give his sympathetic attention to the much-revised manuscript.

Home From Sea must have been already at the printers, if not out, but for the next fortnight I waited for the telephone to ring as anxiously as if I were awaiting a call from my own publishers. But when the call came at last, it was from the author himself. I could not have felt happier had he been a member of my own family – and, after all, we were fellow craftsmen – as he described every detail of his first meeting with a real, live publisher.

'We haven't ordered a taxi,' the clerk had said in the outer office.

'No, the boss wants to see me,' the driver was able loftily to answer.

What ecstasy, what joy to be savoured for a long time afterwards. 'And the funny part about it was,' Maurice added, 'or rather is, that my mother won't be able to read my book – yes, your friend likes the title very much – when it comes out. No, of course she's not blind. She just can't read English. You see, she's never had time to learn.'

We were speaking on the telephone that evening, and he did not ring off until he had made a date for dinner. He himself chose *The Ivy* restaurant, because he had dropped off so many clients there, including the man he really admired in the world of Letters, James Agate. There was a cabman's café a few yards away, where he would often wait, too, for the commissionaire's whistle. This particular restaurant, in his imagination, was like a citadel, and now he was about to storm it.

'The food must be good,' he remarked, 'because the customers always seem to be in a better temper when they leave.'

Well, he would be able to find out for himself now. We drove up in the taxi and parked it round the corner. I watched the commissionaire's face with amusement, when Maurice, again attired in the suit he had worn at the first of our many working sessions, announced blandly that he had booked a table.

'Of course, I know your face, sir, but just for the moment I can't remember your name,' the commissionaire replied with automatic politeness.

A few minutes later, my host was looking round in vain for his hero, all of whose editions of *Ego* he possessed, little realising that in a few months time he would open the *Daily Express* and find the major part of the column of their literary critic of that time devoted to a eulogy of *The Trouble With Yesterday*. However, I was able to lessen his disappointment, and at the same time assuage his thirst for celebrities, by pointing out Herbert Morrison dining with Ellen Wilkinson across the room.

'What's that they're drinking?' he demanded.

I mistook his interest. I imagined that he was contemplating following their lead.

'Hock,' I replied

'Hock,' he repeated, showing acute disapproval in his reaction.

'But you've just offered me champagne.'

'Yes, and I wouldn't have minded if you'd said "yes". This is a CELEBRATION. Like a wedding. And you have champagne then, if you can afford it. And with the advance your friend's given me, I can afford it.'

'Do you seriously mean, Maurice, that in your view, no recognizable official of the Labour Party should be seen drinking anything stronger than lemonade in public?'

'I didn't subscribe my sixpences, when I was really poor, for. . . .'

'For them to spend on hock. But they are not spending *your* sixpences.'

However, I was conscious that it would be impossible to convince him. Something fundamental in his being had been affronted; he refused to accept that this indulgence was not a betrayal of everything in which he had previously believed. Up till that time he had voted Socialist, automatically; he would never do so again; and, it must be put on record, never did.

I could not bear our celebration to be spoilt, and in order to divert the dark looks of disapproval with which he was surveying the other side of the room, I started to recapitulate every step, forwards and backwards – and there had been some despairing patches, too – of our own partnership.

At once his face lightened. 'Just supposing my cab had not been cruising down the end of Portland Place that night. Five minutes later . . . and we shouldn't have been here tonight.'

'Someone else would have turned up,' I assured him.

'You really believe that, Godfrey?'

'I believe,' I said slowly, 'that talent, real talent, always swims to the surface in the end. Sometimes, of course, it takes longer than other times. I agree, for instance, that van Gogh never sold a single picture during his lifetime. Which seems utterly incredible today. Usually, though, it is chiefly a question of having sufficient guts to hang on.'

'I am surprised, really, that you stuck it out. I mean, over my book. I must have been an awful nuisance sometimes, always coming back for more encouragement.'

'But we made a bargain. Your cab whenever I wanted it, as

my own private means of transport. And you've never let me down once.'

'May be. But now you've got a car of your own on the road again, you didn't really need me.'

'Like hell I didn't. My ration of petrol hardly takes me up and down from my home at Esher a couple of times. Besides, I'd become interested. It was a challenge to me as well as to you. And I suppose my vanity came into it, too. I wanted to prove that my original judgment was right.'

There was another reason, too, which I scarcely liked to acknowledge even to myself. The exercise had killed time, of which I had far too much recently on my hands; again, to some extent, all the discussions and the corrections and the marching orders had swallowed up my sense of inadequacy, during that period, in regard to the major conflict, which was everyone's business in some small way.

At the beginning of hostilities, I had been extremely wary of finding myself even a temporary prisoner within the portals of the Ministry of Information. I had avoided, as often as possible, visiting their headquarters in Bloomsbury, lest I should be seduced and sucked into that labyrinth of passages full of hot air, and little else. For to me that white stone building, standing aloof in virginal seclusion, represented the antithesis of action. Still I had had my bellyful of that, so that, unashamedly, I was now grateful when one or two of the departments condescended to employ my services in any capacity at all.

After a while, through showing a suitable humility, I had a rather unusual bone thrown to me to gnaw. Princess Elizabeth was about to be eighteen, her official coming of age. In consequence, the ministry had been commanded from on high to send out all over the Commonwealth, and to every other country not positively under the Nazi sway, a pen-picture of the heir to the Throne, that was, if possible, to be both more personal and more real than any portrait which could be expected to emerge from the scanty material as yet assembled in the library files of newspaper offices. Would I care to have a shot at it? Certain facilities could be arranged.

It was the first time that I had entered the Palace, and I suppose I had a vague expectation of grandeur on an overwhelming scale, even though everywhere else one had grown accustomed to compromise and camouflage. The endless scarlet-carpeted stairs and passages were as I had imagined them, but the marble plinths in the corridors had been beheaded and stripped of their busts for the duration, and at the foot of each one of them was a token sandbag, as a precaution against further emergencies. It was like a stage set, I decided, by a designer renowned for gaining an exact effect with a minimum of props. Even had I not been fully aware, as I followed the footman, whose uniform had become a kind of battledress of a dark shade, that this vast, unmanageable building, which is the least liked of the royal residences by its occupants, had been blooded by bombing, I would have been reminded of the fact the moment that I was ushered into the King's temporary sitting-room.

A writing desk; two comfortable, worn chairs on either side of a small electric fire, and a window that still showed positive signs of recent strife, since the broken panes had only been roughly boarded up.

Standing in front of the fireplace, awaiting my arrival, was one of the Queen's ladies in waiting. There was a birdlike quality about her, and at the same time an unaffected simplicity of manner which instantly endeared me towards this stranger, who had spent so much of her life always walking a few steps behind her royal mistress on ceremonial occasions, never intruding and yet never surrendering her own personality, in the amber glow.

Lady Delia Peel was clearly anxious to be as helpful as she could be, but just as her employer was to remark, when five years afterwards it fell to my lot to write the first biography of her younger daughter – 'But Margaret has not had any life yet' – so it was soon only too apparent, from the conversation which ensued, that, apart from a passionate love of animals, and especially horses, the heir to the Throne had as yet few strongly developed likes or dislikes. Except that it was already noticeable that she had inherited one characteristic from her paternal grandmother, which was to harry her all her working days. This was that, like Queen Mary, she was inherently shy, and possessed none of the extrovert exuberance, and complete unselfconsciousness, of her younger sister. If this important difference had not been pointed out to me, I would have been made aware of it myself when that final Christmas of the war I found myself a member of the invited audience in the Waterloo Chamber, at Windsor Castle, for the pantomime the children had staged with the aid of a Windsor schoolmaster, Mr Hubert Tanner, partly for fun, partly to provide money for a local Service fund.*

The jokes were ghastly, mostly contributed by the Princesses' father, who sat in the front row and laughed uproariously at everything, especially at the reference to the Number 10 army pill for recalcitrant bowels. In her rôle of principal girl, Princess Margaret showed enormous aplomb. Whereas her elder sister, whenever she had to wear tights as principal boy, kept on gazing down nervously at her legs, and never seemed fully at ease. In other scenes, dressed first in Edwardian clothes, and then in a Victorian riding dress, Princess Elizabeth bore such an uncanny likeness to the early pictures of her grandmother, that inevitably the comparison which Lady Delia had made to me came back to me, and I could hear her saying once again, seated opposite me in the Queen's chair in that makeshift sitting-room in the Palace:

'I do hope that now she has to go out, and perform public duties, they will let her do as many young things as possible. Not too many hospitals at first. Now the presidency of the College of Music was perfect. At the next table, at tea afterwards, the students who received their medals from her were such a happy group. Why, they were all laughing loudly.'

And people did not usually laugh loudly in the presence of royalty on any kind of official occasion. Was this then the beginning of a break-through for the future? I did not feel it was the moment to press the point. Certainly there had been no laughter on that occasion a few months before when the Princess had made her first 'grown up' inspection of a battalion of the Grenadier Guards, whose honorary colonel she had just become, and whose crest in diamonds she wore upon the lapel of her teenage coat.

It had meant, with Lady Delia in attendance, a long drive from Windsor Castle, where the Princesses had been incarcerated since the retreat from Dunkirk, to Salisbury Plain, and during the journey the lady-in-waiting became increasingly aware that the girl at her side was tormented with nerves. So much so that, fingering the small gold bracelet with the diamond watch which her father had given her for her last birthday and which she still

* See *The Infirm Glory*, pp. 133–134.

sometimes wears today, she was unable to break the lengthening silence of ominous apprehension between them.

'What did I do, Mr Winn? I'll tell you what I did. I fished in my bag and found the last of my sweet ration. Barley sugar. I gave it to the Princess. Munch it slowly, I told her. Very good for the stomach muscles.'

We used to be given an issue of glucose at sea, as a palliative against sea-sickness. It hadn't worked for me, but on this occasion it did the trick. Everything passed off splendidly. The girl in her simple tweed coat walked up and down between the long lines of guardsmen, as though she had been inspecting troops all her life. The whole battalion marched past twice, but she never moved. Her first ordeal was over. And the anecdote, too, I had imagined, but there I was wrong. There was a postscript, which has often strayed back into my thoughts, when through an open window the scents from the garden and the South Downs behind my house have beckoned me, so that I have longed to play truant from my own desk.

As the car drove back to Windsor Castle, and the young woman, who was still virtually a schoolgirl, was able to relax at last, they passed Stonehenge in the distance. This first glimpse of it was an enchantment.

'I suppose you made a detour, so that the Princess could get out and have a closer view?' I asked.

My guide along the path of royal duty shook her head. 'No, we couldn't stop, even to have a private view of Stonehenge. You see, it wasn't on the day's programme.'

I glanced at my companion keenly. There seemed to be no note of irony in her voice. Was then she herself so utterly indoctrinated? Yet she seemed such a real person, making everything spring to life in the most vivid manner; as, for instance, when at the end of our talk together she described what had happened on the day a bomb had fallen in the courtyard of the Palace. 'The King was sitting where you have been sitting, Mr Winn, and the Queen was here. Her Majesty got up much more quietly than I am doing, and said, "I think we had better go down to the shelter." Then very slowly they walked down the stairs, side by side, so as to prevent any panic. An hour later, as soon as the All Clear came, the Queen drove out to the East End and talked to those whose own homes had received so much worse damage. But at least she was able to tell the women who gathered round the car, "We have been bombed, too, now." '

During another daylight raid, of infinitely worse proportions, a school at Lewisham received a direct hit, and many children were killed. That evening the Queen at Windsor was late coming down to dinner. When she finally appeared, she said, in explanation, to the young Guards officer who was a member of the troop billeted in the Castle at that time, 'I have been talking things out with Lilibet.'

Not talking things over, which can be a smudged and inconclusive exercise, but out – to the absolute finality, embracing every aspect, every possible or impossible argument. An expressive, all-embracing phrase. And there must have been a great deal more of this utterly realistic kind of discussion, behind the high barricades enclosing her family, when the heir to the Throne decided that, like her aunt-to-be, there was one man she was utterly determined to marry, and he, too, despite his mixed foreign blood, was at that moment a serving officer in the British Navy.

I first met Lieutenant Philip Mountbatten, as he then was, in the Chester Street house that was the wartime leave base of his uncle, Lord Louis. As often as he could snatch even forty-eight hours 'up the smoke', he would turn up at the only 'free lodgings' in England, where he was certain of receiving a family welcome. Apart from his outstanding Viking looks, which would have caused him to stand out in any company, and a certain air of authority more usually allied to a higher rank, he seemed no different from any other young serviceman, eager for release, for the soft lights and soft music of dance clubs, and the restoring sight, after much seatime, of pretty girls out for a good time themselves.

Edwina was his ally from the start. It may have been that his uncle already had at the back of his mind the idea of the possible future alliance, but it was his wife who was determined that Philip should first enjoy the freedom of his youth to the full. Overburdened as she was by her own Service duties, she would enlist the aid of anyone she was certain would not bore him to act as his guide and companion, round the Town. He had only his accumulation of meagre pay to spend, and was as yet utterly unaware of the destiny that lay ahead of him, of the invigorating new balance that he would one day bring to the Monarchy, of the windows that he would be able to open at the Palace, both for himself and his children. Of the enormously useful services of such scope and priority that he would increasingly give to the country of his adoption.

Never having had a secure childhood of his own, eternally on the move from one temporary home to another, he was already looking forward, despite his light-hearted gaiety on leave, his seemingly uncomplicated extrovert character, to the time when he would be able to establish roots of his own, put down his anchor at last. But what were his exact prospects in Civvy Street? To a mutual friend who, at Edwina's suggestion, had accompanied him one evening to a night club, he remarked with a self-deprecatory shrug of his shoulders, 'I suppose, if the worse came to the worst, I could always marry an American heiress'.

Of course, he did not intend his mocking aside to be taken except as a joke. Certainly not with the utter seriousness of his description to the same audience of his first tour of duty, on shore, as escort in Edinburgh of Princess Elizabeth. Like any other girl, she had been eager to present her newly-acquired fiancé, both to her friends in the north and to the Scottish people.

One afternoon he had accompanied the Princess on a tour of an Edinburgh hospital. All the excitements of the past weeks, all the public engagements implacably piled one on top of another in too tight a schedule, suddenly caught up with her. Overcome by dizziness, it looked as though she might be about to faint. The officials around her solicitously suggested that she should withdraw to a private room and rest, cutting short the programme. At once she shook her head. It was unthinkable that the patients who had been looking forward so much to seeing her and Philip, should not do so. 'Just give me a few minutes and I shall be all right.' She leant her head against a cold column at the end of a corridor, while the official party provided a protective screen. Only the man who in the years to come, as head of the family, was to bring up their children in turn with the same sense of discipline, had stayed at her side.

Describing the incident later to Peter Stewart, who through Edwina's good offices had become the wartime secretary of the Carlton Club, and who had looked after my own affairs, wise counsellor that he was, for many years, the future consort exclaimed, with both astonishment and admiration in his voice:

'I had no idea it was like this. Why, it was like taking the middle watch at sea and staying on.'

In Service language, that was the ultimate, the most strenuous of tests.

Almost the last time I was to see Edwina Mountbatten alive, Prince Philip was, suitably, at her side, escorting her up the nave of Romsey Abbey on the occasion of the wedding of her younger daughter, Pamela. As this immensely handsome couple passed me, I found myself wondering whether history was about to repeat itself. For Pammy had insisted on choosing an unknown horse from the stable of possible suitors, and my hunch proved right, in that David Hicks, too, was destined to come in a winner in his own particular field.

Pammy was a snow bride. Overnight, the whole landscape had been mantled with white, but the sudden drop in the temperature could not keep the crowds of well-wishers and celebrity-gazers away. At the reception afterwards at Broadlands, the almost inevitable power cut resulted in all the lights temporarily going out, greatly to the delight, in the room where I was drinking the bride's health, of Prince Charles and his sister, one of the giggling bridesmaids. However, nothing could dim the fluorescence of the bride's mother that day. It is something that I have noticed before can happen sometimes, just before the flame is finally extinguished.

Increasingly consumed by the demands of her public work, as though she still refused to accept that she had more than made amends for the locust years, Edwina had of late grown careless about and indifferent to her off-duty appearance. She would dab some powder on her nose, add a little rouge to her cheeks, and pretend that that was enough. But on this occasion she had been persuaded, for her family's sake, to take trouble. Grumbling at the waste of time, she had nevertheless submitted to fittings at Worth's for the sea-green dress that, once acquired, she wore with an air that was *plus royale que royale*. She had imported experts to make her up that morning. The over-all effect was dazzling. In a moment she had become an incandescent beauty again, exactly as I had remembered her when I had been invited to Broadlands for the first time, before the war.

A few weeks later, two days before she was to leave to carry out engagements in the Far East, ending in Borneo, from which she did not return, she had breakfast with me in my Ebury Street home. It was her only free time of the day and she had already written a dozen personal letters before walking across the Square from the house in Wilton Terrace that they had needed for entertaining, when 'Lord Louis', as his own staff still preferred to address him, like a code-word that unlocked the archives, was in supreme charge, co-ordinating all the Defence Ministries. It was here that, at four o'clock in the morning, the telephone was to ring beside his bed, telling him that his wife was dead. It is already a lonely hour for any human being.

On the morning that Edwina came to say goodbye to me, she was dressed once again in her St John's uniform so that she could go straight on to her office desk. She drank a cup of coffee but ate nothing. At the reception, such was her elegance and vivacity, I had not been conscious of how distressingly thin she had become. But now she was clearly not bothering with her make-up again, and the contrast between her appearance then and now was so marked, so frightening, that for no reason – or rather, no exact comparison – a sudden picture came into my mind of Mrs Eddy being propped up in the back of an open carriage and driven through the streets of San Francisco to prove to the faithful followers that the rumours were false; she was not mortally assailed; she was not dying.

'Edwina, cancel this tour and have a long rest,' I burst out, terribly afraid. 'You will kill yourself, if you continue to flog yourself like this. It's not fair on yourself, on your family, on everyone who loves and admires you.'

'But don't you see, Godfrey, that's exactly why I must go. They have been preparing my programme, all the parades, the receptions and the presentations, for months. It would be unthinkable if I let them down.'

Where had I heard those exact words before? Oh, yes, in an account of a tour of an Edinburgh hospital. But then the central figure had been a young woman, still in the full resilience of her youth.

'Don't go, Edwina. Postpone the trip,' I repeated imploringly, only too aware of how desperately tired she looked. At a crucial moment in my own odyssey, she had given me life-saving advice. If only she would in turn take mine.

But she only shook her head and got up to leave. 'I must go. I have promised,' she reiterated. We walked down the stairs to the front door in silence. When we reached it and she turned to embrace me, the last words she spoke appeared to have a curious emphasis, as though she sensed and accepted that she was speaking her own epitaph.

'You know, Godfrey, so many people have got Dickie and myself wrong. Just because he was the last Viceroy, and I was with him in India, and we both openly had such a deep sympathy for the Indian people and their problems, we have been accused of being politically Left Wing.

'But there's no question of my being either Left Wing or Right Wing. The simple truth is, I like meeting people of every world, and working with people of every world, and hearing every possible point of view. It is people, not politics, that I am interested in, and always will be now. . . .'

It was nine years before I went back to Broadlands. And even then my visit was delayed another day, because of the autumn floods, which overnight had submerged large tracts of the southern countryside, in the same extravagant manner as the snow had done for the last of the Mountbatten weddings.

'Floods,' my host echoed, when I rang up to apologize for my non-arrival. 'There are no floods here,' the conqueror of Burma added, almost accusingly.

In a way, it was a relief to hear the strong note of command still in his voice. When the footman in the dark-blue battle-dress brought me through the archway of the drawing-room, where, at the far end of the further room he was, inevitably, sitting at his desk, it was no less of a relief to see at once that time had been much kinder to him than to the contemporary for whom he had once, by accident, provided a plot upon a plate. *In Which We Serve*, by far the best film to come out of the war, based on the life – and the death throes – of H.M.S. *Kelly*, Lord Louis's favourite ship. No living author has written with more understanding of the British matelot than Noël Coward. It is sad, and equally rather strange, that he should now look like a very elderly Chinaman; sad for those who never saw him playing opposite Gertie Lawrence in *Private Lives*, when they were both very much members of the Mountbatten set, and there was an aura about their heads that made one imagine that the gods had granted them all eternal youth.

We walked beside the river, in the last of the autumn twilight. My host told me, in answer to a question, that in his so-called retirement he found himself busier and more in demand than ever. There were close on two hundred committees over which he had to preside, causes near to his heart, campaigns in which all his energies and fighting qualities were still engaged. In addition, he had just completed twelve programmes, lasting an hour each, for a television company, embracing his whole life.

'I suppose you used a teleprompter for all your speeches and commentaries,' I said.

'I did not. I wrote every word myself and then learnt it by heart. It was the only way I could manage. In fact, at first I thought I would never master the medium. I had always had a horror of television or being televised. But I had a first-class team, and they were very patient with me. They had fifty-three shots of the first take. I don't know how I did it. But I did.'

Because you would never be defeated by anything, I thought. He was smiling now, the severity gone which sometimes masked his face and made one feel nervous and nebulous in his presence. I remembered how the first time we had ever met, his whole conversation had been concerned with getting films, free copies of the best current films from the companies concerned, for all the ship's companies serving in foreign waters.

Now the clock had come full cycle, and it was his debut as a television star that we were discussing. He was extremely diffident about it, and appeared to have no expectation of the tremendous stir he was about to make as a chronicler of his times, the conqueror in yet another medium.

'The only thing I regret about the series is that Edwina was not there to speak herself. We had to be content with pictures of her, and of course it is not the same thing. Working on the series made me very conscious all the time of. . . .'

I thought he was going to say – 'how much I miss her'. But that would have been showing too much emotion, and so he changed it to, 'how much she and I, too, were a team.'

Indeed, it was impossible to visualize one without the other.

They were The Mountbattens, indivisible still, I decided, as aloud I asked:

'Do you talk about your father, and the disgraceful way he was treated at the beginning of the First World War? Being turned out of his post as First Sea Lord, just because he had a foreign name.'

'Yes, of course, that comes into it. Everything comes into it.'

'It has always been said. . . .' I stopped.

'Yes?'

'That you were determined to revenge the way he was treated by becoming First Sea Lord yourself one day.'

'Yes, it is said, I know . . . and I accept the legend now with what I hope is a graceful shrug of my shoulders. But if that was part of the motivation, it was only part. I was equally determined to succeed in my own right. Nothing to do with Edwina's money.'

In the television series, which had been shown to me privately, I was very struck by the disarming honesty with which he read out a letter from the then Vicereine of India, deploring that Edwina, a great heiress-to-be, and the granddaughter of a man so close to Edward VII, should have got herself engaged to a young naval officer with such small prospects for ever making a career for himself.

'You must have recalled the contents of that letter again,' I exclaimed, 'when you returned to India as Viceroy yourself, with Edwina at your side.'

'Oh, I never forget that letter ever. I did not have to be reminded of it on our return to India in 1947. All along the line, it acted as a spur.'

'Did you always believe that you would reach the heights you did reach, in the same way, as my brother aged ten, calmly announced, "One day I am going to be a judge"?'

'Yes, I was quite certain,' my companion said quietly, calling his dog, Juno, to heel. 'You see,' he added, 'right from the start I was determined to prove myself a real professional at my job. Not just as someone with royal connections, married to a rich wife, doing time in one of the Services as others go into the Army. . . .'

'To prove yourself in the same manner as Prince Philip has done?'

'Exactly. What has so delighted me is that he should have married whom he did. I was absolutely convinced that it would be good for the country, as it has turned out to be.'

And for themselves, too. I found myself wondering, too, how much the uncle, who had sought to be a statesman as well as a man of action, had deliberately played the part of matchmaker, in the beginning. There was a pause while I did not speak my thoughts aloud. Then my companion continued, again with the smile that one did not often see, and which transformed the granite line of his head.

'I have just come back from staying at Balmoral. Prince Andrew came down in the train with me on his way back to school. His younger brother wanted to kiss him goodbye. "Men don't kiss," was the scathing answer he received.'

We turned back towards the house, with its noble palladian pillars, an eighteenth century addition by the Lord Palmerston of the day. Dating back to the eleventh century, it had not shrunk, as some houses shrink when remembered from one's youth. It was the quietness and the stillness that were different. I kept on expecting to hear Edwina's voice calling, 'Dickie, Dickie,' with an impatient urgency. When I admired, after tea, the glory of the ceiling in the drawing-room, he suggested a tour of the house, but the only insignia of glory that he wanted to show me were none of his mementoes of battles fought and won, across half a century of Service to the Crown, but the case containing all the medals and ribbons of his wife.

'Look, that's the Crown of India, Godfrey, almost the highest recognition that any woman can receive.' He spoke with immense pride in his voice, the next second there was a sudden greyness about his face, and his upright figure in the dark-blue blazer momentarily sagged.

'The news came to me from the duty officer at the Admiralty. The telephone woke me beside my bed. I simply could not take it in, at first. She was the most vital human being I have ever known.

'I just lay there in bed, trying to cut myself off from all outside communication. I suppose I wept. I only remember now feeling utterly numb. And then in the dawn, my son-in-law, John Brabourne, who has become like a son to me, came round. And from that moment the telegrams started pouring in.

'Altogether I received over six thousand letters. Five thousand were from people I had never heard of, who said they were friends. And, of course, they were. She had a fantastic gift of making friends wherever she went . . .'

That night I slept in Edwina's room. The Sargeant drawings were still on the walls from the days when I would be summoned to talk to her in the morning. The other half of the team lingered by the window, as though he was glad of the excuse to enter the suite again himself.

'Neither Patricia nor Pammy care to have this room when they come to stay, although we have turned the furniture round,' he said. 'But I thought you might like to.'

Her personality was still too strong for her two daughters, who were now both people of consequence in their own right. Whereas for me, it did not matter. Indeed, I welcomed the sensation that in a moment I would hear her voice interrupting imperiously, protesting – 'Don't be absurd, Dickie' – as he spoke now of his own efforts to make Edwina rest, to take things more easily, before it was too late.

'Because I was so worried about her, she finally agreed to have a complete check-up six months before she died. She did not want to, but I insisted. Afterwards, I had a long talk with her doctor. He warned me in categorical terms that unless she eased up straight away, she was taking her life in her own hands. But she would not listen either to him, or to me. It was always, "Just one more tour." She was determined to go on, to die in harness . . .'

And in her sleep. If it had to happen, surely that was the perfect way to go, I reminded myself, after my host had gone away to his own part of the house. For a long time I lay awake, not unhappily, pondering on the good fortune that had been hers in passing through the ante-room from this world to the next, still on the brimming tide of her endeavours for people on the other side of the tracks, to be remembered always for that, and for the emanation of beauty and glamour which still surrounded her at her last appearance in public, at her daughter's wedding.

Never to grow wizened and faded and defeated, so that newcomers, jostling on the scene, comment, not so much disparagingly as with genuine surprise in their voices: 'Was she *really* once upon a time considered to be a beauty? How curious.'

That hadn't happened to Vivien Leigh, either, I thought with a sense of overwhelming relief. She had been saved, too. Or, rather, her beauty and her charm were crystallized for ever, in the current fashion, on reels of celluloid. That is, one supposes, a kind of immortality.

Only a few days before my return visit to Broadlands. I had been present at yet another of those innumerable charity film premières, this time at the Empire Cinema in Leicester Square. They had resurrected the 'epic' of all 'epics', the ubiquitous record-breaker, and were displaying it on the wide screen with an impact that was to astonish me. I was only there because much of the money raised was to go to one of Vivien Leigh's own favourite charities. After I had already bought tickets, yet another member of the committee had sent me the advertisement matter, with an inscription added in her own handwriting: '*You loved Vivien, and she loved you. You must be there.*' I did not have to be reminded by such pushing sales talk of the depth of a tie that would not be severed till my own death. If then.

Secretly I had expected to be embarrassed by the over-indulgence of the spectacular side of the picture. All those sequences depicting pillage and burning townships, would they not seem rather old-fashioned? If they did, one was scarcely aware of it, because of the glowing looks and the sheer acting ability, the virtuoso performance of the principal actress. It made me conscious once again of how grudging the critics had always been towards a star who could not help possessing the kind of features that happen to photograph to perfection.

As one of the elders of the critics circle, Alan Dent, puts it in his welcome biography: *

'*. . . there was an axiom in the craft that a good actress had better be a plain Jane, with no beautiful nonsense about her, that pretty features were both a distraction and a handicap, and that the business of a player's face was to register and communicate emotion – and not to reduce the beholder to a state of drivelling adoration, whatever she might be trying to say, register or communicate, with those too lovely features.*'

There is also an idea that someone who by nature has been

* *Vivien Leigh, A Bouquet* (Hamish Hamilton).

endowed with great beauty is automatically inclined to be selfish and spoilt. This was certainly not true of Vivien's character, for she was always far more interested in the lives of her friends than in her own. After her death, a devoted fan who used to stand at the stage door waiting for a glimpse of her divinity wrote to me that on one occasion, the star had enquired where another regular was. On hearing that she was in hospital, she immediately sent flowers the next day, with a note in her own handwriting. An easy enough gesture to make? I agree, except that in this case it was duplicated so many times, and took so many forms. But always with the same basis: a giving of that most precious commodity, time; a sense of caring. As, for example, on the last tour of Australia that she was to make, there came a request from a complete stranger, though a lifetime admirer of her screen performances, that Vivien would come and visit her fan's mother, who was celebrating her ninetieth birthday that week. Vivien not only went to their home, but stayed over an hour, allowing herself to be photographed in a family group. Only one stipulation was made. That her visit should not be released to the local press, in case it might be regarded as a stunt to increase her audiences at the theatre where she was playing *The Lady of the Camellias*. She neither needed publicity nor courted it. Whatever she did came spontaneously from her heart.

In a television programme I was invited to give a list of the souvenirs that I would put in an imaginary box of expanding proportions. I voted at once for a picture of Vivien but found myself choosing, a little to my own surprise, one of her as Lady Macbeth, dagger in her hand, rather than as a more melting Camille. Usually she tended to hide her hands, rather than display them prominently, ever since a critic had spoken disparagingly of them, presumably because he dared not attempt to dismiss the flawless symmetry of her features. It was the only sign of personal vanity that I ever saw her manifest; never once did I catch her even glancing in a passing mirror.

On the first night of the Oliviers' *Macbeth* at Stratford, I had watched her give an electrifying performance which had completely outshone that of her husband, though once again the professional critics could not see it. However, the rest of the audience did, and she received a tumultuous reception. Her success on this occasion with the public proved a theory that I have long since held, that a small, determined woman can be far more frightening and obdurate than a large, galumphing one. And this is how Vivien played Lady Macbeth, compact and controlled in her tigerishness; making of her own physical slightness an asset, because she was able to lean and draw on her own innate courage, her immense tenacity of purpose.

The television interview in which I spoke of this with Kenneth Robinson, recorded in advance, was scheduled to be shown the Saturday evening after Vivien's unexpected death. Should this passage be omitted? I was adamant that it should remain. I knew that she would not mind my speaking of her in the present tense, as though she were still alive, because that is how I should always think of her, though almost from the first time that we met she was plagued with recurring bouts of ill-health, which gradually and inevitably took their toll.

Nevertheless, she went on working to the last. At her death, the manuscript of the play in which she was about to return to the West End stage, Albee's, *A Delicate Balance*, was beside her bed, together with the photograph of the second of her husbands, whom she never fully surrendered. When, in due course, I forced myself to attend the first night at The Aldwych, and watched Dame Peggy Ashcroft giving a far colder and more muted performance in the part than Vivien would have done, I remembered how the latter had said to me, with the typical candour allied to shrewdness that had enabled her to be a most successful 'angel' in the theatre. 'I can't think why I am doing it. Because the lush is going to steal the play.' And as usual her theatrical judgment was right.

In any case, the part was too old for her, and I am glad that I did not see her in it. I prefer to remember her as she was in almost the last of her films, *The Roman Spring of Mrs Stone*. Someone who worked on this production in Rome told me that when she came on to the set for the winding-up party at the end of the picture, the whole camera crew, all the technicians, spontaneously broke into applause. This, I was assured, was unique, though everyone who had ever worked with her, except an occasional jealous and petty actor, had nothing but praise for her professional demeanour. That is the acid test.

In one of the final scenes to be filmed, Mrs Stone had to ride a horse, which, tormented by flies in the noonday heat, unexpectedly bolted. Before any of the startled onlookers could reach its head, it was dragging its rider under some trees, in search of the shade. She could have so easily been scalped, but fortunately her hat, and the wig beneath it, saved her. The moment that they reached her side and disentangled her from the reins, she said at once, without a tremor in her voice, 'Dust me down, and then I will do the scene again'.

A doctor, summoned, insisted that she should rest her bruises in bed for at least twenty-four hours, under sedation. Even so, she was reluctant to do so. And there was something else that she was determined to do, beside complete that particular scene. Some other unfinished business. Discovering that for technical reasons, that had nothing to do with herself, she would not be wanted between a certain Thursday and the following Tuesday, for her ultimate shots to be put in the can, she flew, on a passionate impulse, to New York, to try and persuade the husband she had only recently divorced to change his mind about marrying the girl, half his age, under whose spell he had fallen when they were acting together in *The Entertainer*. It was a vain as well as a self-torturing journey. For the marriage ceremony took place as planned, that Saturday morning. Whereupon, without disclosing any reason for her overnight arrival in America, Vivien, as swiftly and as silently, left again for Rome.

In the empty, bitter aftermath, some of the members of their previous circle, their multitude of acquaintances, sought misguidedly to show their sympathy for the vacuum in which Vivien temporarily found herself, by criticizing the man who, in the early uprush of their feeling for each other, had in New York played Romeo to her Juliet. They were making a grave error to do so. For nothing displeased or alienated her more. No one would ever be allowed to utter a single even slightly disparaging sentence about Larry in her presence, ever. I avoided the mistake myself, partly because I had too great a respect for him as an artist, and partly because the more one is allowed to observe a close relationship between any two human beings, whether married to each other or not, the more shy one becomes of apportioning the blame for the disintegration, if it should happen. Utterly in thrall as I was to Vivien, had I not, with a sharp pang of understanding, heard Larry, with his head in his hands,

H.M.S. *Cumberland* – 'three funnelled bastard' as her crew affectionately called her

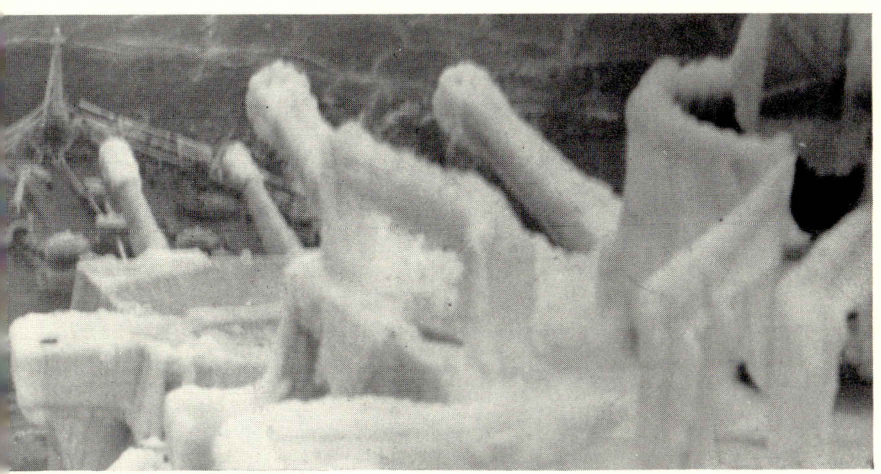

In the Denmark Straits. The guns of H.M.S. *Cumberland*

Memento of my time as an ordinary seaman

My mother's garden at Broom Cottage, Esher. '"Bring back a picture of your garden for my ditty-box," the Sheriff said'

'The Doc.' For him there had been no time for cultivating the soil

cry beseechingly, 'I have ten more years of my career, and I *must* have sleep'.

When I told my own lawyer, David Jacobs, of this revealing aside, I have often thought since of his reaction. 'A wife and a husband come to see me separately about a divorce they are contemplating and settlements involved. I listen to them in turn as they describe the reasons for the break-up, and it is often impossible for me to believe that they are discussing the same marriage.'

For a long time I found it difficult to believe myself that this particular marriage was really over. It had seemed to be eternal and unchanging, like the two figures in Keats' *Ode to a Grecian Urn*. The Oliviers were to the English Theatre what the Lunts – Lynn Fontanne and Alfred Lunt – were to the American stage. To stay with the former at Notley Abbey, their country home just on the Oxfordshire border, was hardly the same experience, I imagine, as staying at Windsor Castle, for Ascot Week, and yet it had something of the same royal exclusiveness.

I was invited there for the first time myself for a week-end during the period when they were playing a double bill at the St James's, with their own company, and Vivien was essaying the two Cleopatras; one night Shakespeare's serpent of the old Nile, the next, Bernard Shaw's vixenish kitten.

That Saturday evening, it was the turn of the Shaw comedy, in which Vivien Leigh had first appeared on the screen, in an adaptation produced and directed by Gabriel Pascal, near the close of the war in Europe. It was not to prove a felicitous partnership, though the star was too loyal to proclaim that in public. I recall going to the gala first night, and coming away acutely disappointed. Instead of allowing the Shavian wit to reach out on its own, and capture the audience, the play had been smothered with too much spectacle that dwarfed the actors. However, I shall always be grateful that the film was made, and at that moment, because otherwise I should not have found myself in Shepperton Studios, interviewing Cleopatra, for the magazine that had me under contract to write every week.

I found her, huddled in a fur coat, in the corner of a giant set depicting Caesar's Palace. She had left home at six o'clock, had been made up by eight-thirty, and had been waiting to rehearse and shoot ever since. It was now eleven o'clock, and not surprisingly she looked wan and frail, though incredibly lovely, in her elaborate Egyptian make-up.

The eternity of the war stretched between us, and I scarcely expected her to remember the day we had spent in a Kentish garden, when all the aeroplanes that were performing gymnastics in the skies were only part of a peace-time Rally at Lympne. But to my astonishment, she not only remembered, she was aware of everything that had happened to me since. Like Edwina Mountbatten, she took infinite trouble to find out about people, and I think that was, perhaps, a major reason why she had so many friends among her own sex, disarming instead of antagonizing them by the genuine warmth behind the shell of her beauty. When I asked her if she did not find these endless waits extremely exhausting, she brushed my enquiry aside with a shrug of her shoulders, and directed the whole conversation back on to myself. I had already acquired the unconscious habit of keeping my hands closed, as far as possible, to hide the ugliness of my broken-off nails. In her gentle, cooing voice she asked me why I did this, and when I held out one hand, in explanation, she took it between both of hers and said simply, 'But these are scars of war. You must never mind.'

And I never did mind, from that moment. Equally from that moment I think we were friends, though one is shy to claim a close intimacy with someone who in a sense belonged to the world. Except that I happened to be the only spectator present, at the moment of ultimate crisis in her fortunes, the death within life that was the overture to the last act. But that was still far away from the morning, on the studio set, when marvelling at her patience and iron discipline, I watched her go over the same small scene, with Claude Rains, again and again.

Every tiny detail comes back to me, like one of those hour-glasses that you find in an antique shop, in which the colours of the landscape are encapsulated for ever. So for ever, Caesar will sit at his desk, with Cleopatra kneeling at his side, as she importunes him to tell her the name of the handsome new young officer whose face and figure have fired her imagination, *The name? Why, it's Marc Antony.* At that, Cleopatra gets quickly to her feet. She is anxious that Caesar should not see the betraying look on her face. She turns away towards the white balustrade from which the smudged spectators could all glimpse the painted outlines of Alexandria's Forum and market place. But it is clear that Cleopatra herself has no eyes for the models set against the backcloth, or the tiny foreshortened figures imprisoned on the Senate steps, like plasticine models, from a child's modelling set. She is lost in her vision, whispering his name. *Marc Antony ... what a beautiful name* ... and now she turns her head to gaze straight at the dazzling arcs and into the camera's face, whispering yet again, *Marc Antony*. . . .

I held my breath. Because of the intensity of the feeling that she was displaying both in her body and in her voice, I half expected at any moment a Freudian slip of the tongue. Marc Antony . . . Larry Olivier. For I was to hear exactly the same intonation so often when she was speaking, off the set, no longer of Cleopatra's great love, but of her own. Play acting and real life. When does one end and the other begin, not only for the professional mummers, but for us all? It is a question often asked, and there is no exact answer. Certainly I had the feeling that first week-end I stayed at Notley of being part of an exquisite charade, performed by an all-star cast (except for myself) whose gaiety and wit and charm carried the whole spontaneous improvisation to a triumphant conclusion.

The other week-end guests, like myself, had a rendezvous in Vivien's dressing-room. I had spent the afternoon performing and on show at a different kind of matinée; I had opened a garden party fête at one of the Sunshine Homes for Blind Babies. The tea for the visitors was laid out on trestle tables at the further end of the lawn. After the opening ceremony I was talking to the Matron, beside the tea urn, at the moment that one of the small inmates, eager no doubt for the 'big eats' which she had been looking forward to all the week, and delighted in her progress towards us, unaided, across the grass, started reaching up towards the plates of food. As her hand continued to flounder in mid-air, I instinctively broke off our conversation to help. But the Matron put out a restraining arm, and shook her head, warningly. Afterwards she explained: 'You would not have been helping, but hindering that child's fight for independence. She must learn, little by little, to do everything for herself. Did you see her face when she succeeded at last in finding the plate of cakes? It was another small victory. That is what we try to teach them, day by day.' I accepted the logic, and the need for it.

Nevertheless, my own appetite had diminished, and I only began to realize how hungry I was when, having gone straight from the party in the country to the theatre, I found myself regretting, at the end of the play, that I had not spent one of the intervals searching for a sandwich. For though there were trays of drinks laid out in Cleopatra's dressing-room, on my finally reaching it through a barrage of admirers, I could spy no food.

The overflow into the passage of those who had been in front, now gradually thinned away, until only the house party was left. Orson Welles, Rex Harrison, who was at that time married to Lilli Palmer, and myself. Eventually we all climbed into two cars, and drove off into the night. One o'clock in the morning before we reached our destination, it was encouraging to find the house blazing with lights, and in the drawing-room more drinks were laid out, though still no sign of a sandwich. I began to panic. How stupid of me. It was all my fault. Of course, the two stars had eaten in their dressing-room, between the matinée and the evening performance, needing sustenance, and the other guests had wisely dined themselves at a sensible hour. Only I was the odd man out. As soon as our hostess gave the signal to go to bed, in a few moments, after the last of the night-caps had been drained, would I be blotting my copybook, on my first visit, if I dared to ask for a biscuit? I was still havering in my mind, and feeling emptier every moment in my stomach, when the doors were thrown open and the butler, making the most of his single line in this part of the script, announced, 'Dinner is served, my lady.'

My relief was enormous. We dined by candlelight, leisurely and with the grace of a bygone age. As though we had all the evening in front of us. Food has never tasted more delicious to me, but it was matched by the conversation. Orson Welles regaled us with fascinating stories about the Emperor Maximilian, getting up at one moment to play the scene better. As the aftermath of appreciation died away across the table, Lilli Palmer said in a soft, apologetic voice, 'Would you mind if I slipped away to bed, Viv?' Her hostess gazed at her in some astonishment. 'You see, last night Johnny and Mary gave a party for us out at Richmond, and it was terribly late when we got back to our hotel.' 'Of course, if you must go.' Lilli Palmer went, gracefully and with the minimum of fuss. The Orson Welles saga continued, a superb virtuoso performance, and the decanter of port was now in circulation. Our hostess did not take this as a signal to leave her own party, and when eventually there was a concerted movement back into the other room, I was surprised to discover that it was broad daylight. Through the windows, still dark against the summer night when I had arrived, I now caught enticing glimpses of the lawn stretching away, down towards the river at the bottom of the garden, and I remember how my hostess had once remarked to me that she must always live close to a stream or lake. 'Godfrey darling, I must show you Larry's lime walk. He trims the trees himself.'

I, in my turn, had always wanted to have a lime walk, in my own garden, together with a mulberry tree. All the same, I pretended not to hear, as I staggered up the stairs to bed, to be embraced in the blessed arms of sleep. What a wonderful evening it had been. I am living to the full at last, I thought, and remembered no more till I was woken by a tap on the door, and Vivien's maid was summoning me. 'Her ladyship would like you to join her for a game of bowls, as soon as it is convenient.'

Bowls. I had brought my tennis racquet. I had not expected bowls. Nor had I expected to find my hostess, after a very few hours sleep, looking as fresh as a girl of eighteen, dressed in jeans and with a scarf tied round her hair. She proceeded to defeat me, without mercy, while a few yards away, seated on the lawn, Orson Welles tapped away at his portable typewriter, working on a film story. After lunch, I slipped away to catch up on my sleep, and when I reappeared for tea, out of doors, it was not to find the company somnolent or silent from the Sunday heat. On the contrary. Bobby Helpmann, who once upon a time had played Oberon to Vivien Leigh's Titania, in a memorable production at the Old Vic, had appeared on the scene and was regaling my fellow guests with his vitality, where Orson had left off. There had been some talk of an early night on Larry's part, but it was not to be. I have a confused recollection of another supper party, this time consisting of bacon and eggs, in the kitchen, at two o'clock in the morning, from which our host tactfully, with the minimum of fuss, extricated himself. He had, he explained, an early call at the studios in the morning, where he was planning a new film. It seemed an early call for myself, too, when again I was roused by a tapping on the door. 'Her ladyship says, please will you join her in the rose garden and help her cut off the dead heads . . .'

This time my hostess was attired in a high-crowned coolie's hat, and wearing matching Chinese trousers. She presented a ravishing sight for tired eyes. She handed me a pair of secateurs and we worked side by side, almost in silence for an hour. It was an extremely pleasant kind of therapy, interrupted only when my host came back from the studios, and we went in to lunch. Afterwards, Larry drove us back to London himself. Orson sat in the back with me, Vivien in front. We meandered through the Buckinghamshire lanes, with their high hedges, glowing with green, in the high noon of another English summer, and it all seemed a very long way from the footlights of the St James's Theatre. But there was another audience waiting to be faced and satisfied, and another and another, and as though that implacable fact was in his mind, I heard our driver remark, 'Thank goodness, we can have an early night this evening, and get to bed directly after the show.'

'Oh, Pussy, not tonight,' murmured Cleopatra, using her own pet name for her husband, and the same voice with which I had heard her apostrophize Marc Antony on the set at Shepperton.

'But for heaven's sake, why not tonight?'

'Because it is Bea's opening at the Café de Paris, and we *promised* to go, *and* to her party afterwards.'

There was a groan from the driver's seat, and the car gave a lurch in sympathy, and for a moment I thought was going to mount the verge. The journey continued in silence, and an hour later I was deposited with my bags in Ebury Street. But I had not the strength to carry them upstairs. So I rang my own bell, and when Bardwell, who has looked after me for over twenty years, appeared, he greeted me: 'There's a message from Queen's Club to ask if you will play in a match at six o'clock. I think one of the team has fallen out.'

I shook my head. 'I am going straight to bed, and don't call me till Wednesday morning,' I said.

'Wednesday morning?' he echoed, conscious that this was Monday afternoon.

'*Wednesday* morning,' I repeated with some firmness.

The next time I stayed at Notley, Rex Harrison was there again, this time with his new wife, Kay Kendall, one of the most enchanting people I have met. Already there hung over her head the question mark of the incurable disease that was to cut short her life and her radiance with such tragic cruelty. She gave love and received love with such abundance that she had a special quality I have rarely found. And it was not surprising that she and Vivien, who had much of the same attitude to life, were so close to each other.

This week-end there was tennis, instead of bowls, because John Mills and his wife Mary, and their elder daughter Juliet, whom I had first held in my arms as a baby, were fellow guests. Johnny is a keen player, and I found myself presiding over a four before lunch on the Sunday, in the capacity of coach as well as performer. It was like the old day at the Villa Mauresque* and my confidence was raised, in such company, especially when Rex persisted in running towards the ball as though his racquet were a butterfly net. His exasperation at the ensuing lack of success was some compensation for the chastening brilliance of his repartee off the court.

We spent a very happy, relaxed Sunday, but that evening a shadow fell over the party, that I realize now was a warning prologue, of all that was to come. We had been dancing to the gramophone; Kay and Vivien, linked arm in arm, had broken into a spontaneous cabaret act, kicking their legs in a vague imitation of stars such as the Dolly Sisters, when suddenly Vivien slipped on the parquet floor and fell to the ground, hitting her head with a considerable bang. Larry, with a look of terror on his face, lifted her and carried her to her room. Her doctor was summoned at once. Such a jolt, it was explained to me, could so easily trigger off one of her recurring bouts of illness. For a while, I stayed behind, talking quietly with Mary and her daughter, the music turned off. But I have no recollection, not surprisingly, of what we discussed, because all our thoughts and all our will-power were directed towards the friend who was consumed by a passion for living to the full every moment of every twenty-four hours, as though she already sensed that time was running out for her. The fear that she might be in pain, or no longer in complete control, was like a naked sword directed

* See *The Infirm Glory*, page 261.

towards our own hearts, only sheathed when at last Larry reappeared to tell us that Vivien was now sleeping, under sedation, and we went quietly away to our own rooms.

In the morning, there was once again the now familiar knock on my door. 'Her ladyship would like you to help her cut off the dead heads of the pinks.' Never have I leapt out of bed with more alacrity. Nothing was said about the previous evening. It was as though the dancing and the dangerous climax of the fall had never happened. My hostess seemed to be absolutely her normal self. I marvelled, and gave thanks.

The pinks, in the borders under the windows, were not decaying yellow stalks, but in full scented splendour, the third and last time that I stayed at Notley. On this occasion, I was the only house guest.

Vivien was rehearsing for the leading part in a typical Feydeau farce, adapted by Noël Coward, and in its English version called *Look After Lulu.* We arranged that she should pick me up, at the end of rehearsals, on the Saturday morning, and drive me down. She arrived at my front door looking as fresh as though she had just got up, though she seemed very tiny in the driver's seat of her larger-sized Rolls. It was the first time, I think, that I had sat beside her when she was at the wheel, but I need have had no qualms. She brought the same unfailing competence to her driving as she did to the running of her homes, both in London and the country, where there was a perfection about every detail, that one will always remember with gratitude and admiration for the trouble that must have been taken, though it was as cleverly concealed as any aids she employed for her miraculous, unchanging appearance.

It was a difficult and tiring drive down through the incessant week-end traffic, and I had expected that my hostess would have wished to rest, but instead, having changed into slacks, she came out into the garden, and lying on a wicker chair gave me the script of the play. She wanted me to hear her in the second act, over and over again. Her concentration seemed to be complete. Only at one moment did she break off to exclaim:

'It's too young for me. It's too young for me.'

I had never heard her express such doubts before. She had always appeared ageless as Cleopatra. But now my instinct told me that it was not so much the play, but a far larger problem, set against an utterly different backcloth, that was consuming her mind. She was forcing herself to repeat her lines, parrot-fashion, to assuage some deeper anxiety. I had a curious, disembodied sensation of being in two places at once, when later I watched the performance, as presented to the public, from the stalls of the New Theatre. Young enough? The play would have been nothing without her; she galvanized the predictable, artificial farce into life, though no one in the audience could have been aware of the agony in her heart, as I was aware of it that Saturday afternoon, offering my services as a prompter, at a private rehearsal.

There was an easy explanation why Larry was not there; he was acting at Stratford. But Shaftesbury Avenue and Fleet Street were full of rumours that the Olivier marriage was perilously near breaking point, and I longed to be of more comfort at that moment than simply the stooge with the prompt-copy in my hand. I could only hope that just being there and trying as best I could to divert her mind, and make her feel that she was not alone, would help.

For dinner she changed into a white Balmain chiffon dress, sweeping the ground, that might have been designed for such a summer's night as this. It was only as irresistibly we were drawn into the garden again, that she mentioned the other name. I had suggested that we walk down to the river, past the lime grove, and usually that gave her great pleasure, but tonight she looked at her watch, and with sudden tenseness in her voice, exclaimed, 'We must stay near the house, Larry has promised to telephone as soon as the curtain is down.'

The scent of the syringa, after the heat of the day, was very strong, mingling with the pinks, in a yearning sweetness that was too hauntingly evocative for this moment. Our footsteps made no sound on the grass. We were like two ghosts, surrounded by a *corps de ballet* of all the other white flowers, the tobacco plants, the night stocks, the spiraea, that Vivien treasured, whose luminosity in the pale light of the lingering dusk possessed a translucent quality which at any other time would have made one exclaim aloud in wonder and delight.

My companion was to create in due course another garden of enchantment; but for this one she no longer had eyes to see. I tried to lessen the tension by asking her if she had ever read an early novel of Compton Mackenzie called *Guy and Pauline.*

'I can't think why it has never been made into a film. The setting is supposed to be Burford, not far from here. Pauline would have been a wonderful part for you.'

'You mean, I'm too old for it now?'

'I . . .'

'Anyway, please tell me the story.'

The politeness in her voice beat at my heart. It made me acutely aware of the supreme effort she was making.

I don't imagine she heard a word of what followed, and I am afraid the author would not have approved of the précis I gave of his plot about the clergyman who lived in a small Cotswold town, where there was a bridge at the bottom of the main street, and the vicarage close by possessed a garden running down to the water's edge of the mill stream. And how the clergyman had three daughters, of which the youngest was called Pauline, who with their mother would play chamber music in the evenings, until one summer an undergraduate poet from Oxford on a walking tour arrived in the town and met Pauline and fell in love at first sight; and how his adored one, to whom he was paying siege, used to creep out of the house when her sister and her parents were asleep, like a moth in her soft white coat, and lie with her lover in the punt, anchored beneath the willow trees.

It was midnight before I reached the end of the story, which you may know is a sad one, so that I wished now I had never embarked upon it, since it was yet another demonstration of how in life one person must always fall out of love again before the other. But the moral, if it was a moral, was lost upon my listener who sat indoors frozen into immobility, with all the beautiful things, which she had collected across the years with love and delicate taste, seeming objects in a cold, impersonal museum, as she went on waiting, with dying hope, for the telephone to ring, even though we knew in our hearts now that it would not ring that night. For the curtain had been rung down at Stratford a long time ago. Not simply after that Saturday evening's performance. But for ever now, where these two players were concerned.

For me, the only good thing that came out of the break-up of the marriage of two people whom I jointly so much admired was that Vivien came, by chance, to be a close neighbour of mine in Sussex. At week-ends we would lunch often in each other's houses, and if I was giving a party for my other neighbours she still preferred to be introduced as Lady Olivier, simply because that meant, symbolically in her eyes, that the link wasn't finally broken. And if I introduced her to the dullest and most undistinguished guest, whispering in her ear 'Please be kind to him for a few minutes,' I would find her half an hour later still talking away brightly, as though he was the one person she had hoped to meet. She had that kind of manners.

Tickeridge Mill was just as romantic a setting as Notley, if on a smaller scale. The lake close to the house provided for her the essential ingredient of water always present, and she assured me that she was comforted by the knowledge that it was there, even when obscured by the mist of autumn, the winter fogs. There was also a miniature wood filled with carpets of anemones and bluebells that she had planted, which burgeoning in the spring might have been created for Titania. Like my mother, Vivien had green fingers, and in an enviously short time, the garden, which had been sadly neglected till the arrival of the new owner, took on the blossoming look of someone who knows that she is cherished.

One learnt to speak of the past now only in terms of present theatrical successes. The Olivier *Othello* was rightly hailed as a masterpiece, the definitive interpretation. Would this still have happened had they stayed together? The only comment I would wish to make is that other people's relationships are surely their own business. I do remember Vivien one week-end speaking with overflowing admiration of a recent visit to the National Theatre, and how she had visited the interpreter in his dressing-room to tell him so. Thus it was good to be made aware that there was a bridge still between the two islands that had broken from the mainland. In her turn, Vivien had conquered Broadway in her first musical, *Tovarich*, the most strenuous acting, singing and dancing rôle she had ever tackled. After a six months run to packed houses, her contract allowed her to take a holiday. But when the management were unable to find any comparable replacement to fill the gap, she agreed to forgo her break so that the theatre should not have to close and the rest of the caste forfeit their salaries. The August heat of New York is proverbially merciless. Not surprisingly, the star of the show collapsed, and another bout of illness followed. It was to Tickeridge she came to find sanctuary, and slowly her strength and her spirits returned. But each attack weakened her defences and her reserves for the final one. She was coming to lunch with me on the Sunday when she had the first intimations that the end was near. 'Vivien has a slight temperature,' a voice said on the phone. Summer 'flu, perhaps? I had no premonition. How seldom one has. After all, I had dined in her company in a friend's house only three nights before in London, and she had seldom looked more serenely beautiful. That was how I saw her and will always see her, as I put down the telephone that day, or stand in front of the picture by Sickert that she left me in her will, so suitably entitled *The Belle of the Ball,* where the central figure is whirling round the room in a hooped party dress to the sound of the music from the piano, the waltz that will never entirely be stilled.

I shall always recall, too, one early summer's day that I spent with her at Tickeridge. No work this time for her guest, in the garden. No dead heads to be decapitated and deposited on the rubbish heap. Instead, the slopes of the lawn on to which her bedroom looked out were carpeted with white daisies. The white flowers of any shape and form, that she loved above all else. I had brought George Douglas with me, one of the best of the younger school of photographers. On our arrival, our hostess was already busy tying up a climber at the side of the porch. She looked down from the steps, and seeming as young as Pauline, in her lime-green cotton shift, with no make-up on her face, exclaimed, 'Oh, dear, I am afraid I look awful.' She then proceeded to be as professional as always and to put herself into the photographer's hands. I suggested that some of the pictures should be taken on the lake, and she at once entered into the spirit of that, fetching a large straw hat, such as Camille might have worn on her ill-fated visit to Armand in the country. The difference being, though, that whereas Camille was simply playing at being a milkmaid and was urban to her finger tips, Vivien was at her happiest in the country, especially when she had time to work herself in the garden. I awaited my moment, to announce, with a casual flourish of one-upmanship, that I had just heard to my delight that Harry Wheatcroft was going to name a new rose after me, to be on show next day at Chelsea. To which Vivien rejoined, with the sweetest of smiles, 'Oh, how lovely for you, Godfrey. But I only hope it won't hang its head like the one named after me. So mortifying when I gave it to my friends at Christmas.'

Still, it remains a kind of immortality, and at least, she herself never hung her head. There was a moment, before we left after tea, when George was stacking away all his cameras and equipment in the car, and my hostess and I walked away towards the bed of bush roses, that included the scarlet and white Ragusas ordered by me as a surprise house-warming present and planted during her Australian tour. Already they had grown almost as tall as we were, and that I took – wrongly as it turned out – to be a good omen.

'I agree with you,' she said quietly, 'that all life consists of a continuous compromise, for everyone. This is a breathing space for me, while I refill the reservoir. I shall never marry again. I am certain of that. Larry still possesses too much of me. But as long as I am well enough to go on working, I shall be all right.

'You remember the first day we met at Jeanne's for the air rally, and the wonderful party Noël gave that evening, and Ruth Chatterton was there? I was making *Fire Over England* then, and Larry was in it, too. Flora Robson was playing Queen Elizabeth. It was in that film that Larry and I met, too. I wonder whether – if the film was shown again – you would see it in our faces, the confrontation with our destiny. I don't think I have ever lived quite as intensely ever since. I don't remember sleeping, ever; only every precious moment that we spent together.

'We were so young. I mean all of us were so young. Like those who went to the war and did not come back. I trusted everyone and I imagined, like the very young always do, that everything lasts for ever. I mean that a day like this would be followed by another and another and another.

'But now I know differently, of course. I know everyone has to face periods of despondency and that one must not always trust everyone, or else one can be very hurt. At the same time, I have learnt who really are my friends, and that can be very comforting, and gives one confidence for whatever lies ahead. Nevertheless, immutably, it is always easier for a man to grow old than for a woman.'

I put my arms round her, not speaking any more, and then I drove home through the quiet Sussex lanes, wondering what sort of impression the day had made upon my companion, so much younger than myself, who was meeting Vivien Leigh for the first time. George Douglas had captured on his lens most of the leading characters on the contemporary scene, and was inclined to be pessimistic and apprehensive. Therefore I awaited his verdict with some trepidation.

'It is refreshing,' he said, 'to meet a star who is exactly what I hoped she would be.'

That was praise, indeed. For a photographer, operating at his level, has an acutely critical eye, in the same way as an architect, entering a house for the first time, instinctively visualizes the alterations and improvements he would make if he could get his hands on the property. Or again, a celebrated plastic surgeon, such as Sir Archibald McIndoe, automatically, even as he is introduced socially to a fellow guest at a party, is taking in a tuck here, and eliminating a sag there. All the inexorable, unwanted signs of the outward decay that often does not match the inner fire. On one occasion, I asked Archie McIndoe if he considered that the faces of all women would be improved, at a certain stage of the journey, by surgery; it is not surprising that I have not forgotten his reply.

'There is one face that I would not want to touch. It needs no help from me. It is the face of Vivien Leigh.'

I am not sure if Vivien visited the East Grinstead hospital, which became Archie McIndoe's base for operating on his 'guinea-pigs', during the war. However, I recall often seeing there another actress, Frances Day, whose signed picture had been a much coveted pin-up in Mess 16, and who with her flowing mane of palest ash-blonde hair, a style first created by Jean Harlow, came little by little to be an affectionate mascot for the patients, representing everything that men who have been through the fire, with parched tongues, and scorced faces and hands, long for, epitomizing the bright lights and the fantasy life of a West End Musical, so far removed from all that they have been compelled to endure.

Frances had a number that she made her own, called *Silver Wings*, which, sung out of its context today, with all the emotion that it engendered at the time dribbled away, would no doubt strike a new generation as being over-soft and sentimental; but at the period of which I am writing it assumed the same significance for all Royal Air Force personnel, counting the days till leave, as Violet Lorraine's *Let the great big world keep turning*, from *The Bing Boys are Here*, had possessed for the foot-sloggers earning a brief respite from the mud of the Somme in the First World War.

As soon as I came back from the wars myself, instinctively I gravitated towards East Grinstead, for the head of the operating theatre had assured me that I would be a welcome visitor at any time. Before, I had been there principally for propaganda reasons; to make the public conscious of exactly what work was being done, in the hope that it might stifle some grumbles at the black-out, or the dreary sameness and scarceness of rations, in the rush of overwhelming relief that one's own face and limbs were still whole and unscarred. I had also, at Archie's direct request, made a broadcast appeal for bicycles for those who felt up to exploring the environs of the town itself, where in every pub drinks for a patient were usually on the House. It was a small enough gesture to make, but the sense of understanding and mutual goodwill that grew up between the local inhabitants and the transient inmates of the hospital created ties that will never be severed. It is not simply that as many as can of the 'guinea pigs' return every year for their annual dinner. In a sense, their unconquered and unconquerable spirit is always there. As is the memory of their chief, who, before hostilities were over, became as much a practising psychologist as he was a surgeon.

For example, under the pretext that I needed some physiotherapy for my back and neck, still stiff with fibrositis, he kept me in the hospital for a week, putting me to sleep in the ward where the worst cases, needing grafting operation after grafting operation, had created a community of mutual self-protection, with instant antagonism directed towards anyone whose eyes flinched from meeting theirs. Some of the patients, I noticed, did not even talk to each other for days on end, and I was careful not to speak myself, unless directly addressed. I imagine the man whom they trusted implicitly had explained my unexpected arrival in their midst. Or perhaps they had grown indifferent to anything except their own progress towards being patched up into a semblance of normality again. Certainly no one challenged my right to be there, and this other subtler treatment, which, undiscussed between us, was being prescribed for me, was to have more permanent results than the heat lamps and the violet rays.

There was one boy – because despite all the dogfights in which he had participated before having been shot down in flames, he still had the air of someone both unfledged and defenceless – who, before he was through, had to endure over thirty operations of varying severity. A long, slow arduous journey towards rehabilitation of a sort. It was not surprising, therefore, that he would sit all day hunched up on the side of his bed, his back to the room, too listless and despairing to take any part in the day-to-day eddies of the enclosed life of this little community, with its sudden, haphazard storms of gaiety or distemper swiftly over, remaining himself remote, morose, a small private promontory of grief and loneliness.

I did not dare to make a move towards breaking down the formidably high barriers. Where even the chief had failed, it would have been impertinent for me to have attempted something so likely to prove abortive. Nevertheless, I was aware that the man who to them all was as absolute an authority as God, was growing increasingly anxious about the continued strain on this patient's mental control, and the effect that his sullen numbness of spirit must be having on the healing and the grafting of his body tissues. In consequence, it was with a sense of almost personal relief and thankfulness that later I was to hear the end of the story.

A woman from America, on a tour of Britain, asked specially if she might visit the hospital at East Grinstead. A brutal illness, leaving utter destruction in its wake, had attacked her soon after her birth, depriving her, in one fell swoop, of her sight, her hearing, and the power to communicate in the manner that other mortals do. Yet somehow, aided by the stubborn, unyielding persistence of a dedicated teacher and helpmate always at her side, she had found a way to conquer her infirmities, which at first had seemed unsurmountable, and to lead, astonishingly, a full life. In doing so, she had already become a legend and an inspiration to all her fellow pilgrims.

I am speaking, of course, of Helen Keller, and when the moment came that her guide took her into the ward, where briefly I had slept, he made instinctively in a direct line, he explained to me afterwards, for the bed of the patient who was in his usual slumped position, staring at the blank wall. Turning his head, this airman suddenly found a little circle round him, and was forced, against his will, to pay attention, even to make some response. Though when he was asked by Miss Keller's companion where his home town was, he replied, as briefly as possible, in one word, 'Oxford.' At once Miss Keller took her companion's hand, and in the sign language, through touch which they had perfected between them spelled out her answer. It was this:

'I have visited your city, and I sat beside the river . . . and it smelt good.'

She had called upon the one sense that was left to her, beside that of feeling, to hit upon something that was both true and honest where she herself was concerned, and that at the same time might prove a bridge between them. As indeed it did. Everything else had been taken from her, in an arbitrary action that could only be explained in medical terms, just as, equally haphazardly, it would seem his good looks had been destroyed before he had time really to relish and enjoy his youth. Nevertheless, the recognition of the life force flowing between them, and for him, too, the recognition of the supreme effort that this complete stranger had made to reach his inner being, by finding a concrete form in which to praise the town of his birth, made such an instant and such a deep impression on him that from that moment he started to recover his own zest for living; to wish consciously to make something of the future, and separate it from the past; to help both his physician and himself. No one, I was assured, had prepared or briefed this particular visitor for what she might find. Once again, the inspiration had stemmed from the head of the Guinea-Pig Club. It had been a chance in a thousand. The kind of miracle for which they all, in their different ways, secretly prayed.

Even so, one is shy to use that word. Perhaps, on second thoughts, it is better simply to record exactly what happened, as it happened, and to leave it at that. There had been another fellow in that ward with whom, for me, it had been easier to make contact. A member of the Australian Air Force, Charles Butler had one untouched profile and one that was needing much delicate surgery at the hands of the master to whom he had been despatched by his own doctors, after they had done the preliminary patching. In between operations, he was allowed out. Indeed, Archie urged all his patients to take as much sick-leave as possible, and to get away as far as possible also. This was easier for those with homes and friends in Britain, than for those from overseas. It was good to feel that one could be of some use, to repay Archie even a little for all that he had done for me, and certainly Charles seemed to enjoy coming to stay with us at Esher, where he endeared himself to my mother by volunteering to act as an unpaid gardener. And most excellent he was at it, too, swiftly restoring the lawns to their pre-war shape and splendour.

Outside in the open air, I am sure he completely forgot what profile he was presenting to the world, because, anyway, he was on his own, in contrast to the crowded ward, or the even more crowded theatre when I took him to see Frances Day, in her show at The Prince of Wales. In the darkened auditorium, he could turn his face ardently towards the line of chorus-girls in the instinctive reactions of a healthy young man. It was only when the house lights went up again in the interval that he crouched back in his seat, burying his head in his programme. I could not help noticing this, just as I could not help noticing that as soon as he came indoors from the garden, he became self-conscious once more. As though playing a game, of which the rules were never mentioned, one tried to show that one was on his side by manoeuvring so as always to be facing his untouched profile.

I think my mother found an outlet, too, for much bottled-up gratitude to those who had defended the skies above her home, in fussing over her guest and plying him with all the bottles of beer and the whisky that I was never encouraged to touch. But then Charles's own scars were so much more apparent than those of her younger son, and infinitely harder to bear. Rightly, she referred to none of them. All the same, with Charles she appeared to be more at ease, and he so much with her, that he paid her the considerable compliment of showing her a picture of himself, taken after his passing-out course, a pilot as yet unblooded in battle. 'I would like to write to your mother,' was all she said. After Archie had done all that there was to be done, and Charles had sailed for home, she was very pleased when we received a letter, in turn, from Charles's parents, thanking us for something that it had been a privilege to be allowed to do. To provide, for a short while, a stepping stone.

For a few Christmases after that, there would be a card, and then as inevitably happens with so many wartime friendships, a year came when there was nothing from 'Down Under', and I imagine the year after that, I fell out, too. Only one friendship, in correspondence, from those times, has never wavered, and that has been with the messmate who originally had no letters to answer. The Sheriff has been keeping his hand in ever since. There was a card, with the ship's crest on it, the first Christmas after the war, and from then on there has been a succession of holiday postcards, unconsciously mapping the progress of his fortunes, starting at Butlin's, when my godson, named after me, was still an infant, and the latest of a brilliantly coloured beach in Majorca. While in between, there have been long letters of family news, marking the passage of time, but without pain or regret. On the contrary, for here is an extract from one that I received a few days ago:

'Godfrey is serving an apprenticeship at an engineering firm, Edward also works at an engineering firm. They are grand lads. You want to hear us when we have all been to see Bolton play. Jean says we must have seen different matches.

'Am doing very well at work. Have just been promoted in a managerial position to Plant Superintendent, a new meaning in today's modern world. Will have five foremen under me, and a lot more responsibility, but I think I can cope. To think in the Navy I only rose from 1st class Boy to Able Seaman, but I have a family to support now. . . .'

Charles Butler has a family to support now, too, and is doing equally well in his own line of country. I discovered this in an unexpected fashion. I had not expected to hear any more, after a gap of so many Christmases, and it came as a complete surprise when, on the Sunday evening, three years ago, as soon as I reached my suite in the hotel at Melbourne, the telephone began to ring in the sitting-room, and on the other end of the line was Charles's voice, bidding me welcome to his home town. 'I wanted to be your first caller,' he said, going on to explain that he had been watching my progress on his television screen, and in the Australian papers. And what about dinner tomorrow night?

I only wish the original sponsor of the Guinea Pig Club could have been there when this member walked into the room twenty-four hours later. Charles was whole again. That was my first and last impression. This was a whole man. The two profiles had become one face again, one person. It was not simply that there was a feeling of ease, of relaxed confidence, about his every movement, every stance that he took, but equally everything that he had to tell me about his life today, as we picked up the threads over dinner, was equally reassuring. It was over twenty years since we had last met, and he had taken out of the private pocket of his wallet the pictures that he had wished to show my mother. Now as we talked about the business that he had inherited from his father, and was maintaining successfully, he was producing a different set of photographs that he was eager for me to see: pictures, this time, of his wife, his teenage children, and the horses that he raced and owned.

In his turn, of course, all his questions about England kept on returning to one target; one place; one person. Charles had read some of the obituaries for the greatest plastic surgeon of them all, who had taken the techniques that he had learnt from his own tutor and fellow New Zealander, Sir Harold Gillies, so many steps forward. But, nevertheless, he still found it difficult to believe that someone who possessed so strong and vital a personality, and with such a voracious appetite for living each twenty-four hours to the full, and who was so skilful in handing out sensible advice to his own patients, should, having survived a serious coronary attack, have been taken in the end unawares, in his sleep. For to Charles Butler, as to so many of his fellow 'guinea-pigs', no doubt, Archie McIndoe had seemed immortal.

'And to me, too,' I agreed, as we sat for a long time over our meal. There was a pause now, while neither of us spoke, and then, as can happen at a reunion like this, when something is released in one, and a torrent of memories overflows across the tablecloth, I found myself blurting out:

'The extraordinary thing is that Archie's life and mine, although we were such utterly different kinds of people, ran on close parallel lines. Not once, but twice. It's a bit complicated, but I think you might be interested.

'You wouldn't know, Charles, but twelve years ago, I had a very severe coronary, too. In fact, I had a fantastic escape, because had the pain been a little less overwhelming I should have got up out of bed, and gone to the bathroom in search of anti-acid remedies, imagining it was that which was causing the effect of a couple of elephants trampling on my chest. The specialist told me afterwards that had I moved, the extra strain on the valves of my heart at that moment was likely to have been fatal. Fortunately, I just passed out, and was found in a semi-conscious state the next morning, and carted off to hospital. But enough about that. . . .

'The summer after Archie had his coronary, I was having a holiday at Cannes, and went to lunch on board the Simon Marks' yacht in the harbour. You remember all that Simon and Miriam did for your hospital, both during the war and afterwards? I found that Archie was staying with them. After lunch, we had a long talk, lying on the deck, and he stressed to me how important it is never to look back on any illness in one's life. You must take precautions, of course, to try and prevent a repetition. But at the same time, you must ignore what's over and done with, and try to pretend to yourself that you never had your coronary. Otherwise, it will catch up with you again . . .'

'As it did with Archie?'

'Certainly something caught up with him. I suppose you could say he had had one postponement too many of his appointment in Samarra. The night before I had my attack, I had gone as the guest of Billy Butlin to the annual dinner of the Saints and Sinners Club. It is always a magnificent affair, with the top speakers of the day. It goes on, in consequence, for a very long time. I am always amused by the gimmick which greets all the guests on their arrival. You are offered your choice of either a white or red carnation.

'I don't know which shade Archie chose, but I do know that he also went to the annual dinner of the Club, the guest of the same host as myself, on a previous occasion, and no doubt sat in my seat, because Billy always had the same table. And when it was all over and the last speaker had had his say, and everyone had finished their brandy, he went home and got into bed . . .'

'But didn't wake up, as you did?'

'Exactly.'

'H'm. I wonder if you also chose the same carnation for your buttonhole? He may have been a sinner, but he was a bloody saint to us.' The mouth joining the two profiles opened in a generous smile. 'I bet you won't go to that dinner again, in a hurry.'

'Oh, I don't know . . .

As I shrugged my shoulders, I was also remembering the other occasion when the course of the life of Charles's hero and that of my own had run uncannily close together. It happened near the end of the war.

For some time, Archie had been increasingly aware of a discomfort, flaring into bouts of pain, on the right side of his body. It sounded as though it was exactly the same as I had had at sea. Hopelessly overworked, and exhausted far more than he would ever admit by the continuous challenge of pouring out all his reserves of strength and optimism to bolster up his patients, he finally decided that he could stand the nagging uncertainty, as well as the pain, no longer. Consulting his fellow-physicians, they tried to reassure him that there was nothing wrong except a recurring contraction of the colon, caused by the continuous overstrain he subjected himself to, standing sometimes for eight hours almost at a stretch in the operating theatre.

Fatigue had made him the worst of patients. He began to imagine that there was a growth at the top of his bowels, and finally demanded, against all advice, on an exploratory operation in London. Nothing sinister was found. His relief should have been enormous, he should have swiftly mended, but the more his colleagues jovially assured him he must be feeling better, he continued to complain that he could still sense the alien presence, the enemy in his side. 'Nonsense, my dear boy, what you need is a real holiday, war or no war.'

So in the end he consented to take one long-overdue leave. It was arranged that he should be the guest of the Air Force Command in Egypt, who were delighted with the prospect of having an opportunity to show hospitality towards the man who had done so much for their Service. And for the Navy, too, who came into the picture by offering him a free ride in a destroyer from Portsmouth to Gibraltar, where a plane would be waiting to fly him on his way to Cairo. The only pedestrian part of the journey would be the passage by train from Waterloo to the coast. Almost inevitably, because of wartime hazards, the train was late coming into the departure platform. To keep himself warm, Archie began to walk up and down. Suddenly a pain far fiercer than anything he had endured before, seized his abdomen, doubling him up. Acutely alarmed, he insisted on being taken straight back to the sick bay from which he had so recently been discharged. 'Open me up again,' he demanded. And this time, the operation was not in vain. They did find something. A swab left over from the first operation.

'If the train had been punctual,' he told me, 'the crisis would probably have occurred when we were going through the Bay of Biscay, pitching and tossing, and no doctor on board to perform an emergency operation.'

A narrow squeak. A last-minute postponement. Even as I listened, with the sour breath of death upon my own cheek, I could feel the pain increasing in my own side. Was it imagination, a sympathy for a fellow suffering? What was it that for so many months had made me so wretchedly off-colour, however hard I tried to concentrate on other things, such as the writing of *Home From Sea*?

My own doctor, who was also the official consultant for Scotland Yard, had short shrift for malingerers at any time. So when he decreed that I took myself off to a clinic in North Wales, where elaborate tests could be done without any menacing interruptions from doodle-bugs, I became increasingly anxious. Especially when he avoided my eyes, as I pestered him with questions that he could not, or would not, answer.

The afternoon that I arrived at Ruthin Castle, I came upon some patients playing bridge in the library. One of the four, with a high colour in his cheeks, was expostulating testily at his partner's play. They broke off to survey the newcomer. After the long, slow, railway journey, I felt at my worst, and no doubt looked it. As soon as I had been led away to my room, the bridge players held a different kind of post mortem from the cards. Recognizing me, they asked the one whose voice had been raised, whom I had mistaken for a peppery retired major in the Artillery, but who in actual fact was himself a member of the medical profession, what was his opinion. 'I have no idea,' he said cautiously, 'but he is certainly a very bad colour.'

'I thought you were a gonner. I thought you had cancer.'

'I thought you looked disgustingly well.'

How stupid of me. I mustn't get the dialogue out of place. This comes later. First there is another encounter that I must record, because in this clinic, which I have never visited again, I was destined to meet two people who were to have an overwhelming and lasting influence on my life.

It was the day that they had put a thin rubber tube reaching down through my mouth into my entrails, that Matron, having me now completely at her mercy, bustled into the room and announced that there was a very frail, little old gentleman, with a room on the next corridor, who kept asking for me. I shook my head. It was an automatic reaction. I did not want to see anyone. And when she persisted, telling me that the other patient was a fellow-writer, called Carl Mayer, I only shook it again. To my shame, I had forgotten the credit titles on those film masterpieces that came out of Germany before the Nazis deprived their country of all its Jewish talents, *Warning Shadows*, and *The Cabinet of Dr Caligari*. So when Matron continued briskly to suggest that I would be doing myself a kindness, if as soon as my tests were finally completed I put on my dressing gown and walked the length of a couple of passages, I simply turned my head away towards the wall.

Of course, the moment that I heard the final results of all the exhaustive X-rays, it was different. Nothing was organically wrong with me. I had a tricky gall bladder that could flare up at any time, and was at the moment suffering from the same kind of colonic spasms as Archie had had; but get that right with rest and diet, and my appetite would return, together with my colour and my vigour. I felt it already doing so, and was at once eager to put on my dressing gown, and to do what Matron had asked of me. And I understood why, the moment that I knocked on the door and entered to discover a small Jack-in-the-box figure, his head moving all the time from side to side, propped up in a bed that already seemed too large for the shrinking figure of its occupant.

'It was good of you to come and see me, my friend.'

Instantly something in me responded. It was as though I had never heard those last two words given their full meaning before. His parchment skin was the colour of his nightdress and the sheets. Only his ever-brilliant eyes and the shock of grey hair still possessed any life of their own. Describing the scene later, it did not seem extravagant to suggest that this was how Christ Himself might have looked, the agony and the forgiveness in the melting eyes, if He had lived to be twice His age on earth.

My other first impression was that everything seemed on too large a scale and uncomforting for someone who was obviously so very ill. In contrast, my own bedroom was like a cell, but I was not going to die. I am not going to die, I told myself, as I looked past the head propped against the pillows, at the wide expanse of window, with its vista of hundreds of daffodils, trumpeting their own brief glory across the grass. As if he could sense the direction of my thoughts, he whispered, 'There is always so little time . . .'

A spasm shook him, and he rang frantically for the nurse, his restless, ivory hands plucking at his stomach. When he began to groan, to try to hasten her arrival I opened the door into the passage. The moment she reached the threshold, he called out imploringly, 'An injection, please'. The nurse, so clean and hygienic, appeared to have no feeling. If he had asked for a bed-pan, it would have been the same. It had to be like that. 'Please come again, my friend,' he whispered, as she shooed me out of the room.

After that, I went every day, and gradually pieced together how it had come about for him to be here. Someone in the film world had recognized the emaciated figure, with the dark, unquenchable eyes, one night on an underground station platform. He had a W.V.S. mug of tea in his hand and was preparing to doss down for the night. There was nothing in the pockets of this great artist, who had refused countless offers from Hollywood because he was afraid the purity of his art would be corrupted, preferring to remain in England throughout the war. But because of the war, none of his kind of films were being made. However, the moment that Del Guidice, the head of Two Cities, one of the Rank subsidiaries, heard of the plight of his fellow exile, he immediately offered him a consultant post in his own organization. But first he must get well; so they sent him off to Ruthin Castle, with a rough shooting script to work on, to make him feel wanted and in no debt for all the medical and other expenses.

'So little time . . .' he repeated, day after day. Already the daffodils were nearly over. Now it was the turn of the tulips. Soon it would be the roses, and I would be back at Esher, helping my mother with the weeding of the herbaceous border, now that Charles had gone home. And where will you be, my friend, I wondered.

'We are already behind schedule. I try to work on the script, but I do not find that I can concentrate as I should. But you will help me, my friend. You will be very kind and help me.'

I mistook his gesture. 'How can I help you?' I protested, eternally on guard against pity. 'I know nothing about script writing. I'd love to learn, to have a shot at it, but not at your expense, Carl. In any case, I do not see Two Cities giving me a job, when I am released from my cell.'

'But, my friend, this is a sea story, and you were at sea, and I was not. It is the script that Leslie Howard was planning to do just before they shot down the plane in which he was a passenger, near Lisbon. Now we must finish it as best we can. The heroine is someone rather different from one of those synthetic Hollywood creations. She is a Liberty ship, in a convoy to Russia. Now you cannot say that is not up your street.'

'At this moment, I don't want ever to think about the sea again,' I protested.

'But today your eyes are as blue as the sea, when it is calm. That means that you are getting better, my friend.'

He had, as well as his gentleness and goodness, a directness of approach such as St Francis of Assisi must have had when talking to his birds. Then why did I not straight away take seriously the project of professional collaboration that he held out to me? I suppose because I had been brought up in the world of the theatre, and was only too aware of all the extravagant promises that are made and never kept. Again, the life of a clinic is like a religious order. You have no inhibitions about pouring yourself out in the various confessionals that are provided, as part of the treatment. Afterwards, you return to the outside world, and swiftly forget the long weeks of isolation, together with their accompanying loyalties and sudden, violent devotions.

I was week-ending at Brighton, which many consider the best doctor of all, when the telegram reached me: *'Two Cities wish to get in touch with you. Please communicate with me.'* Then the number of the house in Hanover Square, and the signature, Carl Mayer, the name that I had disdained the first time that I had heard it, in the clinic. I should not easily purge that memory, I thought, as I hurried back to London. I found him looking tinier and frailer than ever, huddled up beneath a huge mound of bedclothes. The next day he was to have the familiar exploratory operation, but in this case they were to discover a growth of the pancreas, defying the surgeon's knife, not visible on the X-rays, that must have racked him beyond human forbearance. Mercifully, this tortured man died under the anaesthetic. Almost the last thing that he did was to give me an exquisite cup and saucer of Worcester china from beside his bed, which he had come upon in a curio ship on the only excursion he had made to a neighbouring Welsh village during his incarceration at Ruthin. 'I want you to have it,' he said. 'Men make such beautiful things.' And do such abominable, monstrous things to each other, I thought, swearing to myself that no one in my presence would ever heap curses or criticism on any member of his race again. First there had been the example of the taxi-driver and the pogrom, and now there was the concrete help I was receiving from a complete stranger, in his death agonies.

When a few weeks later I signed a contract for five thousand a year with the Rank Organization, which was to run, with options being taken up, for the next five years, I heard once again my sponsor's valedictory voice, admonishing me in his broken English, but with such uncloying sweetness.

'My friend, you see I kept my promise. Always believe in people. It is the best way. Sometimes, you will be disappointed, but more often not. Life has been very good to me. Always when things were bad, something happened to make me believe again in the bounty of the world and the fellowship of man. So it will be for you, too, my friend.'

And it has been.

On the day that I was due to leave the clinic, I happened to go into the library, to find sitting at the writing desk a member of the bridge four who had scrutinized me on my arrival, the middle-aged man with the crumpled shoulders, the high colouring, and fierce blue eyes, whom I had now come to know as the Doc.

After the departure of Carl Mayer, who had done so much, and with such generosity of spirit, to restore my own belief in my creative powers as a writer, and as with returning physical strength and confidence I began to go for walks in the grounds, and in the neighbouring countryside, I had gravitated, *faute de mieux*, to the side of 'The Doc', since he was one of the few patients also allowed out of doors. He was only able to walk at a slow pace, which suited my own powers at that time. In a way, I suppose we must have seemed an incongruous pair, not so much for the disparity in our height, and our ages, as for the vast difference in our approach and experience of life up till that moment. There was an excellent rule of the establishment, much emphasized, that none of the patients should discuss their symptoms with each other; in consequence, I had no idea why, in his own apologetic words, my fellow inmate, whom I had mistaken at first as having seen much army service, should be 'a bit slow on my pins'. Was he, like myself, some sort of a casualty of the war?

Actually, we never spoke of the events of the last five years as they had affected ourselves. I imagine that from his skill with his own patients, he was conscious that I had had enough of that. Instead, he produced a constant stream of anecdotes of his own life, as a general practitioner, in that part of the north that was like a petrified forest from the unending erosions of the industrial revolution. No professional man is a more enthralling talker on his own subject than a doctor. One afternoon, when we had ventured a little further afield to a hillock blazing with gorse bushes, and, while he rested, I was amusing myself searching for wild orchids, he had made a most revealing remark which, in a sense, told me everything. 'Nothing will grow in my garden except laurels.' In a second, I could place and picture the whole scene. The doctor's house in Torrington, near Bury, its red brick blackened and corroded by the implacable smoke from the surrounding chimneys, its brass plate, with the name of Doctor Leach on it, cloudy again like the stanchions on the quarter-deck of the *Cumberland*, almost as soon as it had been cleaned. The endless struggle to keep external shabbiness at bay, the endless stream of patients to the surgery, all seeking a panacea, all eternally below par, searching for reassurance and a private audience for their anxieties. Again, unlike the other local landmarks, the butcher and the baker, and the fish and chip shop, himself on call, all day and all night. The repository of so many secrets, the wise man of the neighbourhood, as well as the magician who doled out pills, with their magical properties. The gyrations of life and death made their unpredictable pattern; the figure of the Doc alone remained, stable, immutable. And though the seasons would fluctuate like the health of the community, nothing really flourished in that smoke-ridden atmosphere, buffeted by those biting northern winds, except the evergreens, the ubiquitous laurels in the drive. Besides, there had been no time for cultivating or coaxing the soil; all his energies were given up to sustaining those who depended upon him absolutely.

The Doc looked up from the letter he was writing, as I came

and stood beside him. He was aware that I was about to leave, and had been receiving my headmaster's report, and a homily for the future in the world outside once more. 'Hello, Goff. Got your clean bill of health?' When I nodded, he gave me an appraising look over the top of his old-fashioned, steel-rimmed spectacles. Like an actor playing the medical role, in a T.V. advertisement for some tonic wine. 'You certainly look very different from the day you arrived. You know, privately, I thought you were a gonner. I thought you had cancer.'

'While I, in my turn, thought you looked so disgustingly well, I couldn't believe you were an inmate. But instead, a visitor just passing the time at the bridge table while a relative had an operation. By the way, how much longer are you going on convalescing in this extremely comfortable hotel, considering there's still a war on?'

The brick-red colour remained static in his cheeks. It did right until the end, but his eyes, as he took off his reading glasses and put them down on the desk, had lost some of their intensity of blue. 'Oh, I've got a few more tests to be done, but they are mere formalities. I really knew what the answer would be when I came in. I heard the result of the really important test a couple of days ago. My kidneys have completely packed up.'

'What does that mean?'

'It means,' he said, no longer using the rough-edged voice I had heard that first day at the bridge table, 'that I have just about a year to live.'

My first reaction was one of complete astonishment. Throughout our growing acquaintance, our daily walks, he had been so invariably cheerful and relaxed. In fact, I had come to believe that he was simply having a rest and a holiday, away from any fear of bombing. Better rations and quiet nights. And why not? It was clear, without fear of contradiction, no civilian on the home front had worked harder since the beginning of the Emergency. And now this . . .

With the gentle consideration that was so much part of his make-up, lying deep beneath the bluff, deceptively hearty exterior, he changed the subject quickly, before there was really time for me to stutter out any attempt at sympathy.

'If you come north this autumn, to speak for the Ministry of Information, and your meeting is anywhere in Lancashire, please let me know. I don't say my hotel rates as many stars as this one, but I have one great advantage. My butcher is one of my best friends, because of past medical aid for his family. So I can promise you a steak. And I can meet your train in Manchester. So don't forget, Goff.'

'You mean, you are going on working?'

'Of course I am going on working,' he replied in his testiest voice, picking up his pen as though about to write a prescription for a patient who had already taken up too much of his time. At that, I took the hint, and left him in peace. But back home in the south again, I did not forget 'The Doc'. I had a curious sensation that like the other magician, who had waved his wand on my behalf, we had not been thrown together by chance, but there was an important reason for our meeting, and something still to be resolved.

As it happened, it was several months before I did go north, and then to pick out his face among the blurred figures at the platform barrier was like a beacon. My heart leapt; I could have embraced him with joy. It had all been a false alarm. Even the most brilliant of medicos could make a faulty diagnosis. And then a few moments later, I had to register that he was now walking with a stick, and had considerable difficulty in heaving himself back into the driving seat of his car. His niece Nan, a charming girl who kept house for him, told me sadly that her uncle's legs were slowly but inexorably atrophying. All the same, he insisted, thanks to his butcher, and having saved up a month's meat ration, on hosting a splendid gathering that evening of all his old cronies from the Bolton Conservative Club. I don't know what they thought of the writer in their midst, but they reminded me of the gaggle of merchant skippers, who, passengers in the destroyer bringing us back from Russia after P.Q.17, had an unanimously undefeatable air about them, though all their own ships had sunk under them. Or again, of the commodores at the convoy conference I had attended on one occasion in Liverpool; most of these were naval veterans from the first war, retired admirals some of them, returned to pool their expertise, but cautiously considering what lay just ahead of them, with incongruous goloshes over their civilian shoes. My fellow guests that night had come to terms, too, one gathered, with their northern environment, and would never be caught napping, whatever Government was in power, or whatever the weather – or the enemy – chose to do. It was moving for the outsider to sense how, under all the chaffing, and the outrageous stories, in what respect and affection they held their host.

The next day, the Doc insisted on driving me himself to my speaking engagement with a luncheon club in Bradford, and the morning after that to Halifax, where he assured me I could expect to see far more Rolls-Royces on the streets than in the West End of London. At least, in peace-time. I didn't argue the toss about anything, I was too happy to be with him again, though the landscape, for all its austere grandeur, reminded me uncomfortably of *Wuthering Heights.* My companion snorted, and scoffed at me for that. Not only did he refuse to make any reference to his own approaching doom, but he was adamantine in his defence of the pitted landscape of the county that he had come to look upon as his own native heath, pointing out, rightly, that as you drop down into Bolton, there is one of the most open and inspiring stretches of country in the whole of Britain.

Yes, but we returned to find the laurels looking even more pinched than usual in the drive, and how thankful I was for the luxury of the coal fire that Nan had stacked up for the evening. As we stood side by side, thawing out after the long drive, my host exclaimed:

'I can't remember when I last took a day off, and left the surgery entirely to my assistant. Except when I was at Ruthin, of course. But I'll tell you what, Goff. If you'll invite me here and now, I'll come and spend a week with you in the south next summer, when your mother's roses are at their best. That'll be something to look forward to.'

'It's on, Doc,' I said, instinctively trying to mimic his jovial tone as I avoided the eye of Nan, who was laying the table for our supper.

But he made it.

The week of his July visit coincided with a stretch of celestial weather. So often, when the recurring arguments about the relative climatic merits of the north versus the south are put to the test, one is ignominiously defeated by a sudden depression on the charts, bringing rain in its train. However, on this occasion the gods were magnanimous. The borders had assumed that special look that they always seem to wear when they are about to

Football team of H.M.S. *Cumberland*. The Sheriff is top left

A. B. Burgess, alias The Sheriff

Outside Hut No. 10 at Mearnskirk Hospital

Sir Archibald McIndoe

Sir Archibald with Squadron Leader 'Bill' Simpson

A Guinea-Pig Reunion Dinner

be admired by an appreciative visitor, who may not be much of an horticulturist but at least can recognize a rose at sight. My mother, too, took to my new friend at sight. She liked his very clean appearance, and even more his uncomplicated personality, of which she could, without reservations, approve. At the same time, I suspect that she was surprised that he should so openly approve of her younger son, who lacked the authority and the comforting conventionality of his elder brother. I bore no resentment about this. It was quite natural on her part. Instead, I was delighted to see how she began to blossom herself the moment that breezily, and full of appreciation for the white walls everywhere, the colour of the flower arrangements, the antique furniture with its loving patina, our guest crossed the threshold, and through the wide windows of my mother's drawing-room glimpsed the terraces of roses stretching away towards the top of the garden and the open fields beyond.

'Well I will say this for you, Goff. You didn't exaggerate,' he said gruffly.

I had, of course, warned her of the prophecy that the Doc had made a year before in North Wales, on my last day in the clinic, but she was always inclined to regard any author as being given to flights of histrionic fancy. Was I not, after all, the storyteller in the family? Besides, when our guest arrived – having been driven down by Nan, who was herself having a holiday – he looked, apart from the obvious difficulty with his legs, a virile picture of robust health. A bit battered but, on the whole, extremely well-preserved for his age.

Their approval, at first sight, was mutual. 'I only wish I had met your mother ten years ago,' the old war horse, turned gallant, announced as we sat on the lawn after lunch, having our coffee. Like all very feminine women, my mother could never resist compliments. With a certain amusement I watched her quickening interest, and listened to her starting to make plans for the Doc's retirement. All he needed for the restoration of his health was to come and live in the south. Now that the hostilities in Europe were over, there was bound to be a spate of rebuilding and replanning. She would find him a nice, small, modern house, easy to run, somewhere in Surrey, not too far from London or the coast, not too far from Esher, either. As the week unfolded in a round of theatre going, my mother's favourite treat, and drives to beauty spots on the Doc's extra petrol allowance, and even an expedition to the races, from which I cried off, I began to realize that her mind was beginning to leap ahead, and that she was even envisaging his coming to share our home, thus assuaging her longing for a man at her side once more. For by this time, just as Charles Butler had not been slow to confide in her, and show her his family snapshots, so had the Doc explained fully and frankly what he had only hinted to me; how his wife, many years ago, had been taken from him, not by the clean break of death but by an illness, incurable in her case, which had kept her incarcerated in a Home that had to be a living tomb. While he himself had been forced into the barren existence of a celibate, too busy and too withdrawn to seek other outlets for his emotions. At the eleventh hour, the chance encounter with my mother, their being thrown into each other's company, against this setting of the warmer south in the high noon of summer, was making him overwhelmingly, intoxicatingly conscious of all that he had been long compelled to discard through the self-imposed discipline of his long working hours. While she, in her turn, who had once exclaimed bitterly to me, after my stepfather's death, 'It is impossible for you to understand what it is like for a woman – to travel always alone, to have no one to drive her any longer in the car, to enter a restaurant without a man at her side, no one of her own age to advise her, or talk things over with at the end of the day,' had overnight shed all the strain of the war years and was miraculously transformed, gay and laughing, instinctively resuming the coquettish play that had so enchanted my stepfather. She had had her second chance, after my father's betrayal. Was there to be a third? Her happiness had always been the most important consideration in my life. I could not bear to assume the title now of kill-joy, as I watched her, with a new-found, extravagant abandon, start opening all the tins in her secret store cupboard, the parcels full of wartime luxuries, that had been sent to her by her younger sister, my Aunt Nanciebel, living in the States. Women are born hoarders, and she had hoarded them against the final Emergency that had never happened. Instead, we were all three now enjoying a gala, and I hoped our guests appreciated just what he had achieved in so short a time.

One evening we cancelled a trip into London, because the day had been like a summer's one of one's childhood, and instead lingered on in the garden while the dusk enfolded us. At the Doc's request, I had played some records on my radiogram, in my writing room which looked out on to the yew hedges, and the giant sentinel beech tree beyond. The music filled the enclosed reaches of the terrace, this safe territory, with enchantment. I had not been certain what kind of music he would most enjoy, but when Yehudi Menuhin, playing the Elgar Violin Concerto, came to the end of the first movement, with its dying fall that seems to epitomize the beauty and the ecstasy of all transient, mortal things, the Doc asked, to my surprise, if I would play it again.

The machine turned itself off. I did not move. In the ensuing friendly silence, our guest began to speak his thoughts aloud.

'I am beginning to understand now all that I have missed . . . I can't remember when I last felt really warm, in my bones. In the north, it's very rare that there's a night when it's hot enough to sit out of doors. And if there has been, I've been too occupied attending to my patients, called in to a confinement, or falling asleep in my chair over the latest number of *The Lancet*.

'Mind you, the people themselves in the north are so warm-hearted, that makes up for everything. When you are young, you don't mind missing the other things, and when you are getting on, well, it doesn't matter any more.'

'But you aren't old,' my mother protested vehemently. 'You are just tired and need a rest. You told us you hadn't had a single holiday all through the war.'

'And you haven't had one either, ma'am. You've just sat here at night, listening to the bombers going over, waiting for the All Clear, often alone in the house. I simply don't know how you've stuck it out. Women like yourself have had the hardest time of all in the war. Goff appreciates, that, don't you?'

I did, but I had been unable to put it into words, because I knew that my mother would have been embarrassed if I had tried to do so. Even now, three months after V.E. Day, she still found it difficult to discard the blackout curtains and allow the lights of the house to blaze forth at night. However, it was different when this newcomer into her life, heralding the peace, paid such a tribute. What had seemed quenched in her for ever, the dampened fires, had been rekindled.

'You know, ten years ago,' the Doc was saying, 'my fellow medicos told me that if I were to sell my practice and come south, and retired to some place like Eastbourne, and potter through the days, I might conceivably survive till I was the biblical three-score years and ten. But I could not face such a prospect. I had seen too many people in bath-chairs in my time to want to join the brigade. I should have felt so damn idle, too. It's good for a man to feel that he is still in harness. Then you enjoy a week like this all the more.'

On the other hand, what he did not enjoy was the shock which came towards the end of that July week of 1945, with the one-sided results of the first post-war General Election. It was soon apparent that, thanks to the Forces' vote from over-seas, there was an overwhelming landslide in favour of the Socialists. The Doc was a staunch Churchill man, so that he was both shocked and appalled by what he regarded as monstrous ingratitude towards the architect of the Allied victory. My mother, not surprisingly, held exactly similar views. It was another bond, to bring them yet another step closer together; whereas I did not like to disturb the week's harmony by admitting that for the first and only time in my life I had voted for the local Socialist candidate in the Westminster Division. It was a gesture, nothing more, because this always had been and always will remain, I imagine a safe Tory seat. However, having spent most of the last six years in the company of servicemen and women, I was only too aware of the cauldron of their resentment, buried beneath the surface, but ever on the boil, fuelled by their anger at having been precipitated into the situation in which they found themselves. This war, without glory for the victor or the vanquished, was, in their eyes, entirely the fault of the politicians, who had re-armed too late and too little, and who when they had not actually lied through their teeth had nevertheless been vacillating and muddleheaded. A clean sweep of them all, and that had to include 'Winnie', Colossus though he had proved himself in the crisis of our fortunes, because unfortunately he was tarred with the pre-war Conservative brush. To all the arguments that he had been the Man of the Hour, and Civilization's saviour, they retorted that Dunkirk was far behind them. What they were concerned with now was a world fit for the returning forces to live in. They did not seek to receive a hero's welcome, but they did expect to be regarded on their return as adult citizens. New ideas and energy, new faces at the top, above all, new ideals of undiluted socialism were needed as much now as at the lowest ebb of the war. The battle for a Brave New World had begun.

I admit freely that I believed this just as ardently myself as any footslogger stationed on the Rhine. And I often think now, with relief, how glad I am that the Doc at least was spared the disillusionment of the aftermath, though I suppose it would only have been human for him to have rejoiced in declaring, 'I told you so.' All the high hopes dashed by the onrush of bureaucracy, monstrously expanding into the threat of a Gestapo state, of spying and being spied upon, into which we have finally been landed. Yet surely we have only ourselves to blame. Not long before my mother herself died, she said to me, sadly:

'I never think of the "good old days" or the "bad old days", but instead of the days when there was no envy. If people saw someone driving past in a car, they were not envious, but instead ambitious to work harder so that they would possess one themselves. Or a better home, or better education for their children. To achieve it by their own efforts, not to have it handed to them on a platter, by the Welfare State. Nowadays, eaten up with envy, they throw stones and jeer at those who through their own initiative and their own talent have outstripped the others in the race.'

I wanted to refute her argument, because it was not a very pleasant picture of one's own countrymen and women, but in my heart I knew that there was considerable truth in what she said. Envy did stalk the land. Together with a 'couldn't care less' attitude, that is vastly different from that over-publicised, ludicrous picture of 'Swinging London'. We are fast becoming a nation not so much of self-respecting shopkeepers, as of hypnotized formfillers, apathetic television spectators, and, nastiest of all, informers. At the dictates of a Socialist Government in power, as I write, everyone and everything must be reduced to the same level. Only the other day, in conversation with a high-up official in the Inland Revenue Service, I was as appalled as the Doc would have been by his volunteered disclosure that his desk is showered, week after week, with a spate of anonymous letters, denouncing neighbours, giving uninvited information as regards new acquisitions like a more expensive motor car or a fur coat, and demanding that an investigation should be instigated as to how 'they' can afford it.

In one sense, the Welfare State had passed by Doctor Leach's surgery. For all the time that he had practised at Torrington, he had charged his private patients modest fees, which they paid if they could, and if through illness they were having a bad patch, he went on attending them just the same. His rewards came in their friendship and in the knowledge that he could look any man in the face who challenged him as to whether he had done an honourable day's work. I am afraid his is a dying breed.

On the last evening of the Doc's visit, I drove him into London to a party at the Dorchester, being given by Jay Llewellin. It had been intended as a celebration after the election, but as in the case of so many others, ministers and ordinary M.P.s alike, what had seemed a safe majority had been swept aside by the tide so strongly, for the moment, going the other way. So the evening could have been a wake, but instead our host, pink-cheeked like the Doc, was taking his defeat with a dignity and an equanimity which one could only admire. 'I shall be glad of the rest,' he said, and clearly meant it. After all he had hardly been out of office since the beginning of hostilities, and that night he told a story, which particularly pleased the Doc, of the occasion that he had been received by the King, on taking over as Minister of Food.

'Sir, I can promise you, at any rate, a pound of oranges.'

To which the Monarch had pointedly replied, 'You mean, you can promise a pound of oranges to each of us with a ration card, including myself?'

'And of course, that is precisely what I did mean,' our host concluded, pouring out fresh drinks all round. I saw the Doc take another whisky, long since forbidden him, but I made no effort to restrain him when he gave me a puckish grin. He was like a schoolboy, on the last day of his holidays. Let no one deny him anything.

After the party was over, he was too keyed-up to want me to drive him straight back to Esher, and asked, instead, if I would stop the car on Westminister Bridge. When I did, he climbed out laboriously and leant over the parapet. Big Ben started to strike midnight, and we gazed towards the illuminated building of the Mother of Parliaments, that view with all the lights reflected in the water that catches at one's memory and one's heart when one is far from England. There was a look upon his face that I could not fathom. One moment it seemed like pity, the next like exultation.

As the last of the strokes died away, he said in a voice so strong, that it must have carried far across the water, 'I'll tell you why I wanted you to drive me here, Goff. I haven't stood on Westminster Bridge since I was a medical student, walking the hospitals. Just to stand here again brings the strength back to my legs. Like most of the others in my year, I started off with such high expectations. I was absolutely confident that I would only be going north for a few years, and then I would be coming back to London, with my plate one day in Harley Street. I would specialize in gynaecology. I couldn't count how many babies I have assisted into the world, or how many maternal lives I have saved, but I am still an unknown G.P. It doesn't matter any longer. In the past, time and again I have tried to comfort myself with the saying that within twenty miles of Manchester lies the real heart of Britain. But on a night like this, standing here, you know it's not true. It's here' – he raised an arm to point across the water to Big Ben, whose unbroken beat had been a symbol of hope, to hang on a little longer, to so many underground resistance fighters after the Nazis had over-run Europe. 'The poor bloody fools. They don't know where they are going, but I do.'

I took this outburst as a concluding reference to the election results, but I made no answer. I did not want the shining surface of our last night together to be even slightly chipped. My mind was too full, anyway, of the picture of the young man, with ardent and eager limbs for the journey ahead, the journey that was for him almost over. I wanted him to know how much his trusting acceptance of myself and all my blemishes had meant to me, what reassurance he had given me for the rest of my own Odyssey. But I was learning reticence from him fast. All I could do was to help him back into the car and drive him peacefully home.

The next day Nan came for him, and after his departure my mother comforted herself by reminding us both that he had assured her that he had enjoyed himself as much as his Torrington patients always did at their Blackpool Wakes Week. He had had his own vision of the Golden Mile.

Nan wrote afterwards to say they had had a comfortable journey, and that on Sunday evening, instead of resting, he had insisted on driving into Bolton to see his cronies at the Conservative Club, and to recite every detail of the glorious binge he had had. 'I see you sods want cheering up,' he had bellowed, calling for drinks all round. It was late when he got back and crawled into bed. He must have still been enveloped in a state of euphoria, because he did not wake his niece. However, some time during the night, the final, implacable process took over, and in the morning he was already in a coma.

Only once did he rally during the few lingering days. His niece was with him, leaning over his bed to hear his whisper. There was something very important that he wanted to say, that everyone must know. Suddenly his bruised, darkening face broke into a beatific smile. 'Tell Goff,' he said, 'that it was worth it. Everything has been worth it. And it was a wonderful week.'

At first after the Doc's death, my mother and I found it difficult to make conversation with each other. Whenever I had come home on leave I had instinctively taken care to guard my tongue; and she in her turn not to encourage me in any careless talk, which, as the posters reminded us, could cost lives. Now when at last we had a safe subject in common to discuss, ironically we were silent. In a strange way, the Doc's death affected me more strongly than that of almost any of the chance companions with whom I had made friends during the last six years. He was so utterly a different kind of person from myself, and yet we had found ourselves right from the start in absolute concord. This sometimes happens with complete opposites. Moreover, he had represented something that was passing from the English scene for ever. Would there be a place for his kind of patriotism and political views in the peace? For my mother his abundantly masculine presence in her house had thawed her frozen heart. Her womanhood had been roused in a manner that she had imagined was over for her, for ever. All the deprivations and the overriding darkness of the war she had accepted with the stoical calm of a Roman matron. I had never heard her grumble or complain once. But now this loss, on top of all the others, was more than she could bear. When they had come to photograph her in her garden, because I was supposed, in the street where I worked, to be 'missing', she had managed to smile into the camera, and control her feelings. But now it was not only sadness, but anger against Fate which consumed her. Inevitably I suffered from the backwash, since, in a curious way, she blamed me for having been bang on the target for once, in my prophecy. He *had* had exactly a year to live. Fact, not fiction, this time. But why this time of all times? Though she never put her resentment into actual words, I could guess only too easily the reason for the tension between us, and once again as after the death of my stepfather, whom she adored, I was filled with an overflowing sense of pity for her sadness, which I longed to be able to translate into practical terms. All I could lamely suggest was that I took her away for the holiday she had forgone all the war years, regarding the terraces of her garden as an observation post that must never be unmanned for a single day. Many of the wire entanglements, guarding the landmines on many of our own beaches, had not yet been removed, and the sands officially passed as being safe again, but some coastal towns were already free and welcoming visitors again. 'You always like Brighton. Shall we go there for a bit?' I suggested, knowing her affection for the Regency architecture of the town. She simply shook her head.

And yet she had known the Doc for such a short time, I thought. But then it is strange how, looking back on those days now, one so often seems to have a more vivid recollection, some tiny incident or remark implanted in one's consciousness for ever, concerning those once encountered for only a brief moment, than about those close to one in the previous peacetime, who became casualties in the conflict. For instance, I shall always see in my mind the brown boots that the newly-appointed American Ambassador, John Winant, was wearing when I went to interview him at his Embassy in Grosvenor Square. Everything else about this noble man, with the carved head so closely resembling that of his countryman, Abraham Lincoln – his suit, his shaving marks, his eyes and untidy hair – were dark and black, except his boots. Looking down at them, he explained, without embarrassment, that he had been wearing them when he had been brought over as a passenger, with the minimum of luggage, in a USA bomber being delivered to our shores, and there just hadn't been any time for him since his arrival to go out and shop for the expected sort of shoes for someone in his position to wear. We spoke for an hour about his hopes for a free world, and about civilization's last chance when Nazidom had finally been exorcised from the face of the Globe, but it is his boots which at this moment I can almost bend down and touch.

Just as I cannot pay a flying visit to Oxford, to speak to some Society, without reliving one week-end of all the week-ends that I have stayed there across the years. Yet this was a week-end without parties or excitements of any kind. I was the guest of Nevill Coghill, then an English don at Exeter, immersed in the placid life of the University, though he was to be precipitated into a vastly different sort of world as the producer of Marlowe's *Faustus,* with the Richard Burtons in the cast, and as the author of the book for the musical version of *The Canterbury Tales.* All this was to come much later; instead, that particular week-end the academic calm of the college, undisturbed by the smallest ripple serenely flowed over me. Seated at the high table in the hall, swiftly surrendering to the immemorial atmosphere, it became impossible for me to believe that only forty-eight hours earlier I had been unable to enjoy the last of my ham sandwiches during my daytrip over Stavanger. I could not even bring myself to take out of my pocket book the wings that Ginger, the Hudson's pilot, had cut off his tunic, so that I could show my host the citation on the back. '*Happy Landings.*' It would have seemed too incongruous.

Just as I cannot go to a London concert without remembering the black scarf at her throat, again so incongruous, so startling a contrast with her white dress, that my guest had worn that July day of 1940 when she had come, a stranger and yet not a stranger, to lunch with me at Ebury Street. Did she still enjoy listening to a concert more than any other form of entertainment? And did the civil servant whom she had eventually married, after her first love had been swallowed up in the Battle of Britain – the boy with a taste for classical music, whose hut and confidence I had shared at Hornchurch – accept and echo her taste?

Just as I cannot go into any outfitters, where there is a display of shorts and singlets, without touching again the silk of the German parachute which my mother, returning one afternoon from her W.V.S. duties, found had arrived mysteriously on her doorstep. Treasure-trove indeed. It had been deposited there by yet another Spitfire pilot, on his way up the Portsmouth Road, in his vintage MG sports model, for a few hours respite in the London clubs. How fantastic it had seemed at the time, the joking promise he had made one week-end, lounging in our garden, that he would bring my mother the next German parachute he could rightly claim as his personal booty, provided that she and her fellow workers cut it up into strips, for handkerchiefs, to sell for the local R.A.F. Savings Drive. Which in due course she did, and made such a huge success with the results that it was only reluctantly that she kept the other part of her bargain, to set aside sufficient to make a pair of silk briefs for her son. These became the highlight of my wartime wardrobe, and though they have long since disintegrated and disappeared, I still cannot buy myself a new pair of shorts today, coupon free, without seeing again Q's face, sunburnt and always smiling, as though he had just returned from holiday. My mother never spoke of him again, either, because he was her favourite of all my wartime friends who came and went.

Just as I could not watch them on the television screen, making the draw for the World Cup without feeling that I was leaning once again over Jimmy Campbell's palliasse, in that barren corridor in the Archangel hospital, filled with the stench of frostbite, recalling not so much his courage and astonishing cheerfulness in the face of his cruel injuries, as that compelling, vivid phrase he had produced so spontaneously about lacking nothing except a football to kick around the ward. Just as I cannot take my place at the table of the judges for the Miss World Contest without being back once again in that small cabin on board H.M.S. *Leda*, turning over in my hands the faded newspaper cuttings that had been produced with such pride by the ship's navigator, since they proclaimed the victory of his wife as the beauty queen of Oslo.

That autumn, after the horror of Hiroshima had ended hostilities in the East as well as the West, I spent compiling, at my publishers' suggestion, a *Scrapbook of Victory*, as a sequel to the earlier volume I had produced, *Scrapbook of the War*, just before I had disappeared into the anonymous ranks of the Lower Deck.

Like Aarl, the Norwegian navigator, I had studiously collected, though moved by other compulsions, a vast array of newspaper cuttings, pictures, articles, vignettes, a headline here, a slogan there. Re-published and re-edited, it seemed to me that they would possess, if not a historical, at least an evocative interest for some, and for those who had never been stifled by the claustrophobia of the blackout nor had had to endure rationing, a curiosity value, if nothing more. There had been so many descriptions of the battles, too few, perhaps, of the civilian front, because it had an inevitably certain sameness and familiarity. For that reason I am choosing now, as almost the last verbal picture in this book, and in the hope that it may reach a wider audience, a letter written by an American soldier named Robert Arhib. He specifically stated at the time that he was putting down all his impressions of our country, in case he did not himself return from the wars. I wish I knew whether he has survived or not, but this is what he had to say:

'The blackout astonished us. It was so oppressively black. It still gives us a feeling that the houses behind the staring windows are abandoned, lifeless. The atmosphere of rural Suffolk, the workers in the fields, the stillness, the emptiness of the roads, the quiet of your village streets – these things made us feel that we had come to a country where all but the remnants of the people had moved away. But we changed our minds when we saw the teeming towns on market day, and walked in the streets on Saturday evenings.

'Memorable days . . . watching our first cricket match on the fields of St Albans, within sight of the Roman ruins . . . the Buckinghamshire village of Chalfont St Giles . . . Boxford, where two girls waited at their window every morning for eight months to watch us as we drove past. We never once spoke to them, but we were friends . . . I shall remember a Sunday in June, punting on the river at Cambridge and talking to a don who badly needed a shave, haircut and press . . . Cycling to Lavenham with Vivien for a look at the perfect Tudor village, and a drink at the Swan . . . walking across the meadows with Joan to listen to the skylarks, those most irresponsible of sun-struck birds. Then there were churches . . . Lincoln and Peterborough and Ely, the beautiful, smaller churches at Cransley and Long Melford and Melton Mowbray, and the chapel at Windsor Castle . . . above all, Boston Stump, lit by the last rays of the

setting sun and shining across the fens like a white sword.

'We shall remember Piccadilly Circus, after dark . . . the swarms of people, the fifty different uniforms . . . the girl who sang operatic arias on the Bakerloo platform as everyone cheered . . . the sailor who played his violin and danced in the Morden train when everyone joined in Dear Liverpool. But we shall remember, too, our Christmas parties for the orphans and the evacuees. No one could ever forget those parties with the kids yelling and gobbling ice-cream, sitting on our shoulders and singing for us. Fifteen hundred we had at one party.

'Mind you, it wasn't all fun. There was the mud of the airfields, the tents that leaked, the north wind that blew, and lots of rain . . . there were haunting scenes . . . the mist hanging on the silent mountains round Loch Lomond that day when everything dripped, and the solitude of the spot was heightened by the wail of the bagpipes. Sombre pictures, too. The shelters each night in the London Underground stations; the faces of the children sleeping on the floors under the feet of passers-by in draughts of dusty air. The battered face of Hull and Bristol and Liverpool, with their exposed, embarrassed scars. You who have lived here and watched the damage grow cannot know the shock of one who suddenly comes on it around the corner.

'There you have the face of Britain as we have seen it in these two years. We have met you all now, the workers and the teachers, the bishops and the soldiers, young girls, farmers, miners, publicans and children, even an earl or two and an M.P.

'We thank you all for your hospitality, for opening your homes to us, for smiling at us and dancing with us, for marrying some of us, for being patient with our faults, for listening to our talk with tolerance, for struggling with our quaint tongue, and then adopting our expressions. For playing host to the vast army of foreigners without letting it get you down. For showing us quiet courage and stamina and the patience that is your greatest virtue and worst handicap. We will remember England.'

I wonder if other authors have the feeling which often assails me, that everyone else seems to write so much more arrestingly than oneself. But in the very necessary process of finding one's own level, I have often been comforted by a story which my literary mentor, Somerset Maugham, once told me. He came into the smoking room of his London Club to be confronted by one of the oldest members, seated beside the fire in a tall-backed arm chair. In search of fresh material for his travellers' tales, the author of *East of Suez* had spent two whole years sailing up rivers in China, visiting Bangkok and Ankor Wat, the one place which he wished to revisit in his own extreme old age, Singapore and Malaya and Hong Kong. In the course of his restless travels, he had come upon the plots of *Rain* and *The Letter*, and now well satisfied with his literary loot, he was back in the metropolis again.

Before he could produce a civil 'Good morning', or comment on the weather, his fellow member, who clearly regarded that particular chair by the fire as his private territory, cut the intruder down to size. 'Hello, Maugham,' he growled, 'Haven't seen your face recently. Been to Brighton, I suppose, for the week-end . . .'

I went to Brighton for the week-end, that Christmas, back to the hotel where I had spent the first Christmas of the war. In one way, it seemed like only yesterday that my mother and Angie Fox and myself had sat in a box at the Theatre Royal, to watch Ivor Novello act in his own play, but in another way there had been a whole lifetime of experience between. So much had happened to us all. I stood at the window of my bedroom in The Old Ship, exulting in the curtains flung back, in a position now to watch with complete equanimity the heaving motion of the small vessels, ploughing their way, through the Channel. No Dover Patrol for me next week, or ever again. I gazed down at the lamps lit along the promenade, and my heart was full of thankfulness and joy. At that moment Brighton seemed the most beautiful place in the world, the embodiment of peace. And how good it was to note the change in my mother, the way that she was really relaxing at last, no longer in the evening half-listening for the sound of aeroplanes overhead. Instead, accepting that they were *all* friendly ones. Through a friend in the trade, I had scrounged some material that would make badly-needed new curtains for the drawing-room at Esher, and I don't think I had ever succeeded in producing a Christmas present which gave her more obvious pleasure.

But equally, in her turn, she gave me something which will never fade or wear out. We had been invited by Archie McIndoe to eat our Christmas dinner in his company, together with the occupants of the ward where, for a few days, I myself had lodged. At first I was doubtful whether my mother would appreciate such a challenge, but she welcomed the idea at once, having received a card from Charles Butler's parents. She would take it with her to show the current batch of patients. We were to eat our turkey and plum pudding in the ward itself.

On the way over, in the car, I stupidly lost my way between Brighton and East Grinstead. Such a small domestic journey, after all the others of the last six years. It would have been farcical had it not been so exasperating. And my mood of irritation with myself was scarcely soothed by my mother's efforts to put us back on to the right road. By the time I finally turned in at the gate of the hospital, flustered and late, there was little of the Christmas spirit left, as far as I was concerned.

'Now remember to look them all straight in the eyes. It will be all right then,' I said curtly.

As she got out of the car she turned, and with one of her rare gestures, touched my arm. At that moment she looked as she used to do at other Christmases in Worcestershire, returning, in her outdoor clothes, from church, tantalizingly standing guard over the drawing-room door till everything was finally in place to her satisfaction, and the children and grownups alike could crowd in to search out our presents, stacked beneath the tree.

'It will be all right. For you, too, my dear. Because you can look everyone in the eyes now, also.'

It was the only reference she ever made to the events of this chronicle as they concerned her younger son. But it was enough.

'A happy Christmas,' I exclaimed, bending to kiss her cheek.

And it was. A very happy one.

The Mill House,
Falmer,
Sussex.
January 1969 – January 1970

Index

References in **bold** type are to illustrations